D1105445

Advances in Identity Theory
and Research

Advances in Identity Theory and Research

Edited by

Peter J. Burke

University of California, Riverside
Riverside, California

Timothy J. Owens

Purdue University
West Lafayette, Indiana

Richard T. Serpe

California State University San Marcos
San Marcos, California

and

Peggy A. Thoits

Vanderbilt University
Nashville, Tennessee

Kluwer Academic/Plenum Publishers

New York, Boston, Dordrecht, London, Moscow

ISBN: 0-306-47741-6 (hardbound)
      0-306-47851-X (paperback)

© 2003 Kluwer Academic/Plenum Publishers
233 Spring Street, New York, New York 10013

http://www.wkap.nl/

10 9 8 7 6 5 4 3 2 1

A C.I.P. record for this book is available from the Library of Congress

All rights reserved

No part of this book may be reproduced, stored in a retrieval system, or transmitted in any form or by
any means, electronic, mechanical, photocopying, microfilming, recording, or otherwise, without written
permission from the Publisher, with the exception of any material supplied specifically for the purpose
of being entered and executed on a computer system, for exclusive use by the purchaser of the book.

Permission for books published in Europe: permissions@wkap.nl
Permission for books published in the United States of America: permissions@wkap.com

Printed in the United States of America

CONFERENCE PARTICIPANTS: *Back row (from left)*: Matthew O. Hunt, Peter J. Burke, Edward J. Lawler, Lynn Smith-Lovin, Peggy A. Thoits, George J. McCall; *(second row)*: Anna LoMascolo, K. Jill Kiecolt, Linda E. Francis, Kay Deaux, Alicia D. Cast, Peter Callero, Jan E. Stets, Timothy J. Owens; *(front row)*: Sheldon Stryker *(center)*, Richard T. Serpe, Dawn Robinson; *(not pictured)*: Kristen Marcussen, Michael D. Large

Contributors

Peter J. Burke, University of California, Riverside, Riverside, California 92521-0419

Peter Callero, Western Oregon University, Monmouth, Oregon 97361

Alicia D. Cast, Iowa State University, Ames, Iowa 50011

Linda E. Francis, State University of New York at Stony Brook, Stony Brook, New York 11794

Matthew O. Hunt, Northeastern University, Boston, Massachusetts 02115

K. Jill Kiecolt, Virginia Polytechnic Institute and State University, Blacksburg, Virginia 24061

Michael D. Large, California State University San Marcos, San Marcos, California 92096

Edward J. Lawler, Cornell University, Ithaca, New York 14850–2488

Anna LoMascolo, Virginia Polytechnic Institute and State University, Blacksburg, Virginia 24061

Lynn Smith-Lovin, University of Arizona, Tucson, Arizona 85721, and Duke University, Durham, North Carolina 27708

Kristen Marcussen, Kent State University, Kent, Ohio 44242

George J. McCall, University of Missouri-St. Louis, St. Louis, Missouri 63121

Timothy J. Owens, Purdue University, West Lafayette, Indiana 47907

Richard Serpe, California State University San Marcos, San Marcos, California 92096

Jan E. Stets, University of California, Riverside, Riverside, California 92521–0419

Sheldon Stryker, Indiana University, Bloomington, Indiana 47405

Peggy A. Thoits, Vanderbilt University, Nashville, Tennessee 37235

Preface

This project grew from a set of discussions between Richard Serpe and Tim Owens in 1997 on how best to honor Sheldon Stryker, whose long career has given exemplary service to social psychology, symbolic interactionism, and identity theory. In particular it seemed that his influence on the development and continued discourse on identity theory was especially worthy of noting. With that thought in mind, Peter Burke, Shel's longtime colleague at Indiana University and Peggy Thoits, a more recent colleague of Shel's at IU, joined to plan and complete the project. The team thus represents a student and three current or former colleagues of Shel. While the order of editorship is alphabetical, Peter served as the corresponding editor (e.g., developed and maintained a project website, corresponded with the publisher and the contributors, and assembled the final volume.). Peggy and Tim did much of the conference organizing work while Tim and Peter wrote conference grant proposals.

We do not conceive of this volume as a static or strictly laudatory tribute to one man's life work. It is thus not a *Festschrift* in the traditional sense. Rather, we sought to honor one of the field's pioneers by critically examining and thoughtfully extending identity theory and research. We pursued this goal by first convening an academic mini-conference in Bloomington, Indiana in the spring of 2001. We invited approximately 14 social psychologists including ourselves (some senior and established, some mid- or early-career, and some graduate students) who were interested in a wide range of theories, methodologies, and substantive issues involving identity.

Each participant was initially instructed to orient his or her chapter around some aspect of Stryker's identity theory and research and then extend, criticize, rebut, or rethink identity in any way they saw fit. Thus, while Stryker's contributions are a springboard for the volume, they are not its exclusive focus. All the conference participants came with working drafts of their papers and presented them for comment and feedback from the editors, the other contributors, and the many other people in attendance. It was a signal professional experience for many, with lively and bountiful debate, engaging conversation, and camaraderie. While this book grows out of that conference and the follow-up discussions and critiques, it is not simply a set of conference proceedings. Each chapter went through several drafts as the contributors worked diligently afterwards to incorporate the comments and criticisms of their initial draft. Our technique has hopefully resulted in a unified and cohesive volume of papers that digs deeply and critically into many facets of identity theory and research, thereby setting a course for future research in a new century.

We owe thanks to many people, but would especially like to identify Rob Robinson, chair of the sociology department at Indiana University, for his valuable and unstinting support; Kevin Vryan for helping with the A/V media and serving as the conference photographer; and Jan Stets, also a contributor, for helping with the conference and book in numerous ways.

The conference and book would not have been possible without the generous assistance of several individuals, departments, and organizations. We gratefully acknowledge the support and contributions made by the American Sociological Association Fund for the Advancement of the Discipline, the Department of Sociology at Indiana University, the Indiana University Office of Research and the Graduate School, Indiana University's Vice-President for External Affairs' Hospitality Funds, the Indiana University Conference Bureau, Vanderbilt University and the Teaching and Learning Center at Vanderbilt, Purdue University, and anonymous individual donors.

Contents

PART III: IDENTITIES, EMOTION, AND HEALTH

PART IV: MULTIPLE IDENTITIES

Introduction

PETER J. BURKE

The concept of identity has become ubiquitous within the social and behavioral sciences in recent years, cutting across disciplines from psychoanalysis and psychology to political science and sociology. Each of these disciplines, however, has one or more conceptualizations of "identity" that make a common discourse difficult.

In political science and some fields within sociology, when examining intergroup conflicts and negotiations for example, the term is often taken to refer to one's national identity or ethnic identity within a national boundary. In this context, the term identity is nearly synonymous with a social category, and all persons within the social category are assumed to have the "same" identity. Here, the term identity is used to denote a group with self-interested motivation and is used in a similar fashion as Harrison White's (1992) discussion of identity and control where an identity is viewed as an organized, coherent force with its own goals and oppositions. The papers in Calhoun's (1994) collection, for example, primarily equate ethnicity with identity, while Snow and Oliver (1995) speak of the common culture within a social movement.

Another use of the term *identity* draws upon the work of Erikson (1968) to denote an individual's subjective sense of personal sameness and continuity, paired with some belief in the sameness and continuity of some shared world image—a sense of being and becoming. When that sense is threatened, Erikson speaks of an identity crisis. Such identity crises are often associated with changes in life stages, as for example in adolescence when individuals may loose their sense of self in role confusion. Unlike the former view of identity as a social category, here identity is ultra-individualistic with each person being and becoming his or her own unique self (Cote, 1986; Streitmatter, 1993).

In the present volume, the use of the term *identity* grows out of the structural symbolic interactionism perspective (Stryker, 1980). Here identity is used in a sense somewhat between the view of identity as a social category and the view of identity as a unique individual. In this view an identity is contained in the meaning of the self—what it means to be who one is. To say "I am a student," is to classify the self, but that alone does not tell us what it *means* to be a student. These internalized meanings vary from person to person, but such variations center on a commonly agreed upon set of core meanings and expectations that are part of the general culture. Nevertheless, these meanings are always a part of the self—who I am. They tell me what to expect of myself and how to respond to myself. Because they are shared, they also tell others how to respond to me.

In the earliest work in this tradition, such meanings were based in the roles that one plays: being a mother, a steelworker, a president, or a friend. These are role identities, and

1

we learn their meanings from cultural knowledge (shared) as well as from our own (more personal) experiences in the roles, negotiating the meanings through our interactions with our role partners. One doesn't fully know what it means to be a mother until one is a mother and has the experiences that accompany the playing out of that role.

Over time two additional bases for the identity meanings were set forth. The first of these additional bases lies in the social categories or groups to which one belongs: being White or Black, being an American or a college graduate. Each of these membership groups helps to provide meanings defining who one is. Identities based on groups or categorizations have been called social identities (Abrams & Hogg, 1990; Stets & Burke, 2000).

A third basis of identity lies in those personal characteristics that are not necessarily shared with others: for example, being assertive, or honorable, or trustworthy—each to one's own preferred level. These more individualized identities are termed personal identities (Stets, 1995). By seeing all of these identities (social, role, and personal) as theoretically isomorphic, but having different bases or sources, a unification of the different uses of identities might better be achieved.

THE PERSPECTIVE OF STRUCTURAL SYMBOLIC INTERACTION

While a full exploration of the structural symbolic interaction perspective is beyond the scope of these introductory remarks, a brief exposition will help set the stage for understanding identity theory and the term identity as used in this volume. All of the reports in the volume draw to a greater or lesser extent on that perspective. The main outlines of this perspective were laid out by Sheldon Stryker in an early paper on identity salience (1968). In following Mead's dictum that self and society are linked, Stryker proposed a conception of identity, based on the symbolic interaction framework, that brought some theoretical coherence to these concepts. This view was set forth in a number of premises that became elaborated over time.

First, he suggests, "Behavior is premised on a named or classified world. The names or class terms attached to aspects of the environment, both physical and social, carry meaning in the form of shared behavioral expectations that grow out of social interaction. From interaction with others, one learns how to classify objects one comes into contact with, and in that process also learns how one is expected to behave with reference to those objects" (Stryker, 1980:53-54). While this is a basic symbolic interaction premise, it should be noted that not all is symbolic. There are indeed "objects" that one comes into contact with and learns to respond to, and that these responses give meaning to them.

His second proposition states, "Among the class terms learned in interaction are the symbols that are used to designate 'positions,' which are the relatively stable, morphological components of social structure. These positions carry the shared behavioral expectations that arc conventionally labeled 'roles'" (p. 54). Important here is the notion that the roles are not just created out of the interactions and negotiations of people, but exist out there enough to be seen, reacted to, and labeled within society.

In his third and fourth propositions, we see how actors with identities fit into the scheme. In the third proposition we see that people in society are named or labeled in terms of the positions they occupy. In the fourth proposition we see that we also name ourselves with respect to these positional designations, and that these labels and the expectations attached to them become internalized and become part of our self. In this way, we become a part of the social structure that is named in proposition two. Cooley

(1902:2) described this as the "collective and distributive aspects of the same thing" when characterizing society and the individual. We are thus identified and defined by self-labels in terms of positions in society, which positions are tied together structurally and serve to tie individuals together. For example, father is tied to son or daughter through structural positions in the family. This is reflective of James' (1890) notion that we have as many selves as we have relationships to others.

Fifth, social behavior emerges through the role-making process that involves negotiating, modifying, developing, and shaping expectations through interaction. In this way, each person's identities are uniquely shaped by the person's experiences and interactions with others.

SALIENCE AND COMMITMENT

In setting forth these ideas, Stryker notes that it is essential to recognize that the self is not an undifferentiated whole, but involves multiple and diverse parts, reflecting the multiple and diverse character of society (James, 1890). Given the multiple positions a person holds in society, that person has multiple identities: father, husband, voter, salesman, fraternal organization member, etc. Identities thus exist to the extent that persons are participants in structured social relationships. In this way the self, composed of multiple identities, not only reflects society, but identities, through the role-making process, also recreates the society in which the identities are embedded.

Stryker (1968) went on to suggest that the multiple identities that individuals hold are organized within the self into a salience hierarchy reflecting the likelihood that each identity would be activated. The concept of salience provides another way in which individual identities differ. Members of the same social movement, for example, each have an identity formed around their position in the movement. And, even though they may occupy very similar positions, the impact of their identities may be quite different because for one person their movement identity is much more salient than the other's—much more likely to be invoked or called up across a variety of situations. The other may have a more salient spousal/family identity, and in situations in which both may be invoked, one may play out the implications of their movement identity, the other play out the implications of their spousal/family identity. The hierarchy of salience of the identities held by an individual represents a unique characteristic of that individual, making him/her different from others.

Finally, Stryker (1968) introduced the concept of commitment, which has a very strong structural component. Commitment represents the connections that one has to others because one has a particular identity. Two aspects of commitment were suggested. One aspect has to do with the number of others to whom one is connected—the extensiveness of the commitment. The other aspect has to do with the strength or depth of the connection to those others—the intensiveness of the commitment. Commitment may also be thought of in terms of the costs of giving up a particular identity. By losing more and stronger attachments to others when an identity is given up, one incurs a greater cost. An illustration may be helpful. When one has a job, say a salesclerk, one not only has the identity of salesclerk, but also becomes connected to others because of that job: one's associates and co-workers, and all the others one maintains contact with in the carrying out of the job. Some of these connections become very strong. If one loses the job, gets laid-off for example, then all those connections are gone; one loses one's place in the scheme. These are often very severe costs that come from losing the identity, and they are greater as the commitment (the number of persons one is tied to and/or the strength of the connection to those others) is greater. Commitment marks the degree to which one is embedded in the social structure as a function of the identity that one holds and it represents society in the individual-society relationship.

Stryker (1968) hypothesized a particular link between these components in suggesting that commitment (the social structural aspect) has a strong influence on salience (the individual aspect), such that greater commitment leads to greater salience for the identity involved. The more people one is tied to because of a particular identity, the higher that identity becomes in the salience hierarchy and the more likely it will be invoked in any situation.

It is the meanings of and expectations for a particular identity that lead one to behave in a manner consistent with the identity when the identity is invoked in a situation. By acting in a manner consistent with their identity, people verify and confirm their identities, and because meanings are shared, these identities (meanings and expectations) as they are portrayed in interaction with others are thus presented to others for verification and confirmation. This is also part of the self-verification process. For example, Serpe and Stryker have shown (1987) that freshman students arriving on campus tend to recreate the symbols and relationships that had defined them before coming to college. Those who do this successfully are able to maintain their previous self-structure, but the self-structures of those who were not able to do this successfully began to change to accommodate to the new surroundings (Ethier & Deaux, 1994).

INTERNAL DYNAMICS

But more than simply presenting the self, as the just described work of Serpe and Stryker shows, people tend to resist changes in their self—both the structure (e.g., current salience hierarchy) and the meanings defining the identities they hold. The dynamics of this process have been spelled out in a series of papers by Burke and others (Burke, 1980, 1991, 1997; Burke & Reitzes, 1981; Burke & Stets, 1999). The social, role, or person based identities that people hold, each constitute a set of meanings and expectations that function as a standard or stable reference defining who one is. When an identity is activated in a situation, that standard serves as a basis for judging the perceived self-relevant meanings in the current situation. The basic idea is that people act to keep these perceived meanings consistent or semantically congruent with the standard. Thus, in general, behaviors are chosen to convey meanings that are consistent with the identities people hold. And, when people see that the situational self-meanings are not congruent with who they are because of some situational disturbance, they act to restore such congruency by counteracting the disturbance. This is the self-verification process (Swann, 1983).

This process is understood to work for all activated identities, whether they are based on group affiliations, role performances, or personal characteristics (Stets & Burke, 2000). The comparator is a function that compares self-relevant meanings from the situation with the self-meanings held in the identity standard and outputs an error signal. The error is zero if there is no difference between the standard (who a person is) and the perceived situational meanings, but gains in magnitude as the difference increases. By counteracting disturbances that arise in the situation, people keep their perceived self-relevant meanings close to their identity standard and thus keep the error close to zero. Emotional responses are tied to the error. When the error is not zero or is increasing, people feel distressed; when the error is decreasing or zero, people feel happy and content (Burke, 1991; Burke & Harrod, 2002; Cast & Burke, 2002; Stets & Tsushima, 2001).

To put the above in slightly different words, because these internalized meanings and expectations *are* the self, people defend them against change and misinterpretation. For example, a student who defines herself as academically oriented would counteract any attribution that seemed to indicate she is a partier (Burke & Reitzes, 1981). Not only that, but when people get feedback that is discrepant with the self-meanings held in their identity, they feel bad. They feel angry or depressed, and their self-esteem suffers (Cast & Burke, 2002). Thus, we see emotional as well as behavioral responses to self-discrepant feedback.

THE PRESENT VOLUME

The chapters in the present volume all begin with this view of identities and seek to extend and apply our understanding of that concept. Some of the papers are more theoretically oriented, proposing new conceptualizations and research agendas, others are more empirically oriented, developing and testing ideas that grow out of the theoretical approach. While each paper was written to deal with its own issues and purposes, there are, nevertheless, some general themes that run through them, in part because these themes are the central foci in the field. Consequently, we have divided the book into four sections corresponding to these themes.

Part I deals with the sources of identity and the mechanisms by which one becomes each of the identities constituting the self. McCall points out that part of gaining an identity means *dis*identifying with other social objects that differ from that one identifies with. Being male is not being female. Being white is not being black. The implications of this for identity theory are explored. Kiecolt and LoMascolo examine the way in which physical resemblances to parents influences the family identity of children. They look at physical resemblances as both an outcome (under what conditions do children see greater resemblances?) and as a factor influencing the formation of the self (which may be especially important for biracial youth). In the last paper in this section, Cast notes that what we *do* has implications for who we are, though often these are indirectly felt. Because of our locations in the social structure, our behavior influences the identities of our role partners, which in turn comes to influence who we are.

Part II of the volume addresses issues concerning the tie between identity and the social structure. Callero develops a conceptualization of the self that focuses more directly on power and the political aspects of identities. He examines the implications of such a conceptualization for macro processes such as democracy. Hunt continues this theme with an examination of the embeddedness of identities within the social structure, with an explicit focus on positions within the stratification system. He looks at both the consequences of the stratification system on the self, as well as the impact of embedded identities on the social stratification system. Owens and Serpe examine the role that self-esteem plays in building commitment to the family identity and making that identity more or less salient for White, Black and Latino individuals.

In Part III of the volume, the authors explore some of the non-cognitive outcomes of identity processes. Stets tests some predictions that identity theory makes about the emotional consequences of the identity verification process and shows that such hypotheses must be conditioned upon the nature of the relationships between people. Francis takes up the question of why expressing emotion to others has beneficial health consequences and suggests the answer may be found in identity theory and the role of affect in that theory. Lawler looks at the role of emotion in the emergence of collective identities that arise when individuals engage in repeated, successful interactions. Marcussen and Large merge Higgins' (1987) self-discrepancy theory with identity theory to explain depression versus distress outcomes from a failure in the self-verification process.

Part IV contains three papers that make explicit the idea that people have multiple identities. Thoits extends her work on the beneficial consequences that holding multiple identities have for the individual by noting that such consequences can depend upon whether the identities are obligatory (not easily gotten out of: spouse, parent, worker) or voluntary (churchgoer, club member, friend). Smith-Lovin, drawing on the embeddedness of identities in the social structure, begins to develop a theory about the structural conditions under which multiple identities are likely to be activated in the same setting and become intertwined in a composite identity with certain consequences for felt emotions. Burke examines the relationship between multiple identities held by an individual and how that relationship may be influenced by the position of the individual within the social structure.

CONCLUSION

This volume presents a series of papers that build upon a particular view of self and identity growing out of a structural symbolic interactionist perspective called identity theory. These papers contribute directly to neglected aspects of that theory such as the influence of one's social structural location, emotion, and multiple identities on identity processes. Indirectly, these papers contribute to a view of identity that will find use in a variety of theoretical concerns in a variety of disciplines. For example, although studies of national or ethnic identity can focus on the commonality that is inherent in a social identity, variations in the levels of salience and commitment that individuals have with respect to such identities are obviously crucially important to movement success. Additionally, the perspective allows for individuals to vary in the meanings of these identities, which might help to explain the emergence of conflicts within movements.

For another example, studies of the identities of individuals from a more psychological point of view could recognize that individuals are members of groups and categories, and they play particular roles within these larger aggregates with the consequence that there is much of identity that is created and shared with others, rather than being unique. Meaning is most often found in social contexts and the way one is tied into those contexts. Thus, identity crises may reflect dislocations in the social structure more than personal problems, and a sense of unified, continuous self may reside in stable, organized relationships with others.

By recognizing the multiple bases of identity that are found in group, role, and person and by taking into account variation in levels of commitment and salience of these identities as people are tied into the social structure differentially, the complexity of society is reflected in the complexity of the self. This complexity of the self as it is played out in behavior occurring in different locations within the social structure acts to reproduce that social structure, or on occasion change it. Because it captures the complex dynamic aspects of identity well, identity theory helps to bridge some of the gaps between psychological and sociopolitical approaches to self, identity, and social change, as many of the chapters in this volume will show.

REFERENCES

Abrams, D., & Hogg, M. A. (1990). *Social identity theory: Constructive and critical advances*. London: Harvester-Wheatsheaf.

Burke, P. J. (1980). The self: Measurement implications from a symbolic interactionist perspective. *Social Psychology Quarterly, 43*, 18–29.

Burke, P. J. (1991). Identity processes and social stress. *American Sociological Review, 56*, 836–849.

Burke, P. J. (1997). An identity model for network exchange. *American Sociological Review, 62*, 134–150.

Burke, P. J., & Harrod, M. M. (2002). *To good to be believed?* Chicago: Annual Meeting of the American Sociological Association.

Burke, P. J., & Reitzes, D. C. (1981). The link between identity and role performance. *Social Psychology Quarterly, 44*, 83–92.

Burke, P. J., & Stets, J. E. (1999). Trust and commitment through self-verification. *Social Psychology Quarterly, 62(4)*, 347–366.

Calhoun, C. (Ed.). (1994). *Social theory and the politics of identity*. Cambridge, MA: Blackwell.

Cast, A. D., & Burke, P. J. (2002). A theory of self-esteem. *Social Forces, 80*, 1041-1068.

Cooley, C. H. (1902). *Human nature and social order*. New York: Charles Scribner's Sons.

Cote, J. E. (1986). Traditionalism and feminism: A typology of strategies used by university women to manage career-family conflicts. *Social Behavior and Personality, 35(5)*, 133–143.

Erikson, E. H. (1968). *Identity: Youth and crisis*. New York: Norton.

Ethier, K. A., & Deaux, K. (1994). Negotiating social identity when contexts change: Maintaining identification and responding to threat. *Journal of Personality and Social Psychology, 67(2)*, 243–251.

Higgins, E. T. (1987). Self-discrepancy: A theory relating self and affect. *Psychological Review, 94*, 319–340.

James, W. (1890). *Principles of psychology*. New York: Holt Rinehart and Winston.

Serpe, R. T., & Stryker, S. (1987). The construction of self and reconstruction of social relationships. In E. Lawler & B. Markovsky (Eds.), *Advances in group processes* (pp. 41–66). Greenwich, CT: JAI Press.

Snow, D. A., & Oliver, P. E. (1995). Social movements and collective behavior: Social psychological dimensions and considerations. In K. Cook, G. A. Fine & J. S. House (Eds.), *Sociological perspectives on social psychology* (pp. 571–600). Boston: Allyn and Bacon.

Stets, J. E. (1995). Role identities and person identities: Gender identity, mastery identity, and controlling one's partner. *Sociological Perspectives, 38(2)*, 129–150.

Stets, J. E., & Burke, P. J. (2000). *Identity theory and social identity theory. Social Psychology Quarterly, 63*, 224–237.

Stets, J. E., & Tsushima, T. (2001). Negative emotion and coping responses within identity control theory. *Social Psychology Quarterly, 64*, 283–295.

Streitmatter, J. (1993). Gender differences in identity development: An examination of longitudinal data. *Adolescence, 41(4)*, 55–66.

Stryker, S. (1968). Identity salience and role performance. *Journal of Marriage and the Family, 4*, 558–564.

Stryker, S. (1980). *Symbolic interactionism: A social structural version*. Menlo Park: Benjamin Cummings.

Swann, W. B., Jr. (1983). Self-verification: Bringing social reality into harmony with the self. In J. Suls & A. Greenwald (Eds.), *Psychological perspectives on the self* (pp. 33–66). Hillsdale, NJ: Erlbaum.

White, H. C. (1992). *Identity and control: A structural theory of social action*. Princeton, NJ: Princeton University Press.

Part I

Sources of Identity

Chapter 1

The Me and the Not-Me
Positive and Negative Poles of Identity

GEORGE J. MCCALL

INTRODUCTION

Symbolic interactionists have long regarded identification of Self and Other as a key feature of social interaction (Blumer, 1962; Cooley, 1902; McCall & Simmons, 1978/1966; Mead, 1934).

> Establishment of one's own identity to oneself is as important in interaction as to establish it for the other. One's own identity in a situation is not absolutely given but is more or less problematic. (Foote, 1951, p. 18)

For just such reasons, symbolic interactionists have similarly considered identity to be a key feature of the self. As Kuhn put it, "a person interiorizes his roles and statuses, and with these the expectations that significant others have of him" (Hickman & Kuhn, 1956, p. 242). Adding to this foundation a Cooley-esque emphasis on imagination, McCall and Simmons (1978/1966, p. 65) proposed that "a role-identity is his imaginative view of himself *as he likes to think of himself being and acting* as an occupant" of a particular social position. These components remain central to the concept today, as Stryker and Burke (2001) stated that "identities are internalized role expectations" (p. 286) and that "self-meanings develop in the context of meanings of roles and counter roles" (p. 287).

Self-identification has traditionally been viewed as attempts to answer the question "Who Am I?" (Howard, 2000; Strauss, 1959). Accordingly, one of the most direct measurement devices for discovering an individual's multiple identities has been the Twenty Statements Test of Self-Attitudes, or TST, in which one is given a paper with 20 numbered lines and invited to enter on those lines one's open-ended responses to the question, *Who am I?* Respondents are instructed "to answer as if you were giving the answers to yourself, not to somebody else. Write the answers in the order that they occur to you. Don't worry about logic or 'importance.' Go along fairly fast, for time is limited." The resulting open-ended responses are taken to characterize the self as an object, an aspect of self that Mead designated the Me as over against I, or self as subject. The substantive richness of these characterizations of the Me are illustrated, for example, in Kuhn (1960) and in Gordon (1968).

Even though various methodological difficulties were explored early on (Gordon, 1969; Tucker, 1966), quite an extensive body of TST research developed (Spitzer, Couch, & Stratton, 1971) and even today continues to illuminate the contours of the "Me" in just that fashion (Rentsch & Heffner, 1994; Turner & Schutte, 1981; Yardley, 1987).

POSITIVE AND NEGATIVE POLES

Logically speaking, however, identifying with one social object entails *dis*identifying with other social objects that differ from that one—a logical point accepted by several SI theorists.

> Identity is established as a consequence of two processes, apposition and opposition, a bringing together and setting apart. To situate the person as a social object is to bring him together with other objects so situated, and, at the same time to set him apart from still other objects. (Stone, 1962, p. 94)

Structural symbolic interactionists (Stryker, 1980) have typically employed the role-set as defining the relevant set of social objects: "as roles are defined by their relation to counter-roles . . ., an identity (as the internal component of a role) is defined in relation to counter-identities." (Burke, 1980, p. 19) Similarly, situated identity theory (Alexander & Wiley, 1981) has focused on the contrastive meanings of a small set of discrete and alternative courses of action contained within a single social situation.

The present paper proposes that the twinned processes of self-identification and self-disidentification be regarded as positive and negative poles of identity, perhaps more conveniently labeled the Me and the Not-Me. While the concept of the Me is quite familiar from Mead's writings, the concept of the Not-Me may require some further clarification. Most importantly, the Not-Me must be distinguished from Sullivan's (1953) "not-me"—a rudimentary, parataxic personification within the self-system of early and dreadful experiences. Similarly, the Not-Me is to be distinguished from the Sullivanesque concepts of the "undesired self" (Ogilvie, 1987) and the "feared self" (Markus & Nurius, 1986). Unlike all of these, the Not-Me need not engender either uncanny emotions or fear; just as the Me can evoke some self-feelings without necessarily being emotionally stirring, so can the Not-Me. Rather, the Not-Me more closely resembles a sum of the "not me" responses (indicating that a personality-trait word is "not descriptive" of the self) as investigated by Paulhus and Levitt (1987).

To explore self-disidentification, a parallel "Who Am I NOT?" test was devised to illuminate the "Not-Me." Apart from inserting the word *not* into the fundamental identity question, the procedure and instructions did not differ from those of the TST:

> Please write twenty different answers to the simple question "Who Am I NOT?" in the blanks below. Answer as if you were giving the answers to yourself, not to somebody else. Write the answers in the order that they occur to you. Don't worry about logic or "importance." Go along fairly fast, for time is limited.

The resulting *I am not . . .* statements were regarded as self-disidentifying statements, proper content of the Not-Me. For as Goffman (1961b, p. 108) has noted, "A shorthand is involved here: the individual is actually denying not the role but the virtual self that is implied in the role for all accepting performers."

The Grammar of Identity

> Central to any discussion of identity is language . . . a proper theoretical account of men's identities and action must put men's linguistics into the heart of the discussion (Strauss, 1959, p. 15)

From this point of view, *any* utterance can be read as revealing something about speaker's identities, but especially revealing are sentences in which the pronoun *I* serves as the subject. Any such "*I*-sentence" does disclose something about a person's self-conception, but what is revealed, and how, depends partly on the syntax of the sentence. The pronoun *I*, like any other subject, may name either "that which is identified" or "that which takes action" (Fries, 1952). The former sense, of course, is more directly revealing of identity, and both the TST and the WAIN test are designed to differentially elicit that use of the pronoun by pairing it with the verb form *am*. Unfortunately, that verb form, too, has two senses: a linking verb (i.e., linking *I* with some subjective complement—as in the sentence *I am a woman*) or an auxiliary participle (i.e., modifying another verb—as in the sentence *I am trying hard*) (Fries, 1952). Here too, the former usage is considered more directly revealing of identity.[1]

Even within the preferred syntactical form (*I* + linking verb + subjective complement), the subjective complement may be either a noun phrase (as in *I am a woman*) or an adjectival phrase (as in *I am rich*). In the former case, the person identifies self with some social object, usually a status or role. In the latter case, the person identifies self with some distinctive characteristic or disposition. Both are important forms of identity claims: "the question 'Who am I?' is one which might logically be expected to elicit statements about one's identity; that is, his social statuses, and the attributes which are in his view relevant to these." (Kuhn and McPartland 1954, p. 72)

Of particular interest here is the grammar of *not* and related adverbs of negation, such as *never, no longer*, etc. A sentence of the form (*I* + linking verb + *not* + subjective complement) serves to distinguish self from that object and/or characteristic named within the subjective complement. Such a self-disidentifying sentence form is specifically elicited in the WAIN test.

Some identity researchers have proposed that self-disidentification can alternatively be achieved through an utterance referring to a "negative identity" of the speaker, a concept widely (and often loosely) employed in the literature. In linguistic terms, a "positive identity" would have to mean a "positive" (or at least non-negative) subjective complement and a "negative identity" would have to mean a "negative" subjective complement. Three conceivable ways in which a subjective complement could acquire a negative flavor would be for it to include: (1) no noun but a semantically "negative" adjective,[2] as in *I am rotten*; (2) a semantically "non-negative" noun modified by a semantically "negative" adjective, as in *I am a terrible cook;* or (3) an unmodified "negative" noun, as in *I am a slut*.

Thus, to classify identities as positive or negative would require classifying nouns and adjectives as semantically negative or non-negative. Such a project is far from straightforward, for a number of reasons. First of all, as any dictionary will reveal, many words have multiple meanings; such denotative ambiguity undermines any attempt to establish the connotative meaning (e.g., favorableness) of a word (Mosier, 1941). Second, such connotative

---

[1]In highly formal English, apposition may eliminate the linking verb, as in *I, a woman, dislike football.*
[2]One class of semantically "negative" adjective is grammatically defined, through incorporation of a negative prefix, as in *unprofessional*.

meanings vary significantly across contexts, both linguistic and social, as affect control theory insists (Smith-Lovin and Heise, 1988). But connotation varies even much further as a function of the personal values, mood, and relationship between speaker and audience; such factors must be understood in order to judge whether a term such as *liberal* is intended, or heard, as a positive or a negative.[3] Third, frame analysis (Goffman, 1974, 1981) would insist that many apparently positive words are being used euphemistically rather than literally.

As a further sociolinguistic complication, a person may—on the same occasion—simultaneously embrace (or simultaneously reject) both a positive identity and its corresponding negative identity. For example, the person may state on the TST both *I am fat* and *I am thin* (or, on the WAIN, *I am not fat* and *I am not thin*). By claiming the same relationship to both extremes of a bipolar continuum, a person effectively places self somewhere in the middle range.

Nevertheless, despite all these difficulties and more, some researchers will persist in the attempt to classify identities as "positive" or "negative" and their attempts at classification cannot be simply overlooked. Even in this chapter I will need to speak of positive and negative identities, however those might be determined.

But it remains the case that assigning a semantically negative flavor to a subjective complement is not the same as the linguistic operation of negation. That is to say, asserting a "negative" identity (e.g., *I am a slut*) is not a form of self-disidentification (e.g., *I am not a good girl*). Moreover, the Not-Me is not a set of negative identities; rather, it is a set of various self-disidentifications. In fact, as will be seen below, negative identities can appear in the Me as well as in the Not-Me.

A final concept, related to that of positive and negative identities, is that of positive and negative self-conceptions, usually measured in terms of high and low levels of global self-esteem (Wright, 1999). Building on the linguistic scheme developed here, a positive self-conception would instead be one numerically dominated by "positive" identities (empirically, the more typical case) whereas a negative self-conception would be one dominated by "negative" identities. Of course, this distinction then similarly rests on the same, very difficult project of classifying nouns and adjectives as either non-negative or negative. But again, the Me cannot be equated to a positive self-conception, nor can the Not-Me be equated to a negative self-conception.

Pilot Study

A convenience sample of students was asked to take the WAIN test and also, four weeks later, the TST. A total of 16 students completed both tests, allowing some preliminary comparison of what might be taken as the Me and the Not-Me.

If each of these tests yields a self-image—i.e., a situationally contextuated view of an underlying self-conception (Burke, 1980; Turner 1968)—what is the relationship between these two self-images?

Equivalent Self-Images?

One obvious possibility is that the Me and the Not-Me are essentially mirror images of the same self-conception, like views of our planet from satellites above the North Pole and

---

[3]That is to say, the rating assigned a word by the "generalized other" may differ from the rating assigned that same word by a specific audience.

South Pole respectively. After all, the TST response *I am a man* is logically equivalent to the WAIN response *I am not a woman*, and the positive statement *I am honest* is logically equivalent to the double-negative statement *I am not dishonest*.

This "mirror-image" hypothesis did receive some empirical support from the pilot study data, in that every one of the sixteen subjects did report at least one TST response that was logically equivalent, in this fashion, to a WAIN response. On the other hand, for no subject were more than 60% of responses to the two tests logically equivalent in this way. Indeed, the average over all subjects was more like half that top figure.

But assessing logical equivalence of responses to the two tests is considerably less straightforward than it may seem, since the validity of such logical inference depends on whether the relevant opposition (e.g., man vs. woman, or honest vs. dishonest) is considered a dichotomy. If so, logical equivalence can validly be attributed, since the opposed terms represent an exhaustive binary set of mutually exclusive categories. However, counter-roles are not always dichotomous; indeed, in some contexts *man* and *woman* are not regarded as an exhaustive set of gender categories. Similarly, personal attributes (e.g., honesty) may be regarded as a bipolar continuum rather than a dichotomy.

For such reasons, assessing logical equivalence of responses to the two tests often requires some role-taking to infer how the responding person was construing the relevant role-set or personal attribute. The numerical results I have reported above reflect quite a conservative mode of assessing equivalence; if a bit more interpretive liberty is taken, the percentage of equivalent responses will be rather higher. For example, many of the female subjects seemed to be striving to indicate on the TST that they were not yet mothers, by listing all (or most of) their other female kinship statuses (e.g., daughter, sister); virtually every one of these women, on the WAIN, did explicitly state that they were not a mother.

Perhaps then, by a more liberal standard of logical equivalence, the average percentage of equivalent responses on the two tests might rise to something nearer half. If so, one would have to admit that, based on studies of the reliability of the TST (Spitzer, Couch, & Stratton, 1971), such a degree of equivalence is pretty much what one might expect from adminstration of the same form four weeks apart.

Different Images?

But if one should conclude that they are not logically equivalent, are, then, the Me and the Not-Me systematically different self-images?

Grammar

Grammatically speaking, *I*-statements in response to the TST and the WAIN did differ systematically, but only in certain respects. First of all, *am*-less sentences (where *I* serves as "that which takes action") did occur in the TST (mean = 0.5) but not in the WAIN (although that difference may have been affected by one formal noncomparability in the two formats). Second, and conversely, sentences using *am* as an auxiliary participle were less common in the TST than the WAIN (means: 0.1 vs. 1.2). Third, although sentences using *am* as a linking verb were equally frequent in both tests (means: 18.7), the two tests differed systematically in the syntactic form of the subjective complement. Whereas nominal phrases dominated these identity statements in the TST (mean:12.5) but were secondary in the WAIN (mean: 5.4), adjectival phrases dominated in the WAIN (mean: 13.3) but were secondary in the TST (mean: 6.2).

Grammatical complexity can be reckoned in many different ways, but the most economical, generally useful index is a simple word count (Preston 1984). By that index, the TST (mean: 52.2 words) and the WAIN (mean: 54.1 words) were virtually identical, even though previous research (e.g., Collier, Kuiken, & Enzle, 1982) had suggested higher grammatical complexity for affectively negative content.

Content

The pilot study results on the relative distributions of nominal and adjectival phrases within the subjective complements in the TST and WAIN responses confirm that the Me is framed more in terms of roles and statuses whereas the Not-Me is framed more in terms of characteristics and dispositions.

Semantics

Connotative meaning is perhaps no less important a standard than logic for the meaning equivalence of the Me and the Not-Me. Even when responses on the two tests are identical in truth value, they may differ significantly in axiological value; most English speakers will judge that the positive statement *I am a good mother* is a stronger claim than the double-negative statement *I am not a bad mother*.

Ceteris paribus, the Me would seem to outrank the Not-Me in the evaluation, potency, and activity connotations (what affect control theorists refer to as "EPA meaning") of their respective identity statements.

With respect to evaluation, the Not-Me would be expected to contain more semantically negative expressions, if for no other reason than that a person with a positive self-concept should more frequently resort to double negatives in the WAIN than in the TST. Pilot study results sustain that expectation, for the WAIN responses did contain more words of negative connotation, even taking strict account of the formidable difficulties of semantic classification mentioned above. Using a very conservative standard, and drawing upon Anderson's (1968) likableness ratings whenever possible, I judged that WAIN tests averaged 4.9 negative adjectives and 0.63 negative nouns, while TSTs averaged 1.2 negative adjectives and 0.13 negative nouns. Strongly reinforcing that differential in negatively-judged words is the difference in the undeniably negative adverb, *not*. By fiat, all 20 WAIN responses contained the word *not*, as compared to an average of 0.69 responses on the TST. Conservatively, then, WAIN tests averaged 26.1 negative-flavored words while TSTs averaged 1.45.

This finding has relevance to the relative potency of the Not-Me, since sentences with negatives in them are harder to understand (Evans 1972) and negation and a reluctance to affirm assertions are key components of the "non-immediate language style"(Kuiken, 1981) that psycholinguists set over against the more potent "immediate language style."

The picture is less clear regarding the activity dimension, in view of the facts (reported above) that *am*-less sentences (where *I* serves as "that which takes action") did occur in the TST but not in the WAIN, while sentences using *am* as an auxiliary participle were less common in the TST than the WAIN.

Overlapping Images?

Despite these characteristic differences between the self-images elicited by these two tests, it can yet be claimed that they are significantly overlapping images. While the WAIN is grammatically constrained to tapping the Not-Me, the fact is that the TST taps both the Me and the Not-Me. In this sample, there occurred only a dozen self-disidentifying statements across the 16 TST respondents, but in the experience of most TST researchers, that mean can often be considerably higher.

Complementary Images?

If purely measured, perhaps the self-images here labeled Me and Not-Me would be most usefully regarded as complementary to one another.

Certainly, as impurely measured by the TST and WAIN, the resultant self-images do exhibit an incomplete but impressive degree of equivalence, through logical translation, yet they also display significant and systematic differences—in grammar, content, and semantics. Perhaps, then, the two poles of identity—self-identification and self-disidentification—are not so much like the North and South poles of a static desk globe (opposed viewpoints affording logically equivalent perspectives) but are instead more functionally asymmetrical (like the North and South poles of a bar magnet—such as Earth itself). Unlike the symmetrical but passive geographical poles, the asymmetrical magnetic poles generate lines of motive force that structure the surrounding space through defining its potentials.

The tension between the Me and the Not-Me, the complementary poles of identity, does motivate and direct actions of the individual, striving to enact the Me and to avoid enacting the Not-Me. Without at least some knowledge of each, we fail to appreciate the significance of that person's performance.

PROACTIVE AND REACTIVE ASPECTS OF IDENTITY WORK

How do these positive and negative poles of identity influence actual social conduct? More specifically, how do they relate to proactive and reactive aspects of identity?

Proactive Identity Work

There are many actions an individual can take to help define and to maintain his or her own self-concept (McCall & Simmons, 1978/1966). All of these amount to, in some sense, adapting one's self-image to other persons and social situations that constitute positive or negative opportunities. Recent history and present opportunity structures interact with one's relatively enduring prominence hierarchy of identities to yield a very fluid salience hierarchy—the *situational self*, i.e., one's own preferences as to the subset of roles one will enact in the situation. Even this situational self—the key to understanding proactive identity work—very much involves both the Me and the Not-Me, as some identities are included in this preferred subset and others are definitely excluded. Indeed, sometimes one cares much more deeply about these exclusions, such as *I am not a sissy*, than about which positive nuances may be elaborated in one's gender role-identity (Freitas et al., 1997; McCall, 1976).

How does proactive identity work unfold? First of all, one must work from clues to discern the identities that others in the situation are likely to claim. When we use a person's behaviors as a basis for our inferences about that person's identities, we are employing the widely-analyzed process of "role-taking" (Stryker, 1962; Turner, 1962). Once we have imputed an identity-set to other, we modify our own lines of action on the basis of the meanings of those identities for our own manifest and latent plans of action. That is to say, based on the opportunity structure that the putative identities of situated others constitutes, we then improvise an identity-set for ourself—a set of preferences emerges.

These twin cognitive processes then drive a corresponding pair of expressive processes—altercasting and presentation of self—whereby the identities we have chosen to attribute to other and to oneself are more or less openly communicated in a social influence attempt (Figure 1).

Self-Presentation

Since Goffman's (1959) seminal work on the presentation of self there has developed considerable literature on strategic self-presentation (Jones & Pittman, 1982; Rhodewatt, 1986) or impression management (Schlenker, 1980; Tedeschi, 1981). Is there, as these literatures suggest, a preferential tendency for individuals to assert positive identities and to deny negative identities? If such a tendency were very strong, three implications follow. First, the test that mainly asserts identities (TST) should elicit a higher proportion of non-negative identities than does the test that is framed to deny identities (WAIN). Second, non-negative identities should be most often asserted while negative identities should be most often denied. Third, most of the identities asserted should be non-negative while most of the identities denied should be negative.

Sensitive to the many objections raised above concerning classification of identities, I more liberally employed my (rather slender) acquaintance with these sixteen respondents to judge whether or not the several components of the various subjective complements were intended as negative.

On that basis, I found that the first of the three implications is confirmed by the pilot study results, as just over 90% of TST identities are non-negative as compared to 63% of the WAIN identities.

The second implication is only partially confirmed. On the TST, 97% of the non-negative identities were embraced, while only 17% of the negative identities were rejected. (The WAIN test, of course, did not allow for assertion of any identities, positive or negative.)

Similarly, the third implication is only partially confirmed. Of the identities asserted (TST only), 95% were indeed non-negative, but of the identities denied (TST) only 42% were negative (comparable to the figure of 37% on the WAIN).

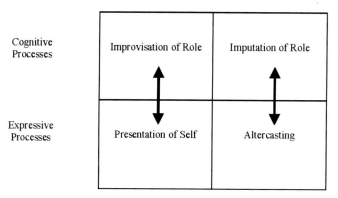

Figure 1.   Interpersonal Processes.

Unless my encodings of subjective complements are quite faulty, the latter findings clearly suggest that the Not-Me, in particular, is very incompletely captured in any simple "social desirability" picture of persons asserting positive identities and denying negative identities.[4]

What, then, might be reasons for asserting negative identities, an act that seems likely to diminish the social desirability of the person? One reason might be to reduce expectations on the part of others; by asserting *I am fat* a person tells others that he or she is not too attractive or athletically inclined. A related reason might be to deflect demands; by asserting *I am a terrible cook* (which does not go as far as the denial *I am not a cook*) a person tells others that "you won't want to ask me to cook for you."

Similarly, what might be reasons for denying positive identities, another act likely to diminish the social desirability of the person? By stating *I am not a doctor* a person is perhaps telling others that he or she is striving, or aspiring, to achieve that status. On other other, such a statement might be made to instead indicate that he or she has achieved departure from that status, has "moved on."

These two off-diagonal cells affect, differently, both the TST and the WAIN. Thus, we again conclude that neither test is purely a measure of Me or Not-Me.

Support-Seeking

But announcing identities is only the beginning of proactive identity work , for supporting evidence must be marshalled if such identity claims are to be personally and socially sustained. Performance (Burke & Reitzes, 1981) is the most direct form of evidence, and proactive identity work includes efforts to design and manage a proper stage and cast for relevant performances. Of course, a validating response from audience can be obtained through other means as well. One of the most frequently studied means is to seek out those others who are especially likely to provide such a validating response, even if only through ingratiation or a cash nexus (Swann, Pelham, & Krull,1989; Swann & Read, 1981).

Much of the research on support-seeking has employed a "self-enhancement" model of humans, wherein they seek positive support of all their identities. Unfortunately, in tests of this model, "negative identity" has been nothing more than low levels of (unidimensional) self-esteem, not even differentiating a positive and negative dimension of self-esteem as distinguished by Owens (1993).

If the self-enhancement model were to treat of negative identities in the more meaningful sense developed here (i.e., a "negative" subjective complement), it would hypothesize—counter to the evidence in the previous subsection—that individuals seek to increase social desirability and will hence assert positive identities but deny negative identities.

Other research on support-seeking has instead employed some sort of "self-verification" model, rooted in symbolic interactionism or affect control theory, holding that individuals will seek favorable comment on their positive identities but unfavorable comment on their negative identities. This hypothesis has usually stood up to empirical tests, even though some of these studies, regretably, have adopted from the self-enhancement

---

[4]In thus "passing" (Goffman 1963), "It is not so much that he is passing himself off as something he is not, but that he has passed himself off as not being some other things that he also is" (McCall & Simmons 1978/1966, p. 183). To deny one's identities, even if only one's negative identities, is to render oneself discreditable.

tradition a treatment of negative identity as low self-esteem (e.g., Robinson & Smith-Lovin, 1992). Happily, however, a number of studies in the symbolic interaction tradition have treated positive and negative identities in a fashion somewhat similar to that proposed here, and have supported the self-verification hypothesis (e.g., Burke, 1991).

But even these best-designed studies suffer the serious limitation of examining only the proactive aspect of identity work, that is to say, only action rather than interaction.

Reactive Identity Work

From an interaction point of view, identity is more than meanings or a cognitive schema, it is most centrally a social object that is negotiated through social interaction.

> Identities are thus strategic social constructions created through interaction, with' social and material consequences. (Howard, 2000, p. 371)

Negotiated identity, the social object, must even be distinguished from the very fluid and situational self-concept we have just been discussing, for:

> The situational self constitutes merely the person's own preference as to the subset of role identities he will enact in a given situation, whereas his character—being a social object—represents the set that is actually interactively negotiated and ratified for him in the situation by all the participants. (McCall & Simmons, 1978/1966, p. 84)

In this sense, scholarly attention should focus, not on the cognitive and expressive behaviors of the individual, but rather on the negotiation process through which participants strive to achieve some sort of reciprocal correspondence of Person and Other's cognitive/expressive processes. Whenever the expressive processes of one party can be brought into rough correspondence with the cognitive processes of the other, there results a working agreement on their respective identities (Figure 2).

Reactive identity work can be equated to an individual's negotiating with others about their respective identities. The novel component that distinguishes this reactive aspect is having to confront, and respond to, the other's representation of who each is. When that representation by other imputes to us identities we had excluded from our situational self, we view those as Not-Me. When it imputes to us identities that we had included in our situational self, we regard those as Me.

Emotional Responses

> . . . the reflected or looking-glass self . . . seems to have three principal elements: the imagination of our appearance to the other person; the imagination of his judgment of that appearance; and some sort of self-feeling, such as pride or mortification (Cooley, 1902).

Even before Cooley's perfection of this "looking-glass" model, confronting others' views of us had been linked with a variety of self-feelings, emotions, and sentiments, including pride, shame, and guilt (Baldwin, 1897; James, 1890). Among more modern sociologists, attention has focused on the emotional impact of other's unwanted views of us and how confronting such views can generate in us embarrassment (Goffman, 1956; Gross & Stone, 1964) or even rage (Scheff, 1995).

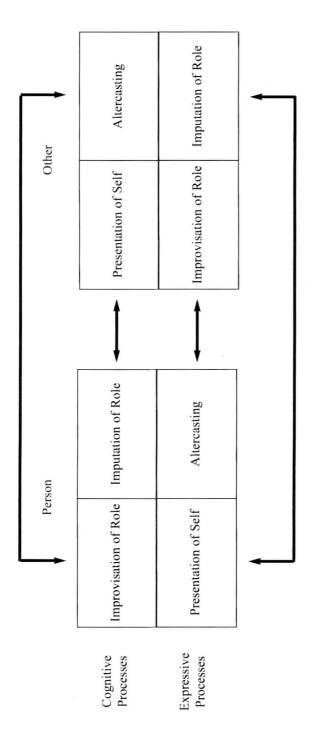

Figure 2. The Working Agreement on Identities.

But what exactly do we mean when we gloss other's view of us as an "unwanted" view? Do we mean that other's representation of us imputes to us a "negative identity" (in the specific sense developed here)? The TST and WAIN data we have considered earlier cast doubt on that interpretation, since it shows that people do reliably choose to assert some negative identities. More likely, I suggest, other's view of us is "unwanted" to the extent it imputes to us identities (positive or, perhaps especially, negative) that we had excluded from our situational self. That is to say, it is unwanted in that it attributes to us identities that we ourselves had relegated to Not-Me. Perhaps lending some weight to this latter interpretation is the suggestion (Smith-Lovin, 1990) that emotion can often be linked to confirmation or disconfirmation of identity.[5]

Identity-Bargaining Responses

Much has been written on the tactics of identity-bargaining (Blumstein, 1975; Weinstein & Deutschberger, 1964) to achieve a working agreement on identities. Two matters need to be emphasized here.

First, it is one's involvement in this bargaining process that constitutes the reactive aspect of one's identity work. Second, this bargaining process confers a distinctive twist on the by-now familiar matter of asserting or denying identities. In this specific context, to assert an identity (and thus to make a claim about Me) amounts to accepting other's altercasting (i.e., accepting the received identities). To deny an identity (and thus make a claim about Not-Me) amounts to resisting other's altercasting (i.e., denying the received identities). Negative identities, in my sense of the term, may be particularly difficult to resist (Prus, 1975; Rogers & Buffalo, 1974,). Perhaps the most familiar illustration of these difficulties is Richard Nixon's pained, repeated, and largely unsuccessful cry, *I am not a crook!* Despite his many denials, his claim about Not-Me, most Americans continue to impute to Nixon that negative identity.

Encounter Phases and Facework

Of course, even an apparently solid working agreement about identities is always threatened, by apparently discrepant events and disclosures, and often it collapses, requiring renegotiation of the identities of all present. Many encounters thus display sequential phases, much like growth rings, reflecting successive working agreements on identities.

In that context identity work takes the form of "facework," or identity management—i.e., situational communication practices that enact, support, or challenge a working agreement on identities (Tracy, 1990). According to Goffman (1955, 1959), these divide into "corrective practices"—what people do after there has been a challenge to a participant's identity—and "preventative practices"—actions taken to avoid such challenges. Corrective practices thus amount to reactive identity work, while preventative practices equate to proactive identity work.

To challenge an already negotiated agreement about identities is essentially either to deny an identity that has been already attributed to a participant (thus challenging other's Me) or to attribute an identity that has been already excluded from other (thus challenging

---

[5]Indeed, that point lies at the heart of affect control theory (Heise, 1979; MacKinnon, 1994). At issue, actually, is whether emotions generated by events that exceed relevant identity standards will be positive or negative in content (Burke, this volume; Carver & Scheier, 1998).

other's Not-Me). In either case, a remedial interchange follows, in an attempt to somehow "explain away" the apparently disconfirming event or condition. The variety of such "accounts"—including excuses, justifications, apologies, disclaimers, and the like—and factors that affect the probability of their acceptance have been well studied by social psychologists (Cody & McLaughlin, 1990).

CONCLUSIONS

In the future, I suggest, identity theory and research will want to take account of the negative pole of identity, the Not-Me, in addition to its more familiar positive pole, the Me. But in doing so, our attention must not be confined to situation-scale timespans, as it has been in this chapter, for the self is an enduring, fairly stable system. The self as object—the Me, but also the Not-Me—responds situationally but is constructed (and reconstructed) over substantial spans of time.

One of the most interesting facts about the longitudinal, "career-scale" view of self (McCall & Simmons, 1982) is that, quite often, what was Me becomes Not-Me, and what was Not-Me becomes Me. Roles with which the person identified self become foci of self-disidentification, and vice versa. Usually these changes reflect typical career sequences, organized by ordinary social institutions (Hughes, 1958; McCall and Simmons 1978/1966; Strauss, 1959), and are termed "alternations" of identity (Travisano, 1970). Occasionally, however, changes between the Me and Not-Me are quite unexpected developments (Goffman, 1961a; Rambo, 1995; Scott, 1979), or true "conversions" in identity (Travisano, 1970). Career-scale changes in the Me and Not-Me always involve processes of "role dispossession" (Goffman, 1961a) and "role exit" (Ebaugh, 1988) on the one hand and the complementary processes of resocialization (Fein, 1990) on the other.

Identity work, whether career-scale or situation-scale, is always a social (not merely a personal) undertaking, with some very interesting consequences for the grammar of identity.

REFERENCES

Alexander, C. N., & Wiley, M.G. (1981). Situated activity and identity formation. In M. Rosenberg & R. H. Turner (Eds.), *Social psychology:Sociological perspectives* (pp. 269–289). New York: Basic Books.

Anderson, N. H. (1968). Likableness ratings of 555 personality-trait words. *Journal of Personality and Social Psychology, 9*, 272–279.

Baldwin, J. M. (1897). *Social and ethical interpretations in mental development.* New York: Macmillan.

Blumer, H. (1962). Society as symbolic interaction. In A. M. Rose (Ed.), *Human behavior and social processes* (pp. 179–192). Boston: Houghton Mifflin.

Blumstein, P.W. (1975). Identity-bargaining and self-conception. *Social Forces, 53*, 476–485.

Burke, P.J. (1980). The self: Measurement requirements from a symbolic interactionist perspective. *Social Psychology Quarterly, 44*, 83–92.

_____. (1991). Identity processes and social stress. *American Sociological Review, 56*, 836–849.

Burke, P. J., & Reitzes, D.C. (1981). The link between identity and role performance. *Social Psychology Quarterly, 43*, 18–29.

Carver, C. S., & Scheier, M.F. (1998). *On the self-regulation of behavior.* Cambridge: Cambridge University Press.

Cody, M. J., & McLaughlin, M.L. (1990). Interpersonal accounting. In H. Giles & P. Robinson (Eds.), *Handbook of language and social psychology* (pp. 227–255). New York: Wiley.

Collier, G., Kuiken, D., & Enzle, M.E. (1982). The role of grammatical qualification in the expression and perception of emotion *Journal of Psycholinguistic Research, 11*, 631–650.

Cooley, C. H. (1902). *Human nature and the social order.* New York: Scribner's.

Ebaugh, H.R. F. (1988). *Becoming an ex: The process of role exit*. Chicago: University of Chicago Press.

Fein, M. L. (1990). *Role change: A resocialization perspective*. New York: Praeger.

Edwards, A. L. (1957). *The social desirability variable in personality assessment and research*. New York: Dryden Press.

Evans, J. St B. T. (1972). Reasoning with negatives. *British Journal of Psychology, 63*, 213–219.

Foote, N. (1951). Identification as the basis for a theory of motivation. *American Sociological Review, 16*, 14–22.

Fries, C. C. (1952). *The structure of English: An introduction to the construction of English sentences*. New York: Harcourt, Brace & World.

Freitas, A., Kaiser, S., Chandler, J., Hall, C., Kim, J., & Hammidi, T. (1997). Appearance management as border construction: Least favorite clothing, group distancing, and identity . . . not! *Sociological Inquiry, 67*, 323–335.

Gecas, V., & Burke, P.J. (1995). Self and identity. In K. S. Cook, G. A. Fine, & J. S. House (Eds.), *Sociological perspectives on social psychology* (pp. 41–67). Boston: Allyn and Bacon.

Goffman, E. (1955). On face-work: An analysis of ritual elements in social interaction. *Psychiatry, 18*, 213–231.

_____. (1956). Embarrassment and social organization. *American Journal of Sociology, 62*, 264–274.

_____. (1959). *The presentation of self in everyday life*. New York: Doubleday Anchor.

_____. (1961a). *Asylums*. New York: Doubleday Anchor.

_____. (1961b). *Encounters*. Indianapolis: Bobbs-Merrill.

_____. (1963). *Stigma*. Englewood Cliffs, NJ: Prentice-Hall.

_____. (1974). *Frame analysis*. New York: Harper & Row.

_____. (1981). *Forms of talk*. Philadelphia: University of Pennsylvania Press.

Gordon, C. (1968). Self-conceptions: Configurations of content. In C. Gordon & K. J. Gergen (Eds.), *The self in social interaction*, Vol. 1 (pp. 115–136). New York: Wiley.

_____. (1969). Self-conceptions methodologies. *Journal of Nervous and Mental Disease, 148*, 328–364.

Gross, E., & Stone, G.P. (1964). Embarassment and the organization of role requirements. *American Journal of Sociology, 70*, 1–15.

Heise, D. R. (1979). *Understanding events: Affect and the construction of social action*. New York: Cambridge University Press.

Hickman, C. A., & Kuhn, M.H. (1956). *Individuals, groups, and economic behavior*. New York: Dryden Press.

Howard, J. A. (2000). Social psychology of identities. *Annual Review of Sociology, 26*, 367–393.

Hughes, E. C. (1958). *Men and their work*. Chicago: Aldine.

James, W. (1890). *Principles of psychology*. New York: Holt.

Jones, E. E., & Pittman, T.S. (1982). Toward a general theory of self-presentation. In J. Suls (Ed.), *Psychological perspectives on the self*, Volume 1 (pp. 231–262). Hillsdale, NJ: Erlbaum.

Kuhn, M. H. (1960). Self-attitudes by sex and professional training. *Sociological Quarterly, 1*, 39–55.

Kuhn, M. H., & McPartland, T.S. (1954). An empirical investigation of self-attitudes. *American Sociological Review, 19*, 68–76.

Kuiken, D. (1981). Non-immediate language style and inconsistency between private and expressed evaluations. *Journal of Experimental Social Psychology, 17*, 183–196.

MacKinnon, N. J. (1994). *Symbolic interactionism as affect control*. Albany: State University of New York Press.

Markus, H., & Nurius, P. (1986). Possible selves. *American Psychologist, 41*, 954–969.

McCall, G. J. (1979, April). *The functions of deviant identities in the formation of role-identity*. Southern Sociological Society, Atlanta, GA.

McCall, G. J., & Simmons, J.L. (1978/1966). *Identities and interactions*. New York: Free Press.

_____. (1982). *Social psychology: A sociological approach*. New York: Free Press.

Mead, G. H. (1934). *Mind, self, and society*. Chicago: University of Chicago Press.

Mosier, C. I. (1941). A psychometric study of meaning. *Journal of Social Psychology, 13*, 123–140.

Ogilvie, D. M. (1987). The undesired self: A neglected variable in personality research. *Journal of Personality and Social Psychology, 52*, 379–385.

Owens, T. J. (1993). Accentuate the positive—and the negative: Rethinking the use of self-esteem, self-deprecation, and self-confidence. *Social Psychology Quarterly, 56*, 288–299.

Oyserman, D., & Markus, H. (1990). Possible selves and delinquency. *Journal of Personality and Social Psychology, 59*, 112–125.

Paulhus, D. L., & Levitt, K. (1987). Desirable responding triggered by affect: Automatic egotism? *Journal of Personality and Social Psychology, 52*, 245–259.

Preston, J.M. (1984). Referential communication: Some factors influencing communication efficiency. *Canadian Journal of Behavioural Science, 16*, 196–207.

Prus, R. C. (1975). Resisting designations: An extension of attribution theory into a negotiated context. *Sociological Inquiry, 45*, 3–14.

Rambo, L. R. (1995). *Understanding religious conversion.* New Haven: Yale University Press.

Rentsch, J. R., & Heffner, T.S. (1994). Assessing self-concept: Analysis of Gordon's coding scheme using "Who Am I?" responses. *Journal of Social Behavior and Personality, 9*, 283–300.

Rhodewatt, F.T. (1986). Self-presentation and the phenomenal self: On the stability and malleability of self-conceptions. In R. F. Baumeister (Ed.), *Public self and private self* (pp. 117–142). New York: Springer Verlag.

Robinson, D., & Smith-Lovin, L. (1992). Selective interaction as a strategy for identity maintenance: An affect control model. *Social Psychology Quarterly, 55*, 12–28.

Rogers, J. W., & Buffalo, M.D. (1974). Fighting back: Nine modes of adaptation to a deviant label. *Social Problems , 22*, 101–118.

Scheff, T. J. (1995). Socialization of emotions: Pride and shame as causal agents. In T. D. Kemper (Ed.), *Research agendas in the sociology of emotions* (pp. 281–304). New York: SUNY Press.

Schlenker, B. R. (1980). *Impression management: The self-concept, social identity, and interpersonal relations.* Monterey, CA: Brooks/Cole.

Scott, R. A. (1979). *The making of blind men: A study of adult socialization.* Rutgers, NJ: Transaction Books.

Smith-Lovin, L. (1990). Emotion as confirmation and disconfirmation of identity: An affect control model. In T. D. Kemper (Ed.), *Research agendas in the sociology of emotions* (pp. 238–270). New York: SUNY Press

Spitzer, S., Couch, C., & Stratton, J. (1971). *The assessment of self.* Iowa City, IA: Sernoll.

Stone, G. P. (1962). Appearance and the self. In A. M. Rose (Ed.), *Human behavior and social processes* (pp. 86–118). Boston: Houghton Mifflin.

Strauss, A. L. (1959). *Mirrors and masks: The search for identity.* New York: Free Press.

Stryker, S. (1962). Conditions of accurate role-taking: A test of Mead's theory. In A. M. Rose (Ed.), *Human behavior and social processes* (pp. 41–62). Boston: Houghton Mifflin.

_____. (1980). *Symbolic interactionism: A social structural version.* Menlo Park, CA: Benjamin Cummings.

Stryker, S., & Burke, P.J. (2001). The past, present, and future of an identity theory. *Social Psychology Quarterly, 63*, 284–297.

Sullivan, H. S. (1953). *The interpersonal theory of psychiatry.* New York: Norton.

Swann, W. B., Jr., Pelham, B.W., & Krull, D.S. (1989). Agreeable fancy or disagreeable truth? Reconciling self-enhancement and self-verification. *Journal of Personality and Social Psychology, 57*, 782–791.

Swann, W. B., Jr., & Read, S.J. (1981). Acquiring self-knowledge: The search for feedback that fits. *Journal of Personality and Social Psychology, 41*, 1119–1128.

Tedeschi, J. T. (Ed.). (1981). *Impression management theory and social psychological research.* New York: Academic Press.

Tracy, K. (1990). The many faces of facework. In H. Giles & P. Robinson (Eds.), *Handbook of language and social psychology* (pp. 209–226). New York: Wiley.

Travisano, R. V. (1970). Alternation and conversion as qualitatively different transformations. In G. P. Stone & H. A. Farberman (Eds.), *Social psychology through symbolic interaction* (pp. 594–606). New York: Wiley.

Tucker, C. (1966). Some methodological problems of Kuhn's self theory. *Sociological Quarterly, 7*, 345–358.

Turner, R. H. (1962). Role-taking: Process versus conformity. In A. M. Rose (Ed.), *Human behavior and social processes* (pp. 20–40). Boston: Houghton Mifflin.

_____. (1968). The self-conception in social interaction. In C. Gordon & K. J. Gergen (Eds.), *The self in social interaction,* Vol. 1 (pp. 93–106). New York: Wiley.

Turner, R. H., & Schutte, J. (1981). The true self method for studying the self conception. *Symbolic Interaction, 4*, 1–20.

Weinstein, E., & Deutschberger, P. (1964). Tasks, bargains, and identities in social interaction. *Social Forces, 42*, 451–456.

Wright, D. E. (1999). *Personal relationships.* Mountain View, CA: Mayfield.

Yardley, K. (1987). What do *you* mean "Who Am I?": Exploring the implications of a self-concept measurement with subjects. In K. Yardley & T. Honess (Eds.), *Self and identity: Psychosocial perspectives* (pp. 211–230). Chichester: Wiley.

Chapter **2**

Roots of Identity
Family Resemblances

K. Jill Kiecolt and Anna F. LoMascolo

According to "Miss Manners," most families have at least one relative who "can give you the provenance of your entire face, telling you the source of your eye color, curls, freckles and the angle of your ears. Furthermore, they can tell you why you are so stubborn, passive or restless, whether you will turn out to be no good, and at what age you can expect to lose your figure, hair, teeth, and memory" (Martin, 2000, p. F5).

Family resemblances to one's parents are part of most individuals' self-concepts, yet they have received little attention in research on self and identity. Family resemblances can include physical appearance, attributes such as personality traits, role identities, and sociodemographic characteristics, and they can be actual or possible selves (Markus & Nurius, 1986).

In this paper we explore the nature of family resemblances between parents and children as an aspect of individuals' self-concepts. We describe three mechanisms by which family resemblances can enter individuals' self-concepts. We then propose a theoretical model of the perceived degree of family resemblances that draws on identity theory (Stryker, 1980, 1987; Stryker & Burke, 2000) and role-identity theory (McCall & Simmons, 1978). Along the way, we also address several related questions: Does it matter if individuals embrace or dislike their resemblance to a parent? Does the perceived degree of resemblance decrease or matter less as young adults become independent of their parents? How might perceived family resemblances affect identity formation? Among children of interracial marriages, how might perceived resemblance to one's parents serve as a basis for identity construction?

FAMILY RESEMBLANCES AS ASPECTS OF IDENTITY

How should we conceive of family resemblances as aspects of the self-concept? We argue that they are both individual identities and collective identities. A collective identity refers to the portion of one's self-concept that is based on one's perceived "membership in a social group (or groups) together with the value and emotional significance attached to that membership" (Tajfel, 1981, p. 255). Put differently, collective identities answer the question

"Who are we?" These "we's" are "identifications of the self with a group as a whole" (Thoits & Virshup, 1997, p. 106). Individual identities, in contrast, are self-descriptions of oneself as an individual—"who I am."

Collective identities are formed through identification with a social group. To date, most research has investigated collective identities formed through identification with large-scale social categories such as race, ethnicity, class, and nationality (Thoits & Virshup, 1997). Perceived family resemblances entail identification of the self with specific family members, or perhaps with only one other person. No research of which we are aware treats identification with a parent as a collective identity, but some research has investigated identification with a partner in a romantic relationship. In this context, too, an individual essentially has a collective identity, a "we-feeling" with another person that occurs when the individual "includes [another] in the self" (Aron et al., 1991, p. 242). This means that an individual comes to see self and other as sharing characteristics (Aron et al., 1991). Individuals may perceive resemblances to their parents on any sort of identity (Thoits & Virshup, 1997, p. 125): physical appearance (tall), mannerisms (gestures), personality or character traits (honest, hard-working), social types of person (intellectual), role identities (Presbyterian ministers), or even sociodemographic groupings (African American). These types of identities are the possible "meanings" of family resemblances. That is, the "meanings" of family resemblances are themselves identities, and as discussed below, some identities can be nested in or attached to others (Reid & Deaux, 1996).

First, attributes—personality or character traits and associated behaviors—can form the basis of perceived family resemblances. What identities "mean" usually has been defined in terms of the personality traits associated with them (e.g., Burke & Reitzes, 1981) or the traits that distinguish complementary identities (e.g., gender identities) from each other (Burke & Tully, 1977). Similarly, individuals' personality traits and behaviors ("personal identities") can be attached to their various role identities ("social identities") (Reid & Deaux, 1996) or can overlap in meaning with role identities (Stets, 1995). In our case, the "meanings" of perceived family resemblances—the characteristics that family members share—are personality or character traits and associated behaviors, such as "talkative" or "hard-working."

Second, physical characteristics and mannerisms can form the basis for perceived family resemblances just as personality characteristics do. A man, for example, sees that he has "his mother's eyes" and "his father's nose." Third, role identities—self-designations based on occupying particular social positions—are another basis of perceived resemblances to a parent. A child may take up a parent's occupation (as sociologist Robin Stryker, daughter of Sheldon Stryker, has done) or assume a parent's role identity as a blood donor (Piliavin & Callero, 1991). As with all collective identities, a "we feeling" is involved: A child perceives similarity to a parent because they share a role identity.

For shared role identities to be thought of as family resemblances, they must distinguish family members from outsiders (Turner et al., 1994). Shared occupational, recreational, and civic role identities may form the basis for perceived family resemblances, because children in the United States do not necessarily follow in their parents' footsteps. Family role identities (e.g., "parent") that children and parents share will not be seen as "family resemblances" because they are so common across families. Moreover, shared role identities probably do not become part of a family identity unless they also are central and salient individual identities.

Finally, perceived resemblances to a parent can be based on social categories such as race, ethnicity, or country of origin that not only describe who "we" are as parent and child, but also convey information about families' sociodemographic group memberships. Perceiving a family resemblance based on a sociodemographic characteristic is more likely when the social category is of high centrality. Ethnic identity often is a master status for members of racial and ethnic minority groups, but is of low centrality for "white ethnics" in the United States (Alba, 1990).

Perceived family resemblances are not only collective identities, but also individual identities that describe "who I am" (Thoits & Virshup, 1997). Individual identities, too, can refer to one's physical characteristics, mannerisms, personality or character traits, social types of person, role identities, or sociodemographic groupings. Like Thoits and Virshup (1997), we focus on individual identities that people might share with others, rather than on "unique or highly specific details of biography and idiosyncratic experiences" (p. 107).

How me states and we states relate to one other is an important, unresolved issue (Thoits & Virshup, 1997, p. 127). Social identity theory argues that at any given moment, an individual's attention is focused either on a me state or a we state (Thoits & Virshup, 1997; Turner et al., 1987). As Thoits and Virshup (1997, p. 127) argue convincingly, however, "people may simultaneously be aware of themselves" at both levels. For example, a woman sees herself as determined and patient, just as her father is; and she sometimes thinks of that resemblance as she sees herself showing determination and patience. Nevertheless, people probably experience we states much less frequently than me states (Tajfel, 1981; Thoits & Virshup, 1997).

Because "me's and we's are qualitatively different states, . . . they probably do not merge," for merging implies that they fuse into a single entity (Thoits & Virshup 1997, p. 129). Instead, in the case of family resemblances, "we's" may *modify* "me's" in an important way: A sense of "who we are" as family members may strengthen an individual's core sense of "who I am." Most individuals have some sense of how they resemble a biological parent. Not knowing how one resembles one's biological parents may be problematic, because of the primacy and legitimacy that blood relations are accorded in society (Wegar, 1999). Specifically, research on identity formation among adoptees, though limited, implies that knowing "who I am" may depend partly on knowing "who we are" (e.g., Haimes, 1987). Some adoptees say that they do not know who they are because they lack ties to biological kin. The following quote illustrates this dilemma as well as the dual individual and collective nature of family resemblances:

> When I found my natural mother, I felt deep inside me that I had finally found myself. I could fill so many empty pockets: who I looked like; where my ancestors came from; where I got my interests, talents and even allergies (Grotevant, 1997, p. 13).

Hence, some components of the self-concept may seem more authentic (Turner, 1987) or may be more crystallized—more firmly held (Markus, 1977; Rosenberg, 1981)—when they can be linked or attached to a source such as one's parents. Similarly, some adoptees claim that finding their biological parents enables them to "place themselves socially" and to "compile a consistent biography" (Haimes, 1987, p. 363).[1]

Family resemblances differ from other aspects of the self-concept in that they range from being ascribed to being achieved to some degree. Most often they are neither strictly voluntary nor strictly involuntary. Like other identities, they arise in interaction.

---

[1]In order to fill in those "missing pieces," many adoptive parents of girls from the People's Republic of China construct "origin stories" that positively portray the circumstances surrounding their daughter's birth and de-emphasize abandonment (Miller-Loessi & Kilic, in press). Adoptees may construct their own stories as well.

HOW FAMILY RESEMBLANCES ENTER THE SELF-CONCEPT

Perceived family resemblances are an outcome of interaction among a child and parents and others. Three mechanisms by which family resemblances may enter a child's self-concept are (a) ascription; (b) identification, when children claim or cultivate similarity to a parent; and (c) discovery of resemblances between oneself and a parent. That is, the impetus may come from either a parent or others, or from a child. Furthermore, like socialization more generally, the process may be more or less deliberate or inadvertent (Turner, 1970).

First, in ascription, parents, other family members, and family friends point out resemblances between parents and children. Probably the most important motive for parents and other kin is to signal a child's belonging to a family: ." . . the group's acceptance of the individual as a member" (Ellison, 1993, in Stets & Burke, 2000, p. 233). Before babies are born, parents often imagine which of their characteristics their offspring will inherit and frequently express their hopes for their baby (e.g., "I hope s/he gets my eyes." "I hope s/he is not as temperamental as her/his father." "I hope s/he gets the thin gene from the Joneses, instead of the fat gene from the Smiths.") When the child is born, the parents almost immediately begin to assign features ("he has your dimpled cheeks") and label qualities ("she has her father's laid-back personality"), and they continue to do so as children develop. A parent might also claim a resemblance between her or his child and the other parent in order to signal the child's "membership" in the other parent's family. For example, some researchers have found a bias among mothers toward claiming resemblances between infants and their fathers, which the researchers interpret as a strategy for promoting fathers' confidence in their paternity (McLain et al., 2000; Regalski & Gaulin, 1993; Daly & Wilson, 1982). Similarly, a parent might ascribe her or his spouse's characteristics to a child in order to foster closeness between the child and the other parent.

A parent also may call attention to resemblances between herself or himself and a child to shape the child's self-concept and behavior in desired directions.[2] This is a form of altercasting: The parent ("ego") casts the child ("alter") into a particular identity or role type so that the child will enact a desired behavior (Weinstein & Deutschberger, 1963, p. 456). Although altercasting typically refers to ego's assigning alter a complementary role (Weinstein & Deutschberger, 1963; Blumstein, 1991), it can be extended to assigning alter a collective identity, based on similarity between ego and alter (Stets & Burke, 2000). In this case, a parent claims resemblance with her or his child to reinforce a desired behavior or deter an undesired behavior. A parent might say to a child, "Don't give up. We are not quitters!"

Parents also might point out resemblances between themselves and their child to influence an audience's perceptions. In these cases, noting a family resemblance is a figurative form of investiture (Stone, 1962), which originally referred to parents' dressing infants to signal their gender, thereby evoking desired "responses of the world toward the child" (p. 106). Investiture simultaneously assigns an infant a gender and publicly claims that identity. It is impression management from without. Similarly, when parents point out family resemblances to an audience, they "invest" a child (and themselves) with attributes. For example, a father admires his daughter Jane's sculpture at an art fair. He comments to Jane and a family friend, "Jane is a terrific artist, isn't she? I think she inherited some of her mother's artistic ability."[3]

---

[2]Wylie (1987) finds in a small-scale observation study that as mothers interact with their child, they make numerous attributions, usually with evaluative content, about what the child is like. These attributions are tailored to the child's level of development.

[3]A more contemporary term for this process is "identity work" (Snow & Anderson, 1987).

Sometimes parents engage in investiture to redefine a negative characteristic as a more positive one. A mother might tell her daughter's teacher, "I know that Lily has a hard time sitting still in class. I was just like her—very high energy," and tell her daughter also. At times the audience is the other parent. For example, a child's father might say, "Sam is obstinate," and his mother might say, "Sam isn't obstinate. He's fiercely independent, just as I am."[4]

The family resemblances that parents and others ascribe to children do not instantly become part of children's self-concepts, however. Over time, parents and others call attention to specific ways in which a child resembles one parent or another ("John doesn't obey because, like me, he hates being told what to do"). They then attribute some of the child's behaviors to a shared characteristic ("John is willful just like his mother"). This process of attribution should lead the child to see a family resemblance (e.g., "In this way, I'm like my mother") that not only incorporates "willfulness" into his self-concept as an individual identity, but also establishes a sense of belongingness and connection to his mother.

A second mechanism through which children may come to perceive family resemblances is identification, in which children imitate a parent or look for resemblances to parents on desirable characteristics. Identification reinforces a child's feeling of belonging to her or his family. By perceiving ourselves to be similar to others, we feel connected to them (Schimel et al., 2000, p. 446). In addition, "[b]y virtue of being associated with some individual, one's own identity takes on characteristics from the identity of the other" (Turner, 1970, p. 67), resulting in lasting change in the self-concept.

The third mechanism by which children may discern family resemblances is self-attribution (Bem, 1967) or discovery (Turner, 1987). As children grow up and assume new roles, they may discover qualities in themselves that they attribute to parental resemblance. A college student might find that like her grandfather, she wants to pursue a military career. An individual might hear himself telling his child, "You will do this because I said so," just as his father used to tell him. In these instances, individuals suddenly see similarities to a family member, perhaps thinking, "I'm a lot like that person." As in identification, this feeling of likeness involves incorporating another into one's self-concept and changes an individual's self-concept. The mechanism of self-attribution extends Bem's (1967) self-perception theory to social identity theory. In this case, an individual not only infers her or his own characteristics from her or his behavior, but infers the attached collective identity as well.

Not all self-attributions, or discoveries of similarity to a parent, result from long-term relationships, however. Sometimes self-attributions quickly occur among adoptees who have just obtained information about their pre-adoption selves and their biological kin. This information typically leads adoptees to reappraise who they are. Some adoptees regard the new information as embellishments that do not fundamentally change their existing identities. Others see the new information as constituting their "real" selves, heretofore hidden, and assign it centrality in their self-concepts (Haimes, 1987, p. 365). In either case, adoptees have established a new collective identity, in which they feel similar to at least one of their biological parents.

As a result of these three processes, children tend to believe that they resemble their parents to some degree. It is difficult for children to resist their parents' definitions of them. Young children (ages 8 to 11), especially, place greater faith in their parents' knowledge of

---

[4]Such responses also indicate a parent's identification with her or his child (Turner, 1970, pp. 66–67).

what they are like on visible characteristics (intelligence, attractiveness) than they do their own. The older the child, the greater the reliance on the self for such information (Rosenberg, 1979, pp. 243–244).

INFLUENCES ON PERCEIVED FAMILY RESEMBLANCES

In this section we consider how to explain the degree of perceived family resemblances. Two theories in sociology, Stryker's identity theory (1980) and McCall and Simmons' role-identity theory (1978), have addressed the relative prominence of self-concept elements. Components of those two theories also can explain perceived resemblances to one's parents.[5]

Briefly, Stryker's identity theory (Stryker, 1980, 1987; Stryker & Burke, 2000; Stryker & Serpe, 1994) proposes that role identities are ranked on a hierarchy of salience. Salience, defined as "readiness to act out an identity" (Stryker & Serpe, 1994, p. 17), in turn depends on (1) *interactional commitment*—the number of relationships owing to a given role identity, and (2) *affective commitment*—the strength of ties to others involved in the role identity. Put another way, commitment to social relationships affects identity salience (Stryker, 1987, p. 89).

In McCall and Simmons' role-identity theory (1978, pp. 74–77), the prominence of a role identity depends on its reward value, which is a function of others' support of the identity and of the extrinsic and intrinsic gratifications of competently performing the identity. *Support for a role identity* refers to how favorably other people evaluate an individual's role performance, or by extension, a personality trait or physical characteristic. *Extrinsic gratifications* from performing a role identity include money, goods, and favors. Some personality traits and physical characteristics could net extrinsic rewards in combination with particular role identities. For example, being extraverted is apt to be financially rewarding for a sales representative. Other personality traits may receive even broader support. For example, "favored personality configurations" are tendencies that facilitate persons' mobility in the stratification system via selection mechanisms (Turner, 1988, p. 5). *Intrinsic gratifications* from role performance include self-perceived competence as well as more role-specific rewards, as when chefs enjoy what they cook. Personality traits and physical characteristics also may be intrinsically gratifying, either across role identities or in connection with specific role identities.

Together these two theories suggest a model, shown in Figure 1, in which salience depends on affective commitment, interactional commitment, and the rewards from enacting a role identity. Burke and Reitzes (1991) and Brennan et al. (2000) have tested similar combined models. In the case of perceived family resemblances, Stryker's identity theory would predict that the greater the interactional and affective commitment to one's parents and to other relationships surrounding the parent-child relationship, the higher the degree of perceived similarity to one's parents. McCall and Simmons' role-identity theory would predict that the more rewards from perceived family resemblances, the more such resemblances children will perceive.

---

[5]We also believe that the same model can help predict the salience of family resemblances as both individual and collective identities, but do not develop this idea here.

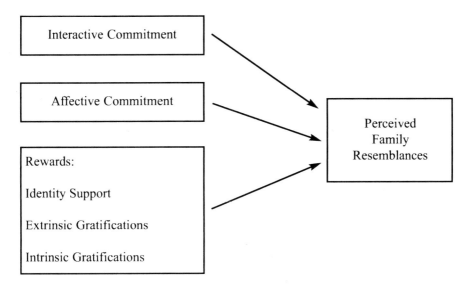

Figure 1. Model for Perceived Family Resemblances.

Commitment and Family Resemblances

Interactional commitment—here the ties premised on children's filial role—should positively influence children's degree of perceived resemblance to their parents. Interactional commitment (and hence the salience of the filial role) has been predicted to decline over time as children reach adulthood and acquire occupational, marital, and parental roles (Roberts & Bengtson, 1993, p. 264). Even earlier, as children grow up, they acquire more alternative sources of information and evaluation about the self (Rosenberg, 1979, pp. 243–244). Moreover, children are less bound by traits ascribed to them as they learn how to engage in self-affirmation, "an effort to construct a particular kind of self" (Turner, 1987).

Applied here, interactional commitment also refers to the costs of relationships foregone if children were unable to play their filial role. This can be a matter of degree. In general, interactional commitment, and hence perceived resemblance to parents, is predicted to change when children's identities change along dimensions that are bases for family resemblances *and* in ways that threaten (or enhance) their ties to parents and kin. Here are four examples: A member of a Christian family converts to Judaism (*sociodemographic characteristic*). The son of two writers quits bodybuilding, which his parents deplored, and writes a book about his experiences as a bodybuilder (Fussell, 1991) (*role choice*). A man rejects his insouciance, which he learned from his hippie parents, and becomes very "serious" about life (*personality characteristic*). A former beauty queen's daughter, who was a tomboy in her youth, begins conforming to her mother's standards of feminine appearance by wearing makeup, feminine clothes, and so forth (*appearance*). These changes either lessen or enhance individuals' ties to parents and kin, and in some cases, other social ties as well. At any given time, perceived resemblance to one's parents should be positively related to ties to parents and to others who positively reinforce those resemblances.

Interactional commitment may have a stronger effect on perceived resemblance for children who grow up with both biological parents. Even if both parents remain close to their children after a divorce, they are probably less likely than other parents to point out resemblances between their children and their former spouse. Parents of adoptees may be less likely to search for and find resemblances between themselves and their children, and other people may be less likely to do so as well. One study finds that parents of adopted children ascribe more influence to heredity and less to environment in forming human characteristics than other parents do (Meerum Terwogt, Hoeksma, & Koops, 1993).[6] As discussed above, some adoptees regard the characteristics on which they resemble their biological parents as more "real" than their other characteristics, perhaps including those they share with adoptive parents. In such cases, interactional ties to adoptive parents may carry less weight.

Affective commitment also should be positively related to the degree of family resemblance. A study of college students from two-parent families and their parents (Fox, 1999) found that the stronger the students' emotional attachment to a given parent, the more similar students and that parent were on the Big Five personality dimensions. Moreover, students thought they resembled a given parent less when they and the other parent were in a coalition against the given parent. In another study, the closer young Israeli adults felt to their grandparents, the more similar they felt to them (Romano, 1997). Perceived similarity may increase closeness as well. Nevertheless, family dynamics that influence children's affective attachment to their parents and other family members may influence the salience of the identities, particularly the personality traits, involved in those family resemblances.

The mechanism by which commitment results in perceived family resemblances is a type of identification based on role-taking. Identification can imply that "[o]ne person sees events as if he were in another's shoes" (Turner, 1970, p.169). Over time, a child who identifies with her or his parent will come to respond to some events and situations as the parent would, because the child defines situations from the parent's perspective. Such responses can become perceived similarities with parents when children label their responses as an individual identity, and one that they share with a parent. Turner proposes that similarities owing to this kind of identification are less exact than similarities arising from imitation, but less easily eradicated (p. 169). They may even be embodied as physical resemblances: A longitudinal study of couples married twenty-five years finds that spouses resemble each other more over time, presumably because of the "habitual use of facial musculature" in the process of "repeated empathic mimicry" (Zajonc et al., 1987, p. 335).[7] Role-taking, then, can reinforce genetic similarities between biological parents and children and create similarities between adoptive parents and children.

Rewards and Family Resemblances

From McCall and Simmons' role-identity theory, we predict that the greater the rewards from perceived family resemblances, the more similar children will perceive they are to their parents. The rewards depend heavily on whether given identities or characteristics are viewed as desirable or undesirable. As noted above, rewards can be of several types. The first is support for an identity. The more favorably parents evaluate a shared identity or attribute, the more they should support it in their children. Probably most family resemblances that parents and others point out in children are positive or neutral. Just as

---

[6]A belief in heredity over environment has gained ground among adoption advocates, some of whom urge parents to accept their adopted children's inherited traits rather than trying to change them (Wegar, 1997). To the extent that adoptive parents accept this dictum, they may be less likely to search for or to construct resemblances between themselves and their children.

[7]We are indebted to Janice Kiecolt-Glaser for this reference.

parents search for signs that their children have their positive attributes, however, they also may watch for signs of undesirable attributes. Sometimes parents see in their child a characteristic that they dislike in themselves.[8] For example, a parent who feels handicapped by shyness might hope that her child would not be shy. Depending on how mutable parents believe a negative identity or attribute to be, they might try to eradicate it or minimize it through rewards or punishments.

The extrinsic and intrinsic gratifications associated with an identity also depend on how desirable the attribute is. Perceived family resemblances should be stronger for identities that bring extrinsic gratifications, such as money, or intrinsic gratifications, such as self-perceived competence or a sense of moral worth. Not surprisingly, individuals are more likely to perceive themselves as similar to persons who have positive attributes (Schimel et al., 2000). Children probably tend to embrace resemblances to their parents on desirable characteristics and to deny resemblances on negative ones as "Not-Me" (McCall, this volume). If a resemblance is undeniable and children believe it is mutable, they may do identity work to appear different from their parent (Snow & Anderson, 1987) or try to change themselves to avoid becoming a "feared self" (Kiecolt & Mabry, 2000). If an undesirable attribute seems immutable, one has an excuse for it.

Children may distance themselves psychologically from a parent "with undesirable attributes, particularly when they have reason to fear that they may possess those attributes themselves" (Schimel et al., 2000, p. 447). For example, some adoptees are ambivalent about discovering who their biological parents are. The fear of turning up a disreputable biological parent seems linked to the fear of resembling the disreputable biological parent without having realized it.[9]

Because people tend to distance themselves emotionally from someone with whom they share a negative attribute, Schimel et al. (2000) propose that children and parents who share personality traits that they dislike in themselves often have difficulty getting along with one another. If this hypothesis is correct, sharing a negative attribute could lessen children's affective commitment and perhaps even their interactional commitment to a parent.[10]

CONSEQUENCES OF PERCEIVED FAMILY RESEMBLANCES FOR THE SELF-CONCEPT

The extent and nature of perceived family resemblances may have consequences for other aspects of the self-concept. First, our analysis suggests a possible interpretation for the identity problems that some adoptees report (and some psychologists expect [Wegar, 1999]): Adoptees may have fewer self-schemas than non-adoptees. We suggested above that perceived similarity to one or both parents in personality, appearance, and so forth may help crystallize self-concept elements. We also suggested that people are less likely to search for and find resemblances between adoptive parents and children, because they believe that characteristics are primarily hereditary. Adoptees, too, may ascribe their

---

[8]Of course, parents may unwittingly support negative attributes as well. Parents also may unconsciously project their negative attributes onto their children, in the Freudian sense (Swanson, 1988). The latter process is outside the scope of the analysis.

[9]Ralph H. Turner, personal communication.

[10]Although identity theory links interactional and affective commitment (Stryker & Serpe, 1994), they are somewhat independent. Silverstein and Bengtson (1997), for example, find that some parent-child relationships involve reciprocal exchanges, but lack emotional closeness.

characteristics primarily to heredity, viewing their "real" selves as inhering in the biological link to their "real" parents. If they have no knowledge of what those parents are like, they may have fewer self-schemas than non-adoptees. This hypothesis also could apply to children who are reared by one biological parent instead of two, or even to children who have little contact with their extended kin.

Adoptees, however, may construct self-schemas involving heritable characteristics. They may draw on origin stories (Miller-Loessi & Kilic, in press), or they may deduce such self-schemas by attributing characteristics they share with adoptive family members to learning and unique characteristics to heredity.[11] Similarly, adoptive parents may point out adoptees' unique traits (e.g., musical ability) and ascribe them to heredity.

Second, perceived resemblances between oneself and a parent not only provide information about one's "actual self," but also can represent "possible selves" that foretell "who I will be" (Markus & Nurius, 1986). A young man with a receding hairline might have a bald possible self, modeled on his father. Hence, individuals who cannot or do not construct family resemblances may have fewer or different possible selves.

Third, a lack of family resemblance on physical characteristics that are markers of ethnic status has been thought to hinder ethnic identity formation—at both the individual and collective levels—among transracial and transethnic adoptees (Bausch & Serpe, 1997; Simon & Roorda, 2000). For example, Bausch and Serpe (1997) find that about half of Mexican Americans surveyed in California feared that Latino children adopted by non-Latinos would have an ethnic identity conflict or fail to participate in Latino culture. They cite findings that interracially adopted children of color often feel uncomfortable with their physical appearance or lack pride in their ethnic heritage. Studies of Black adoptees in White families suggest, however, that adoptees do not lack an ethnic identity. For example, "Donna Francis," an African-American adoptee, describes herself as "the opposite" of her White family (Simon & Roorda, 2000, p. 35): "I never took my blackness for granted because I was the opposite of everyone related to me. I had a heightened awareness of my blackness" (pg. 37). Hence, a lack of family resemblance can heighten the salience of ethnic identity.[12] In another case, Chinese girls, most of whom have been adopted by White U.S. families, also are unlikely to lack a Chinese ethnic identity. Adoptive parents have formed associations with other adoptive parents in most large United States cities, in which they "exchange information about adoption experiences . . . and suggested 'origin stories'. They also sponsor Chinese cultural celebrations [and] Mandarin language training" (Miller-Loessi & Kilic, in press).

Because family resemblances are linked to ethnic identities, they also have been viewed as problematic for biracial individuals. Adolescents with one White and one Black parent tend to identify more with the parent they resemble physically, especially on skin color, and with that parent's ethnic culture (Gibbs, 1987). They often adopt visible features of the culture, such as style of dress,[13] and they sometimes reject the other parent's ethnic culture. Perhaps biracial individuals are led by physical resemblances to look for or construct other types of resemblance to that parent as well. How, then, might biracial individuals who do not identify more closely with one parent than another construct an ethnic

---

[11]J. Beth Mabry, personal communication.

[12]Donna Francis's self-description as "the opposite" of her relatives indicates that to her, their characteristics (perhaps physical appearance, demeanor, personality, values, and so forth) are "Not-Me" (McCall, this volume). Her case shows, though, that one need not identify with family members to construct an ethnic identity.

[13]Some teenagers, however, identify with the dominant majority status of their white parent even though they physically resemble the black parent more.

identity? Of note, biracial individuals are not completely free to choose their ethnic identity. They perceive that others assign racial labels to them based on their skin color, and those labels have more influence on their racial self-identification than their own perceptions do (Brunsma & Rockquemore, 2001).

CONCLUSION

We have described family resemblances as both individual and collective identities, outlined three mechanisms by which family resemblances might enter individuals' self-concepts, and proposed a theoretical model of children's perceived degree of resemblance to their parents. Based on Stryker's identity theory (1980), we have proposed that the greater the interactional and affective commitment to one's parents and to other relationships surrounding the parent-child relationship, the greater the perceived similarity. Based on McCall and Simmons' role-identity theory (1978), we have proposed that the greater the rewards from perceived family resemblances in the form of identity support, intrinsic gratifications, and extrinsic gratifications, the greater the perceived similarity. Moreover, as undesirable attributes are not usually rewarded, sharing an undesirable attribute with one's parents will tend to lessen one's affective commitment and even perhaps one's interactional commitment to a parent.

We also have suggested that perceived family resemblances have consequences for other aspects of identity. Persons who lack perceived family resemblances, such as adoptees, may have fewer or less crystallized self-schemas. Such persons also may have fewer or different possible selves. The social significance of physical resemblances to parents may influence ethnic identification among transracial or transethnic adoptees and biracial individuals.

The nature of family resemblances as self-concept elements needs investigation. One question is whether, or under what conditions, people regard characteristics shared with a family member as more indicative of their "true self" than some other parts of their self-concept. As noted above, some adoptees assign greatest authenticity to characteristics they share with their biological parents, perhaps because current fashion ascribes a more personality-determining influence to biology than was true a few decades ago. In contrast, some adults who do not know their biological father view many of their characteristics as less a part of their "'own personality'" because they were inherited (van Kampen et al., 1990, p. 283). The larger question is how much the authenticity of self-concept elements depends on whether they result from ascription, identification, discovery, or one's own efforts.

Second, when do children begin to perceive resemblances between themselves and their parents? Children under age seven apparently do not understand the concept of biological inheritance (Solomon et al., 1996), but they may be able to identify with their parents and to grasp attributions of how they resemble their parents. Third, do family resemblances involve clusters of traits? Empirically, "perceptions of similarity to a person on any given dimension increase the subjective likelihood that one is similar on other dimensions" (Schimel et al., 2000, p. 460). Hence, seeing a resemblance between oneself and a parent on one trait (e.g., being funny) may lead to seeing resemblances on other, related traits (e.g., being outgoing and fun-loving). Perceived similarity on one negative trait also could lead one to fear similarity on related negative traits. Fourth, does the proposed model apply in cultures in which self-construals tend to be more collective and less individualistic than in the United States (Markus & Kitayama, 1991)? Such cultures may be more familistic as well. Are family resemblances more extensive, central, or salient in such cultures than in more individualistic, less familistic cultures?

Testing our model and addressing these questions will require measuring the nature and extent of perceived family resemblances. As a beginning, the Twenty Statements Test (Kuhn & McPartland, 1954) could be modified to elicit perceived resemblances to a given parent, and the "Who Am I NOT?" test (McCall, this volume) could be modified to discover how much and in what ways children differentiate themselves from their parents. Measuring the salience and centrality of such resemblances will be complex, because of their dual individual and collective nature.

Our model of perceived family resemblances may be most useful for investigating the larger context of family interaction. Research on the family emphasizes role-identities and neglects "we-feelings." Yet perceived family resemblances may affect not only individuals' self-concepts, but also family cohesiveness.[14] Lawler (this volume) combines an exchange theory of commitment with structural identity theories to explain the salience of collective identities. His theory also outlines conditions under which collective identities and role-identities influence each other. Our model could be combined with Lawler's theory to investigate the emergence and salience of collective identities within families and the effects of such identities on family solidarity within and between generations. Understanding how such "we-feelings" develop may be especially important in an era in which family affiliations have become more voluntary.

REFERENCES

Alba, R. D. (1990). *Ethnic identity: The transformation of white America.* New Haven: Yale University Press.

Aron, A., Aron, E., Tudor, M., & Nelson, G. (1991). Close relationships as including other in the self. *Journal of Personality and Social Psychology, 60,* 241–253.

Bausch, R. S., & Serpe, R. T. (1997). Negative outcomes of interethnic adoption of Mexican American children. *Social Work, 42,* 136–143.

Bem, D. (1967). Self-perception: An alternative interpretation of cognitive dissonance phenomena. *Psychological Review, 74,* 183–200.

Blumstein, P. (1991). The production of selves in personal relationships. In J. A. Howard & P. L. Callero (Eds.), *The self-society dynamic: Cognition, emotion, and action* (pp. 305–322). New York: Cambridge University Press.

Brennan, K. M., Ritter, C., Salupo, M. M., & Benson, D. E. (2000, August). Measuring identity processes: A reinterpretation and application of Stryker's and Burke's identity theories. Paper presented at the meeting of the American Sociological Association, Washington, D.C.

Brunsma, D. L., & Rockquemore, K. A. (2001). The new color complex: Appearances and biracial identity. *Identity, 1,* 225–246.

Burke, P. J., & Reitzes, D. C. (1981). The link between identity and role performance. *Social Psychology Quarterly, 44,* 83–92.

Burke, P. J., & Reitzes, D. C. (1991). An identity theory approach to commitment. *Social Psychology Quarterly, 54,* 239–251.

Burke, P. J., & Tully, J. C. (1977). The measurement of role identity. *Social Forces, 55,* 881–897.

Daly, M., & Wilson, M. I. (1982). Whom are newborn babies said to resemble? *Ethology & Sociobiology, 3,* 69–78.

Fox, J. M. (2000). Parent-offspring similarity on five personality dimensions: moderating effects of family dynamics. Unpublished doctoral dissertation, University of Connecticut, Storrs.

Fussell, S. W. (1991). *Muscle: Confessions of an unlikely bodybuilder.* New York: Poseidon.

[14]Edward Lawler, personal communication.

Gibbs, J. T. (1987). Identity and marginality: Issues in the treatment of biracial adolescents. *Orthopsychiatry, 57*, 265–278.

Grotevant, H. D. (1997). Coming to terms with adoption: The construction of identity from adolescence into adulthood. *Adoption Quarterly, 1*, 3–26.

Haimes, E. (1987). 'Now I know who I really am.' Identity change and redefinitions of the self in adoption. In T. Honess & K. Yardley (Eds.), *Self and identity: Perspectives across the lifespan* (pp. 359–371), London: Routledge and Kegan Paul.

Kiecolt, K. J., & Mabry, J. B. (2000). Agency in young adulthood: Intentional self-change among college students. *Advances in Life Course Research, 5*, 181–205.

Kuhn, M. H., & McPartland, T. (1954). An empirical investigation of self-attitudes. *American Sociological Review, 19*, 68–76.

Markus, H. (1977). Self-schemata and processing information about the self. *Journal of Personality and Social Psychology, 35*, 63–78.

Markus, H. R., & Kitayama, S. (1991). Culture and the self: Implications for cognition, emotion, and motivation. *Psychological Review, 98*, 224–253.

Markus, H., & Nurius, P. (1986). Possible selves. *American Psychologist, 41*, 954–969.

Martin, J. (2000, November 17). Guard dogs at the family gate. *The Washington Post*, p. F5.

McCall, G., & Simmons, J. L. (1978). *Identities and interactions* (Rev. ed.). New York: Free Press.

McLain, D. K., Setters, D., Moulton, M. P., & Pratt, A. E. (2000). Ascription of resemblance of newborns by parents and nonrelatives. *Evolution and Human Behavior, 21*, 11–23.

Miller-Loessi, K., & Kilic, Z. (in press). Imagined and real: The families of Chinese girls adopted by Westerners. In M. Chamberlain & S. Leydesdorff (Eds.), *Gender and transnational families*. London: Routledge.

Piliavin, J. A., & Callero, P. L. (with Keating, L., Koski, B., & Libby, D.). (1991). *Giving blood: The development of an altruistic identity*. Baltimore: Johns Hopkins University Press.

Regalski, J. M., & Gaulin, S. J. C. (1993). Whom are Mexican infants said to resemble? Monitoring and fostering paternal confidence in the Yucatan. *Ethology & Sociobiology, 14*, 97–113.

Reid, A., & Deaux, K. (1996). Relationship between social and personal identities: segregation or integration? *Journal of Personality and Social Psychology, 71*, 1084–1091.

Roberts, R. E. L., & Bengtson, V. L. (1993). Relationships with parents, self-esteem, and psychological well-being in young adulthood. *Social Psychology Quarterly, 56*, 263–277.

Romano, I. (1997). The relationship between young Israeli adults and their grandparents: Feelings of sameness and emotional closeness. Unpublished doctoral dissertation, Adelphi University.

Rosenberg, M. (1979). *Conceiving the self*. New York: Basic Books.

Rosenberg, M. (1981). The self concept: Social product and social force. M. Rosenberg & R. H. Turner (Eds.), *Social psychology: Sociological perspectives* (pp. 593–624). New York: Basic Books.

Schimel, J., Pyszczynski, T., Greenberg, J., O'Mahen, H., & Arndt, J. (2000). Running from the shadow: Psychological distancing from others to deny characteristics people fear in themselves. *Journal of Personality and Social Psychology, 78*, 446–462.

Silverstein, M., & Bengtson, V. L. (1997). Intergenerational solidarity and the structure of adult child-parent relationships in American families. *American Journal of Sociology, 103*, 429–460.

Simon, R. J., & Roorda, R. M. (2000). *In their own voices*. New York: Columbia University Press.

Snow, D. A., & Anderson, L. (1987). Identity work among the homeless: The verbal construction and avowal of personal identities. *American Journal of Sociology, 92*, 1336–1371.

Solomon, G. E. A., Johnson, S. C., Zaitchik, D. & Carey, S. (1996). Like father, like son: Young children's understanding of how and why offspring resemble their parents. *Child Development, 67*, 151–171.

Stets, J. E. (1995). Role identities and person identities: Gender identity, mastery identity, and controlling one's partner. *Sociological Perspectives, 38*, 129–150.

Stets, J. E., & Burke, P. J. (2000). Identity theory and social identity theory. *Social Psychology Quarterly, 63*, 224–237.

Stone, G. P. (1962). Appearance and the self. In A. M. Rose (Ed.), *Human behavior and social processes* (pp. 86–118). Boston, MA: Houghton Mifflin.

Stryker, S. (1980). *Symbolic interactionism: A social structural version*. Menlo Park, CA: Benjamin/Cummings.

Stryker, S. (1987). Identity theory: Developments and extensions. In K. Yardley & T. Honess (Eds.), *Self and identity: Psychosocial processes* (pp. 89–103). Chichester, UK: John Wiley and Sons.

Stryker, S., & Burke, P. J. (2000). The past, present, and future of an identity theory. *Social Psychology Quarterly, 63*, 284–297.

Stryker, S., & Serpe, R. (1994). Identity salience and psychological centrality: Equivalent, overlapping, or complementary concepts? *Social Psychology Quarterly, 57*, 16–35.

Swanson, G. (1988). *Ego defenses and the legitimation of behavior.* New York: Cambridge University Press.

Tajfel, H. (1981). *Human groups and social categories: Studies in social psychology.* Cambridge: Cambridge University Press.

Terwogt, M. M., Hoeksma, J. B., & Koops, W. (1993). Common beliefs about the heredity of human characteristics. *British Journal of Psychology, 84,* 499–503.

Thoits, P. A., & Virshup, L. K. (1997). Me's and we's: Forms and functions of social identities. In R. Ashmore & L. Jussim (Eds.), *Self and identity: Fundamental issues* (pp. 106–133). New York: Oxford University Press.

Turner, J. C. (with Hogg, M. A., Oakes, P. J., Reicher, S. D., & Wetherell, M. S.). (1987). *Rediscovering the social group: A self-categorization theory.* Oxford, UK: Basil Blackwell.

Turner, J. C., Oakes, P. J., Haslam, S. A. & McGarty, C. (1994). Self and collective: Cognition and social context. *Personality and Social Psychology Bulletin, 20,* 454–463.

Turner, R. (1970). *Family interaction.* New York: John Wiley.

Turner, R. (1987). Articulating self and social structure. In K. Yardley & T. Honess (Eds.), *Self and identity: Psychosocial processes* (pp. 119–132). Chichester, UK: John Wiley and Sons.

Turner, R. (1988). Personality in society: Social psychology's contribution to society. *Social Psychology Quarterly, 51,* 1–10.

van Kampen, L., Koops, W., Terwogt, M. M., & Reijnders, C. (1990). Onbekendheid met de biologische fader als een belemmerende factor in de identiteitsontwikkeling: Een empirische exploratie (Lack of knowledge of the biological father as an obstructing factor in the development of identity: An empirical study) (Abstract). *Nederlands Tijdschrift voor de Psychologie, 45,* 283–288.

Wegar, K. (1997). *Adoption, identity, and kinship: The debate over sealed birth records.* New Haven, CT: Yale University Press.

Weinstein, E. A., & Deutschberger, P. (1963). Some dimensions of altercasting. *Sociometry, 26,* 454–466.

Wylie, R. (1987). Mothers' attributions to their young children. In T. Honess & K. Yardley (Eds.), *Self and identity: Perspectives across the lifespan* (pp. 77–92). London: Routledge and Kegan Paul.

Zajonc, R. B., Adelmann, P. K., Murphy, S. T., & Niedenthal, P. M. (1987). Convergence in the physical appearance of spouses. *Motivation and Emotion, 11,* 335–346.

Chapter **3**

Identities and Behavior

ALICIA D. CAST

INTRODUCTION

Since the early works of such influential scholars as William James (1890), George Herbert Mead (1934), and Charles Horton Cooley (1902), research within the tradition of symbolic interactionism has focused on the various ways the self produces meaningful behavior. While two distinct perspectives on the self and how it is related to behavior currently exist (Demo 1992; Gecas and Burke 1995), both share the general idea that in interaction, individuals seek to project an identity and consequently, that behavior reflects that identity.

While the effect of identity on individuals' behavior has received a great deal of attention, less attention has been given to the effects that behavior might have on identity. Given that the self is a process that both shapes and is shaped by interaction, it seems likely that not only should identity affect behavior in interaction, but that those behaviors should, in turn, have consequences for identity. Indeed, research in other areas suggests that behavior is particularly likely to have an impact on an individual's identity during times of identity acquisition and negotiation and when behaviors are enacted repeatedly over time in stable social structures.

Given that identity theory recognizes the important ways that social structure organizes the self and social behavior through the production of patterned interaction, identity theory is an appropriate framework in which to develop an understanding of how identity and behavior are interrelated. According to identity theory, individuals seek to verify role-based identities in interaction with others in counter-roles. In the most general scenario, individuals should behave in ways consistent with their identity so that perceptions are consistent with identity meanings. However, the identities and behaviors of others may also shape our behavior and if interactions and behaviors with others are stable and sustained over time, small adjustments to the identity may be made in an effort to create as much consistency between identity meanings and perceptions as possible. That is, identities may come to reflect the behaviors that individuals engage in.

These ideas are investigated over time using a sample of newlymarried couples. The use of newlymarried couples to study the reciprocal relationship between identities and behavior is advantageous for several reasons. First, while new couples may have a generalized understanding of what it means to be a "spouse" (husband or wife), this understanding is often vague. When individuals take on this new role of spouse, meanings of self and other are likely to undergo a dramatic transformation as identities are negotiated. The negotiation process modifies and ultimately stabilizes the identities for individuals and their spouses (Berger and Kellner 1970; Blumstein 1992). As this process unfolds, individuals evaluate the self as an occupant of that role, using both feedback from others as well as making their own inferences about who the self is.

Second, while all role transitions have the potential to significantly alter the self because they involve changes in the social situation (Elder and O'Rand 1995; Stryker 1989; Wells and Stryker 1988), the transition into the spousal role is one of the most important and significant role transitions due to the centrality of the family in the formation and maintenance of the self-concept (Berger and Kellner 1970; Clausen 1986; Heiss 1968). Family-based roles (and their identities) are influential because they tend to be highly salient identities that individuals are highly committed to, providing structure to interaction (Stryker 1968). This structure provides consistency and stability to family interaction making repetitive behavior probable, increasing the likelihood that behaviors will contribute to identity change. For these reasons, newlywed couples are an appropriate context in which to develop and investigate the possible reciprocal relationship between identity and behavior.

PREVIOUS RESEARCH

The idea that behavior has an impact on individuals is not a new idea. Research conducted in a variety of different areas suggests that behavior itself can effect long-term changes in the individual. First, cognitive dissonance theorists have suggested that behavior may change attitudes, including self-attitudes, when behaviors and attitudes are inconsistent (e.g. Aronson 1999; Festinger 1957; Harmon-Jones 1999). If persons perceive that they have recently behaved in ways that are inconsistent with previously formed self-attitudes, these attitudes may change in order to eliminate this inconsistency, particularly during the initial stages of formation when self-attitudes are weak.

Second, researchers interested in the connections between social structure and personality have addressed the relationship between social structure and psychological functioning (e.g. Kohn and Schooler 1983; Pearlin et al. 1981), the relationship between occupational characteristics and self-esteem and self-efficacy (Mirowsky and Ross 1992; Ross and Wright 1998), and the construction of new identities within institutions (Rose et al. 1979; Schmid and Jones 1991; Vaught and Smith 1980). What this research suggests is that the behaviors individuals engage in when adjusting to new roles in structured interactions are a critical element in helping individuals define themselves as occupants of a particular position, leading to changes in the self-concept, including identities.[1]

Third, the effects of behavior on identity have been the focus of researchers working in the tradition of Bem's Theory of Self-Perception (1972) and Secord and Backman's (1961) Theory of Interpersonal Congruence. This research suggests that while individuals may use the behavior of others to infer who and what *others* are, they may also use their own behavior to infer who and what *they* are, particularly when self-attitudes are uncertain or ambiguous as is likely during the early stages of role acquisition (Bem 1972). When individuals repeatedly

---

[1] Indeed, changes in self are exactly what such structured environments such as prisons and mental institutions are designed to accomplish (Goffman 1961; Schmid and Jones 1991).

engage in new behaviors as occupants of a new role, they see themselves (when they reflect upon the self as an object) engaging in certain behaviors and eventually infer that these behaviors reflect a "true" expression of the self. As a result, self-definitions are altered and these behaviors become "ossified" into the self (Blumstein 1991). Here, it is emphasized that when individuals engage in new behaviors repeatedly, their behavior not only provides a clue to others as to who and what they are, but it is also a source of information to the self about who and what the self is, ultimately altering how individuals think of themselves.

In sum, previous research suggests that behavior can provide insights to the individual as to who and what he or she is. This occurs much in the same way that individuals determine who others are based on others' behavior. These inferences about self and other that are based on behavior are likely to produce changes in identity when individuals are making the transition into a new role as views about the self and others are likely to be only loosely formed and relatively weak. However, such changes are only likely to occur when interaction and the behaviors within it are relatively consistent over time. Therefore, behavior is more likely to affect inferences about self and other in social environments that are relatively stable.

IDENTITY THEORY

Identity theory was developed to address how social structure organizes and constrains actors in social interaction (Stryker and Statham 1985). According to identity theory, an identity is a set of meanings applied to the self in a social role or situation, defining what it means to be who one is in that role or situation (Burke and Tully 1977; Stryker 1980). Identities are organized into a hierarchy of salience and commitment, reflecting the embeddedness of the individual in the social structure (Stryker 1980). Through interaction with others in counter-roles (Burke 1980), individuals seek to verify self-meanings (Burke 1991; Swann 1990). Identities are "verified" when perceptions of the social environment match identity meanings.

In general, the verification process is ongoing and in most cases, only small adjustments in behavior are necessary to create consistency between identity standards and perceptions of the social environment. One reason for this is that individuals work to create "opportunity structures" (Swann 1983; 1990) where feedback about the self is generally consistent with how individuals view themselves. Because feedback is consistent with identity standards, drastic changes in behavior are unlikely and behavior is likely to be consistent with the identity. Therefore, in the most general scenario, identities serve as behavioral guides for individuals (Burke 1991; Foote 1951). Consequently, individuals will choose behaviors that reflect their identity in order to maintain consistency between perceptions and identity meanings. In other words, behaviors should reflect identity.[2] Thus, it is hypothesized:

> H1: The more an individual's identity implies involvement in spousal role behaviors, the more the individual will engage in those behaviors.

---

[2]Ideally, one would investigate behavior as function of the discrepancy between identities and perceptions of the environment rather than a direct result of the identity (Burke and Cast 1997). However, adequate measures are not available and therefore, the effects of a mismatch between identity standards and perceptions cannot be effectively investigated. Furthermore, the main purpose of this paper is to suggest how behavior might influence identity. Because large discrepancies tend to disrupt identity processes more than small discrepancies, it is likely that the effect of behavior on identity is likely to be greater when there are large discrepancies between identity standards and perceptions. Therefore, estimates here may be conservative.

However, it is important to note that behavior in interaction is not simply a function of the individual's identity standards. Roles are social in nature and they imply the existence of counter-identities; for example, the role of mother implies the role of child (Burke 1980). Individuals respond to the identities and behaviors of others in interaction because the identities and behaviors of others in interaction are part of individuals' perceptions of the social environment. Consequently, the behaviors individuals choose in an effort to verify their identities are not simply a function of one's own activity, but one's activity in relation to others. We may become aware of the identities of others through the process of altercasting, whereby through their behavior, others "cast" us into an identity (Weinstein and Deutschberger 1963). We may also become aware of the identities of others through reflected appraisals (Kinch 1963), role-taking (Mead 1934), and the looking-glass self (Cooley 1902). Thus, the behavior of individuals within marriage is not only influenced by individuals' identities, but also the identities and behaviors of the spouse.[3]

The spousal role is somewhat unique in that the existence of a counter-role in heterosexual unions not only has meanings that are relevant to one's position as a spouse in a marriage, but it is also a "gendered" role. As such, the meanings in these identities tend to have an "opposing" dimension to them due to the dichotomous nature of gender in contemporary society (Bem 1993). This quality of the spousal role is particularly relevant when considering the division of household labor. As couples seek to define who they and their spouse are in the marriage, spousal roles tend to become differentiated through the creation of a division of labor (Blumstein 1991). Indeed, simply the idea that a "division" exists implies an opposing and dichotomous dimension to the spousal role. In this case then, when an individual in a marriage claims a certain identity in the spousal role (say, primarily responsibility for laundry) they imply an opposite identity in the other (not primarily responsible for laundry). Given that the identities and behaviors of those interacting are interrelated, for husbands and wives, an individual's identity related to the household division of labor has direct implications for the behavior and identity of the spouse and in turn, the spouse's identity and behavior has direct implications for the individual's identity and behavior. Thus, it is hypothesized:

> H2: The more identity of the spouse implies involvement in spousal role behaviors, the less involved the individual will be in spousal role behaviors.

> H3: The more the spouse engages in spousal role behaviors, the less involved the individual will be in spousal role behaviors.[4]

Effects of Behavior on Identity

While research on how the self shapes behavior has dominated much of the research in symbolic interactionism, the latter has received less attention. There are, however, some

---

[3]It is difficult to determine exactly how the identities of others may affect self-perceptions. The role of behavior in this process is easier to distinguish. It is assumed that when the effects of behavior are controlled for, the remaining influence of identities on an individual's behavior and identity are the result of processes much like those suggested by Mead (1934), Cooley (1902), and Kinch (1963). Thus, the identity of the spouse serves as a proxy for these influences on self-perceptions.

[4]The wording of these hypotheses suggests that identities have a zero-sum quality to them. This is not meant to imply that all identities have this quality. The particular identity investigated here is perhaps one in which many of the meanings are zero-sum in nature given the dichotomous nature of the husband and wife role. Therefore, the wording used here reflects these concerns and is not meant to imply that identities in general have a zero-sum quality to them.

exceptions. First, research on the effects of behavior on the self is seen in research addressing the role of attributional processes in the development of self-esteem (Bandura 1977; Gecas and Schwalbe 1983; Rosenberg 1979, 1990), particularly self-efficacy, one component of global self-esteem. Efficacious behavior produces a feeling of efficaciousness in the individual (self-efficacy). Second, Stryker (1987) has suggested that the performance of a role identity will affect the salience of the identity. Performance of an identity serves as an indication to the individual as to how salient a particular identity must be to them. If behavior can provide important insights to the individual as to his or her efficaciousness, self-esteem, and the salience of the identity, it seems plausible that behavior can also provide important insights into who and what one is more generally.

As mentioned previously, our identities and the identities and behaviors of others influence our behavior. However, identities may change when there is a persistent discrepancy between identity standards and perceptions of the social environment (Burke 1991).[5] At such times, identity standards shift so that they more closely match perceptions. While large discrepancies are likely to produce large changes in identity, even small changes in behavior over time may produce change as individuals continually reflect upon who they are. Reflections about the self and others are likely to change when individuals make the transition into new roles. Indeed, the major task for husbands and wives when they are first married is to define themselves (and consequently, each other) as an occupant of their new positions. It is a time when loose understandings of what it means to be a certain type of person (in this case, a spouse) become settled (Berger and Kellner 1970). As they negotiate their respective identities, the feedback they receive from their spouse informs the individual as to the identity the spouse is claiming and the identity that the spouse expects in the individual. These shape individuals' conceptions of themselves with a given role. Again, the identities and behaviors of both husbands and wives inform and reflect to each other their respective identities. Thus, it is hypothesized:

H4: The more the identity of the spouse implies involvement in spousal role behaviors, the less an individual's identity will imply involvement in those activities.

H5: The more the spouse engages in spousal role behaviors, the less the individual's identity will imply involvement in those activities.

H6: The more the individual engages in spousal role behaviors, the more the individual's identity will imply involvement in those activities.

THEORETICAL MODEL

Symbolic interactionists view the self as both social product and social force, reflecting the idea that the self is fundamentally a process, shaped by and shaping interaction (Rosenberg 1990). Thus, it is important to consider both how the individual is influenced by others in interaction but also how the individual influences others. As Weinstein and Deutschberger (1963) suggest, any effective analysis of the self must have "interaction built in." By using longitudinal couple data, including the identities and behaviors of both husbands and wives, it is possible to consider how identities and behaviors might affect each other over time and effectively "build interaction into" the model. Thus, the model in Figure 1 includes the identities and behaviors of husbands and wives.

---

[5]When individuals are confronted with a persistent mismatch between identity meanings and perceptions of the social environment, one possibility is to simply exit the role. This is unlikely, however, when the identity is salient and the individual is highly committed to the relationship as is common in intimate relaitonships.

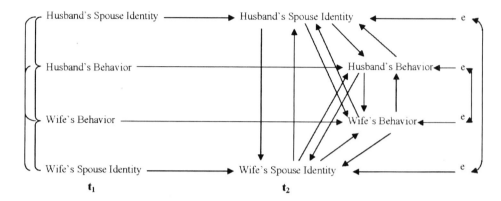

Figure 1. General Model of the Reciprocal Relationship
between Identities and Behavior for Husbands and Wives.

Looking at the estimated model in Figure 1, we see that there are paths leading from an individual's identity at t_1 to their identity at t_2 and a path from behavior at t_1 to behavior at t_2. These paths represent the stability of identities and behavior over time. At t_2, we see paths from an individual's identity to his or her behavior. This path represents the relationship between identities and behavior that has been the focus of most research—that is, where behavior reflects identity. There are also paths to an individual's behavior from the identity and behavior of the spouse reflecting how the spouse may affect the individual's behavior. Paths are also seen to an individual's identity from the identity of the spouse and from the behavior of the spouse, reflecting the idea that the identities and behaviors of others affect our own identities. Last, there is a path from the individual's behavior and the behavior of the spouse to the individual's identity. Specifically, this path represents the idea that individuals may use their own behavior and the behavior of their spouse to make inferences about who they are.

METHODS AND MEASURES

The reciprocal effects between identity and behavior are examined using data from a longitudinal study investigating marital dynamics in the first two years of marriage (Tallman et al. 1998). Each data collection period included a 90-minute face-to-face interview, a 15-minute videotaping of a conversation focused on solving an area of disagreement, and four consecutive one-week daily diaries kept by each respondent. The present analysis is based on information gathered during the face-to-face interview and daily diaries right after the coules was married (t_1) and approximately two years later (t_2).

The sample was drawn from marriage registration records in 1991 and 1992 in two mid-size communities in Washington State. Of the 1,295 couples registered to marry, 574 met the criteria for involvement (both were over the age of 18, were marrying for the first time, and had no children living with them). These couples were contacted and asked to participate; 286 completed all data collection processes in the first period. There was a 15% attrition rate from the first data collection period to the second period and an additional 4.2% attrition rate from the second to the third period of data collection. Couples who dropped out of the study before completing the final phases of data collection were more likely to be young ($p < .05$), less educated ($p < .05$), and of a lower socioeconomic status (p < .05).[6] Because of missing values on some items, the present analyses are based on the 164 couples for which there was complete data at both time points.

Measures

Spousal Identity

Higgins (1989) has suggested that identities contain two main standards: ideal and ought. For a given role-identity, an individual is likely to have some sense of the responsibilities inherent in the social position he or she occupies (ought standards). However, the individual also engages in role-making (Turner 1962) reflecting more or less what he or she would ideally like to do as an occupant of that position (ideal standards). Thus, identities are likely to contain meanings relevant to both ideal and ought standards (Burke and Stets 1999; Stets and Burke 2000).

The role identity investigated here is the spousal role identity. It is measured using items related to three household activities: cooking and food preparation, cleaning and housekeeping, and shopping for the family. To assess ideal standards, respondents were asked to indicate the extent to which they would take responsibility for the specific activity *if they were completely free to choose* their level of involvement in the activity. Responses range from 0 to 10 with 0 indicating "none of the time" and 10 indicating "all of the time." To assess ought standards, respondents were asked to indicate the extent to which they felt they *should be responsible* for each of the three household activities. Response categories ranged across a 5-point scale from doing all of the activity in the relationship (coded 4) to doing none of the activity (coded 0). Items representing both the ideal and ought dimensions were factor analyzed to confirm their unidimensionality (see Table 1). The omega reliability for the spouse identity measure is .87 at t_1 and .90 at t_2. Items were standardized and summed to create the scale scores. A high score on each scale indicates that the identity implies high levels of involvement in the activity.[7]

Spousal Role Behavior

Behavior in spousal role activities was measured using self-reported daily involvement in the above three activities (cooking and food preparation, cleaning and housekeeping, and shopping). Respondents indicated in their daily diary how much time they had spent that day in these activities. Because not all respondents completed all 28 days of their diaries, a daily average for each individual was calculated based on the days completed and used to represent an average amount of time spent in these three activities. Responses ranged from 0 (indicating "no time") and 6 (indicating "more than 10 hours"). The three items were factor analyzed to confirm their unidimentionality (see Table 1). The omega reliability for the scale is .69 at t_1 and .79 at t_2.

---

[6] A full description of the data collection process and the data itself can be found elsewhere (Tallman et al. 1998).
[7] While these items do not represent all dimensions of the spousal role or its related behavior, they do reflect what has been referred to as the "housekeeper role." (Slocum and Nye 1976). Given the amount of theoretical and empirical attention given to the division of household labor in the family, it would seem that while it may be only one dimension, it is an important dimension. Consistency between identity meanings and behavioral meanings are critical in linking identities to role performance (Burke and Reitzes 1981). Since the items for the identity and behavior measures are similar, the measures are consistent in this manner.

Table 1. Factor Loadings for Measures (N = 164)

Item	Loadings	
	t_1	t_2
Spousal Role Identity		
Ideal		
Cooking	.74	.68
Cleaning	.61	.56
Shopping	.63	.72
Should		
Cooking	.67	.76
Cleaning	.57	.72
Shopping	.59	.69
Omega Reliability (Ω)	.87	.90
Spousal Role Behavior		
Cooking	.67	.77
Cleaning	.64	.72
Shopping	.47	.62
Omega Reliability (Ω)	.69	.79

Analysis

Structural equation modeling was used to estimate the model seen in Figure 1. The maximum-likelihood procedure of AMOS (Arbuckle 1997) is a full-information method; equations are estimated simultaneously, using information from all equations to estimate parameters rather than estimating one parameter at a time. Given proper specification of the model, full information methods produce estimates with smaller mean-square errors. This method also estimates correlation among the errors as correlated errors are likely among husbands and wives because both are likely to be affected by the same factors not included in the model.

When estimating reciprocal effects, instrumental variables are necessary for identification. Variables at t_1 are used here for this purpose. Several constraints in the final model should be noted. First, effects for husbands and wives were constrained to be equal as it is assumed that the processes investigated here operate similarly for husbands and wives; tests of equality confirm this (chi-square = 5.88, df = 8, p > .05). Second, stability coefficients for the spousal identity and behavior are not significantly different (chi-square = 1.64, df = 1, p > .05) and were constrained in the final model.

Furthermore, this model estimates simultaneous effects. While identity change occurs slowly over time, estimating both cross-lag and simultaneous effects leads to problems of identification in the model so only simultaneous effects are estimated here. Estimation of cross-lag effects may not capture any effects if the time between data points is long as is here (Finkel 1995). So, although these effects are undoubtedly occurring over time, given the time between data collection points here (two years), simultaneous effects capture these relationships most effectively.

RESULTS

Table 2 presents results from the final model. In this table the estimated reciprocal effects between the identities and behaviors of husbands and wives are presented. As one might expect, there is significant stability in the spousal role identity and spousal role behavior (b = .51), but these coefficients also suggest that there are changes occurring in the spousal role identity and in spousal role behavior in the first two years of marriage.

Previous models relating identities to behavior suggest that behavior reflects identity. Thus, the spousal role behavior of husbands and wives should be influenced by their respective identities (Hypothesis 1). Surprisingly, individuals' spousal identity is not significantly related to their behavior in the spousal role. However, consistent with Hypothesis 2, the behavior of husbands and wives is influenced by the identity of their spouse. Indeed, the more the identity of the spouse implies involvement (implying less involvement for the other), the less an individual engages in spousal role behavior (b = -.11). The spouse's behavior also affects the individual's behavior. The more a spouse engages in spousal role behaviors, the less the individual engages in those activities (b = -.11). This is consistent with Hypothesis 3. These two coefficients (identity of the spouse and the spouse's behavior) are not significantly different (chi-square = 1.1, df = 1, p < .05). Thus, an individual's behavior is influenced by the spouse's identity and behavior but not the individual's own identity.

Not only do we see that identities and behavior have an impact on behavior, but they also impact individuals' identities. As seen in Table 2, the more the identity of the spouse implies involvement in spousal role behaviors (implying less involvement for the other), the less the identity of the individual implies involvement in those activities (b = -.11) confirming Hypothesis 4. In support of Hypothesis 5, Table 2 also suggests that the behavior of the spouse also has a significant impact on the individual's identity. The more an individual's spouse engages in spousal role behaviors (suggesting less involvement for the individual), the less an individual's identity implies involvement in those activities (b = -.11). The effects of the spouse (through identity and behavior) are not significantly different (chi-square = 1.26, df = 1, p > .05). Furthermore, these cross-effects between the identities and behaviors of husbands and wives are not significantly different (chi-square = 2.26, df = 1, p > .05).

It was also suggested that the behaviors individuals engage in may also influence their identities (Hypothesis 6). The results in Table 2 also support this hypothesis. The more individuals engage in spousal role behaviors, the more their identity implies involvement in these activities (b = .25). Thus, the behavior of both the spouse and the self informs individuals as to who and what they are, although the influence of individuals' behavior on their identity is significantly stronger than the influence of their spouses' behavior or identity (chi-square = 11.28, df = 1, p < .05).

Table 2. Standardized Coefficients of Reciprocal Effects between Identity and Behavior (N = 164)

	Husband's t_2		Wife's t_2	
	Identity	Behavior	Identity	Behavior
Husband's Identity t_1	.51*			
Husband's Behavior t_1		.51*		
Wife's Identity t_1			.51*	
Wife's Behavior t_1				.51*
Husband's Identity t_2		ns	-.11*	-.11*
Husband's Behavior t_2	.25*		-.11*	-.11*
Wife's Identity t_2	-.11*	-.11*		ns
Wife's Behavior t_2	-.11*	-.11*	.25*	

chi-square = 20.70, df = 16, p = .19

* $p < .05$

DISCUSSION

A central concern in symbolic interactionism is how the self produces meaningful behavior in interaction. Consequently, research has largely focused on how identities influence behavior and largely neglected the possibility that behavior might also influence identity. Given the symbolic interactionist perspective that the self is a process, a reciprocal relationship between identity and behavior is possible, particularly when the role is newly acquired and associated identities are still being formed. During such times, the identities of others and the behaviors of self and others can be an important source of information to the individual about who and what he or she is.

Change in identity requires a stability in the social environment and the emphasis on the role of social structure in understanding the self within identity theory makes identity theory an especially appropriate framework in which to develop an understanding of how the behaviors of self and other influence identity. Results presented here suggest that among these couples, individuals' identities have an insignificant amount of influence on the degree of involvement in spousal role behaviors. However, an individual's behavior is influenced by the identity and behavior of the spouse. The more the identity of the spouse implies involvement in spousal role behaviors (implying less involvement for the individual), the less the individual engages in those behaviors; and, the more the spouse is involved in spousal role behaviors, the less the individual engages in those behaviors. If we look at what factors influence identity, the individual's identity is also influenced by the identity and behavior of the spouse. The more the identity of the spouse implies involvement in spousal role behaviors, the less the individual's identity implies involvement in those activities; and, the more the spouse engages in spousal role behaviors, the less the individual's identity implies involvement in those activities. However, the individual's identity is also influenced by what the individual is actually doing during the first two years. This suggests that during the first two years of marriage, what individuals do affects what they want to do and think they should do.

In spite of what might be considered to be a surprising lack of direct effects of identity on behavior, should we conclude that identities do not influence behavior? Definitely not. Tests of the generally applicability of identity theory have provided support for the linkages between identities and behavior. So, how we explain that individuals' identities did not affect their behavior? First, we can look to the items that were used to measure the spousal identity. The items used here reflect only certain aspects of what it might mean to be a spouse. These three items largely reflect what one might refer to as structural requirements of this position. Given that these are things that have to be done, these may be dimensions of the spousal role that individuals do nott have a lot of control over in terms of their accomplishment. These activities have to be done.

Second, it is important to remember that one of the main ways that social structures reproduce themselves is by producing selves that reflect those social structures. Social structure influences who we are by constraining some behaviors and facilitating others (Stryker 1994). To the extent that social structure (such as the cultural expectations attached to roles) patterns early behaviors in social roles, then such behaviors are likely to have a powerful impact on how individuals come to see themselves within that role. It is likely that early on, individuals' understandings of who they are within a role is vague and very loosely organized. As individuals try out different behaviors and respond to the influence of others, individuals' conceptions of themselves as occupants of a particular role become crystallized. If roles and associated identities require time to be negotiated, identities may become more important in understanding behavior later once the identity has stabilized. To these extent that identities stabilize, the effects of behavior on identity over time should decline and the influence of identity on behavior should become stronger.

Seemingly, two years would be long enough to make the transition into a new role and develop a fairly strong sense of self in that role, but there are certain qualities to the role of spouse that may make this more difficult. Some roles may be more contested than others and may require a longer period of negotiation and the "housekeeper" role (Slocum and Nye 1976) is one of the most contested roles within the family. Furthermore, individuals in new marriages are likely to have very strong feelings for their spouse and in an effort to maintain positive relations, they defer to the wishes of the spouse rather than do what they would like to do. Thus, it may be several years before individuals truly "grow into" their role and it becomes an organized, stable aspect of the self that provides clear direction for behavior.

There may also be other aspects of social structure that might be relevant to the ideas developed here and these particular results. Individuals occupy a variety of different positions in society and thus, there may be more than one identity that is relevant to a particular behavior or particular context (see the chapters in Part IV in this volume). For example, the role of spouse is very much imbued with gender meanings in our society (if not most societies). That is, the role of husband and wife and mother and father are tightly connected to one's sense of self as a man or a woman. Research on the division of labor within the family has illustrated that the division of labor is influenced by factors outside of the activities themselves, one of which is gender (e.g., Berk 1985). This would suggest that there may be other identities or other aspects of that may be more important in understanding how the spousal identity manifests itself in behavior. For example, Kroska (1997) suggests that a gender ideological identity may function as a type of master identity and thus be crucial in examining the relationship between family identities and the division of household labor.

However, the goal of this paper was not to provide evidence for the effects of identity on behavior, but rather to investigate the influence that behavior might have on the formation of identity. This research suggests that we send ourselves further down the path first tread by Mead and Cooley and in recent years has benefited from the contributions of Sheldon Stryker. First, as was the initial intention of this paper, by incorporating the possibility or the idea that identities and behavior are reciprocally linked to each other, a picture of the self as a complex and truly dynamic process is clearer. Furthermore, the ideas developed and the results presented in this research produce a variety of different questions that are relevant to the different ways that social structure provides a context for interaction that have been brought to our attention recently (e.g. Stryker and Serpe 1982; Stryker 1987; Stryker 1989; Stryker 1994). Overall though, the ideas developed here and the questions they raise underscore the importance of social structure in understanding the self, a simple and powerful point that Sheldon Stryker has impressed upon us throughout his career.

ACKNOWLEDGMENTS: The research reported in this paper is part of a larger longitudinal study of newly married couples, "Socialization into Marital Roles," funded by a grant from NIMH (MH46828), under the direction of Irving Tallman, Peter J. Burke, and Viktor Gecas. During part of the preparation of this manuscript, the author was supported by a National Research Award from the National Institute of Mental Health (Indiana University Training Program in Identity, Self, Role, and Mental Health—PHST 32 MH 14588).

REFERENCES

Arbuckle, J. L. (1997). *Amos Users' Guide, Version 3.6*. Chicago: SmallWaters.

Aronson, E. (1999). Dissonance, Hypocrisy, and the Self-Concept. In E. Harmon-Jones and J. Mills (Eds.) *Cognitive Dissonance: Progress on a Pivotal Theory in Social Psychology* (pp. 103–126). Washington, D.C.: American Psychological Association.

Bandura, A. (1977). *Social Learning Theory*. Englewood Cliffs, NJ: Prentice-Hall.

Bem, D. J. (1972). Self-Perception Theory. In L. Berkowitz (Ed.) *Advances in Experimental Social Psychology* (pp. 1–62). New York: Academic Press.

Bem, S. L. 1993. *The Lenses of Gender*. New Haven: Yale University Press.

Berger, P. and H. Kellner. (1970). Marriage and the Construction of Reality. In H. P. Dreitzel (Ed.) in *Recent Sociology, No. 2* (pp. 50–72). New York: Macmillan.

Berk, S. F. (1985). *The Gender Factory: The Apportionment of Work in American Households*. New York: Plenum.

Blumstein, P. (1991). The Production of Selves in Personal Relationships. In *Self-Society Dynamic: Cognition, Emotion, and Action* (pp. 305–322). Cambridge: Cambridge University Press.

Burke, P. J. (1980). The Self: Measurement Implications from a Symbolic Interactionist Perspective. *Social Psychology Quarterly, 43,* 18–29.

Burke, P. J. (1991). Identity Processes and Social Stress. *American Sociological Review, 56,* 836–49.

Burke, P. J. and J. E. Stets. (1999). Trust and Commitment Through Self-Verification. *Social Psychology Quarterly, 62,* 347–360.

Burke, P. J. and D. C. Reitzes. (1981). The Link Between Identity and Role Performance. *Social Psychology Quarterly, 44,* 83–92.

Burke, P. J. and J. C. Tully. (1977). The Measurement of Role-Identity. *Social Forces, 55,* 880–897.

Clausen, J. A. (1986). *The Life-Course: A Sociological Perspective*. Englewood Cliffs, NJ: Prentice-Hall.

Cooley, C. H. (1902). *Human Nature and Social Order*. New York: Charles Scribner's Sons.

Demo, D. H. (1992). The Self-Concept Over Time: Research Issues and Directions. *Annual Review of Sociology, 18,* 303–326.

Elder, G. H. and A. M. O'Rand. (1995). Adult Lives in a Changing Society. In K. S. Cook, G. A. Fine, and J. S. House (Eds.) *Sociological Perspectives on Social Psychology* (pp. 452–475). Boston: Allyn and Bacon.

Festinger, L. (1957). *A Theory of Cognitive Dissonance*. Evanston, IL: Row, Peterson.

Finkel, S. E. (1995). *Causal Analysis with Panel Data*. Thousand Oaks: Sage.

Foote, N. N. 1951. Identification as the Basis for a Theory of Motivation. *American Sociological Review, 16,* 14–21.

Gecas, V. and P. J. Burke. (1995). Self and Identity. In K. S. Cook, G. A. Fine, and J. S. House (Eds.) *Sociological Perspectives on Social Psychology* (pp. 41–67). Boston: Allyn and Bacon.

Gecas, V. and M. L. Schwalbe. (1983). Beyond the Looking-Glass Self: Social Structure and Efficacy-Based Self-Esteem. *Social Psychology Quarterly, 46,* 77–88.

Harmon-Jones, E. and J. Mills. (1999). An Introduction to Cognitive Dissonance Theory and an Overview of Current Perspectives on the Topic. In E. Harmon-Jones and J. Mills (Eds.) *Cognitive Dissonance: Progress on a Pivotal Theory in Social Psychology* (pp. 3–21). Washington, D.C.: American Psychological Association.

Heiss, J. (1968). An Introduction to Elements of Role Theory. In J. Heiss (Ed.) *Family Roles and Interaction: An Anthology* (pp. 1–34). Chicago: Rand McNally.

Higgins, E. T. (1989). Self-Discrepancy Theory: What Patterns of Self-Beliefs Cause People to Suffer? *Advances in Experimental Social Psychology, 22,* 93–136.

James, W. (1890). *The Principles of Psychology*. New York: H. Holt.

Kinch, J. W. (1963). A Formalized Theory of the Self-Concept. *American Journal of Sociology, 68,* 481–86.

Kohn, M. and C. Schooler, with the collaboration of J. Miller, K. A. Miller, C. Schoenbach, and R. Schoenberg. (1983). *Work and Personality: An Inquiry into the Impact of Social Stratification*. Norwood, NJ: Ablex.

Mead, G. H. (1934). *Mind, Self, and Society*. Chicago: University of Chicago Press.

Mirowsky, J. and C. E. Ross. (1992). Households, Employment, and the Sense of Control. *Social Psychology Quarterly, 55,* 217–35.

Pearlin, L. I., M. A. Lieberman, E. G. Menaghan, and J. T. Mullan. (1981). The Stress Process. *Journal of Health and Social Behavior, 22,* 337–356.

Rose, P. I., M. Glazer, and P. M. Glaser. (1979). In Controlled Environments: Four Cases of Intensive Resocialization. In P. I. Rose (Ed.) *Socialization and the Life Course* (pp. 323–325). New York: St. Martin's Press.

Ross, C. E. and M. P. Wright. (1998). Women's Work, Men's Work, and the Sense of Control. *Work and Occupations, 25,* 333–55.

Rosenberg, M. (1979). *Conceiving the Self.* New York: Basic Books.

Rosenberg, M. (1990). The Self-Concept: Social Product and Social Force. In M. Rosenberg and R. H. Turner (Eds.) *Social Psychology: Sociological Perspectives* (pp. 593–624). New Brunswick, NJ: Transaction.

Schmid, T. J. and R. S. Jones. (1991). Suspended Identity: Identity Transformation in a Maximum Security Prison. *Symbolic Interaction, 14,* 415–432.

Secord, P. F. and C. W. Backman. (1961). Personality Theory and the Problem of Stability and Change in Individual Behavior: An Interpersonal Approach. *Psychological Review, 68,* 21–32.

Slocum, W. L. and F. I. Nye. (1976). Provider and Housekeeper Roles. In F. I. Nye (Ed.) *Role Structure and Analysis of the Family* (pp. 81–99). Beverly Hills: Sage.

Stets, J. E. and P. J. Burke. (2000). Identity Theory and Social Identity Theory. *Social Psychology Quarterly, 63,* 224–237.

Stryker, S. (1968). Identity Salience and Role Performance. *Journal of Marriage and the Family, 4,* 558–64.

Stryker, S. (1980). *Symbolic Interactionism: A Social Structural Version.* Menlo Park: Benjamin Cummings.

Stryker, S. (1987). Identity Theory: Developments and Extensions. In K. Yardley and T. Honess (Eds.) in *Self and Identity: Psychosocial Perspectives* (pp. 89–103). New York: John Wiley & Sons.

Stryker, S. (1989). Further Developments in Identity Theory: Singularity Versus Multiplicity of Self. In J. Berger, M. Zelditch, M. L. Borgatta (Eds.) in *Sociological Theories in Progress: New Foundations* (pp. 35–57). New York: Macmillan.

Stryker, S. (1994). Freedom and Constraint in Social and Personal Life. In G. M. Platt and C. Gordon (Eds.) *Self, Collective Behavior, and Society: Essays Honoring the Contributions of Ralph H. Turner* (pp. 119–138). Greenwich, CT: JAI Press.

Stryker, S. and R. T. Serpe. (1982). Commitment, Identity Salience, and Role Behavior. In W. Ickes and E. Knowles (Eds.) *Personality, Roles, and Social Behavior* (pp. 199–218). New York: Springer-Verlag.

Stryker, S. and A. Statham. (1985). Symbolic Interaction and Role Theory. In G. Lindzey and E. Aronson (Eds.) *Handbook of Social Psychology* (pp. 311–378). New York: Random House.

Swann, W. B., Jr. (1983). Self-Verification: Bringing Reality into Harmony with the Self. In J. Suls (Ed.) in *Psychological Perspectives on the Self* (pp. 33–66). Hillsdale, NJ: Erlbaum.

Swann, W. B., Jr. (1990). To Be Adored or to Be Known? In R. M. Sorrentino and E. T. Higgins (Eds.) *Motivation and Cognition, Vol. 2* (pp. 408–448). New York: Guilford.

Tallman, I., P. J. Burke, and V. Gecas. (1998). Socialization into Marital Roles: Testing a Contextual, Developmental Model of Marital Functioning. In T. N. Bradbury (Ed.) *The Developmental Course of Marital Dysfunction* (pp. 312–342). Cambridge: Cambridge University Press.

Turner, R. (1962). Role-Taking: Process Versus Conformity. In A. Rose (Ed.) *Human Behavior and Social Processes* (pp. 20–40). Boston: Houghton Mifflin.

Vaught, C. and D. L. Smith. (1980). Incorporation and Mechanical Solidarity in an Underground Coal Mine. *Sociology of Work and Occupations, 7,* 159–187.

Weinstein, E. A. and P. Deutschberger. (1963). Some Dimensions of Altercasting. *Sociometry, 26,* 454–66.

Wells, L. E. and S. Stryker. (1988). Stability and Change in Self Over the Life Course. In P. B. Baltes, David L. Featherman, and R. M. Lerner (Eds.) *Life-Span Development and Behavior* (pp. 191–229). Hillsdale, NJ: Lawrence Erlbaum.

Part II

Identities and Social Structure

Chapter 4

The Political Self
Identity Resources for Radical Democracy

PETER L. CALLERO

THE POLITICAL SELF: IDENTITY
RESOURCES FOR RADICAL DEMOCRACY

The theoretical tradition of symbolic interactionism is often criticized by more macro-oriented sociologists for its failure to consider and develop issues of power that go beyond the dynamics of interpersonal relations. During the decades of the 1960's and 70's critics such as Gouldner (1970) and Huber (1973) chastised symbolic interactionists and micro-oriented sociologists such as Goffman, as irrelevant, and naïve when it came to the larger and more central concerns of sociology. The publication of Stryker's (1980) *Symbolic Interactionism: A Social Structural Version*, can be read at least in part as a response to these criticisms. By merging key elements of role theory with a symbolic interactionist theory of self, Stryker was able to construct a conceptual framework more open to main-stream (i.e. macro) sociological concerns. While his theory does not explicitly focus on social forces of domination and control, Stryker (1980: 151) does stress that "there is nothing inherent in symbolic interactionism that necessitates either naivete with reference to, or denial of the facts of differentially distributed power."

Stryker was correct in his assertion that the tradition of symbolic interactionism does not *preclude* an analysis of the political, nevertheless, it is still very much the case that institutionally sustained power is a secondary concern for most symbolic interactionists. This deficiency is clearly evident in contemporary conceptualizations of the self—the central concept in most symbolic interactionist frameworks. Influential theorists such as Stryker, Burke, Rosenberg and Blumer, have generally followed the paradigm established by Mead, which is to focus on the cognitive and intersubjective processes of the self independent of the actual, historically specific events, social forces and institutions that provide for particular selves in specific economies of power and politics. Although it is not fair to say that Mead's social psychology is completely apolitical (as some critics charge), it is true that his naturalism and behaviorist orientation directs attention away from social structural processes and particular political forces. For Mead and many contemporary theorists of the self,

57

politics is an exogenous force that varies in intensity. The political in this manner is no different from any other variable that may or may not influence the actor's identity, social network or social action.

To be sure, there are some exceptions to this delimited approach to the political.[1] Some studies working from a symbolic interactionist framework do hint at a more fundamental importance of historically specific events tied to a political economy that come to define the structure of self development. Turner's (1976) study of the self as institution and impulse suggests that the very structure of the self can be tied to shifts in cultural processes. Hochschild (1983) shows how similar cultural shifts and basic emotional responses can be linked to alternations in markets from industrial production to service orientation. And Elder's (1974) longitudinal study of a cohort of depression era youth reveals the fundamental impact that this particular political economy had on "personality." But all of these examples are missing a sophisticated conceptual understanding of the self in which the political is built into the very framework of the theory and where relations of power are presumed to be constitutive.

In this chapter I propose a conceptualization of the self in which the political is seen as constitutive. More specifically, I call for a return to the central political themes found in the tradition of American pragmatism and the Enlightenment values of classical sociology. I also push for the adoption of an emancipatory agenda and a praxis orientation toward theory.

In building this framework I am guided by the following principles:

- The conceptualization of the self must be historically grounded
- It must have a normative standpoint from which a foundation of social and political critique can be built
- It should address the social and political conditions that facilitate positive self development
- It should speak to the identity resources required of an emancipatory political system

My intent is to develop a conceptualization of the political self that privileges a radical, deliberative democracy for the development of critical identities that can serve both as resources for insurgent movements and anchors for a normative standpoint.

THE POLITICAL AS ESSENTIAL

The sphere of politics and the political, broadly conceived, includes all social processes, social forces and social relations associated with the institutional deployment of power. This would obviously include social processes connected to formal structures of government, but would also extend to social relations tied to the political economy (e.g., market, workplace), religious institutions, education, the culture industry (e.g., entertainment, news, art, music), even the family. Any time power is deployed, either legitimately or illegitimately, in a patterned, organized or regular manner, politics is involved. Conceptualized in this manner, it is not difficult to recognize the fundamental place of politics in modern society. Indeed, the greater challenge becomes finding a social experience that is

---

[1]This is particularly true for approaches to the self that are influenced by post-structuralism, post-modernism and cultural studies. See Callero (2003) for a critical review of this literature.

independent of political influence. Sociologists have been central in demonstrating the insidious deployment of power in gender relations, family structure, education institutions, religion and the workplace, and symbolic interactionists accept the premise that language can transmit and enforce systems of dominance in subtle but effective ways.

Given that most sociologists, symbolic interactionists included, recognize the elementary role of politics in modern society, it is surprising that the political is absent from most conceptualizations of the modern self. This failure to articulate and develop an understanding of the self as fundamentally political is problematic for at least three different reasons.

First, it means that many theoretical frameworks focusing on the structure and dynamic processes of the self and self-development are incomplete. Without an explicit development of the self in relation to power and politics contemporary conceptualizations are basically inaccurate. It is inconceivable today that any theory of society with a macro, institutional or system level focus, could be taken seriously in the discipline if it failed to develop the essential role of politics. Yet this is where many micro-oriented theorists find themselves. If symbolic interactionists are to take the dictum "self reflects society" seriously, we will appreciate the incomplete and therefore inaccurate, picture created by most extant models of the self.

A second reason for developing an understanding of the self as essentially political has to do with the politics of science. We must recognize that academic and intellectual pursuits are not protected from political implications. Sociological theory contributes to relations of power through the construction of theoretical models that proffer a particular understanding of the social world. These models can and have been used to legitimate and extend institutional practices of domination and control. This was the case, for example when Social Darwinism was employed by intellectuals and policy makers to sustain class advantage and maintain control during the Gilded Age of industrial capitalism in the U.S. But our theories also contribute to political processes through acts of omission as well as commission. In other words, the exclusion of topics and ideas in a theoretical model or conceptual framework can also be used to support or legitimate domination and control. Self theory and research on the self that ignores essential political processes is unintentionally protecting the dominance of particular status quo political arrangements. When control, domination and power are unacknowledged the implication is that the existing state is part of the social background and can be taken-for-granted as a set of orienting assumptions. For example, a theory of social relations in the ante-bellum south that fails to recognize or address the institution of slavery would no only be considered incomplete, it would also be considered politically suspect and in the service of the (now) obvious forces of domination. Once we recognize the self as essentially social, we must also accept the self as essentially political. To do otherwise is to risk contributing to oppressive systems and the hegemony of their supporting ideologies.

A third problem with an apolitical self-theory is that it risks being dismissed as sociologically irrelevant. Durkheim's (1938:104) analytical dictum that "every time a social phenomenon is directly explained by a psychological phenomenon, we may be sure that the explanation is false" may be oversimplified, but it does serve as an apt warning. As the discipline of sociology moves increasingly away from 'variable analyses" of gender, race, sexual orientation and class, and develops sophisticated understandings of the complex and dynamic conjuncture of economic power, cultural privilege and identity difference, a corresponding theory of self is needed. So far, the tradition of symbolic interactionism has failed to meet this intellectual challenge. As a consequence, much of self theory today is oriented toward either completely apolitical psychological theories that focus on self as subject, or postmodern conceptualizations of identity that reject the self as nothing more than a modernist construct and a cultural fantasy (Callero, 2003). The increasing dominance of certain postmodern statements on identity is due in large part to the explicit and central importance these theories give to the question of power. Foucault (1965), for example, offers a fascinating description of the dispersed and amorphous "capillaries of power" that limit freedom in modern society. But Foucault's philosophy dissolves the agentic self and offers little hope for resistance and no framework for constructing an emancipatory theory.

RECOVERING THE POLITICAL THROUGH RETROSPECTION AND REVISION

The strategy that I propose for building a conceptualization of a political self begins with a call to adopt key emancipatory themes that were born of the Enlightenment and nurtured in the tradition of classical sociology. In particular, I believe that those of us working within a symbolic interactionist framework must establish a clear and explicit commitment to achieving freedom and liberty by way of reason and critical analysis of established systems of power. Critique, however, can not stand alone. Critical analysis without a corresponding commitment to social change is hollow and impotent. We must also seek to move truth to action by adopting a praxis orientation where political objectives are not opaque and particular emancipatory solutions are defended and advocated.

This is the vision articulated by Mills (1959:177) in his advocacy of a "sociological imagination":

> There is no necessity for working social scientists to allow the political meaning of their work to be shaped by the "accidents" of its setting, or its use to be determined by the purposes of other men (sic). It is quite within their powers to discuss its meaning and decide upon its uses as matters of their own policy.

What is especially ironic about Mill's position is that he builds his case on the same philosophical principles of pragmatism that serve as the foundation for symbolic interactionism. Yet, despite Mills' appreciation of the political nature of the self-society relationship, his radical political pragmatism with its praxis orientation never became the basis for an elaborate theory of self. Nor did his early work have much influence on symbolic interactionists or other sociologists developing theories of the self.

To locate an emancipatory theory of self-society we must turn to the school of thought known as Critical Theory where the most historically persistent and vital legacy of the Enlightenment agenda can be found. The formal institutional origins of Critical Theory begin in Germany during the 1930's at the Frankfurt based Institute for Social Research, but the intellectual roots of the school can be traced to Marx and Weber and their concern with the nature and trajectory of capitalist modernity

Critical theorists are committed to developing a theory of liberation through the identification and explication of social systems of domination (Kellner, 1989). For critical theorists the economic, institutional and cultural changes characteristic of modernity are complex and dialectical, exhibiting both oppressive and emancipatory tendencies. On the one hand the expansion of bureaucratic control, the concentration of economic capital and the growth of corporate power have produced serious limits on individual freedom and equality. On the other hand the emergence of democratically oriented politics and the decline of traditional gender, ethnic and sexual divisions are taken as evidence of a growing social and cultural liberation.

The first generation of Critical Theorists was generally pessimistic about the liberating promise of modern political institutions. The rise of the German Fascism lead to a profound disillusionment with bourgeois democracy and the emancipatory potential of an increasingly rationalized state. In the view of theorists such as Horkheimer (1978), democracy was inherently incapable of fostering a liberated self or the political legitimacy required for its continuance. As they saw it the promise of rationalism had given way to an authoritarian personality, and modern liberal state that reproduced systematic barriers to liberty (Shalin, 1992).

The pessimism of Horkheimer, however, stands in stark contrast to the optimism of his most famous student, Jurgen Habermas. In his *Theory of Communicative Action*, Habermas (1987) recognizes the systematic distortions of the democratic process associated with modernity, but he breaks with his mentors in professing a commitment to the emancipatory potential of "communicative rationality."

For Habermas, the foundational justification for democracy is evident in the very structure of ordinary language. The intersubjective prerequisite of the speech act reveals the liberating potential of reason, rational discourse and public communication. This theoretical commitment to the communicative rationality of intersubjective communication allows Habermas to argue that the disruptions of democracy under a capitalist political economy can be resisted and reformed by extending and deepening discursive democratic practices.

The work of Habermas has generated an immense intellectual debate (too large to review here) and his contributions to contemporary theory are sizeable. For the purposes of this paper, however, Habermas is important for two reasons. First, he recognizes that political critique and advocacy requires a normative standpoint, or philosophical foundation found in a sociological understanding of communication. And second, he is committed to an emancipatory agenda and praxis orientation through the enhancement of radical participatory democracy.

By merging elements of Habermas' theory with the work of philosophical pragmatists such as Dewey, Mead and Mills, we have the foundation for building a conceptual framework for the political self.

A GOOD SELF FOR THE GOOD SOCIETY

To engage in critical political analysis and to be committed to an emancipatory agenda presumes a normative standpoint. It presupposes the existence of a standard that can be used to differentiate acts of control and domination from acts of liberation and emancipation (Antonio, 1989). It short, it requires a conception of the "good self" for the "good society." But what is the good self and what criteria do we employ to assess and advance this ideal?

Critical theorists such as Habermas, as well as social pragmatists in the tradition of Dewey offer a general answer to these questions; namely, *the good self is a democratic self*. This is not simply because we can claim the normative superiority of democracy in the present political environment, but rather because democracy as a social practice provides the context necessary for the emergence and development of the defining capacities of the self. When relations of power stunt the development of the uniquely human capacities of objectification, creativity and self-expression we can say that power is in opposition to positive self-development.

The idea that the practice of democracy enhances and facilitates positive self-development is found in the work of political theorists as diverse as Marx, Gramsci, Jefferson, Emerson, John Stewart Mill, Dewey and Habermas. According to Warren (1995: 167) these "radical democrats" share the view that "more participation will produce more individuals with more democratic dispositions—individuals who are more tolerant of difference, more sensitive to reciprocity, better able to engage in moral discourse and judgement, and more prone to examine their own preferences." These positive interpersonal skills and capacities are valuable not only because they facilitate understanding and cooperation but also because the mature democratic self is better able to recognize domination and assert claims of emancipation against stultifying forces of control.

The good, democratic self, should not, however, be mistaken for the independent individual represented in classical theories of liberalism and lionized in American popular culture. Nor should the good self be equated with a consensus oriented moral agent in the manner depicted by some recent advocates of "communitarianism" (Etzioni, 1998). Rather, a democratic self must be able to appreciate, understand and desire a common good and just community where both personal interests and collective identities are valued. In short, the democratic self is ideally able to achieve a balance between agency and solidarity where individualism does not give way to alienation, and collective identity does not limit or detract from personal freedom.

Radical participatory democracy is transformative in that it assists in the development of the good political self—a democratic self. It is equally important to recognize, however, that democratic selves are critical to the deepening of democratic practice and the building of democratic communities. This is the point that Dewey (1927) makes when he says "A society which makes provision for participation in its good of all its members on equal terms and which secures flexible readjustment of its institutions through interaction of the different forms of associated life is in so far democratic." Dewey's emphasis on "flexible readjustment" is one key to understanding how democratic communities facilitate the "good society"

The good self is not an obedient or conformist self, and dissent and disagreement in discourse are not taken as indicators of failed communication in pragmatist theory. Nor do pragmatists equate rationality with universal consensus. On the contrary, for theorists such as Mead and Dewey dissent is taken as a necessary component of rational, democratic discourse. Shalin (1992: 263), for example, points out that for pragmatists, the absence of consensus is actually positive in that "it can be taken as a sign that participants are free to express their view and to engage in debate from their perspective." Consensus for the pragmatist is only a temporary pivot point in an iterative process that moves toward an agreement that can only be provisional and should not be an ultimate goal or communicative ideal. While pragmatists recognize that dissent can be procedurally unproductive at times, they also emphasize that dissent, if organized correctly can be procedurally productive. The welcoming of dissent flows out of the pragmatist assertion that normative validity is founded on culturally specific, intersubjective understandings. Consequently, moral principles and actions do not require justification across culture and history. Agreement, when achieved can serve as a resource for the tentative grounding of future deliberation that must include disagreement, which is itself a resource for future explorations of tentative truths. This "modest universalism" expects communication to produce shared attitudes as actors employ role-taking capacities, but mutual understanding does not imply or depend upon similar values or common beliefs. Understood in this way it is possible to see how the complexity of modern society is not necessarily a barrier to rational democratic discourse. An increase in social diversity can lead to more frequent cross-group contact which compels active role-taking and the production of "workable" intersubjective understandings. With this comes an appreciation of tolerance and the value of plural meanings. Group differences, multiple understandings, variety in tradition are rightly understood as resources for the pursuit of "tentative truths." From a pragmatist's perspective, truth is more than finding good reasons and building consensus. Truth must also be redeemed in practical accomplishments of the real world.

MODERNITY, IDENTITY AND RADICAL DEMOCRACY

Despite the pragmatist assertion that the self can only be fully comprehended in the actual experience of real world interaction, symbolic interactionists have placed relatively little emphasis on the historically specific, real world contexts that shape the modern self. A commitment to an emancipatory agenda and praxis orientation requires the identification of the actual socio-cultural forces that hinder the development of democratic selves and a political strategy for advancing the good society. In this final section I will offer a general framework for approaching both of these goals.

Modernity and the Segmented Self

A general defining feature of the process of modernization is the progressive increase in societal complexity, differentiation and specialization resulting from the forces of capitalism, bureaucracy and the decline of tradition. For the self, societal complexity is reflected in the process of role segmentation, or the increasing differentiation and specialization of social life (Frank and Meyer, 2002; Hage and Powers, 1992). For the modern actor it means a separation of one's lifeworld into numerous distinct social locations with little in common. The classic historical example of role segmentation is seen in the separation of work and family life that has produced a clear differentiation between what it means to do family and what it means to do work (Hareven, 1976). This type of role segmentation is not simply the process of isolating traditional roles, but rather it also includes the reconstruction of traditional roles and the creation of new roles. In this way modernity produces different cultural definitions of, say, work and family as well as the physical separation of work and family. Similar specialization, differentiation and segmentation continue to occur along other institutional settings such as religion, education, health care and politics (Brint, 1994).

When traditional lifestyles are disrupted and challenged by the forces of modernity, the modern actor faces a dilemma. On the one hand, the decline of traditional institutional and cultural orders releases a pervasive "social reflexivity" which means greater self-direction and autonomy. As old power structures crumble certain barriers to democracy and positive self-development are removed. On the other hand, the growth of personal agency comes with certain risks. Paramount among these is the loss of social identity. In modern societies self-identity is problematized in a manner unknown to traditional communities. This results in new experiences of ontological insecurity and self-anxiety. Giddens (1991:3) makes this point when he notes that:

> Doubt, a pervasive feature of modern critical reason, permeates into everyday life, as well as philosophical consciousness, and forms a general existential dimension of the contemporary social world. Modernity institutionalizes the principle of radical doubt and insists that all knowledge take the form of hypotheses . . . the self, like the broader institutional contexts in which it exists, has to be reflexively made.

The political implications of existential uncertainty can be mixed. A defensive response to such "detraditionalization" is to resort to a fundamentalist stance by asserting truth while at the same time refusing to accept principles of dialogue demanded by democracy. This is evident in the growth of religious fundamentalist movements and reactionary political regimes. Swatos (2001), for example, sees a direct path between the economic and cultural processes of globalization and the growing sectors of "ultraorthodoxy" in Islam, Judaism and Christianity.

Absent a retreat to conservative religion and politics, there is a value in detraditionalization. Issues such as gender equality, religious authority and sexual orientation that went "unseen" under the momentum of tradition are gradually "exposed" in a modern context. As a consequence we find the emergence of a "life politics" which is concerned with how we should live in a world where everything that was once traditional must now be decided about (Giddens, 1994). Although not an adequate emancipatory project, a politics of lifestyle and identity does provide an opening for the construction of democratic communities and democratic selves.

Role as Identity Resource

When traditional ascriptive anchors of identity are lost, actors must make a conscious effort to achieve a sense of self. In other words, the question of identity is a modernist concern (Taylor, 1989). With the autonomy to search for new sources of identity, modern actors initiate a search for resources to construct the self (Warren, 1995). A fundamental source for identity is found in the culturally available roles that are either freed from traditional ascriptive limits or have been newly created in modern society. As a result, actors find a multiplicity of distinct role-identities to use as resources for building a coherent self. Thus the reservoir of cultural roles that structure modern society are at the same time resources for the creation of a personal repertoire of role-identities. The detraditionalization of society motivates a search for self while the process of role-segmentation provides the modern solution. Taken together it is possible to see how even though role-segmentation is associated with doubt and existential uncertainty, it is reproduced as actors employ roles as identity resources. In this way the segmented and increasingly rationalized structure of society is mirrored in the segmented and rationalized structure of self (Frank and Meyer, 2002).

Still, the autonomy and agency implied by the search for identity is only part of the picture. Actors are not free to be whatever they want to be. Some roles are certainly more powerful and enabling than others are and unless one has access to these, agency is limited. The obvious limits of roles tied to class, gender, race and sexual orientation standout. Still other roles require the availability of different symbolic resources (especially economic and cultural capital). One needs money and good grades, for example, to get into college. In both senses the modern self is limited in its freedom and autonomy. In addition, the modern self is often "colonized" by the same process.

> Family roles are articulated, with detailed instruction and legal regulation (e.g., of spousal abuse) on how to manage newly liberated desires and choices. Informal recreational activities are formalized, so that one can take detailed lessons in the right and wrong way to golf or sing . . . Traditional religious and ethnic cultures are rationalized in role performances (on holidays, in particular) that can be taught in school and specified for any outsider in the press (Frank and Meyer, 2002: 91).

To the extent that the strategic rationality of economic and state bureaucracies define the culturally available roles, the use of certain roles as a basis for identity will further limit the modern self. This is most clearly evident in the traditional occupational identities of artisans and other craftspeople who expressed creativity and self through their labor. Industrial production processes that routinized, segmented and dehumanized work resulted in alienated and colonized selves.[2] More recently one can think of what it meant to be a medical doctor in the early part of the 20th century in comparison to the meaning of the same role as defined by modern health maintenance organizations. But even in these two examples of a colonized self, it is important to emphasize that the modern actor never becomes a complete automaton of role expectations. Numerous interactionists have consistently established the creative and ingenious strategies for crafting personal identity amidst the limits of modern society (see especially the work of Goffman, 1961a, 1961b). Thus while a role may limit what we do and how we define our self, we are still able to use the role as resource in certain creative ways. Finally, it is also possible for actors to initiate the establishment of new role-identities that are not limited by a strategic rationality. This form of resistance, however, faces a stiff challenge in modern society where the encroachment of undemocratic system forces threatens to dominate and co-opt even these roles.

IDENTITY RESOURCES FOR RADICAL DEMOCRACY

In the conceptual language of Jurgen Habermas, the strategically rational and undemocratic system forces of modern society have colonized the lifeworld of the modern actor. That is to say, the taken for granted assumptions of a culture based on principles of communication have been replaced by rationalized motives of profit and promotion. As a result, the promise of emancipation associated with the communicative reason of radical democracy is at risk. Using the concepts of role and identity we can articulate with more precision how the good, democratic self is threatened and, more importantly, how resistance and democratic change is possible.

The two dominant trajectories that I have described above can serve as an important analytical frame for understanding the opportunities for a radical democratic resistance. In the first instance, the modern self reacts defensively to the destabilizing forces of modernity by clinging to reactionary identities constructed from idealized images of a traditional society where "truth" was secure. This "solution" is limited in that the communities that anchor these identities are usually undemocratic, are unsympathetic to the values of tolerance, sympathy, dissent and diversity and therefore can not sustain the democratic identity resources needed to construct a democratic self.

The other self trajectory is one that is open to the forces of modernity but is colonized by the dominant system forces. This occurs when the increasingly isolated and alienated self is constructed using undemocratic system roles associated with an increasingly bureaucratic and capitalistic political economy. This version of the modern self alternates between moments of existential security and feelings of isolation and alienation. The colonized self may recognize the need for "change" but is usually passive and politically

---

[2]Technology and other nonhuman apparatus can also become a part of the self in a manner that is usually dehumanizing and controlling (Callero, 2003). Ironically, this form of colonization often occurs against a backdrop of marketing hype that promises liberation, as in a recent ad for a laptop computer that read: "Get a More Mobile Notebook; Get a More Mobile You!".

adrift. At times, democratic identities associated with "alternative lifestyles" develop but these may not provide the required resources for change. With the decline of free public spaces untouched by a corporate culture, there are fewer democratic resources for building a good self.

The good self requires a good society where democratic identity resources are developed and sustained. But it would be sociologically naïve to assume that a particular revolutionary movement or vanguard political party could provide the necessary resources. The democratic self cannot be built from a predetermined plan since by definition such a strategy violates the essential principles of participatory democracy. The good self requires public forums that privilege dissent and participation unencumbered by power. For this reason, communities guided by principles of radical participatory democracy hold promise as an insurgent alternative avenue of political reform.

Radical democracy as an alternative mode for organizing political action is not a utopian political plan. Consistent with the arguments of Habermas, radical democracy can be seen as an empirical consequence of a society that increasingly recognizes the illegitimacy of tradition and coercion. The promise of such a change is evident in the growth of so-called new social movements organized around issues of the environment, feminism, sexual orientation, militarism and global labor, among others. These movements are unique in that they occupy the sociological space between the informal, private spheres of family and the more formal public sphere of the state and the market. It is a space of relative freedom, often referred to as civil society (Cohen and Arato,1992) where structures are generally decentralized and action is highly participatory.

From the perspective of the political self, radical democratic communities are important for the positive political identities that they provide. They can be at once a source of solidarity and a resource for agency (Klandermans and de Weerd, 2000). And because they are sustained in a dynamic of participatory democracy they assist in the development of the good self. Insurgent democratic communities, or what Nancy Fraser (1992) calls "subaltern publics" can serve as a medium of political change by activating and organizing collective action. At the same time it would be sociologically naïve to assume that significant social change would result from simply sustaining the good self in an alternative political community. Alternative communities are at risk of becoming isolated from the more dominant political culture. They can become too parochial, issue oriented and inward looking. When the security of identity and solidarity becomes the endpoint, social movements may simply serve as "lifestyle enclaves" (Bellah, Madsen, Sullivan, Swidler and Tipton, 1985). To mount significant resistance against the antidemocratic forces of capitalism, corporate culture and bureaucratic rationalization it is necessary to confront the momentum of status quo political arrangements. History provides illustrations and hope for the growing resistance of democratic movements. Yet we know relatively little about the micro processes that accompany the positive shifts in the decentralization of power and the democratization of culture. Missing is a conceptual formula for thinking about the mutual generation of agency and structure.

GENERATING SOCIAL CHANGE

Habermas' systems language is not sufficient for articulating the possibility of structural change that is generated from micro level processes. A more conducive approach is offered by Sewell (1992: 16) who argues that

[a] theory of change cannot be built into a theory of structure unless we adopt a far more multiple, contingent, and fractured conception of society—and of structure. What is needed is a conceptual vocabulary that makes it possible to show how the ordinary operations of structures can generate transformations.

Sewell's conceptual vocabulary builds on the work of Anthony Giddens (1984). According to Giddens, structure is "carried" in reproduced practices and relationships and, therefore, depends highly upon interaction for its maintenance. More specifically, it is argued that structure exists in two distinct but mutually dependent dimensions, what Sewell refers to as "schemas" and "resources." Schemas are the taken for granted rules and cultural assumptions that serve as principles of action (recognized injustices, violation of rights), while resources are human qualities (e.g., strength, knowledge) and nonhuman objects (e.g., weapons, tools) that serve as a source of power.

We can think, for example, of a typical U.S. state legislature where schemas are evident in the assumptions that structure the relation among legislators (e.g., seniority and experience has leadership privileges), among legislative staff (e.g., one takes direction from legislators, public challenges are unacceptable) and between legislators and constituents (e.g., deference is owed to legislators, legislative rules, statutes must be obeyed and accepted). Resources are evident in both the nonhuman material conditions of a legislative assembly (e.g., weapons of security personnel, the structure of seating in the assembly, public address systems, computers) as well as the human qualities of legislators (knowledge of parliamentary procedure, relationships with particular lobbyists).

While schemas and resources combine to form structure, there is an important difference between these two dimensions. Schemas are said to have a "virtual" existence in that they are not reducible to any particular location in space and time. The schemas that serve to distinguish the relations among legislators and citizens, for example, are generalizable procedures that can be put into practice in a range of different settings. Resources, on the other hand, are conceptualized as having an "actual" existence, meaning they are observable in time and space. The State Capitol building, the weapons of guards, the acts of voting, the counting of votes all have an actual existence and serve as a source of power. Nevertheless, it should be reemphasized that the two dimensions cannot be maintained independently. The actualization or enactment of cultural schemas produces the observable human resources, and the use of resources validates the reality of the schemas. Resources are the products of schemas and schemas are generated from resources. Once structure is conceptualized in this way, the micro processes of social change are more evident.

Role as Social Structure

I have argued elsewhere that roles can be conceptualized as micro social structures that exist as both schema and resource (Callero, 1994). As a schema, a role has a virtual reality in the sense that it exists at a transcendent level, available for use in different intersections of space and time. A role, therefore, is not dependent upon a particular status or position and is not simply a set of expectations. It is a generalizable set of meanings or principles (Callero, 1994). It is at this level that we can say a role has a cognitive dimension (Callero 1991), and serves as an image (Schwalbe 1987) or gestalt (Turner 1962) that directly or indirectly guides action. When employed as a resource, a role also has an actual existence, and is the basis of power. At this level a role is observable as it is enacted in particular encounters and becomes a real object of interaction.

I want to suggest that the dual nature of roles corresponds to the dual nature of social structure and that linking role and social structure in this way has certain advantages over more familiar conceptualizations of role. For example, it avoids the overly deterministic approach to action characteristic of traditional structural approaches (e.g., Linton, 1936), while at the same time it offers a conceptual link to a dynamic theory of social structure, a quality absent from most interactionist approaches (e.g., Turner, 1962). As a consequence, the role as resource approach is better able to articulate processes of social change as they emerge from collective action. The essential insight of the resource perspective is straightforward: roles are used as tools for creative action, agency and change, and the agency experienced from using roles is limited and structured by the meaning or type of role. In addition, the cultural variation in role type (virtual existence) is reproduced through role use (actual existence).

Transposing Social Roles

If we conceptualize roles as sets of schemas and resources, as I have suggested, we can get a more specific understanding of how the importing or generalizing of roles from one structure of common use to another structure is key to understanding social change. Sewell (1992) suggests that agency can be defined as the ability of an actor to transpose a schema—that is, to apply it creatively, in an unfamiliar context. The enactment of schemas in unfamiliar settings creates unpredictability and the potential for change in the reproduction of schemas and the accumulation of resources. Robin Stryker (1994) has most recently demonstrated support for this principle. In an analysis of legal and scientific rationalities, Stryker shows that the generalizing of scientific schemas into the domain of law can account for specific types of change in the legitimacy of legal institutions. Following Sewell and Stryker, then, I want to suggest that attempts to alter dominant political structures may be enhanced by collective acts of agency in which social roles are transposed or imported from communities of radical democracy. The use of novel roles may create unpredictability and provide new opportunities for action.

Conceptualized in this manner we can see how insurgent communities that develop radical, democratic role-identities can facilitate positive social change if they are used in settings that are undemocratic and exploitive. We can think for example of the democratic advances achieved in the U.S. civil rights movement, the anti-apartheid revolution in South Africa, women's suffrage and the global labor movement. In all instances acts of civil disobedience were used to confront and make visible taken-for-granted systems of domination. At the micro level, oppositional democratic communities served as resources for legitimating emancipated role-identities which then served as resources for resistance. When Rosa Parks took her seat in the front of the bus she was transposing her black democratic identity onto a white community of exclusion. Although her act demonstrated individual bravery, she was empowered by a "subaltern public" that sustained democratic schemas and resources. We can see similar resources at work today as communities across the globe organize to resist the growing dominance of multinational corporations. On university campuses, students have had success in challenging sweatshop labor practices by forcing college administrators to face the exploitation of laborers who produce garments bearing university logos. Students in this instance employ identity resources defined by the values of open discourse, the free-exchange of ideas and internationalism to expose inconsistencies in university policy.

CONCLUSION

The modern self is a political self. This is true whether or not an explicitly recognized political identity is part of the self-structure. Gender, occupation, sexual orientation and religion, are all essentially political and are employed as resources to construct the self. When symbolic interactionists ignore the politics of self, our theories are incomplete, our relevance to sociology is diminished and we unintentionally assist in the reproduction of oppressive social systems.

The framework developed in this paper is intended as a broad outline for orienting empirical work and theoretical debate. It reflects a commitment to the emancipatory agenda of classical sociology and a belief in the necessity of adopting an explicit normative standpoint. Consistent with the tradition of American pragmatism and Critical Theory, I have argued that the standpoint for assessing the "good self" as well as the "good society" is radical participatory democracy. It is important to emphasize that this is a position derived from an empirical understanding of the mature self and is not simply a particular cultural preference.

Guided by these general principles I have suggested a political strategy for achieving positive social change. This strategy emphasizes the value of developing relatively independent insurgent role-identities within social movement communities that privilege radical participatory democracy. Once secure, these role-identities can be employed as resources for doing politics as they are transposed onto more hegemonic structures. Transposing roles from a normatively secure context onto a structure that is novel will necessarily generate resistance, but power is never relinquished without a struggle. When social structure is altered the self is implicated and the foundation for social identity is more or less threatened. Discourse may become uncivil, reactionary, and defensive and may even result in an initial increase in control and domination. But movement towards debate and public dialogue is itself a measure of victory in that it signals the nascent promise of radical democracy.

ACKNOWLEDGMENTS: I want to thank Dean Braa for his many important contributions to the ideas represented in this paper and for his careful reading and helpful comments on an earlier draft. I also want to recognize the contributions of all who participated in the mini-conference on The Future of Identity Theory and Research, held in honor of Sheldon Stryker at Indiana University, April, 2001.

REFERENCES

Antonio, R. J. (1989). The normative foundations of emancipatory theory: Evolutionary versus pragmatic perspectives. *American Journal of Sociology*, 94, 721–48.

Bellah, R., Madsen, R., Sullivan, W.M., Swidler, A. & Tipton, S.M. (1985). *Habits of the heart: Individualism and commitment in American life*. Berkeley: University of California Press.

Brint, S. (1994). *In an age of experts: The changing role of professionals in politics and public life*. Princeton, NJ: Princeton University Press.

Callero, P. L. (1991). Toward a sociology of cognition. In J. A. Howard and P. L. Callero (Eds.), *The self-society dynamic: Cognition, emotion and action* (pp. 43–54). New York: Cambridge University Press.

Callero, P. L. (1994). From role-playing to role-using: Understanding role as resource. *Social Psychology Quarterly*, 57, 228–43.

Callero, P.L. (2003). The sociology of the self. *Annual Review of Sociology*, 29, 115–133.

Cohen, J. & Arato, A. (1992). *Civil society and political theory*. Cambridge, Mass.: MIT Press.

Dewey, J. (1927). *The public and its problems*. New York: Henry Holt.

Durkheim, E. (1938). *The rules of sociological method*. New York: The Free Press.

Etzioni, A. (Ed.). (1998). *The essential communitarian reader*. Lanham, MD.: Rowan and Littlefield.

Elder, G. (1974). *Children of the great depression: Social change in life experience*. Chicago: University of Chicago Press.

Foucault, M. (1995). *Discipline and punish: The birth of the prison*. New York: Vintage Books.

Frank, D.J. & Meyer J.W. (2002). The profusion of individual roles and identities in the postwar period. Sociological Theory, 20, 86–105.

Fraser, N. (1993). Rethinking the public sphere: A contribution to the critique of actually existing democracy. In C. Calhoun (Ed.), *Habermas and the public sphere* (pp. 109–42). Cambridge, MA: MIT Press.

Giddens, A. (1984). *The constitution of society*. Berkely: University of California Press.

Giddens, A. (1991). *Modernity and self-identity: Self and society in the late modern age*. Stanford, CA: Stanford University Press.

Giddens, A. (1994). *Beyond left and right: The future of radical politics*. Stanford, CA: Stanford University Press.

Goffman, E. (1961a). *Asylums: Essays on the social situations of mental patients and other inmates*. New York: Anchor Books.

Goffman, E. (1961b). *Encounters: Two studies in the sociology of interaction*. Indianapolis: Bobs Merrill.

Gouldner, A. (1970). *The coming crisis in western sociology*. New York: Basic Books.

Habermas, J. (1987). *The theory of communicative action, vol. 2, Lifeworld and system: A critique of functionalist reason*. Boston: Beacon Press.

Hage, J. and Powers, C. (1992). *Post industrial lives: Roles and relationships in the 21ˢᵗ century*. Thousand Oaks, CA: Sage.

Hareven, T. K. (1976). Modernization and family history: Perspectives on social change. *Signs: Journal of Women in Culture and Society*, 2, 190–206.

Hochschild, A. R. (1983). The managed heart: Commercialization of human feeling. Berkeley: University of California Press.

Horkheimer, M. (1978). Dawn and decline: Notes, 1926–1931 and 1950–1969. New York: Seabury.

Huber, J. (1973). Symbolic interaction as pragmatic perspective: The bias of emergent theory. *American Sociological Review*, 38, 278–84.

Kellner, D. (1989). *Critical theory, Marxism and modernity*. Baltimore: Johns Hopkins University Press.

Klandermans, B. & de Weerd, M. (2000). Group identification and political protest. In S. Stryker, T.J. Owens & R. W. White (Eds.), Self, identity, and social movements (pp. 68–90). Minneapolis: University of Minnesota Press.

Linton, R. (1936). *The study of man*. New York: D. Appleton-Century-Crofts.

Mills, C. W. (1959). *The sociological imagination*. New York: Oxford University Press.

Schwalbe, M. L. (1987). Mead among the cognitivists: Roles as performance imagery. *Journal for the Theory of Social Behavior*, 17:113–133.

Sewell, W. H., Jr. (1992). A theory of structure: Duality, agency, and transformation. *American Journal of Sociology*, 98:1–29.

Shalin, D. N. (1992). Critical theory and the pragmatist challenge. *American Journal of Sociology*, 98, 237–79.

Stryker, R. (1994). Rules, resources, and legitimacy processes: Some implications for social conflict, order, and change. *American Journal of Sociology*, 99: 847–910.

Stryker, S. (1980). *Symbolic interactionism: A social structural version*. Palo Alto, CA.: Benjamin/Cummings.

Swatos, W. H. (2001). Globalization and religious fundamentalism. In P. Kivisto (Ed.) *Illuminating social life, 2ⁿᵈ edition* (pp. 361–84). Thousand Oaks, CA: Pine Forge.

Taylor, C. (1989). *Sources of the self: The making of modern identity*. Cambridge, MA: Harvard University Press.

Turner, R. (1962). Role-taking: Process vs. conformity. In A. M. Rose (Ed.), Human behavior and social processes (pp. 22–40). Boston: Houghton Mifflin.

Turner, R. (1976). The real self: From institution to impulse. *American Journal of Sociology*, 81, 989–1016.

Warren, M. E. (1995). The self in discursive democracy. In S. K. White (Ed.), *The Cambridge companion to Habermas*. New York: Cambridge University Press.

Chapter **5**

Identities and Inequalities
Exploring Links Between Self and Stratification Processes

Matthew O. Hunt

INTRODUCTION

Self-concept theory and research (Rosenberg, 1979; Gecas and Burke, 1995; McCall and Simmons, 1966) takes as a central goal demonstration of the fact that the self "matters" (i.e., is not an epiphenomenon) for social behavior and the organization of society. In this chapter, I explore some ways in which self and identity matter—as both "social product"and "social force" (Rosenberg, 1981)—for the study of social stratification and inequality. The goal of this paper is to review some existing research lying at the intersection of the study of self and stratification, and to suggest several ways in which such scholarship can be further developed. Special emphasis is placed on integrating key concepts from "identity theory" (Stryker and Burke, 2000) into our understanding of stratification processes.

We can start with the observation that sociological and social psychological research into phenomena such as legitimation processes (Della Fave, 1980; Stolte, 1983; Shepelak, 1987), "stratum identification" and "consciousness" (Gurin, Miller, and Gurin, 1980), and the determinants and consequences of an array of socio-political attitudes (Kluegel and Smith, 1986; Schuman, Steeh, Bobo, and Krysan, 1997) has a mixed record regarding the use of the self-concept. Further, when the "self" is invoked—and particularly when the focus is on some aspect of "identity"—it is typically used in a relatively rudimentary way from the standpoint of what has come to be known as "identity theory" within sociological social psychology (Stryker, 1968, 1987).[1]

As developed by Stryker and colleagues (e.g., Serpe and Stryker, 1987), identity theory conceptualizes "identities" as internalized self-designations based on the meanings (role expectations) attached to positions in social structure (role involvements). Building on thinkers such as Mead (1934) and James (1890), identity theory views the

---

[1]See Stets and Burke (2000) for a useful discussion of the differences and similarities between "identity theory" (i.e., role-identity theory) and its psychological cousin, "social identity theory."

self as a multidimensional construct whose structure reflects the institutionally differentiated nature of societies. Further, the multiple identities comprising the self are held to be
organized into a "salience hierarchy" (Stryker and Burke 2000), having direct implications
for outcomes such as role-choice behavior. While empirical support has been found for
these ideas (Stryker and Serpe, 1982), as well as for the more cognitively-focused aspects
of "identity theory" developed by Burke and colleagues (Burke, 1980; Burke and Reitzes,
1981), most symbolic interactionist research on the self is still subject to the criticism of
having ignored issues of power, inequality, and the stratified nature of modern societies
(Callero, this volume; Gouldner, 1970; Hollander and Howard, 2000; Howard, 2000. For
an important exception, see: Stryker, 1980).

Thus, our knowledge of both social stratification and self/identity could be augmented with greater attention paid to (1) the social structural sources of variation in identity
structures and processes, and (2) the influence of identity structures and processes on stratification-related outcomes such as persons' perceptions of the stratification order and other
socio-political attitudes (Kluegel and Smith, 1986). To this end, after briefly outlining
some ways in which the self *has* been incorporated into the study of stratification-related
phenomena, I explore a proposed line of research—by way of an extended application of
Thoits (1992) operationalization of "identity structure" (i.e., "claims," "salience," and
"combinations")—concerning how key concepts from identity theory could help expand
our knowledge of the self as both (1) the *product* of social structural arrangements (Stryker, 1980), and, conceivably, (2) a social *force* shaping consciousness of, and attitudes
about, social inequalities (Kluegel and Smith, 1986; Hunt, 1996).

HOW HAS STRATIFICATION RESEARCH "CONCEIVED THE SELF"?

Self-Evaluation

A good starting point for answering the question of how self has been incorporated into
research on socially structured inequalities and intergroup relations is the notion of "self-
evaluation" (e.g., self-esteem, self-efficacy)—arguably the most widely researched dimension of the self-concept (Rosenberg, 1979; Owens, Stryker, and Goodman, 2001). As a
social *product*, research on constructs such as self-esteem has documented the impacts of
"larger social structural" features of society such as social class (Rosenberg and Pearlin,
1978) and race/ethnicity (Hughes and Demo, 1989; Porter and Washington, 1979), as well
as the effects of interpersonal environments as in the case of the consequences of the racial
homogeneity of classrooms for the self-esteem of black schoolchildren (Rosenberg, 1981).

As a social *force*, Della Fave (1980) conceptualizes self-evaluation as a key factor
facilitating the legitimation of stratified social orders. Specifically, Della Fave argues that
the congruence between objective status (control over "primary resources") and subjective
status ("self evaluation"—understood as the perception of one's own ability to control the
aspects of the larger social and political environment) shapes peoples' sense of just-
deserts in ways supportive of the maintenance of the status quo.[2] Empirical support for

---

[2]According to Della Fave (1980), advantaged and disadvantaged actors alike perceive advantaged persons' societal "contributions," and ability to control their environments, as greater, resulting in higher self-evaluations for
the advantaged than the disadvantaged, and, ultimately, an across-strata consensus that existing inequalities in
reward-levels are legitimate (i.e., lower status actors with low self-evaluations are unlikely to challenge the
legitimacy of inequality).

this argument has been mixed, however, generally hinging on the failure to substantiate the prediction that lower status actors will perceive their reward levels as just/deserved (Stolte, 1983; Shepelak, 1987).[3] Also viewing self-evaluations as a social force, Hunt (2001) documents that self-esteem and mastery shape ideological beliefs about the causes of poverty; self-esteem is the more consequential aspect of self-evaluation shaping support for "individualistic" beliefs about inequalities, while mastery is the key aspect of self-evaluation shaping system-challenging, "structuralist" beliefs.

Self-Attribution

The determinants and consequences of "self-attributions" (Crittenden, 1983), or people's lay perceptions—in causal terms—of self-relevant events, is another aspect of self-concept that has received attention by social psychologists interested in social stratification. Kluegel and Smith (1986) document that "self-explanations" for personal outcomes (i.e., personal socio-economic positions) exist along an internal/external dimension reminiscent of the "locus of control" construct (Rotter, 1966), and are shaped by social structural factors similar to those shaping beliefs about the larger stratification order. For example, higher incomes lead to greater use of "internal," individualistic explanations for both personal outcomes and for issues such as why poverty exists (Kluegel and Smith, 1986), while women and racial minorities have been observed to favor the use "external" self-attributions more than their male and white counterparts, respectively (Crittenden, 1983), mirroring women and minorities' greater endorsement of structuralist beliefs about the causes of inequality.

As a social force, self-attributions have been shown to impact persons' perceptions of the causes of inequalities. For example, Kluegel and Smith (1986) and Heaven (1989) observe a pattern of "attributional consistency" regarding the generalization of attributions for personal outcomes to attributions about the causes of issues such as poverty (i.e., "internal" self-explanations lead to "individualistic" beliefs about the poor, while "external" self-explanations lead to "structuralist" beliefs about the poor). Some of my own work replicates these patterns among whites (Hunt, 1996), however, I observe reversals of the earlier documented patterns for African-Americans and Latinos, suggesting the need to incorporate race/ethnicity (and other social structural factors) more fully into our theories and models of social psychological processes (see: Hunt, Jackson, Powell, and Steelman, 2000 for an extended treatment of the implications of social psychology's failure to more centrally incorporate issues of race/ethnicity into its research).

Social Identities

A final source of examples of research on intersections of self and stratification include studies of the determinants and consequences of various "social identities" (Tajfel,1982; Stets and Burke, 2000) flowing from persons' identification with social categories such as racial, ethnic, and social class groupings (rather than with roles). For example, Harris (1995) links childhood interracial contact to "black adult identity," documenting that

---

[3]Della Fave (1986) argues that some of the failure to support key tenets of the self-evaluation theory of legitimation may stem from inadequate measures of self-evaluation as he conceptualizes it (i.e., the use of self-esteem scales in past empirical tests fails to capture the evaluation of self vis a vis the ability to influence the larger socio-political environment).

interracial contact during childhood weakens adult feelings of closeness to other blacks. And, more recently, Brown (1999) traces patterns in racial "label preferences" among African-Americans to several social structural factors, finding, for example, that the label "African-American," compared to "black," "negro," and "colored," is preferred by younger respondents and those with higher levels of education and income ("negro" and "colored" were particularly likely to be endorsed by older blacks and those with lower socioeconomic status).

Further, as a social force, Brown (1999) documents how racial identity (label) preferences shape policy-relevant attitudinal outcomes such as "protest ideology" (i.e., support for use of "laws and persuasion," vs. "non-violent protest" vs. advocating violence) and perceptions of the intentions of whites (i.e., whether whites are generally supportive of, or opposed to, blacks' advancement). Brown observes, for example, that African-Americans favoring the label "black" are most likely to support the use of laws and persuasion, and are the most optimistic with regard to perceptions of the intentions of whites.

Another "social identity" that has been examined extensively is "social class identification" (SCI) or "subjective" social class membership (Vanneman and Cannon 1987). As a social product, Jackman and Jackman (1983) show how social structural factors such as occupation, race, and socioeconomic status (hereafter SES) impact SCI (as well as the salience or "intensity" of SCI where, for example, objectively poor and working class persons feel more intensely about class label than do their more advantaged counterparts). And, as a social force these authors demonstrate how SCI shapes economic ideologies in ways consistent with an "underdog" thesis (Robinson and Bell, 1978)—i.e., SCI is inversely related to "liberal" positions on number of issue attitudes such as support for social welfare activities (job guarantees, minimum income), and on attitudes regarding desirable levels of income inequality.

Ethnic identity (or identification) has also been studied as both social product and social force. As a social product, Nagel (1995) has documented increases in rates of ethnic identification among Native Americans over the past several decades—patterns termed "ethnic renewal" and attributed to changing political opportunities for these race/ethnic minorities in the United States. In contrast, Alba (1990) documents clear declines in whites' ethnic identifications (e.g., as Italian, Irish, Polish) as a function of structural and demographic changes across the 20th century. Owing to ethnic assimilation through inter-marriage over several generations, Alba characterizes contemporary American society as a context in which whites' ethnic identities are increasingly adopted and discarded by choice. In short, the image of this "twilight of ethnicity" thesis is that white ethnic identity has become an achieved rather than ascribed status.

As a social force, Coverdill (1997) uses data from the General Social Surveys (GSS) to demonstrate that whites who claim an ethnic identification (i.e., who could identify an ethnic ancestry) had more liberal attitudes on racial issues (e.g., support for race-targeted social policies) than whites who did not ethnically identify. Coverdill interprets these findings in direct contrast to Waters' (1990) characterization of the relative racial conservatism of "white ethnics" (based on her in-depth interview study). However, Coverdill acknowledges that some of the disjuncture between his and Waters' findings may be attributable to measurement issues flowing from use of the GSS—i.e., Waters' conceptualization of identity is like that of Alba (1990) in making a distinction between "ethnic identification" (identification of ancestry) and "ethnic identity" (e.g., engaging in ritual or other behavior predicated on an ethnic identification). In short, ethnic identification seen as is a necessary but not sufficient precursor for ethnic identity, and the GSS measures the former.

Finally, some research on intersections of race and religion incorporates a notion of "religious identity" as social product and social force. For example, Hunt and Hunt (2001) find that race influences what they term "denominational identity salience," (based on responses to the GSS item (RELITEN) asking: "how strong a [insert denomination named] are you?"). Specifically, African-Americans, nationwide, demonstrate significantly stronger identification with their denomination than whites. And, as a social force, Hunt and Hunt (1999, 2000) document that, among African-Americans, "denominational identity salience" is significantly more predictive of church attendance in the urban North region (where institutional differentiation is maximized, and thus a wider array of choices for behavioral involvement exists) than in the South—findings supporting the imagery of black church attendance in the South as relatively "semi-involuntary" in nature (Ellison and Sherkat, 1995).

How Can an "Identity Theory" Approach to Self Advance Stratification Research?

While the foregoing review makes it clear that "the self" has been incorporated into some mainstream sociological research into issues of stratification and inequality, a shared shortcoming of the research reviewed is a relatively underdeveloped and/or narrow conceptualization of self (focusing, for example, on one aspect of self-feeling such as "self-esteem," or on one identity in relative isolation from other identities).

In contrast, as outlined earlier, "identity theory" (Stryker and Burke, 2000) conceptualizes the self-concept as a multidimensional construct whose structure reflects that of the differentiated social worlds in which the person is integrated. From the standpoint of a "structural symbolic interactionism" (Stryker, 1980) the self is comprised of multiple identities organized into a "hierarchy of salience," with more salient identities having a higher probability of invocation across a wider variety of settings (and for a person in a given setting). Further, for identity theory, the source of salience is "commitment"—defined as the extensiveness and intensiveness of a person's social networks predicated on playing a particular role. As such, the theory is ultimately concerned with social structural and cognitive factors influencing behavioral choices people make when alternative lines of action are available.

The classic "identity theory" question posed by Stryker, in both the lecture hall and his writings, can be paraphrased as: "Why, given a free afternoon, does one man take his children to the zoo while another plays golf with his buddies?" The answer, according to identity theory, is the differential salience of family-based (e.g, "parent") and friendship or recreation-based (e.g., "golfer") identities of the two men, stemming from differential patterns of commitment to others. Stryker and Serpe (1982) have demonstrated empirical support for the "commitment shapes identity salience shapes role choice behavior" equation invoked by the example above, and perhaps best understood as the "identity theory" corollary to the Meadian dictum that "society shapes self shapes social behavior."

In addition to the concept of "salience," other role-identity theorists have been concerned with how sheer numbers of, and particular combinations of, roles and/or identities impact behavioral and psychological outcomes. For example, research in the mental health field views the accumulation of role-identities as a subjective resource—literally a "cognitive buffer" against mental illness (Linville, 1987; Thoits, 1983, 1986). Further, Thoits (1992) has shown that particular role-identity combinations (e.g. worker and parent)

impact psychological distress, and differently so by gender.[4] In so doing, Thoits opera-
tionalizes several key constructs central to identity theory: identity claims, identity
salience, and identity combinations. After briefly reviewing her methodology, I propose
use of a similar approach to mapping both role *and* social identity configurations, with the
aim of exploring possible advances in our understanding of the self both as social product
and social force in the study of stratification.

Operationalizing "Identity Structure"

Thoits (1992) considers 17 role identities in her study of gender and marital status differences
in the relationship between "identity structures" and psychological well-being. These are:

1. spouse	10. relative
2. lover	11. friend
3. parent	12. neighbor
4. stepparent	13. churchgoer
5. caregiver	14. group member
6. worker	15. community volunteer
7. student	16. hobbyist
8. son/daughter	17. athlete
9. son/daughter-in-law	

As part of the data collection process (which involved face to face interviews with a stratified
random sample of 700 married and divorced urban adults in Indianapolis circa 1988–89), inter-
viewers coded whether respondents were *actually involved* in each role (i.e., establishing patterns of "*objective membership*") in addition to collecting data on identity patterns. To collect
data on identities, a *five question* version of the now-classic "Who am I?" Twenty Statements
Test (TST) was initially employed. Following this open-ended approach to mapping respondents' self-concepts in identity terms, *identity claims* were documented using a series of closed-
ended questions. Specifically, using the 17 roles from the list, respondents were asked about
each: "Do think of yourself as a _____?" Response options included: "yes," "no," or "does
not apply," and each "yes" response was coded as an identity claim (importantly, the respondent had to hold the role for a "yes" to be treated as a role-identity). Next, to measure *identity
salience*, respondents were asked to look over their five "Who am I?" responses *and* their
responses to the 17 closed-ended role-identity prompts. They were instructed: "Suppose you
had to sort these things into three groups: most important to you, second most important, and
third most important." Respondents were allowed to name up to three identities per "level." In
coding identity salience, a value was assigned to each role occupied by the respondent: 3 = the
role was in the "most important" rank; 2 = the role was in the "second most important" rank;
1 = the role was in the in the "third most important" rank; 0 = the role was not ranked (i.e., the
role was held but it did not appear in the respondent's salience hierarchy).[5]

---

[4]Stryker and Burke (2000) make the important observation that "multiple identities" is not the same issue as
"multiple roles" or status inconsistency, since identities require the internalization of "role-related expectations
and their ordering in a hierarchy of salience" (p. 291).

[5]Thoits also examined the effects of various identity combinations (specifically, 24 groups representing all possible "gender by marital status by worker by 'child at home'" combinations). However, owing to space limita-
tions, I focus primarily on identity claims and identity salience in this paper.

Exploring Role and Social Identities: A Proposal

Thoits' (1992) example of the operationalization of identity "claims" and "salience" offers an useful template and starting point for exploring how both role *and* social identities are distributed in society, as well as how they may impact relevant attitudinal and behavioral outcomes. A survey study that employed Thoits' methodology, and that included both role *and* social identities (as well as standard sociodemographic measures and a battery of relevant socio-political attitudes) would advance our understanding of how (1) social stratification influences patterns of role *and* social identity formation; and (2) how identity configurations may shape political consciousness (Gurin, Miller, and Gurin, 1980) and related socio-political attitudes.

What follows is a thought experiment—part proposal, part delineation of questions that identity theorists might consider—designed to facilitate possible future research aimed at advancing the study of self/identity and stratification processes. These ideas represent one *possible* image of how research might proceed, and are designed to highlight key questions that future researchers could pursue. Thus, for the purposes of the remainder of this paper, I proceed as if the goal were to design an "identities" module of a survey research such as the National Opinion Research Center's "General Social Survey" (GSS), a nationally representative survey of roughly 1500 adult Americans (or 3000, beginning in 1994, when the survey became biennial rather than annual) using probability sampling techniques and face-to-face interviewing (National Opinion Research Center, 2002)

As alluded to above, one approach to this task would be to include a list of both role and social identities, employing Thoits' (1992) methodology for measuring various aspects of identity structure. This would, of course, require a list of appropriate social identities to be added to the existing list of 17 role-identities used by Thoits. One such list is provided by the 1972 National Election Study (University of Michigan, 1972), which contains a module on "group identifications." The 16 social categories comprising this list are (with possible language updates/changes suggested in parentheses):

1. Businessmen (Businesspeople)	9. Whites
2. Liberals	10. Blacks
3. Southerners	11. Conservatives
4. Poor people	12. Women
5. Catholics	13. Middle Class People
6. Protestants	14. Workingmen (Working Class People)
7. Jews	15. Farmers
8. Young People	16. Older People

In addition, two other categories/identities that would be useful to include given social trends of the past 30 years in the United States, include:

17. Latinos	18. Fundamentalist Christians

Thus, the resulting list of 35 identities would be comprised of roughly equal numbers of role (17) and social (18) identities.[6]

---

[6]In light of recent events, some combination of: Arabs, Arab-Americans, and/or Muslims, might also be considered for the list of social identities. Thanks are due to Jill Kiecolt for this suggestion.

While past "identity theory" research has focused on *role*-identities, inclusion of social identities tapping ways in which persons locate themselves in social and cultural space not captured by identity theory's institutional focus on statuses or roles, would be useful in exploring the self as social product and social force. Also, including two basic types of identities in a single study would be consistent with the goal of facilitating interchange between the "two social psychologies" (Stryker 1977; House 1977), given the traditional emphasis of psychological social psychologists on social identities and sociological social psychologists on role identities (Stets and Burke 2000).

"What Would We Learn?" Part I—Descriptive Issues

Most basically, such a study would provide descriptive knowledge of three basic issues central to the study of identities, and the social bases of identities: rates of "objective membership," identity claims, and identity salience.

Rates of "Objective Membership" in the Set of Roles and Categories

First, such a survey undertaking would provide data on rates of "objective" role and social category membership, regardless of whether the respondents identifies with the role or category.[7] These data could be used to map patterns of actual involvement in the 35 role/categories explored (with results presented as simple percentages holding each role/category). Thoits (1992) presents such data for 17 role identities, by gender and marital status. This stage of the research would provide a picture of how membership in our list of roles/categories is distributed in the larger adult population, and would give us new knowledge of overall and relative rates of membership in key roles and social categories.

Identity Claims

Second, such data would also allow analysis of patterns in "identity claims"—i.e., whether the identity is claimed by respondents who are "objectively" in the role or category. Thoits (1992) maps such patterns for 17 role identities, documenting that rates of "identity claims" vary between 70%—100%—rates cited as justification of the use of role membership as a proxy for identity in past research on mental health. Two issues come to mind here: (1) are the Indianapolis findings generalizable to a national sample and important subgroups comprising it such as racial minorities (Hunt et al., 2000)?; and (2) would we observe similar rates of "identity claims" for the 18 *social* identities in the list (i.e., are

---

[7]Such data could be collected in one of three ways. First, through direct questions (e.g., having children defines parenthood; occupational information could be used to place persons in "working" vs. "middle" class categories—see Gurin et al., 1980 for an example; information on church attendance could be used to classify persons as churchgoers; reporting one or more friends defines being a "friend," etc. See Thoits (1992), for more discussion on the operationalization of "roles held"). Second, in some cases, objective membership could possibly be assessed using interviewer's observations (sex and race of respondents are collected in this way by the GSS, however if the interviewer is unsure of how to code race, a question is used). Third, the facts of the situation could provide information (e.g., state of residence could be used to classify respondents in regions—e.g., "Southerner" vs. not).

rates of correspondence between objective involvement and subjective identification similar for non-role-based identities?)?[8]

Identity Salience

Finally, we would be able to map how "salient" various claimed identities are. Mirroring Thoits (1992) analyses of 17 role identities using an Indianapolis sample, such data would give us a nationally representative picture of the relative salience of 35 social and role identities—both individually and as types. Key questions that could be answered include whether social or role identities more salient generally, as well as how the individual identities in our list are ranked.

"What Would We Learn?" Part II—Identity Structure as Social Product and Social Force

In addition to providing descriptive data on how objective memberships and identity structures are distributed generally, the proposed survey would provide data for answering key questions concerning the self as both social product and social force.

Identity Structure as Social Product

Regarding the self as *social product*, the key question from the standpoint of a structural symbolic interactionism is whether "larger social structural" variables (termed "external" social structure by Stryker and Burke, 2000) affect rates of objective membership, identity claims, and identity salience for the list of 35 roles/categories. Stryker (1977) argues that a truly sociological social psychology must seek to demonstrate how larger societal factors shape identity processes and other individual-level phenomena (see also: House, 1981). To use Stryker's imagery, these data would enable us to identify how "larger" social structures act as "sorting mechanisms" affecting the probability of having various social relationships, or of occupying various statuses—issues having implications for the formation of both role and social-category based self-designations in identity terms (Stryker, 1980).

The basic analytic issue here is mapping the impact of social structures on role/category occupancy, identity claims, and identity salience.

Social Structure and Role/Category Occupancy. First, regarding rates of objective membership, the basic question is whether "vertical status" variables (race, SES, gender), and other social structural factors such as age, have implications for rates at which persons occupy our 35 roles and social categories? Stryker, Serpe, and Hunt (2000) document such social structural effects on the probability of having familial, work, or voluntary organization involvements. And, Thoits (1992) presents patterns in 17 role memberships by gender and marital status. The proposed study could build on this, and related, scholarship through an analysis of rates of membership in 35 roles/categories by other variables such as race, SES, gender, and age.

---

[8]Inclusion of social identities also raises the issue of whether it would be useful to map identity claims even if objective membership in the category is absent (recall that Thoits (1992) required objective membership for an identity claim). While perhaps of questionable utility for the role-identities (i.e., it might make little sense to ask the childless if they conceived of themselves as a "parent"), one could envision scenarios where objective membership in a social category was absent though an identification with that category is present (e.g., one could be classified as objectively middle class based on occupation and claim a working class identity).

Social Structure, Identity Claims, and Identity Salience. Next, researchers could assess whether "larger" social structures shape whether or not identity claims are made for particular involvements, as well as patterns in the salience of various identities. Thoits (1992) shows such patterns for 17 role-identities, after hypothesizing that, owing to gendered socialization, women would be more likely to value and invest themselves in "primary" relationships (i.e., family, relative, friend identities were expected to be claimed more, and to be higher in womens' identity structures), whereas men would gravitate toward more "achievement-related" or "instrumental" activities (i.e., occupational, organizational, and athletic identities were expected to be claimed more, and to be higher in mens' identity structures).

While these gender patterns were not borne out in the Indianapolis data, the issue of whether gender matters for the *social* identities on our list (e.g., are women more likely to identify with religious affiliations, and men more in occupational terms?) is an important empirical question. Further, data from the proposed study would also facilitate exploration of whether other social factors such as race, social class, and region shape identity structures (e.g., are claims of Latino' "familism" borne out in data on family-based identities? Are past findings of a heightened black religiosity observed for religiously-based identities?) In short, are basic sociological claims and findings regarding group differences in various domains observed at the level of identities? Mapping such patterns would be invaluable to advancing our understanding of the relationship between objective status and subjective orientations (Gurin, Miller, and Gurin, 1980; Jackman and Jackman, 1983).

Identity Structure as Social Force

Regarding the self as social force, this projected line of research would provide a detailed view of how the self may impact outcomes relevant to stratification research such as sociopolitical attitudes, voting behavior, and support for public policies designed to ameliorate inequalities. The first relevant question, from the standpoint of mapping how self may shape political consciousness is:

Does making an "identity claim" matter net of objective membership in the role/category? This "objective vs. subjective" status issue is a critical one in establishing whether self "matters" for political and stratification-related outcomes (i.e., whether it is important to have measures of self/identity *apart from* information on objective membership in social categories). Results such as Brown's (1999) demonstration that blacks' racial label preferences shape protest ideology and perceptions of the intentions of whites, suggests an affirmative answer to this question. Data from the study proposed herein would be useful in determining whether identity claims matter similarly for a wider range of identities and issues.

For example: does *identifying* as a "Southerner" affect racial attitudes net of residence in that region? Research documents that regional residence in the South shapes such attitudes (Tuch and Martin, 1997); however, the issue remains as to whether people who subjectively identify as "Southerners" differ from other residents of the South on issues such as attributions for black/white SES difference (Kluegel, 1990), and in their support for race-targeted social policies (Tuch and Martin, 1997). A similar issue is inspired by Hunter's "culture wars" thesis (1990), where research using denominational and "issue attitude" indicators of "fundamentalism" (Davis and Robinson, 1996) suggests systematic differences between fundamentalists and their more theologically modernist counterparts (i.e., "liberal or moderate Protestants") on a host of social and economic attitudes. But, the question remains: does claiming the "fundamentalist" *identity* shape social and economic attitudes net of objective membership in a "fundamentalist" Christian affiliation? In short, is there variation on these attitudes *among* members of fundamentalist churches that could be explained with a measure of identity claims? Such questions, heretofore unanswered (to my knowledge a the time of this writing), could be addressed with the proposed data collection.

The potential examples are many; however, the basic research issue can be stated in general terms: Does *identifying* in class, race, gender, age, regional, religious, and other terms shape attitudes (and behavior) net of objective indicators of role/category group membership? The notion of "identity claims" (Thoits, 1992) would take us a long way toward answering this question. And, if self/identity is not epiphenomenal for these outcomes, data such as those from the proposed study could help further develop our understanding of which identities matter for which issues (i.e, whether identity/attitude effects are issue or domain-specific).

Does "identity salience" matter net of an identity claim?   The logical next question is whether the *salience* of an identity is relevant for attitudinal (or relevant behavioral) outcomes net of identity claims and other background characteristics? Further, is any such connection issue or domain specific? Possible research questions include: Does a "salient" racial identity differentiate persons from others on racial (or other) attitudes? (e.g., are "salient" blacks different from "non-salient" blacks on support for race-targeted programs such as Affirmative-Action?)? Or, does a salient class identity differentiate persons from others on economic (or other) attitudes (e.g., are the "salient" poor different from those who merely identify as "poor" on support for the redistribution of wealth?)?[9] Or, does a salient gender identity differentiate persons from others on beliefs about gender roles and other gender issues (e.g., are "salient" women different from non-salient women on attitudes toward feminism, the Equal Rights Amendment, gender roles, and workplace issues such as comparable worth?)?

Further, regarding role-identity issues, does a "salient" parent identity differentiate persons from others on education-related issues (e.g., are "salient" parents different from other parents on support for taxation aimed at improving public schools?)? Or, does a salient "spouse" identity differentiate persons from others on attitudes toward social issues relating to families and intimate relationships (e.g., are persons with a salient spouse identity different from other married persons regarding support for abortion rights, gay rights, and no-fault divorce laws)? Or, does a salient church-based identity differentiate persons from others on social and political attitudes (e.g., are "salient" fundamentalists different from other fundamentalists regarding support for abortion rights?)?[10]

---

[9]Another interesting question is whether "salient" working class members are more or less supportive of social welfare than "non-salient" members of the working class? One might argue that "salients" would be especially liberal economically following a "class consciousness" logic; however, a highly salient working class identity might also shape political consciousness in the opposite direction by highlighting difference from the poor rather than common economic interests (Lane, 1959; Lewis, 1978).

[10]Research suggests that fundamentalist Protestants are more conservative on social issues and possibly more egalitarian/populist on some economic issues (Davis and Robinson, 1996). Thus, the issue is whether persons with a salient fundamentalist identity differ from other fundamentalists, and from other types of Protestants? For example, if "salient" fundamentalists were observed to be more conservative than non-salient fundamentalists and other types of Protestants across the board (i.e., on social and economic issues), we would have evidence that the "non-salient" fundamentalists may be the economic populists identified in some previous research.

Put simply, the research issue at this stage is whether the salience of a particular identity shapes outcomes net of an identity claim—a question whose answer would be useful in determining whether the application of key "identity theory" constructs has utility for research on social and political attitudes.

Two Final Research Issues: "Relative Salience" and "Identity Combinations." Two additional research issues arise when considering the possible impact of "identity structure" on political consciousness. First, in addition to the general "salience" issue, data from the proposed study could be used to map whether the *relative salience* (i.e., the relative position of an identity vis a vis other identities in a salience hierarchy) matters for socio-political attitudes. For example: if race is more salient than social class, does this have implications for support for race-targeted vs. class-targeted social welfare policies? Or, if "fundamentalist" is more salient than social class, does this have implications for attitudes toward the range of social and economic attitudes linked to fundamentalism by past researchers (Hunter, 1990, Davis and Robinson, 1996)? Further, if "relative salience" matters, can we identify *which* identities interact with *which* in shaping particular outcomes (e.g., if the relative position of a racial identity is consequential, can we determine which identities interact with race?)?

Second, and relatedly, we could explore whether particular *identity combinations* matter. Role-identity combinations have been shown to be a key variable for explaining psychological outcomes such as distress (Thoits, 1992). What impact might they have on socio-political attitudes? For example: does having *simultaneously* salient race, class, and gender identities shape consciousness differently than if these are salient one at a time? Or, does having simultaneously salient parent, worker, and churchgoer identities shape attitudes differently than in other combinations? If so, are the effects of such combinations issue-specific? Such questions could be pursued if sufficient variation in various identity combinations or configurations were observed in data from a study such as that proposed herein.

CONCLUSIONS

In this chapter, my goal has been three fold: First, I reviewed some research lying at the intersection of stratification and self/identity scholarship to document ways in which self/identity issues have been incorporated into such research. Second, I argue that the self is relatively under-theorized and under-incorporated into mainstream sociological research on stratification-related topics; and, in this context I also briefly discuss "identity theory," and outline an example how key constructs from this research area have been operationalized in past research. Third, I outline and argue, by way of a hypothetical survey project, how incorporation of some basic "identity theory" constructs in a large-scale survey undertaking such as the GSS could help advance our understanding of (1) the influence of stratification variables (and other social structural forces) on identity processes and structures, and (2) the role of such processes and structures in shaping socio-political attitudes such as beliefs about inequalities and related public-policies. In keeping with the intellectual legacy of Sheldon Stryker, it is hoped that the ideas put forth in this paper contribute to the development of more fully sociological social psychology.

ACKNOWLEDGMENTS: This chapter was a paper originally prepared for the Indiana Conference on Identity Theory, Bloomington, IN, April 27–29, 2001. The author thanks Larry Hunt for his comments on an earlier draft of this paper.

REFERENCES

Alba, R. D. (1990). *Ethnic identity: The transformation of white America*. New Haven, CT: Yale University Press.

Brown, T. N. (1999). Predictors of racial label preference in Detroit: Examining trends from 1971 to 1992. *Sociological Spectrum, 19*, 421–442.

Burke, P. J. (1980). The self: Measurement implications from a symbolic interactionist Perspective. *Social Psychology Quarterly, 43*, 18–29.

Burke, P. J. & D. C. Reitzes. (1981). The link between identity and role performance. *Social Psychology Quarterly, 44*, 83–92.

Callero, P.L. The political self: Identity resources for radical democracy. (this volume).

Coverdill, J. E. (1997). White ethnic identification and racial attitudes. In S. A. Tuch & J. K. Martin (Eds.), *Racial attitudes in the 1990s: Continuity and change* (pp. 144–174). Westport, CT: Praeger.

Crittenden, K. S. (1983). Sociological aspects of attribution. *Annual Review of Sociology, 9*, 425–446.

Davis, N. J. & R. V. Robinson. (1996). Are the rumors of war exaggerated?: Religious orthodoxy and moral progressivism in America. *American Journal of Sociology, 102*, 756–787.

Della Fave, L. R. (1980). The meek shall not inherit the earth: Self-evaluation and the legitimacy of stratification. *American Sociological Review, 45*, 955–971.

_____. (1986). Toward an explication of the legitimation process. *Social Forces* 65, 476–500.

Ellison, C.G. & D. E. Sherkat. (1995). The "semi-involuntary institution" revisited: Regional variations in church participation among black Americans. *Social Forces, 73*, 1415–37.

Gecas, V. & P. J. Burke. (1995). Self and identity. In K. S. Cook, G. A. Fine, & J. S. House (Eds.), *Sociological perspectives on social psychology* (pp. 41–67). Boston: Allyn and Bacon.

Gouldner, A. (1970). *The coming crisis in western sociology*. New York: Basic Books.

Gurin, P., A. H. Miller, & G. Gurin. (1980). Stratum identification and consciousness. *Social Psychology Quarterly, 43*, 30–47.

Harris, D. (1995). Exploring the determinants of adult black identity: Context and process. *Social Forces, 74*, 227–241.

Heaven, P. C.L. (1989). Economic locus of control beliefs and lay attributions of poverty. *Australian Journal of Psychology, 41*, 315–325.

Hollander, J. A. & J. A. Howard. (2000). Social psychological theories on social inequalities. *Social Psychology Quarterly, 63*, 338–351.

House, J. S. (1977). The three faces of social psychology. *Sociometry, 40*, 161–77.

_____. (1981). Social structure and personality. In M. Rosenberg & R. H. Turner (Eds.), *Social psychology: Sociological perspectives* (pp. 525–561) New York: Basic Books.

Howard, J. (2000). Social psychology of identities. *Annual Review of Sociology, 26*, 367–393.

Hughes, M. & D. H. Demo. (1989). Self-perceptions of black Americans: Self-esteem and personal efficacy. *American Journal of Sociology, 95*,132–59.

Hunt, M. O. (1996). The individual, society, or both?: A comparison of black, Latino, and white beliefs about the causes of poverty. *Social Forces, 75*, 293–322.

_____. (2001). Self-evaluation and stratification beliefs. In T.J. Owens, S. Stryker, & N. Goodman (Eds.). *Extending self-esteem theory and research: Social and psychological currents* (pp. 330–350). Cambridge, UK: Cambridge University Press.

Hunt, M. O., P. B. Jackson, B. Powell, & L. C. Steelman. (2000). Color-blind: The treatment of race and ethnicity in social psychology. *Social Psychology Quarterly, 63*, 352–364.

Hunt, M. O. and L. L. Hunt. (2000). Regional religions?: Extending the "semi-involuntary" thesis of African-American religious participation. *Sociological Forum, 15*, 569–594.

Hunt, L. L. & M. O. Hunt. (1999). Regional patterns of African American church attendance: Revisiting the semi-involuntary thesis. *Social Forces, 78*, 779–791.

_____. (2001). Race, region, and religious involvement: A comparative study of whites and African Americans. *Social Forces, 80*, 605–631.

Hunter, J. D. (1990). *Culture wars: The struggle to define America*. New York: Basic Books.

Jackman, M. & R. Jackman. (1983). *Class awareness in the United States*. Berkeley: University of California Press.

James, W. (1950). *The principles of psychology*. New York: Dover. (Original work published 1890)

Kluegel, J. R.&d E. Smith. (1986). *Beliefs about inequality*. New York: Aldine de Gruyter.

Lane, R. E. (1959). The fear of equality. *American Journal of Political Science, 53*: 35–51.

Lewis, M. (1978). *The culture of inequality*. New York: Meridian.

Linville, P. (1987). Self-complexity as a cognitive buffer against stress-related illness and depression. *Journal of Personality and Social Psychology, 52,* 663–676.

McCall, G. J. & J. L. Simmons. (1966). *Identities and interactions.* New York: Free Press.

Mead, G. H. (1934). *Mind, Self, and Society.* Chicago: University of Chicago Press.

Nagel, J. (1995). American Indian ethnic renewal: Politics and the resurgence of identity.*American Sociological Review, 60,* 947–965.

National Opinion Research Center. (2002). *General Social Survey.* Retrieved September 15, 2002, from http://www.norc.uchicago.edu/projects/gensoc1.asp

Owens, T. J., S. Stryker, & N. Goodman. (2001). *Extending self-esteem theory and research: Social and psychological currents.* Cambridge, UK: Cambridge University Press.

Porter, J. R. & R. E. Washington. (1979). Black identity and self-esteem: A review of studies of black self-concept, 1968–1978. *Annual Review of Sociology, 5,* 53–74.

Robinson, R. V. & W. Bell. (1978). Equality, success, and social justice in England and the United States. *American Sociological Review, 43,* 125–43.

Rosenberg, M. (1979). *Conceiving the Self.* New York: Basic Books.

_____. 1981. The self-concept: Social product and social force." In M. Rosenberg & R. H. Turner (Eds.), *Social psychology: Sociological perspectives* (pp. 593–624). New York: Basic Books.

Rosenberg, M. & L. I. Pearlin. (1978). Social class and self-esteem among children and adults. *American Journal of Sociology, 84,* 53–77.

Rotter, J. (1966). Generalized expectancies for internal vs. external control of reinforcement. *Psychological Monographs, 80:* 1.

Schuman, H., C. Steeh, L. Bobo, & M. Krysan. (1997). *Racial attitudes in America: Trends and interpretations* (revised edition). Cambridge, MA: Harvard.

Serpe, R. T. & S. Stryker. (1987). The construction and reconstruction of social relationships. In E. Lawler and B. Markovsky (Eds.), *Advances in Group Processes* (pp. 41–66). Greenwich, CT: JAI.

Shepelak, N. (1987). The role of self-explanations and self-evaluations in legitimating inequality. *American Journal of Sociology, 52,* 495–503.

Stets, J. & P. Burke. (2000). Identity theory and social identity theory. *Social Psychology Quarterly, 63,* 224–237.

Stolte, J. F. (1983). The legitimation of structural inequality: Reformulation and test of the self-evaluation argument. *American Sociological Review, 48,* 331–342.

Stryker, S. (1968). Identity salience and role performance. *Journal of Marriage and the Family, 4,* 558–64.

_____. (1977). Developments in "two social psychologies": Toward an appreciation of mutual relevance. *Sociometry, 40,* 145–160.

_____. (1980). *Symbolic interactionism: A social structural version.* Menlo Park, CA: Benjamin/Cummings.

_____. (1987). Identity theory: Developments and extensions. In K. Yardley & T. Honess (Eds.), *Self and identity* (pp. 89–104). New York: Wiley.

Stryker, S. & P. Burke. (2000). The past, present, and future of an identity theory. *Social Psychology Quarterly, 63,* 284–297.

Stryker, S. & R. T. Serpe. (1982). Commitment, identity salience, and role behavior: A theory and research example. In W. Ickes & E. S. Knowles (Eds.), *Personality, Roles, and Social Behavior* (pp. 199–218). New York: Springer-Verlag.

Stryker, S., R. T. Serpe, & M. O. Hunt. (2001). Social structure and commitment: A study of blacks, Latinos and whites (unpublished manuscript).

Tajfel, H. (1982). *Social identity and intergroup relations.* Cambridge, UK: Cambridge University Press.

Thoits, P. A. (1983). Multiple identities and psychological well-being: A reformulation and test of the social isolation hypothesis. *American Sociological Review, 48,* 174–87.

_____. (1986). Multiple identities: Examining gender and marital status differences in distress. *American Sociological Review, 51,* 259–72.

_____. (1992). Identity structures and psychological well-being: Gender and marital status comparisons. *Social Psychology Quarterly, 55,* 236–56.

Tuch, S. A. & J. K. Martin. (1997). Regional differences in whites' racial policy attitudes. In S.A. Tuch and J.K. Martin (Eds.) *Racial attitudes in the 1990s: Continuity and change* (Pp. 165–176). Westport, CT: Praeger.

University of Michigan. (1972). *National Election Study.* Retrieved February 15, 2001 from http://www.umich.edu/~nes/

Vanneman, R. & L. Cannon. (1987). *The American perception of class.* Temple University Press.

Waters, M. C. (1990). *Ethnic options: Choosing identities in America.* Berkeley: University of California Press.

Chapter **6**

The Role of Self-Esteem in Family Identity Salience and Commitment among Blacks, Latinos, and Whites

TIMOTHY J. OWENS AND RICHARD T. SERPE

Despite well established, ongoing, and vigorous research programs in sociological investigations of self-esteem and identity, and the two areas natural kinship and common roots, the self-esteem and identity nexus has nevertheless failed to receive adequate theoretical and empirical attention (see Cast & Burke, 2002; Ervin & Stryker, 2001; Thoits & Hewitt, 2001; Owens & Aronson, 1999 for recent exceptions). In addition, whether considered individually or collectively, both areas have much work to do with respect to understanding the role of race and ethnicity as a cause and correlate of self-esteem and identity (see Hunt, Jackson, Powell, Steelman 2000).

Our study seeks to redress these gaps through a three-part investigation. First, we address the theoretical implications of a conscious effort to bring identity and self-esteem research into closer alignment. Second, we test our theoretical assumptions with data from a large random sample of Southern California adults. Third, because of the importance of race and ethnicity in identity and self-concept processes, we make specific model comparisons between Blacks, Latinos, and non-Hispanic Whites. We also focus our attention on the family because of its importance as a key societal institution.

Self-esteem and identity are aspects of the broader concept of the self. Here we define self as an organized and interactive system of thoughts, feelings, identities, and motives that: (1) stems from self-reflexivity and language, (2) people attribute to themselves, and (3) characterize specific human beings (Owens, 2003, p. 206). Self-esteem may be defined as a "positive or negative attitude toward a particular object, namely, the self" (Rosenberg, 1965, p. 30). When self-esteem is high, one has self-respect and a feeling of worthiness, while still acknowledging personal faults and shortcomings. High self-esteem must therefore not be equated with arrogance or conceit. Indeed, high self-esteem people not only tend to acknowledge their inadequacies, but unlike low self-esteem people, believe they can improve (see Rosenberg & Owens, 2001). When self-esteem is low, however, people lack respect for themselves and see only their weaknesses thus coming to view themselves as "unworthy, inadequate or otherwise seriously deficient" human beings (Rosenberg, 1979, p. 54).

Identity can be broadly defined as internalized social and demographic characteristics attached to people which helps specify who they are by locating them relative to other people. According to Stryker (1980, p. 60) "identities are 'parts' of self [constituting] internalized positional designations . . . [that] exist insofar as the person is a participant in structured role relations." In this sense one's identity is tied to specific social networks such as family or broader social groupings such as ethnicity or gender. In addition, identities carry shared expectations with respect to present and future interaction with role-related others. In this chapter we adhere to Stryker's view of identity.

LINKING SELF-ESTEEM AND IDENTITY

Although a link between self-esteem and identity is often presumed (see Gecas and Burke, 1995), if for no other reason than both are aspects of the self and trace their lineage to James (1890) and the early symbolic interactionists, surprisingly few studies have endeavored to grapple with the intersection of these two distinct though related concepts. Ervin and Stryker (2001, pp. 31–33) have recently outlined a three-point argument for the reasonableness of linking self-esteem and identity. First, it makes intuitive sense. Since contemporary social psychological research attests to the mutual impact of cognition on emotion (Scheff, 1985; Lazarus, 1984; Zajonc, 1984) these two essential aspects of the self—one fundamentally cognitive (identity) the other fundamentally, though not exclusively, affective (self-esteem)—must also mutually influence each other. Second, on metatheoretical grounds, self-esteem and identity should be interrelated. The fact that the self is an organized, interactive, and differentiated system of thoughts, feelings, identities, and motives is beyond dispute. Therefore, if the self is a system of differentiated though interrelated components, self-esteem and identity must be related to each another. Finally, the most convincing reason for linking the two concepts is to advance social psychological theory in general and research and theory in both self-esteem and identity more specifically. These linkages, while suggested in the literature, are too often neglected, in part because theory has lagged behind intention. Another reason is that while identity theorists and self-esteem theorists are often sympathetic to each others' research programs, and sometimes draw from a common literature, they have nevertheless developed more parallel to each other than interactively. Our study attempts to reduce this gap.[1]

Self-Esteem Theory: A Brief Overview

According to Rosenberg (1979, pp. 62–77), four broad principles form the basis of support for "most of the theoretical reasoning employed in the literature to understand the bearing of interpersonal and social structural processes on the self-concept" (p. 62). They include reflected appraisals, social comparisons, self-attributions, and psychological centrality. The four principles can be directly translated into a theory of self-esteem since self-esteem is the evaluative component of the self-concept. The principle of *reflected appraisals* is central to the symbolic interactionist's insistence that the self is a social product derived from the attitudes that others have toward one's self and that one eventually comes to see him- or herself

---

[1]Cast and Burke (2002) have recently attempted to outline a theory of self-esteem based upon Burke's identity control theory, Swann's (1983) notion of self-verification, and a view of self-esteem as "analogous to a reservoir of energy" (Cast & Burke, 2002, p. 1049).

as others do, à la Meadian self theory (1934) and Cooley's looking-glass self (1902). Through *social comparisons*, people judge and evaluate themselves in comparison to particular individuals, groups, or social categories. Social comparisons are further established through criteria and normative bases of comparison. Criteria bases operate when individuals compare themselves to others in terms of being better versus worse or superior versus inferior on some criteria (e.g., saxophonist, poker player, parent). Normative bases operate along dimensions of deviance or conformity (e.g., an adulterous husband, an honest CEO). *Self-attribution* holds that individuals draw conclusions about themselves by observing their own actions and their outcomes (e.g., intelligent, homely, funny). Finally, the principle of *psychological centrality* holds that the self is an interrelated system of hierarchically organized components, with some attributes and identities more important to the self than others. Psychological centrality serves to protect a person's self-concept and thus self-esteem by pushing potentially damaging self-attributes and identities to the periphery of the self system, while keeping enhancing attributes closer to the center.

Identity Theory: An Overview

Stryker's identity theory (Stryker, 1968, 1980; Stryker & Serpe, 1982; 1983; 1994; Stryker & Statham, 1985; Serpe, 1987) shares symbolic interactionism's axiom that people can and do make choices, even though constrained by the situation (i.e., social structure and social interaction). More specifically, his identity theory focuses on the reciprocal relationship between the individual and the larger social structure in which he or she is imbedded as well as the interactions between sets of individuals and society. Stryker's identity theory also sees the self as consisting of a hierarchical ordering of identities, with each identity differentiated according to its salience and one's commitment to his or her role relations. Thus, one is committed not to an identity but to relationships with respect to which the identity is pertinent.

Identity salience is defined as the probability that a particular identity will be invoked by self or others within or across social situations (Stryker 1980). However, while an identity can be invoked willfully by the person possessing it—the aspect we focus on in our study—it can also be invoked without the person's permission. *Identity salience hierarchy* refers to the ordering of identities into a hierarchy such that the higher the positioning of a particular identity, the greater the probability of its activation. (See Stryker and Serpe [1994] for a comparison of identity salience and psychological centrality.) *Identity commitment*, on the other hand, focuses on a person's position in a network of social relations and is marked by two general dimensions: interactional commitment and affective commitment (Stryker & Serpe, 1994; Serpe, 1987; 1991). *Interactional commitment* is the extensiveness of interactions in a social network to which one belongs by virtue of having an identity. Extensiveness in turn is operationalized as the number of persons one interacts with and the amount of time, energy, and resources one expends in a given social network by way of a particular identity. *Affective commitment* is the emotional significance that others in a given social network have for a person via his or her particular identity.

While interactional and affective commitments are related, Stryker and Serpe argue they are nevertheless theoretically and empirically independent (Stryker, 1987; 1989; Stryker and Serpe 1987; 1994; Serpe 1987; 1991). Identity salience with respect to commitment begins with a self composed, in part, of a number of identities, with each corresponding to a role the individual plays. Here identities differ in their salience within the self-system, such that identity salience is dependent on how much commitment one has to a particular identity and how positive one's evaluation of the identity is. *Commitment thus precedes salience.* In a series of papers using a three-wave longitudinal study Stryker and Serpe have found strong evidence that prior commitment has a greater impact on identity salience than the impact of identity salience on commitment (Stryker and Serpe 1987, 1993; Serpe 1987).

DATA AND METHODS

Sample

Our data were collected from telephone interviews conducted between January and March of 1993 of noninstitutionalized adults residing in five southern California counties (Los Angeles, Orange, Riverside, San Bernardino, and San Diego). The Social Science Research Center at California State University Fullerton collected the data under the second author's direction. Random digit dialing and computer assisted telephone interviewing (CATI) was used to obtain an overall sample N of 2,854 people. The study's race and ethnic breakdown is $n = 1,245$ for non-Hispanic Whites, $n = 737$ for Latinos, $n = 646$ for Blacks, $n = 148$ for Asians, and $n = 62$ for respondents who are either in other categories or refused to answer the race self-identification question. In order to maximize participation among the heavily Latino population of Southern California, the survey was conducted in English or Spanish depending upon the respondent's language preference. In all, 433 Latino respondents (58.8%) completed the survey in Spanish.

The overall response rate was 70.1% and was calculated according to the guidelines of the American Association for Public Opinion Research (2000). The response rate represents the ratio of completed interviews to the total of all completed interviews, never completed call-backs, refusals, working numbers at which an answering machined was reached, and working numbers that were never answered. Blacks were purposefully oversampled through telephone exchanges in 1990 census tracts where the Black population was greater than 30%. In the analyses presented here, the Asian category is excluded due to the large degree of cultural heterogeneity among this demographic group. Persons categorized as "other" were also excluded. The final effective sample is 2,631 or, 47.3% White, 28% Latino, and 24.6% Black (numbers do not sum to 100 due to rounding). (See Appendices 1a–1c for correlations, means, and standard deviations for all variables in the analyses.)

Variables and Constructs

Self-Esteem is composed of four items from the Rosenberg Self-Esteem Scale (1965). (1) On the whole, I am satisfied with myself. (2) I certainly feel useless at times. (3) I feel that I have a number of good qualities. (4) I wish I could have more respect for myself. Responses were coded from 1 = strongly agree to 4 = strongly disagree. The negatively worded items (2 and 4) were reverse coded so a high score equates with high self-esteem. Cronbach's alpha was (.63). Between group structural invariance of the self-esteem construct was tested through confirmatory factor analysis using AMOS 4.01. All group pairings were structurally invariant except between Whites and Latinos, however only slightly so ($p < .1$). Given the stringency of this test, the relatively large n's involved (particularly for Whites, and the p-level found, we believe sufficient structural invariance exists between the White and Latino measurement models to make later comparisons in the structural equation models reasonable.

Family Commitment and Identity Constructs

In each of the following commitment and identity domains, respondents were instructed to think of the family thusly: "By family, we would like you to include your parents, brothers and sisters, aunts and uncles, and cousins. In other words, the people you grew up with. Please do not focus only on your spouse/partner and/or children." In order to avoid response set bias, the specific questions within each domain were asked in random order. *Family interactive commitment* is composed of three items. (1) How often do you do things with your family? Responses were coded from 1 = never to 7 = daily. (2) In an average week, how many hours do you spend with your family doing things together, including eating, having a conversation, talking on the telephone, watching TV, etc.? (3) Of the money you do not need for rent, food, clothing and other essentials how much do you spend on family activities? Things like going to the movies and gifts. Responses were coded from 1 = almost none to 5 = almost all. Cronbach's alpha was somewhat below the desired threshold of acceptability (.54). However, structural invariance was found to exist across all three ethnic groups. *Family affective commitment* is composed of four items. (1) How much would you miss your family members if you were not able to spend time or communicate with them? Responses were coded from 1 = not at all to 4 = a great deal. (2) How close (in personal and emotional terms) to the members of your family are you? Responses were coded from 1 = not at all close to 4 = very close. (3) How important are your family members to you? Responses were coded from 1 = not at all important to 4 = very important. (4) After I do things with members of my family I often feel unhappy. Responses were coded from 1 = strongly agree to 4 = strongly disagree. The negatively worded item (4) was reverse coded so a high score equates with high family affective commitment. Cronbach's alpha was (.66). Structural invariance was found to exist across all three ethnic groups. Finally, *Family identity salience* is composed of three items all with responses coded from 1 = almost certainly would not to almost certainly would. (1) Think about meeting a co-worker for the first time. How certain is it that you would tell this person about your family? (2) Think about meeting a person of the opposite sex for the first time. How certain is it that you would tell this person about your family? (3) Think about meeting a friend of a family member for the first time. How certain is it that you would tell this person about your family? Cronbach's alpha was (.66). Structural invariance was found to exist across all three ethnic groups.

Control Variables

Five control or exogenous variables are employed. *Age* is measured in years since last birthday. *Income* is the respondent's estimated annual household income. Responses were coded from 1 = less than $14,999 to 8 = above $100,000. *Gender* is coded as 0 = male and 1 = female. *Education* is measured by years of schooling completed. *Living with any relative* is a dichotomous variable indicating whether or not the respondent was currently living with a relative(s) by blood or marriage. We refer to this variable as "anyrel" hereafter. *Race/ethnicity* is measured through self-identification by the respondent. Our basic theoretical model was estimated separately for the three race and ethnic groups under consideration.

ANALYTIC STRATEGY

Our basic theoretical model is shown in Figure 1. For the sake of simplicity, the figure does not include the covariances that exist among the five exogenous variables or the indicators of the latent constructs, all of which were discussed above and all of which were specified in the actual AMOS modeling. Since our general theoretical model is being applied to three distinct groups (Whites, Blacks, and Latinos) we elected not to estimate correlated errors among the various indicators. Our reasoning is three-fold. First, there is no compelling reason for doing so. While preliminary data analysis indicated that estimating some correlated errors improved the model fit marginally for one group or another, the practical effect of making such estimates did not materially change the parameter estimates among our constructs. Second, we want to keep our model as general as possible, particularly in the face of the divergent groups. Estimating different correlated errors for different groups would defeat the requirement of model equivalence among the race/ethnic groups and prevent us from making direct comparisons between them. Last, without cross-lagged variables, there is no persuasive statistical rationale for doing so.

The controls for self-esteem include income, education, and gender. Income and education are aspects of socioeconomic status and the latter is known to influence self-esteem, particularly among adults (Rosenberg & Pearlin, 1978). Gender differences in self-esteem are also known to exist (Owens and King, 2001). (Unfortunately we were unable to estimate separate gender-specific models for the Latino and Black samples thus necessitating gender be entered only as a control.)

The controls for family interactive commitment are age, "live with any relative," and self-esteem. We reason that younger adults are more likely to live with children or with parents or other family members more than older adults are, thus potentially increasing the younger peoples' interactive commitment in this facet of identity. In addition, living with at least one family member would surely increase regular contact and thereby increase the probability of interactive commitment to the family. Since global self-esteem is relatively stable over time (Owens, Mortimer, & Finch, 1996) and tends to transcend general life domains (Rosenberg & Owens, 2001), we placed it prior to all three facets of identity.

Family affective commitment is controlled by gender, anyrel, and self-esteem. The reasons for including anyrel and self-esteem are the same as those discussed for family interactive commitment. We propose gender as a control for family affective commitment because of the extra emotional demands families often place on women (e.g., Hays, 1996) and because of the general social pressures women often feel to be affectively attached to their families (e.g., Millman, 1991; Hochschild, 1983). Family identity salience—our variable of central concern—is controlled by self-esteem and by both forms of family commitment for reasons noted above and in the identity theory section discussed earlier.

Finally, since family interactive commitment and family affective commitment are subdimensions of an overall family commitment orientation, we assume they are both conceptually and statistically related to each other. Indeed, the combined group simple correlation between family interactive commitment and family affective commitment is .31 ($p < .01$). With this in mind, and because their reciprocality may have theoretical and statistical importance, we initially intended to estimate the mutual influence each had on the other. Unfortunately, a reciprocal effects analysis proved impossible in this context for all but the White subsample. As a reasonable compromise solution, we allowed the latent commitment variables' error terms (zetas) to correlate. This last specification is particularly important on statistical grounds because without doing so, our parameter estimates for the effects of family interactive commitment and family affective commitment on family identity salience would almost surely be biased.

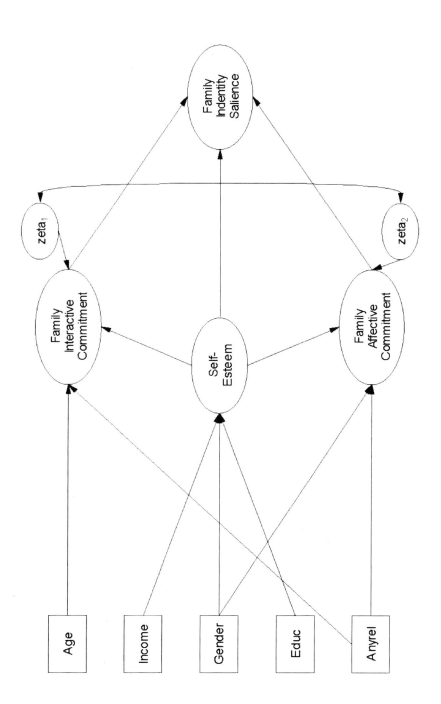

Figure 1. Theoretical Model: Family Identity Salience as a Function of Self-Esteem, Family Interactive Commitment, and Family Affective Commitment.

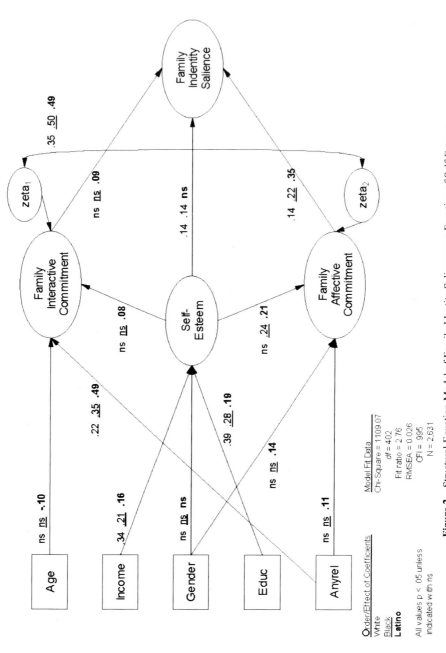

Figure 2. Structural Equation Model of Family Identity Salience as a Function of Self-Esteem, Family Interactive Commitment, and Family Affective Commitment (Standardized Coefficients).

RESULTS

Model Fit

Our three-group model fits the data well (see Figure 2). The fit ratio is 2.76 (χ^2 = 1109.07, df = 402), the RMSEA is 0.026, and the CFI is .99. The RMSEA (root mean square error of approximation) assesses how well a model with unknown though optimally chosen parameter estimates would fit the population covariance matrix (Browne & Cudeck, 1993). Values below .08 but especially below .06 indicate a well-fitting model (Hu & Bentler, 1999; Browne & Cudeck, 1993). The CFI (comparative fit index) ranges from 0 (no fit) to 1.00 (excellent fit) and compares a hypothesized model with an independence model. All three model fit statistics fall well within acceptable ranges for a good fit between our hypothesized model and the observed data (Hu & Bentler, 1999). (See Appendix 2.)

Structural Equation Model Findings

We start with the middle (endogenous) variables in Figure 2 and discuss self-esteem, family identity commitment, and family affective commitment in that order. Income and education, our measures for SES, positively impacted self-esteem across all three racial/ethnic groups, as predicted. Income and education had their strongest impacts on self-esteem first among Whites (β = .34 and β = .39, respectively), next among Blacks (β = .21 and β = .28, respectively), and then among Latinos (β = .16 and β = .19, respectively). The consistency of these results leave little doubt that social structural variables indicative of success and achievement in the U.S. influenced these adults' self-esteems, a finding consistent with prior research (Rosenberg & Pearlin, 1978). Our findings are also consistent with the relative levels of attainment in income and education among the three race/ethnic groups. The mean sample income for Whites was $43,852, for Blacks it was $36,218, and for Latinos it was $26,281. On the other hand, gender had no impact on self-esteem among any of the race/ethnic groups under examination, contrary to prediction.

  With respect to family interactive commitment (hereafter FIC), we find that age only had an impact on FIC among Latinos (β = -.10). Thus, the younger the Latino the higher his or her FIC. However, this finding comports with the general structure of Latino families in both the U.S. population and our sample. According to the 1990 U.S. Census (the census closest to our data-gathering period), the Latino population of the U. S. was considerably younger than either the White or the Black populations. The median age of Latinos living in the western part of the U.S. (our general sampling area) was 24.5 while it was 28.1 for Blacks and 33.6 for Whites (Rogers, 1999, p. 46). Our sample data parallel the census data. In our sample, the median and mean age among Latinos was 30 and 31.7, respectively; among Blacks 39 and 40.7, respectively; and among Whites 39 and 42.5, respectively.[2] Whether or not a respondent was living with a family member at the time of the interview (anyrel) had an across the boards impact on FIC, as predicted. Anyrel's impact was modest among Whites (β = .22), moderate among Blacks (β = .35), and moderately high among Latinos (β = .49). Consequently, for all groups, but especially Latinos and Blacks, living with a relative increased overall FIC. Like age, living with a relative partly reflects differences in family structure among the three groups under consideration. According to 1990 census data, the average number of family members residing together

---

[2]Note that our sample only includes adults 18 years of age or over while the census data includes all ages.

in the western part of the U.S. was 3.08 for Whites, 3.34 for Blacks, and 4.09 for Latinos (Rogers, 1999, p. 50). In addition, the dependency ratio[3] among urbanites in the West was 66.6 for Latinos, 60.7 for Blacks, and 57.3 for Whites (Rogers, 1999, p. 45). This indicates that the proportion of elderly and dependent children in the Latino and Black populations is greater than in the White population, with Latinos having a substantially higher proportion. The implication is that as a population's dependency ratio increases, contact—and thus interaction with dependent family members—should increase as well.

Concerning family affective commitment (hereafter FAC), we find that gender had a small though significant impact only among Latinas ($\beta = .14$). This finding is somewhat surprising given the general presumption that American women tend to exhibit fairly high emotional expressiveness and feelings of intimacy in their families (see Thompson & Walker, 1989). In addition, only Latinos living with a relative had a small though significant increase in their affective commitment to their families ($\beta = .11$). The interesting implication is that even though anyrel had a salutary effect on all three groups' interactive commitments, actually living with a relative only influenced the affective dimension of commitment among Latinos, and it was positive.

Looking just at self-esteem's effect on FIC and FAC, we note the differential influence that self-esteem had on both commitment variables across all three racial/ethnic groups. First, among Whites, self-esteem had no impact on either form of commitment. For Blacks, however, self-esteem was unrelated to FIC but modestly associated with FAC ($\beta = .24$). It appears, therefore, that as self-esteem increased among Blacks, only affective commitment increased, not interactive commitment. However, among Latinos, self-esteem positively impacted both FIC ($\beta = .08$) and FAC ($\beta = .21$), with self-esteem's impact on FAC being over twice as strong as on FIC. Finally, the correlated error terms (zetas) between FIC and FAC are noteworthy. Although they are fairly substantial across all three groups, they are higher among Blacks ($\beta = .50$) and Latinos ($\beta = .49$) than among Whites ($\beta = .35$).

We turn now to the family identity salience construct (hereafter FIS). Beginning with the commitment constructs, we note first that FIC had no impact on Black or White FIS but a small though significant one among Latinos ($\beta = .09$). This is interesting because even though the correlated error between FIC and FIS was smallest among Latinos, it nevertheless persisted after all three significant indirect effects on the FIC-to- FIS path (age, anyrel, and self-esteem) were taken into consideration. In short, interactive commitment truly plays a role in identity salience net other effects in the important domain of the family. Unlike the other aspect of commitment, FAC had a significant impact on FIS across all three groups but more so again among Latinos. The strength of the relationship between FAC and FIS was $\beta = .14$ for Whites, $\beta = .22$ for Blacks, and $\beta = .35$ for Latinos. Affective commitment, a later entrant into Stryker's original identity theory (1968), clearly has an important role to play in identity salience, particularly in the context of the family.

CONCLUSION

Drawing on a survey of Southern Californians that included a large representation of racial/ethnic minorities, we examined the role that self-esteem plays in identity commitment and salience among a broad cross-section of Black, Latino, and White adults. This is

---

[3]The dependency ratio is the number of children under 18 plus the number of elderly persons under age 65 and older per 100 persons of working age (18 to 64).

important because while there has been some though not much research comparing Black and White self-esteem (e.g., Owens & King, 2001; Hughes & Demo, 1989; Rosenberg & Simmons, 1972) there has been almost no research comparing Black and White self-esteem to that of Latinos. Moreover, Latinos as a group tend to be underrepresented in social science research. In addition, we concentrated our efforts on the context of the family because of its significance as a key societal institution. Overall, our results support the assertion that self-esteem and identity have both a natural kinship and an important empirical role to play in bringing the self-esteem and identity literatures into closer alignment, as others have also recently noted (Cast & Burke, 2002; Irvin & Stryker, 2001; Owens & Aronson, 2001).

A number of our predictions were confirmed, one was not, and others had mixed results across the three groups under consideration. First, as predicted we found that income and education both had salutary effects on self-esteem across all three racial/ethnic groups. However, their biggest impact was on White self-esteem, followed by that of Blacks and then Latinos. This finding is interesting for at least two reasons. One, as we showed, our findings follow the general income and education patterns of all three groups, thus illustrating the relative impact of stratification variables on the selves of the three racial/ethnic groups under consideration. Two, just as Rosenberg and Pearlin (1978) found, SES appears to be most influential on the self-esteems of adults. However, the relative impact may be moderated by a groups' actual level of attainment, which is in keeping with the principle of psychological centrality. Indeed, according to the 1990 U.S. Census, 79.9% of Whites 25 years of age and over were high school graduates compared to 66.7 of Blacks and 51.3% of Hispanics (U.S. Bureau of the Census, 1992, p. 144). Contrary to prediction, however, gender had no effect on self-esteem among any of our groups.

Second, as predicted for all the groups, but especially Latinos and Blacks, living with a relative increased the respondents' overall interactive commitment to their families. The impact of living with a relative was strongest among Latinos followed by Blacks and Whites. We offer two possible explanations. One, Latino families tend to stress the importance of family as an integral part of their everyday lives (Julian, McKenry, & McKelvey, 1994; Wilkinson, 1987). Two, the general parenting styles of Blacks tends to emphasize discipline along with high levels of support and open communication (Bartz & Levine, 1978). Together, they may lead to increased familial interaction and commitment. Somewhat contrary to prediction, however, we observed that age was only significant in family interactive commitment among Latinos, where younger Latinos had higher family interactive commitment. This finding accords partly with Julian, McKenry, and McKelvey (1994) in that the relative youthfulness of the Latino sample would place many of our respondents in the parent role, thus increasing interaction. Moreover, the large kinship networks that mark many Latino families should also play an important role in increased family interactive commitment (Horowitz, 1997).

Third, our findings with respect to family affective commitment are somewhat mixed. Its two control variables—gender and anyrel—were only significant among Latinos, with gender being in the direction of Latinas. Although the strength of the effect was not strong it was nevertheless significant. These two finding are not particularly surprising within the Latino family context. However, the reason for the lack of a relationship between anyrel and particularly gender among Blacks and Whites, is unclear and contrary to prediction.

Fourth, the effect of self-esteem on family interactive commitment and family affective commitment is also mixed. Only Latino self-esteem had a small but positive effect on family interactive commitment. Perhaps more interesting, self-esteem had a modestly positive effect on Black and Latino family affective commitment, but no effect on that of Whites. The positive findings are consistent with our prediction and the fact that self-esteem—like family affective commitment —largely tap an affective dimension of self and commitment. However, why it does not predict family affective commitment among Whites requires further research.

Finally, with respect to family identity salience, we note that while family interactive commitment had a small though significant impact on Latino family identity salience, it had no effect on that of Blacks or Whites. Interactive commitment truly plays a role in identity salience net other effects in the important domain of the family, but only among Latinos. However, family affective commitment had an across the boards significant impact on family identity salience, but again more so among Latinos. Although family is important to all three groups, this finding provides additional evidence that family is preeminently important to Latinos. This later entrant to identity theory is clearly the most important, at least in the family context. We conclude by noting that self-esteem's impact on family identity salience was only significant among Blacks and Whites. This is somewhat surprising given self-esteem's consistent role in Latino family interactive commitment and family affective commitment. However, a plausible explanation could be that self-esteem has its major influence in family identity salience indirectly through a consistent impact on family interactive commitment and family affective commitment. Among Blacks, self-esteem has a direct effect on family identity salience but only an indirect effect through family affective commitment. For whites, the two dimensions of interactive commitment we examined appear to play no appreciable role in the formation of family identity salience.

REFERENCES

American Association for Public Opinion Research. (2000). "Standard Definitions Final Dispositions of Case Codes and Outcome Rates for Surveys: RDD Telephone Surveys, In-Person Hosusehold Surveys, and Mail Surveys of Specifically Named Persons." Ann Arbor, MI: APPOR.

Bartz, K. W., & Levine, E. S. (1978). Childrearing by Black parents: A description and comparison to Anglo and Chicano parents. *Journal of Marriage and the Family, 40*, 709–719.

Browne, M. W. & Cudeck, R. (1993). Alternative ways of assessing model fit. In: K. A. Bollen & J. S. Long (Eds.), *Testing structural equation models* (pp. 136–162). Newbury Park, CA: Sage.

Burke, P. J. (1991). Identity processes and social stress. *American Sociological Review, 56*, 836–849.

Cast, A. D. & Burke, P. J. A theory of self-esteem. *Social Forces, 80*, 1041–1068.

Coltrane, S. (1996). *Family man: Fatherhood, housework, and gender equity.* New York: Oxford University Press.

Ervin, L. & Stryker, S. (2000). Theorizing the relationship between self-esteem and identity. In: T. J. Owens, S. Stryker & N. Goodman (Eds.), *Extending self-esteem theory and research: Sociological and psychological currents* (pp. 29–55). New York: Cambridge University Press.

Gecas, V. & Burke, P. J. (1995). Self and identity. In: K. S. Cook, G. A. Fine & J. S. House (Eds.), *Sociological perspectives on social psychology* (pp. 41–67). Boston: Allyn and Bacon.

Hays, S. (1996). *The cultural contradictions of motherhood.* New Haven: Yale University Press.

Hochschild, A. R. (1983). *The managed heart: Commercialization of human feeling.* Los Angeles: University of California Press.

Horowitz, R. (1997). The expanded family and family honor. In M. Hutter (Ed.), *The family experience: A reader in cultural diversity* (pp. 156–187). Boston: Allyn & Bacon.

Hughes, M., & Demo, D. H. (1989). Self-perceptions of black Americans: Self-esteem and personal efficacy. *American Journal of Sociology, 95*, 132–159.

Hu, L. T. & Bentler, P. M. (1999). Cutoff criteria for fit indexes in covariance structure analysis: Conventional criteria versus new alternatives. *Structural Equation Modeling: A Multidusciplinary Journal, 6*, 1–55.

Hunt, M. O., Jackson, P. B., Powell, B. & Steelman, L. C. (2000). Color-blind: The treatment of race and ethnicity in social psychology. *Social Psychology Quarterly, 63*, 352–364.

James, W. (1890). *The principles of psychology.* New York: Henry Holt.

Julian, T. W., McKenry, P. C. & McKelvey, M. W. (1994). Cultural variations in parenting: perceptions of Caucasian, African-American, Hispanic, and Asian-American parents. *Family Relations, 43*, 30–37.

Lazarus, R. S. (1984). On the primacy of cognition. *American Psychologist, 39*, 124–129.

Mead, G. H. (1934). *Mind, self & society from the standpoint of a social behaviorist.* Chicago: University of Chicago Press.

Millman, M. (1991). *Warm hearts and cold cash: The intimate dynamics of families and money.* New York: Free Press.

Owens, T. J. (2003). Theory and research in self and identity. In: J. D. DeLamater (Ed.), *Handbook of social psychology.* New York: Kluwer/Plenum.

Owens, T. J. & Aronson, P. J. (2000). Self-concept as a force in social movement involvement. In: S. Stryker, T. J. Owens & R. W. White (Eds.), *Self, identity and social movements* (pp. 132–151). Minneapolis: University of Minnesota Press.

Owens, T. J. & King, A. B. (2001). Measuring self-esteem: Race, ethnicity, and gender considered. In: T. J. Owens, S. Stryker & N. Goodman (Eds.), *Extending self-esteem theory and research: Sociological and psychological currents* (pp. 56–84). New York: Cambridge University.

Rogers, C. C. (1999). Age and family structure, by race/ethnicity and place of residence. *Economic Research Service, United States Department of Agriculture,* 1 June 1999, 42–53.

Rosenberg, M. (1979). *Conceiving the self.* New York: Basic Books.

Rosenberg, M. (1965). *Society and the adolescent self-image.* Princeton, NJ: Princeton University Press.

Rosenberg, M. & Owens, T. J. (2001). Low self-esteem people: A collective portrait. In: T. J. Owens, S. Stryker & N. Goodman (Eds.), *Extending self-esteem theory and research: Sociological and psychological currents* (pp. 400–436). New York: Cambridge University Press.

Rosenberg, M. & Pearlin, L. I. (1978). Social class and self-esteem among children and adults. *American Journal of Sociology, 84*, 53–77.

Rosenberg, M., & Simmons, R. G. (1972). *Black and white self-esteem: The urban school child.* Washington, DC: American Sociological Association.

Serpe, R. T. (1991). The cerebral self: Thinking and planning about identity relevant activities. In: J. A. Howard & P. J. Callero (Eds.), *The self society dynamic: Cognition, emotion, and action* (pp. 55–73). New York: Cambridge University Press.

Serpe, R. T. (1987). Stability and change in self: A structural symbolic interactionism explanation. *Social Psychology Quarterly, 50*, 44–55.

Serpe, R. T. & Stryker, S. (1987). The construction of self and the reconstruction of social relationships. In: E. J. Lawler & B. Markovsky (Eds.), *Advances in group processes: Theory and research* (Vol. 4, pp. 41–82). Greenwich, CT: JAI Press.

Serpe, R. T. & Stryker, S. (1993). Prior social ties and movement into new social relationships. In: E. J. Lawler, B. Markovsky & J. O'Brien (Eds.), *Advances in group processes: Theory and research:* Vol. 10 (pp. 283–304). Greenwich, CT: JAI Press.

Stryker, S. (1989). Further developments in identity theory: Singularity versus multiplicity of self. In: J. Berger, M. Zelditch, Jr. & B. Anderson (Eds.), *Sociological theories in progress: New formulation* (pp. 35–57). Newbury Park, CA: Sage.

Stryker, S. (1968). Identity theory and role performance. *Journal of Marriage and the Family, 30*, 558–564.

Stryker, S. (1987). Identity theory: Developments and extensions. In: T. M. Honess & K. M. Yardley (Eds.), *Self and identity: Psychosocial perspectives* (pp. 89–104). New York: Wiley.

Stryker, S. (1980). *Symbolic interactionism: A social structural version.* Menlo Park, CA: Benjamin Cummings.

Stryker, S. & Serpe, R. T. (1982). Commitment, identity salience and role behavior: Theory and research example. In: W. Ickes & E. S. Knowles (Eds.), *Personality, roles, and social behavior* (pp. 192–216). New York: Springer-Verlag.

Stryker, S. & Serpe, R. T. (1994). Identity salience and psychological centrality: Equivalent, overlapping, or complementary concepts? *Social Psychology Quarterly, 57*, 16–35.

Stryker, S. & Serpe, R. T. (1983). Toward a theory of family influence in the socialization of children. *Research in Sociology of Education and Socialization, 4*, 47–71.

Stryker, S. & Statham, A. (1985). Symbolic interaction and role theory. In: L. Gardner & E. Aronson (Eds.), *Handbook of social psychology* (3rd ed., pp. 311–378). New York: Random House.

Swann, W. B., Jr. (1983). Self-verification: Bringing social reality into harmony with the self. In: J. M. Suls & A. G. Greenwald (Eds.), *Social psychological perspectives on the self:* Vol. 2 (pp. 33–66). Hillsdale, NJ: Lawrence Erlbaum.

Thoits, P. A. & Hewitt, L. N. (2001). Volunteer work and well-being. *Journal of Health and Social Behavior, 42,* 115–133.

Thompson, L. & Walker, A. J. (1989). Gender in families: Women and men in marriage, work, and parenthood. *Journal of Marriage and the Family, 51,* 845–871.

U.S. Bureau of the Census. (1992). *Statistical Abstract of the United States, 1992.* Washington, DC: U.S. Government Printing Office.

U.S. Bureau of the Census. (2002). Race and Hispanic origin of householder (table F-5) families by median and mean income: 1947 to 2001, published 30 September 2002. Web site: URL http://www.census.gov/hhes/income/histinc/f05.html.

Wilkinson, D. (1987). Ethnicity. In S. K. Steinmetz, & M. B. Sussman (Eds.), *Handbook of marriage and the family* (pp. 345–405). New York: Plenum.

Zajonc, R. B. (1984). On the primacy of affect. *American Psychologist, 39,* 117–123.

	1	2	3	4	5	6	7	8	9	10	11	12	13	14	15	16	17	18	19
Education	1.00																		
Income	.39	1.00																	
Age	-.02	.09	1.00																
Gender	-.14	-.30	.08	1.00															
Any Relative	-.11	-.04	-.04	.12	1.00														
SE 1	.16	.14	-.03	-.02	.04	1.00													
SE 2	.22	.18	-.02	.00	.02	.36	1.00												
SE 3	.11	.06	-.16	-.01	.01	.36	.18	1.00											
SE 4	.15	.15	-.02	-.03	.02	.43	.46	.22	1.00										
FIC 1	.00	-.02	-.00	.07	.28	.11	.01	.10	.08	1.00									
FIC 2	-.00	.12	-.09	.00	.16	.09	.04	.08	.04	.25	1.00								
FIC 3	-.07	-.03	-.08	.05	.43	.06	.01	.08	.03	.51	.23	1.00							
FAC 1	-.05	-.02	.02	.16	.14	.13	.10	.06	.08	.32	.18	.23	1.00						
FAC 2	-.03	-.02	.06	.17	.14	.15	.14	.06	.16	.33	.18	.24	.55	1.00					
FAC 3	-.08	-.05	.06	.10	.12	.14	.13	.00	.12	.27	.14	.24	.64	.58	1.00				
FAC 4	.09	.09	-.05	.03	.08	.22	.24	.16	.27	.23	.12	.22	.34	.35	.34	1.00			
FIS 1	-.02	-.03	-.06	.07	.10	.13	.09	.08	.04	.18	.15	.11	.27	.28	.25	.19	1.00		
FIS 2	.00	-.01	-.09	.07	.06	.10	.08	.11	.04	.17	.13	.08	.27	.24	.24	.17	.63	1.00	
FIS 3	.04	.02	-.06	.05	.08	.14	.11	.10	.09	.16	.16	.08	.26	.25	.22	.19	.61	.54	1.00
Mean	14.8	5.3	40.8	.57	.67	3.1	2.9	3.4	3.0	4.7	2.1	2.4	3.7	3.5	3.8	3.3	2.7	2.9	3.0
S.D.	2.7	3.4	14.8	.50	.47	.60	.76	.50	.75	.19	1.0	1.1	.65	.71	.47	.74	.89	.85	.82

Legend: SE = Rosenberg Self Esteem; FIC = Family Interactional Commitment; FAC = Family Affective Commitment; FIS = Family Identity Salience

Appendix 1a. Correlations, Means, and Standard Deviations for Whites.

	1	2	3	4	5	6	7	8	9	10	11	12	13	14	15	16	17	18	19
Education	1.00																		
Income	.47	1.00																	
Age	.05	.13	1.00																
Gender	-.05	-.13	-.03	1.00															
Any Relative	-.06	-.07	-.06	.12	1.00														
SE 1	.13	.09	.05	.03	.02	1.00													
SE 2	.24	.23	-.02	-.08	-.00	.31	1.00												
SE 3	.16	.14	-.18	-.06	.04	.27	.22	1.00											
SE 4	.24	.24	-.01	-.03	.07	.24	.41	.15	1.00										
FIC 1	.00	-.03	-.03	.11	.22	.08	.09	.01	.11	1.00									
FIC 2	.03	.07	-.16	.07	.19	.00	-.04	.03	.03	.20	1.00								
FIC 3	-.10	-.10	-.01	.12	.29	.00	.01	.01	.04	.49	.22	1.00							
FAC 1	.01	-.05	.07	.06	.05	.08	.03	.01	.03	.25	.16	.15	1.00						
FAC 2	.02	.04	.11	.10	.02	.09	.09	.04	.17	.30	.14	.18	.45	1.00					
FAC 3	.05	-.00	.05	.06	-.07	.04	.04	-.00	.06	.13	.05	.07	.31	.32	1.00				
FAC 4	.09	.13	-.04	.01	.04	.19	.23	.20	.22	.12	.08	.06	.17	.17	.19	1.00			
FIS 1	.06	.04	.08	-.03	.06	.11	.03	.06	.08	.13	.08	.06	.17	.15	.10	.12	1.00		
FIS 2	.06	.05	-.03	-.10	-.03	.11	.05	.11	.10	.11	.09	.01	.16	.09	.06	.14	.64	1.00	
FIS 3	.10	.07	.03	.01	.05	.15	.07	.08	.14	.14	.10	.06	.16	.17	.11	.13	.65	.63	1.00
Mean	14.1	4.2	40.1	.65	.72	3.0	2.8	3.3	3.0	4.9	2.1	2.5	3.7	3.7	3.9	3.3	2.5	2.8	2.8
S.D.	2.6	3.0	15.0	.47	.45	.66	.75	.52	.77	1.9	1.0	1.1	.58	.57	.31	.67	.97	.94	.90

Legend: SE = Rosenberg Self-Esteem; FIC = Family Interactional Commitment; FAC = Family Affective Commitment; FIS = Family Identity Salience

Appendix 1b. Correlations, Means, and Standard Deviations for African Americans.

	1	2	3	4	5	6	7	8	9	10	11	12	13	14	15	16	17	18	19
Education	1.00																		
Income	.39	1.00																	
Age	-.14	.18	1.00																
Gender	-.07	-.26	.07	1.00															
Any Relative	-.11	-.04	.08	.10	1.00														
SE 1	.13	.14	.05	-.05	-.07	1.00													
SE 2	.23	.28	-.05	-.12	-.03	.21	1.00												
SE 3	.32	.21	.02	-.08	-.02	.34	.19	1.00											
SE 4	.31	.24	.01	.06	-.05	.15	.34	.17	1.00										
FIC 1	-.73	.04	.13	.01	.16	-.04	.15	.02	-.05	1.00									
FIC 2	.05	.07	-.07	-.09	-.03	.03	-.03	.03	-.03	.06	1.00								
FIC 3	.01	-.01	.06	-.00	.21	-.07	.01	.01	-.01	.47	.07	1.00							
FAC 1	-.14	-.08	.07	.05	-.03	.01	-.01	.05	-.04	.14	-.03	.12	1.00						
FAC 2	-.12	.02	.15	.01	.02	.04	-.00	.06	.03	.22	.05	.18	.38	1.00					
FAC 3	-.09	-.04	.08	.05	.01	.06	.05	.08	.02	.14	-.03	.13	.44	.34	1.00				
FAC 4	.16	.11	-.00	-.00	.02	.11	.11	.20	.11	-.03	-.05	.03	.17	.15	.24	1.00			
FIS 1	-.04	-.02	-.02	-.04	.05	-.01	.05	.08	.03	.04	.05	.00	.04	.08	.03	.07	1.00		
FIS 2	.12	.04	-.05	-.08	-.03	.06	.01	.15	.06	.01	.01	.04	.06	.07	.01	.10	.62	1.00	
FIS 3	.02	.02	-.03	-.07	.02	.02	.31	.12	.04	.08	.01	.03	.06	.14	.04	.13	.60	.63	1.00
Mean	10.7	2.6	31.7	.56	.88	3.0	2.7	3.1	2.5	5.1	2.1	2.6	3.7	3.6	3.9	3.1	2.5	2.6	2.7
S.D.	3.9	2.3	10.3	.50	.33	.56	.73	.53	.76	1.9	1.2	1.1	.61	.66	.33	.74	.94	.98	.90

Legend: SE = Rosenberg Self Esteem; FIC = Family Interactional Commitment; FAC = Family Affective Commitment; FIS = Family Identity Salience

Appendix 1c. Correlations, Means, and Standard Deviations for Latinos.

	Self Esteem			Interactional Commitment			Affective Commitment			Identity Salience		
	White	Black	Latino	White	Black	Latino	White	Black	Latino	White	Black	Latino
Education	**.188**[c]	**.277**[c]	**.391**[c]									
	.033	.049	.040									
	.006	*.010*	*.006*									
Income	**.160**[c]	**.211**[c]	**.314**[c]									
	.022	.032	.056									
	.006	*.009*	*.010*									
Age				**-.009**[c]								
				-.008								
				.002								
Gender							**.142**[c]					
							.091					
							.019					
Any Relative				**.499**[c]	**.353**[a]	**.223**[c]	**.114**[c]					
				1.391	1.084	.917	.078					
				.100	*.148*	*.194*	*.021*					
Self Esteem				**.083**[a]	**.135**[a]		**.209**[c]	**.241**[c]			**.138**[b]	**.142**[b]
				.225	.409		.135	.116			.231	.253
				.101	*.176*		*.026*	*.034*			*.093*	*.092*
Interactional Commitment										**.091**[a]		
										.049		
										.023		
Affective Commitment										**.349**[c]	**.218**[c]	**.143**[b]
										.793	.761	.471
										.107	*.253*	*.197*

a = p < .05; b = p < .01; c = p < .001

Order of Cells:
Standardized
Unstandardized
Standard Error

Chi-Square = 1109.17
Degrees of Freedom = 402
Chi-Square/df = 2.76
RMSEA = .026
CFI = .995

Appendix 2. Standardized, Unstandardized Coefficients for the Groups Model Comparing Whites, African Americans, and Latinos.

Part III

Identities, Emotions, and Social Health

Chapter **7**

Justice, Emotion, and Identity Theory

JAN E. STETS

INTRODUCTION

In its current form, identity theory has two slightly different emphases and thus two somewhat different programs of research (Stryker & Burke, 2000). In the work of Stryker and his colleagues (Serpe & Stryker, 1987; Stryker & Serpe, 1982, 1994), the focus is on how social structure influences one's identity and, in turn, behavior. Thoits' (Thoits, 1983, 1991, 1995) ongoing research also has this emphasis. In the work of Burke and his associates (Burke & Cast, 1997; Burke & Reitzes, 1981, 1991; Burke & Stets, 1999; Cast & Burke, 2002; Stets & Burke, 1996, 2000; Tsushima & Burke, 1999), the emphasis is on the internal dynamics of the self that influence behavior.[1] Though there are different emphases, both versions of identity theory assume that persons always act within the context of social structure in which others and themselves are named in that each recognizes the other as an occupant of societal positions or roles (Stryker, 1980).[2] Thus, there is the shared view that at the core of an identity is the categorization of the self as an occupant of a role and that within this categorization are the meanings and expectations associated with the role and its performance. This is what is meant by a role identity.[3]

---

[1] As Cast (this volume) points out, most research in identity theory has addressed how behavior is an outcome of identity processes. Cast shows how behavior is not only a consequence, but also a cause of identity processes.

[2] A third form of identity theory may be seen in the work of McCall and Simmons (1978). Though there has not been a clear program of research emerging from this version of identity theory, it has made important theoretical contributions to understanding identities. For example, McCall (this volume) proposes positive and negative poles (The "Me" and "Not-Me") to identity-work. Many identity theorists using either Stryker's social structural approach or Burke's process approach have turned to McCall and Simmons theoretical work that seemingly includes both aspects.

[3] Importantly, McCall and Simmons (McCall & Simmons, 1978) indicate that a role identity has a "conventional" dimension and an "idiosyncratic" dimension. The former is the role of role identity that relates to the expectations tied to social positions while the identity of role identity relates to the unique interpretations individuals bring to their roles. McCall and Simmons point out that the proportion of conventional versus idiosyncratic behavior tied to role identities varies across people and across identities for any one person.

Stryker (1980) suggests that the many role identities that one may have are organized into a hierarchy of salience. A salient identity is an identity that is likely to be played out across different situations. What importantly influences the ranking of an identity in the salience hierarchy is the degree of commitment one has to the identity.[4] Stryker's emphasis within identity theory takes seriously the idea of incorporating social structure into an analysis of the self. His salience hierarchy reflects the idea that as our society is hierarchically organized, so too must we see the self as hierarchically arranged. Because people live their lives in social relationships in society, commitment takes these ties into account when explaining the identities that persons are likely to invoke in a situation.[5]

Burke's emphasis has been on examining the internal mechanisms that operate for a role identity (Burke, 1991, 1996). Since an identity is a set of meanings attached to the self in a social role, this set of meanings serves as a standard or reference for a person. A person acts in a self-regulatory manner with the goal of matching meanings of the self in a situation (often derived from how others see the self as revealed in "reflected appraisals") with the identity meanings in one's standard. This is the hallmark of the *self-verification* process (Burke & Stets, 1999). Individuals seek to confirm their self-views in situations, often by looking at the views and responses of others (Swann, 1990). This self-regulating, self-verifying process is ongoing and continuous, often requiring little attention for an individual. A person becomes more attentive when the normal state of continuous self-verification gets interrupted and a lack of self-verification occurs. In response, persons may either modify what they are doing in the situation or change how they see things in the situation.[6]

There is an important similarity in how Stryker and Burke see the role of emotion in the identity process, and it is this aspect of identity theory that I develop in this research. For Burke (1991, 1996), emotion reflects the degree of congruence between the self-in-situation meanings and the meanings held in the identity standard. Continuous congruence (self-verification) registers positive emotion and incongruence that cannot be handled automatically within the self-regulatory system (lack of self-verification) registers negative emotion (Bartels, 1997; Burke & Stets, 1999; Cast & Burke, 2002). For Stryker (Stryker, 1987), identities that generate positive feelings should be played out more often and move up in the salience hierarchy while identities that repeatedly cause negative feelings should be less likely to be played out and move down in the salience hierarchy. Additionally, identities that are inadequately played out should generate negative feelings, thereby signaling that self-in-situation meanings are not being supported by others.[7] Thus,

---

[4]McCall and Simmons (1978) organize the many different role identities into a hierarchy of prominence, an organization that reflects a person's ideal self. The prominence of an identity depends upon the degree to which one: 1) gets support from others for an identity, 2) is committed to the identity, and 3) receives extrinsic and intrinsic rewards from the role identity. The more prominent the role identity, the more likely it will be performed in a situation. In this way, McCall and Simmons theory also has a social structural emphasis.

[5]While identity theorists assume that actors hold multiple positions in the social structure, and correspondingly, multiple identities, very little research has examined the "'multiple identities' conception of the self" (Stryker & Burke, 2000, p. 291). In this volume, we find identity researchers becoming more attentive to theorizing on multiple identities as revealed in the chapters by Burke, Smith-Lovin, and Thoits.

[6]In successfully performing a role in a situation, McCall and Simmons highlight the importance of negotiation with others in the situation. This is where we see their emphasis on interaction and thus a more process approach to understanding identities. One's expectations associated with a role identity, whether they are normative or personal, may differ from the expectations others' associate with that role identity in the situation. Some degree of compromise is needed between individuals so that proper role performance can be achieved.

[7]Similarly, McCall and Simmons (1978) argue that if a prominent identity has been threatened (by others not supporting one's role performance), an individual should experience a negative emotional response.

the lack of support from others as to who one is registers negative feelings for Stryker in the same way that a lack of self-verification registers negative feelings for Burke.

Importantly, the role of emotion in identity theory is closely aligned to other social psychological theories that link emotional consequences to a discrepancy between self-views and others view of the self in the situation.[8] For example, affect control theory asserts that emotion signals the extent to which events confirm or disconfirm one's identity in a situation (Heise, 1979; Smith-Lovin & Heise, 1988). Fundamental sentiments (culturally derived) are tied to identities and the extent to which identity meanings in a situation differ from fundamental sentiments of that identity determines the amount of deflection. Small discrepancies cause small deflections and weak emotions in these situations reflect the identity that is invoked. Large discrepancies lead to large deflections and strong emotion that signals the need for action to restore fundamental sentiments in the situation.

Current Study

I examine the relationship between emotion and identities more closely by studying the *characteristics of the discrepancy* that leads to an emotional response and the *strength/intensity* of the emotional response.[9] In the former, Stryker (1987) indicates that inadequate role performance leads to negative emotion and adequate role performance produces positive emotion.[10] For example, one may see herself as "academically inclined" in the student identity yet fail on an important test. Others in the situation may have difficulty supporting her as "academically inclined," the individual may feel disappointed, sad, or angry, and she may be less likely to play out the student identity in the future. Alternatively, if she excels on an important exam, others might praise her, she will experience happiness and pride, and she will be more likely to invoke the student identity in the future. In a similar fashion, Burke (1991, 1996) argues that a departure from one's identity standard in a situation or incongruence will result in negative emotion. When input meanings in the situation match the meanings held in the identity standard, positive emotion results. Therefore, Stryker and Burke agree that negative emotion results from not meeting one's identity expectations and positive emotion results from meeting one's identity expectations. I make a similar assumption in this study.

Feelings vary in terms of their strength or intensity and I have recently begun to investigate how identities related to the intensity of emotion.[11] Stryker (1987) argues that the strength of an emotion is a function of how important an identity is in one's salience hierarchy with more important identities producing a stronger emotion. Burke (1991,

---

[8]Lawler (this volume) turns the identity-emotion relationship around by arguing that rather than identities influencing emotion, emotion that is linked to repeated, successful interactions influences the development of collective identities.

[9]Francis (this volume) also examines the relationship between emotion and identities.

[10]This is consistent with the classic work of Cooley (Cooley, [1909] 1962) and the more recent work of Shott (1979) who view negative emotion as emerging when others do not accept one's self-image that has been built up, and positive emotion as emerging when normative, moral conduct receives approval from others.

[11]Using the 1996 General Social Survey which included an emotion's module, Tsushima and I (Stets & Tsushima, 2001) find that more intense anger is associated with the lack of verification of *group-based* identities that are intimate such as the family identity compared to *role-based* identities that are less intimate such as the worker identity. Further, we find that those with a *low status* identity (for example, an employee at work or a child at home) reported more intense anger to the lack of verification than those with an identity equal in status (for example, at co-worker at work or a spouse at home). These findings reveal that the different bases of identities (group and role) and the status of the identity are important predictors of the intensity of emotion.

1996) hypothesizes that repeated interruptions in the self-regulating identity process cause more negative emotion than occasional or infrequent interruptions. The current study tests Burke's hypothesis by examining emotions that emerge from the distributive justice process where justice reflects a congruent state and injustice reflects an incongruent state.

Like Burke's version of identity theory, distributive justice theory conceptualizes the self as acting in a self-regulatory manner with the goal of matching one's actual reward in a situation with one's expected reward (Jasso, 1983; Markovsky, 1985). Congruence registers the experience of justice and incongruence registers the experience of injustice in a situation. If we translate the idea of repeated interruptions, that is, frequently disrupting the verification process, into repeatedly being over-rewarded or under-rewarded in a justice situation, more *intense* emotions should occur as the distributive justice process *persists*.

A laboratory experiment that simulates a work situation and invokes the worker identity is conducted. Subjects (workers) carry out three simple tasks, and they learn that another subject (the manager) in the situation is responsible for the points (reward) they receive following task performance. Subjects are given points that reflect an under-reward, expected reward, or over-reward. The reward is administered at prearranged intervals throughout subjects' task performance (high persistence), or only once after task completion (low persistence). Self-reports on subjects' feelings are obtained after they receive their reward.

THEORY

Recent developments in identity theory conceptualize the identity process as a self-regulating, control system (Powers, 1973). I rely on this conceptualization in this research. When an identity is activated in a situation, a feedback loop is established (see Figure 1 below) (Burke, 1991). There are four important components to this loop. The *identity standard* defines the character of an identity or what it means to be who one is in a situation. The standard stores the self-meanings tied to social roles. The *input* contains the meanings of how one sees itself in a situation. These self-meanings are often derived from how others see the self, labeled the "reflected appraisals." The *comparator* compares the meanings from the input and the meanings from the standard and registers the difference or error between them. The result of this comparison is the *output*. This is behavior that acts upon the environment either to maintain congruence between the input and standard meanings by continuing to act, uninterrupted, or by acting differently when a large error is registered, in order to change the input meanings to match the meanings in the standard. Emotion in the identity model reflects the size of the error in the comparator. Positive emotion reflects a congruence of input and standard meanings. Negative emotion reflects the input meanings not matching the meanings held in the identity standard.

The distributive justice process has been theorized as operating in much the same way as the identity process. In distributive justice theory, there is the assumption of a *standard* that guides the perceived fairness of the allocation of one's outcomes (the just reward), a *comparison process* where an actual outcome is evaluated given an expected (just) outcome, *behavior* which reveals the degree of discrepancy between actual and expected outcomes and is expressed in justice-restoring responses (or the lack thereof), and *emotion* which follows from the evaluation of the discrepancy (Markovsky 1985). Distributive justice, as derived from social exchange theory (Blau, 1964; Homans, 1961) and equity theory (Adams, 1965; Walster, Walster, & Berscheid, 1978) assumes that the evaluation of fair or just outcomes in a situation is based upon comparing one's own ratio of rewards to investments with either another's ratio of rewards to investment (Walster et al., 1978), past outcomes (Thibaut & Kelley, 1959), a referential structure (expectations regarding what people are believed to receive given the social structure and the status value attached to their investments and rewards (Berger, Zelditch, Anderson, & Cohen, 1972; Jasso, 1980)), or the group (Markovsky, 1985). In general, the amount of reward one receives in a situation or one's *actual reward* are compared to one's *just reward* (the referential structure above) (Jasso, 1983) or the *reward standard*, that is, the reward level implied by any one of the sources above (Markovsky, 1985).

Like the *comparator* in the identity model, a *comparison unit* is identified in distributive justice theory; it organizes and stores information on both the reward standard and actual reward (Markovsky, 1985). However, unlike the comparator in the identity model, the comparison unit does not register the degree of difference between the two values. The *congruence evaluation* does this by using the information in the comparison unit to establish the degree of discrepancy (Markovsky, 1985). The subjective impact of the congruence evaluation is the justice experience. Congruence registers the experience of justice and incongruence registers the experience of injustice whether that is an over-reward or under-reward. *Emotions* follow from the cognitive evaluation of (in)congruence. Historically, three emotions have been examined: guilt that results from an over-reward, satisfaction that results from an expected reward, and anger that is due to an under-reward (Hegtvedt, 1990; Homans, 1961; Jasso, 1980).

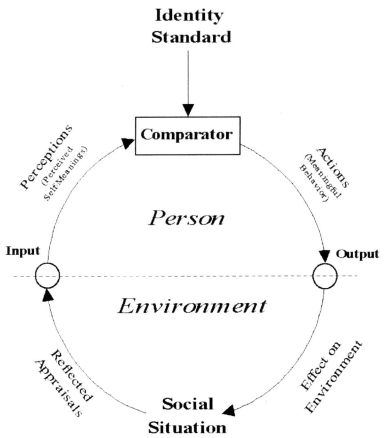

Figure 1. Model of the Identity Process.

In this research, I assume that any difference between one's actual reward and just reward in a situation produces a state of injustice. From the perspective of identity theory, when persons do not receive what they expect, this may be conceptualized as interrupting the smooth flowing cybernetic feedback loop in Figure 1. What persons expect to obtain in the situation, given their standard and behavior following from that standard, is different from what they receive. In identity theory, this may be understood as a *Type 1* interruption: *The Broken Loop* (Burke 1991, 1996). While the loop may be broken at the *output* side (*Type 1a*) (one's behavior has little or no effect) or *input* side (*Type 1b*) (one's behavior has effects but the individual misreads those effects), a state of injustice most likely results from *Type 1a* interruptions. According to Burke, *Type 1a* interruptions involve one's behavior not influencing how others treat the self. Others may not recognize one's efforts. They may not pay attention. Or, they may impose meaning on the person, independent of the person's behaviors and intentions behind those behaviors. Essentially, the person has lost some control over events.

If expectations in the standard do not match the outcomes that persons receive in a situation, then action or meaningful behavior on the output side of the loop is not registering its intended effects. According to Burke (1991), *frequent* interruptions or what I will label *persistent* interruptions, should lead to a *stronger* emotional response than infrequent interruptions because the repeated interruptions reduce the person's ability to enact behaviors that would ordinarily lead to an automatic adjustment in the self-regulating system. Self-verification cannot be achieved. I expect an upper-limit to increasing intensity.

Consistent with identity theory (Burke, 1991, 1996) and distributive justice theory (Homans, 1961; Jasso, 1980), I expect an over-reward to lead to negative feelings. The reward has exceeded the expected standard and this should make one feel bad. For distributive justice theorists, an over-reward is most likely to lead to feelings of guilt given the perception that the reward is at the expense of others (Hegtvedt, 1990). Fear may also emerge as one becomes concerned with retaliation from others for receiving something in excess (Walster et al., 1978). Further, based on identity theory, since negative feelings should intensify with persistent over-rewards, my first set of hypotheses include the following:

Hypothesis 1: An over-reward will lead to negative feelings of: a) guilt and b) fear.

Hypothesis 2: A persistent over-reward will strengthen negative feelings of: a) guilt and b) fear.

Following from identity theory and distributive justice theory, I anticipate an expected (just) reward to lead to positive feelings such as satisfaction (Burke & Stets, 1999; Cast & Burke, 2002; Jasso, 1980). Essentially, the comparator in the identity model does not register any discrepancy between the input and the standard. Indeed, there is empirical support that the perception of equity influences feelings of satisfaction (Cate, Lloyd, & Long, 1988; Utne, Hatfield, Traupmann, & Greenberger, 1984). I anticipate that other positive emotions will result from a just reward such as gratitude and deservedness. Since positive feelings should intensify with persistent expected rewards given identity theory, my next set of hypotheses is the following:

Hypothesis 3: An expected reward will lead to the positive feelings of: a) satisfaction, b) gratitude, and c) deservedness.

Hypothesis 4: A persistent expected reward will strengthen the positive feelings of: a) satisfaction, b) gratitude, and c) deservedness.

Finally, I anticipate that an under-reward will lead to negative feelings. This is consistent with identity theory that incongruence results in negative emotion. It is also consistent with distributive justice theory, particularly the classic work of Homans (1961), who indicated that persons experience anger when they do not receive the rewards they expect. Along with anger, I examine the negative feelings of disgust and resentfulness. Since negative feelings should intensify with persistent under-rewards, my last set of hypotheses include the following:

> **Hypothesis 5**: An under-reward will lead to the negative feelings of: a) anger, b) resentfulness, and c) disgust.

> **Hypothesis 6**: A persistent under-reward will strengthen the negative feelings of: a) anger, b) resentfulness, and c) disgust.

METHOD

Procedure

This study takes place in a laboratory setting. Subjects are paid volunteers recruited from classes at Washington State University. Subjects are told that an advertising agency, HIGH-LIGHTS, has been asked by one of the major automobile manufacturing companies to run an ad campaign, targeted to young families, for a new car that will enter the market in the near future. The agency needs to pretest their planning strategies to see if they are efficient and effective in getting their ad campaign underway. They are seeking feedback from individuals to assess their procedures. Subjects are asked to perform three simple clerical tasks. These are the tasks that HIGHLIGHTS employees will carry out for the ad campaign. Following each task, subjects are asked a series of questions, among them their reaction to the tasks and their reaction to the points they received following their performance.

The three tasks are relatively simple.[12] They include: 1) alphabetizing promotional letters on the new car by the selected family's last name (listed at the top of the promotional letter), 2) writing each family's name and address from the top of the promotional letter onto to a HIGHLIGHTS mailing envelope, and then clipping a return envelope that is addressed to HIGHLIGHTS to the promotional letter and mailing envelope, and 3) taking a new stack of promotional letters, doing task two again, but keeping each promotional packet in alphabetical order as subjects go along. Each task is carried out for six minutes and subjects are videotaped throughout their participation.[13] Each session lasts about an hour. Subjects are paid $10 for their participation.

Three persons are involved in each experiment: 1) a supervisor (a confederate) for HIGHLIGHTS who oversees the study including administering initial questionnaires, assigning subjects to be the worker or manager, and conducting the follow-up and debriefing, 2) a manager (a second confederate) who evaluates the worker's performance on each task and administers a reward (under-reward, expected reward, and over-reward) in the form of points, and 3) a worker (subject) who carries out the three tasks and provides his or her reactions after each task. The supervisor begins the study.

---

[12]Three tasks were incorporated into the study to guard against the possibility of boredom setting in if subjects were to do only one task. Additionally, having three distinct tasks provides three different points in the experiment where rewards can be given following the subject's performance. This establishes the *persistence* condition.

[13]Based on extensive pre-testing, six minutes was found to be long enough for subjects to develop an attitude toward the task.

Two subjects (a subject and a confederate)[14] are ushered into a room where they are introduced to the study and asked to fill out a series of questionnaires. Then, the supervisor "randomly" assigns one subject to be the worker for the study and the second subject (confederate) to be the manager.[15] The subject is then taken to a second room to watch a five-minute instructional video that demonstrates the tasks that he or she will perform.[16] The subject in the video receives 100 points following the manager's evaluation that the subject did average work. This sets the standard/expected reward for the subjects. Whenever subjects are evaluated as doing average work, they should expect 100 points. The subject is told that while he or she is watching the video, the supervisor will instruct the other subject on how to be a manager for the study in another room.[17] After the subject finishes viewing the video, work on the tasks begin.

The manager enters the room and stands in front of where the subject is seated. In the room are two tables. The table off to the right of where the subject is seated has a series of bins where the subject will deposit his or her work upon completion of each task. Also on the table is a scale where the manager will weigh the subject's work after each task. The manager will compare the subject's weighted work in ounces with an evaluation sheet that is posted on a wall in the room that identifies (in ounces) what constitutes below average, average, and above average work.[18] The other table is where the subject is seated. It is in the center of the room and is the subject's "work station." This is the area where the subject will carry out each task. On this table are 300 promotional letters addressed to families,[19] a set of legal size envelopes that have the HIGHLIGHTS return address,[20] and set of letter size envelopes that have the HIGHLIGHTS address as the delivery address.

The manager begins by reviewing with the subject that she will be doing three simple clerical tasks that are the kinds of tasks that HIGHLIGHTS employees will be carrying out. More important is what follows. The manager tells the subject that after task completion, the manager will give the subject 100 points for doing average work, 150 points for doing above average work, and 50 points for doing below average work. To insure that the subject understands this reward schedule, the subject is asked to fill out a brief survey following the manager's explanation. Subjects are asked how many points they will earn for doing average work, above average work, and below average work. If

---

[14]To be clear, subjects do not know that the other is a confederate. Throughout the entire study, they think that others are naive subjects, just like themselves.

[15]Subjects choose a number between 1 and 10. The confederate always chooses first and chooses the number "3". After the subject chooses a number, the supervisor tells the subjects that the folded papers in the box in front of them contains numbers that range from 1 to 10. In reality, all folded papers contain the number "7". Based on whatever number the subject chooses, the supervisor then does a quick calculation in his head. The supervisor explains that whoever chose furthest from the number (if the subject chose "1" or "2") or closest to the number (if the subject chose "4" thru "10") that is picked in the box will be the worker and the other will be the manager. This "fixes" the subject to be the worker and the confederate to be the manager.

[16]Two different "instructional" videos are made to allow for the subject in the video to carry out the tasks under the condition of high persistence or low persistence. If the subject has been randomly selected into the high persistence condition, the subject will see the person in the video carrying out the tasks under high persistence. If the subject has been randomly selected into the low persistence condition, the subject will see the person in the video doing the tasks under low persistence.

[17]Since this subject is the confederate, no instruction occurs.

[18]The manager will always say that the subject has done average work irrespective of how much the subject gets done. If the subject asks how much he or she got done in ounces, the manager always provides an answer that is within the range of someone doing average work.

[19]The 300 families names and addresses are ficticious.

[20]The HIGHLIGHTS address is ficticious.

the managers see that subjects are answering incorrectly, they review the reward schedule to the subjects. The subjects are also asked to identify who will determine how many points they will get. If they do not indicate that it is the manager, the manager again reviews the administration of points, emphasizing that it is the manager who will determine how many points the subject gets.

The above procedure does two things. It sets the expectation/standard of 100 points for average work for the subject. The subject sees this standard being invoked in the instructional video, and it is reiterated before the subject begins the tasks. Additionally, when studying injustice, it is important that another is perceived as responsible for the outcomes one gets. If one were to take responsibility for the outcomes received, then the perception of injustice might not follow. In this study, subjects see the manager giving the points/reward in the instructional video, and this is reiterated before the subject begins the tasks.

Once the study gets underway, male and female subjects are given their points (over-reward = 150, expected reward = 100, or under-reward = 50) either after they complete each task (high persistence) or after they complete all three tasks (low persistence). This is a 2 x 3 x 2 experimental design (gender, reward, and persistence). Subjects are randomly assigned to the reward and persistence conditions. A total of 282 subjects were obtained.

Manipulation Checks

Following receipt of their reward, subjects are asked a series of questions. To see if the standard of "100 points = average work" had been adopted by the subjects, the following question is asked, "After the manager told you how you performed on these tasks, how many points did you expect the manager to give you?" Response categories included "50 points," "100 points," or "150 points." Since the managers always told the subjects that they did "average work," subjects should respond that they expected 100 points. The results showed that the mean response for this question was 100.89. This was not significantly different from the mean value of 100 ($t = .71$, $p = .48$).

In order to determine whether subjects gave the manager responsibility for the rewards they received, following receipt of their rewards subjects were asked, "Who determined how many points you got for these tasks?" Almost all of the subjects (96%) said the manager was responsible for the reward(s) they received.

Measures

Female is coded 1 for women and 0 for men. The reward condition is captured by two dummy variables. An over-reward is coded 1 if subjects are given 150 when they expect 100, and 0 otherwise. An under-reward is coded 1 if subjects receive 50 points when they expected 100 points, and 0 otherwise. Persistence is coded 0 for low persistence and 1 for high persistence. Subjects' emotional reactions to the rewards they receive are gathered. In the high persistence condition, subjects' reactions are obtained three times, following each task and just after they receive their reward. In the low persistence condition, subjects' reactions are obtained once, after they receive their reward at the end of the three tasks. For each emotion listed, subjects are asked to circle the number that corresponds to how they felt after getting the points (reward) for their task(s). Responses ranged from 0 ("Didn't feel the emotion at all") to 10 ("Intensely felt the emotion").

Given that an over-reward is associated with guilt and fear, I investigate the effects of these two negative emotions separately from the negative emotions tied to an under-reward. The correlation between guilt and fear is .42, $p < .01$. I estimate the effects of gender, reward, and persistence on guilt and fear, and then I estimate the effects when these emotions are summed. In the latter, a high score represents greater guilt and fear. The correlation among the three positive emotions that are related to getting what one expects is high (satisfied and grateful r = .78; satisfied and deserving r = .72, grateful and deserving r = .67). Like guilt and fear, I estimate the effects of gender, reward, and persistence for each of these positive emotions and then again when the items are added together (Ω = .89). A high score on the summed items represents more positive emotion. Finally, the correlation among the negative emotions that are tied to an under-reward is high (angry and disgusted r = .77; angry and resentful r = .80; disgusted and resentful r = .78).[21] The items are analyzed separately and then analyzed as a scale with a high score representing more negative emotion (Ω = .92).

RESULTS

Table 1 presents the regression results for guilt and fear. For exploratory purposes, all higher-ordered interaction effects are examined in all the analyses. As revealed in the second column of Table 1, none of the independent variables or higher-ordered interactions influences guilt. In the third column, an over-reward significantly influences fear, but it is in the opposite direction than what is expected. Compared to those who receive an expected reward, those who are over-rewarded are less not more likely to report fear. Thus, Hypothesis 1a and 1b are not supported. Hypothesis 2a and 2b are also not supported. Rather than persistence strengthening the feeling of fear, a prediction that follows from identity theory, persistence dampens the feeling of fear. However, persistently being over-rewarded does not dampen the feeling of fear as much as persistently getting what one expects. This is shown in Table 2. A comparison of the means for fear under low and high persistence shows that the feeling of fear becomes less intense when one persistently gets what they expect than when one is persistently over-rewarded.

Table 1. OLS Standardized Estimates of Guilt and Fear by Reward, Persistence, and Gender (N = 282)

	Guilt	Fear	Total
Independent Variables	β	β	β
Under-reward	.02	-.05	-.02
Over-reward	-.03	-.36**	-.26*
Persistence	-.14	-.37**	-.32**
Female	-.14	-.11	-.15
Persistence x Under-reward	.05	.22	.17
Persistence x Over-reward	.13	.31*	.27*
Female x Under-reward	.04	-.07	-.02
Female x Over-reward	.18	.20	.23
Female x Persistence x Under-reward	.03	.01	.02
Female x Persistence x Over-reward	-.20	-.08	-.16
R^2	.05	.08**	.07*

* $p < .05$, ** $p < .01$

---

[21] Guilt and fear are not as highly correlated with these negative items (guilt and anger r = .23; guilt and resentful r = .19; guilt and disgusted r = .21; fear and anger r = .23; fear and resentful r = .27; fear and disgusted r = .25). This supports the idea that guilt and fear that are often discussed with respect to an over-reward comprise a different dimension of negative emotion than those negative emotions commonly associated with an under-reward (anger, resentful, and disgusted).

Table 2. Means for Fear by Reward and Persistence

Reward	Persistence	
	Low	High
Under-reward	1.4	1.1
Expected reward	1.8	0.3
Over-reward	0.8	0.7

Tables 3, 4, and 5 show the effects of gender, reward, and persistence on positive emotions and address Hypotheses 3a, 3b, and 3c and 4a, 4b, and 4c. First, compared to those who get what they expect, those who are under-rewarded are less likely to report feeling satisfied, grateful, and deserving. Additionally, compared to those who get what they expect, those who are over-rewarded are more likely to report feeling satisfied and grateful. Therefore, satisfaction and gratitude is not simply associated with getting what one expects (Hypothesis 3a and 3b), but it is also associated with getting more than what one expects. Thus, rather than over-rewards inducing negative feelings such as guilt and fear, it appears to induce positive feelings such as satisfaction and gratitude.

The main effect of persistence is once again opposite from what is predicted from identity theory. Thus, Hypothesis 4a, 4b, and 4c are disconfirmed. Rather than persistence intensifying positive emotions, it diminishes positive emotions. This is true for feelings of gratitude and deservedness. However, when one is persistently over-rewarded, feelings of gratitude do not diminish in intensity as much as they do when one persistently gets an expected reward. This is shown in Table 4. Additionally, when one is persistently over-rewarded or persistently under-rewarded, feelings of deservedness do not decrease in intensity as much as when one persistently gets what is expected. This is revealed in Table 5.

Tables 6, 7 and 8 presents the negative emotions commonly associated with an under-reward and address the final set of hypotheses (5a, 5b, and 5c and 6a, 6b, and 6c). Consistent with Hypotheses 5a, 5b, and 5c, compared to getting what is expected, when subjects get less than what is expected, they are more likely to report feeling angry, resentful and disgusted. However, a persistent under-reward does not strengthen these negative feelings. Therefore, Hypotheses 6a, 6b, and 6c are not supported. Though females are more likely than males to report negative emotion as shown in the last column of Table 6, the negative emotion females are more likely to report resentfulness (column 2). The last column in Table 6 also shows that when females are persistently under-rewarded, their negative feelings become less intense. Tables 7 and 8 inform us as to what is occurring.

In Table 7, the mean values for anger reveal that when females are persistently under-rewarded, their anger becomes less intense compared to when they get what is expected. In contrast, when males are under-rewarded, their anger remains relatively constant. Table 8 shows this same pattern for disgust. When females persistently get less than what they expect, feelings of disgust weaken compared to when they get what they expect. However, when males are persistently under-rewarded, their disgust remains relatively the same.

In general, the results do not support the idea that over-rewards will lead to negative emotions such as guilt and fear as identity theory or even distributive justice theory would predict. Rather over-rewards cause individuals to feel good. Only under-rewards influence individuals to feel bad. The effect of persistence as outlined in identity theory is also not supported. Rather than persistence intensifying positive or negative emotion, it actually diminishes or weakens the positive or negative emotion. These unexpected findings challenge current assumptions in identity theory.

Table 3. OLS Standardized Estimates of Satisfaction, Gratitude, and Deservedness by Reward, Persistence, and Gender (N = 282)

Independent Variables	Satisfied β	Grateful β	Deserving β	Total β
Under-reward	-.53**	-.43**	-.57**	-.56**
Over-reward	.21*	.19*	.04	.16*
Persistence	-.06	-.26**	-.27**	-.22**
Female	.10	.10	.09	.11
Persistence x Under-reward	-.01	.14	.21*	.13
Persistence x Over-reward	.17	.24*	.21*	.23**
Female x Under-reward	-.14	-.15	-.13	-.16
Female x Over-reward	-.03	-.01	-.01	-.01
Female x Persistence x Under-reward	.06	.05	-.03	.03
Female x Persistence x Over-reward	-.10	-.11	-.02	-.09
R^2	.57**	.42**	.42**	.56**

* $p < .05$, ** $p < .01$

Table 4. Means for Gratitude by Reward and Persistence

Reward	Persistence	
	Low	High
Under-reward	1.3	1.0
Expected reward	5.5	3.6
Over-reward	7.1	6.8

Table 5. Means for Deservedness by Reward and Persistence

Reward	Persistence	
	Low	High
Under-reward	2.0	2.0
Expected reward	7.0	5.1
Over-reward	7.3	7.2

Table 6. OLS Standardized Estimates of Anger, Resentful, and Disgusted by Reward, Persistence, and Gender (N = 282)

Independent Variables	Angry β	Resentful β	Disgust β	Total β
Under-reward	.37**	.45**	.46**	.46**
Over-reward	-.16	-.15	-.08	-.14
Persistence	-.03	-.09	-.01	-.05
Female	-.16	-.19*	-.15	-.18*
Persistence x Under-reward	.07	.06	.04	.06
Persistence x Over-reward	-.01	.02	-.04	-.01
Female x Under-reward	.23*	.09	.03	.13
Female x Over-reward	.13	.09	.05	.10
Female x Persistence x Under-reward	-.30*	-.13	-.22*	-.23**
Female x Persistence x Over-reward	.01	.01	.03	.01
R^2	.28**	.32**	.27**	.33**

* $p < .05$, ** $p < .01$

Table 7. Means for Anger by Gender, Reward, and Persistence

Gender	Reward	Persistence	
Males		Low	High
	Under-reward	4.0	4.3
	Expected reward	1.9	1.3
	Over-reward	0.7	0.4
Females			
	Under-reward	4.8	2.0
	Expected reward	0.6	0.8
	Over-reward	0.8	0.5

Table 8. Means for Disgusted by Gender, Reward, and Persistence

Gender	Reward	Persistence	
Males		Low	High
	Under-reward	4.0	4.3
	Expected reward	1.9	1.3
	Over-reward	0.7	0.4
Females			
	Under-reward	4.8	2.0
	Expected reward	0.6	0.8
	Over-reward	0.8	0.5

DISCUSSION

Discrepancy Effects

If an over-reward did not lead to negative feelings such as guilt and fear and instead led to positive feelings such as satisfaction, gratefulness, and deservedness, this challenges the assumption in identity theory that when an outcome differs from an expected standard, it leads to negative emotion. Clearly we would expect such positive feelings under conditions of getting what one expects, but such positive feelings were even more likely to emerge when subjects got more than what they expected. Why was there no guilt or fear?

Hegtvedt (1990) found that while guilt was greatest for an over-reward, much lower for an under-reward, and lowest for expected rewards, the overall levels of guilt were very low. In her study, Hegtvedt used a reward structure in which the under-reward ($20) and over-reward ($40) varied by a constant amount ($10) from the just reward ($30). A similar procedure was used in this study. The amount of departure from the standard (100 points) was the same (50 points) for an under-reward (50 points) and over-reward (150 points). However, I did not find guilt significantly higher for those who were over-rewarded or under-rewarded compared to those who got what they expected. This may be because I used points rather than money, and money may mean more to subjects than points, thereby inducing a more intense emotional response.

If the *type* of over-reward (money vs. points) may be important for inducing guilt, the *amount* of the over-reward may be more important. Hegtvedt indicated that the magnitude of an over-reward may be important in inspiring a feeling of unfairness, with a relatively large over-reward inducing more unfairness and thus more guilt than a relatively small over-reward. In this study, the amount of the over-reward (50 points) may not have been enough of a departure from the expected standard to generate a feeling of unfairness and, more importantly, negative emotion. Indeed, while those who were under-rewarded saw their reward as *less fair* compared to those who got what they expected ($\beta = -.65$, $p < .01$), those who were over-rewarded saw their reward as *more fair* compared to those who got what they expected ($\beta = .12$, $p < .01$).

Consistent with the importance of the size of the departure from the expected standard, Jasso's (1980) theory of distributive justice draws attention to the fact that an under-reward of a given amount has a greater impact on the evaluation of an injustice than an over-reward of an equal amount. According to her justice evaluation function, if one wants to estimate injustice with the amount of injustice the same for an under-reward as for an over-reward, it takes more of an over-reward to generate injustice of an equal magnitude to that of an under-reward.[22] However, there may still be other factors that explain the absence of guilt for those who are over-rewarded.

Hegtvedt (1990) suggested that Homans' emphasis on guilt may be overstated because subjects may not fear retaliation for obtaining more than what they expected, or they may not perceive that their over-reward is at the expense of another. Indeed, in this study, rather than an over-reward inducing more fear, it induced less fear. Further, subjects in the present study may not have perceived that getting more meant that others were getting less. There was nothing in the design of the experiment that led them to think that getting more meant that they were "stealing" from others who would then get less. Thus, feelings of guilt and fear may be conditioned upon other factors being present in the situation rather than simply being over-rewarded. If this is true, then the scope conditions for the theory are quite limited.

What is important about the findings in this study is that an over-reward led to emotion that was of the opposite valence: positive emotion. In this study, I dealt with rewards (goods) rather than punishments (bads). Goods inherently are positive, reinforcing, rewarding, and gratifying. Thus, when individuals receive an over-reward, the inherent message is "you are good." When people's standards are somewhat exceeded given an unexpected good, they may quickly adjust their standard to the new level. This adjustment may be easy because the discrepancy is relatively small and it *enhances the self*. The findings of this study do not indicate that subjects felt that they deserved the over-reward, but they were more satisfied and grateful, and they felt that it was more fair compared to getting what they expected. The lack of deservedness may be due to subjects seeing that their outcome was not due to their own effort or how much of the task they completed, but to the manager's biased allocation of rewards.

Self-enhancement or people's pursuit of favorable information about who they are (goods) is considered the most powerful motive underlying people's quest for self-understanding, followed by *self-verification* or people's pursuit of information that confirms their preexisting self-view (Sedikides, 1993). In Burke's (1991) identity model, self-verification is the more important motive; a discrepancy registers negative affect because the definition of the self is incongruent with the identity standard. Based on the current experimental results, I propose that something more complex may be occurring when an interruption occurs in the identity process.

When individuals' outcomes slightly exceed their standard in a positive direction, that is, they get 150 points when they expect 100 points, they are receiving two different

---

[22]Mathematically, this translates into: log (under-reward/just reward) = -log (over-reward/just reward).

messages. On the one hand, they are told that they are a "good person" given the over-reward. This enhances the self and leads to positive feelings. On the other hand, the over-reward creates a discrepancy between individuals' standards (100 points) and what he or she gets (150 points). This incongruence leads to negative feelings. These two competing messages may be resolved in the following way. Individuals may respond to the enhancing aspect of the over-reward and move their standard up. By doing this, they remove the incongruence (that is, that 150 is different from their standard of 100 because they elevate 100 to 150) and the negative feeling associated with it. The result is that individuals report only strong positive feelings.

The *degree* of exceeding the standard is likely to be important in the above process. If the outcome *somewhat* exceeds the standard in a positive direction, it leads to positive emotion, given it's *self-enhancing* nature, the ease by which the standard can be raised, and the removal of discrepant information. If the outcome *significantly* exceeds the standard in a positive direction, it leads to negative emotion because the outcome is too discrepant from the standard, making it too difficult to *self-verify*.

The above resolves the self-enhancement—self-verification debate in the literature in a different fashion than that offered by Swann and his colleagues (Swann, 1990; Swann, Griffin, Predmore, & Gaines, 1987). Swann and his associates argued that *self-enhancement* was dependent upon *immediate affective reactions* to social feedback while *self-verification* was dependent upon *less immediate cognitive reactions* to social feedback. I argue that what is important is the degree of disparity in meanings held in the input and identity standard and the double meaning of a "good." *Self-enhancement* is more highly activated when a small discrepancy occurs in a positive direction. Individuals adjust their standard upward, this facilitates self-verification, and positive emotions result. *Self-verification* is more highly activated when a large discrepancy exists in a positive direction. Individuals may have difficulty adjusting their standard upwards because the incongruence is too large. Consequently, negative feelings result. Therefore, rather than assuming that any discrepancy produces negative emotion because the information is not self-verifying, I suggest that it depends upon the size of the error registered in the comparator and how individuals resolve competing messages that a "good" produces.

Persistence Effects

Identity theory assumes that persistent interruptions will produce more intense emotion. In this study, the observed effects were in the opposite direction, on average, dampening subjects' emotional responses. This was particularly the case for those subjects who got what they expected. The less intense emotional responses from individuals who got what they expected may be due to *uncertainty reduction* (Fiske & Taylor, 1991). Uncertainty has to do with how sure one is in a situation. Uncertainty is an aversive state because it is associated with reduced control over one's circumstances. The aversive state motivates people to reduce their uncertainty. The most common emotion associated with uncertainty is fear. The fear is due to the perception of unpredictability and uncontrollability. In Table 2, we find that those who got what they expected reported more fear than those who got more than what they expected. Further, when individuals persistently got what they expected, this fear was reduced more. This is what we would expect to find if uncertainty reduction were operating.

In general, the less intense emotions that resulted from persistent discrepancies emerged across all reward conditions. This pattern suggests that individuals' simply may be changing their standards, adjusting their standards to the level of rewards they received.

Since a strong emotional response would signal a discrepancy between input meanings and standard meanings, a weaker emotional response over time would suggest a closer correspondence between input and identity standard meanings.

Laboratory studies have had considerable success in changing a person's self-concept unlike non-laboratory studies that have had less success such as clinicians working with their clients for years in intensive therapy (Swann & Hill, 1982). Swann and Hill have argued that what is important in self-concept change is what individuals are able to do after they receive social feedback that tends to disconfirm their self-views. They argued, and found empirical support, that if individuals received feedback that was inconsistent with how they saw themselves and they were given *no* opportunity to refute this feedback, they were more likely to align their subsequent view of themselves to the feedback.[23] Alternatively, if people received feedback that was inconsistent with how they saw themselves and they *were* given an opportunity to refute the feedback through interaction with the other who provided the feedback, little self-concept change occurred. Essentially, by challenging the feedback and defending their self-view, people were more likely to ward off the influence of the feedback on their self-view.

In this study, subjects were not given the opportunity to refute the reward(s) they received from the manager. If they were given the opportunity to interact with the manager and express how they felt about the reward(s) they received, they may not have adjusted their standard and their emotional responses may not have weakened in strength. Indeed, there is the assumption in identity theory that if people cannot change the meanings in the situation to match their standard, the standard will change to match the meanings in the situation. Thus, the effect of persistence as outlined in identity theory may be contingent on the degree to which one has the opportunity to refute information about the self in the situation.

Interestingly, the results of this study showed that there was a gender difference in the effect of persistence for under-rewards. When females were persistently under-rewarded, their negative feelings of anger and disgust became less intense. Essentially, they were feeling less bad (or feeling better), and in this sense *self-enhancement* was occurring. For men, their negative feelings remained constant. The enhancing effects of an outcome may operate differently for under-rewards than over-rewards. When people get an under-reward, they are told that they are "*not* a good person" and the outcomes are not self-verifying. It is only when they get this message *persistently* that their standard may be most likely to change. Thus it may take less time to change a standard in a positive direction when one gets an over-reward than it does to change a standard in a negative direction when one gets an under-reward. However, those with lower status in our society may be more susceptible to a change in their standard in a negative direction than those with higher status. In terms of gender, this would be women.

There is evidence that women have a lower sense of entitlement compared to men (Major, 1987).[24] Given women's lower status in society, they tend to accept less. Others

---

[23] As Swann and Hill (1982) point out, any change in persons' self-views within a laboratory setting may quickly fade after they leave the laboratory. Given the desire for individuals to have their self-views verified or confirmed, any self-discrepant information experienced at Time 1 may be reinterpreted as consistent with self-views in Time 2, especially as they return to the context that has already provided support for those self-views. For a new self-view to endure, individuals in one's social environment must validate this new view. Alternatively, individuals may opt for a new social environment comprised of a new set of individuals who will support their new self-view.

[24] Entitlement should not be confused with deservedness (Steil, 1994). Entitlement refers to *who one is* while deservedness refers to *what one does*.

who are at a power disadvantage in our society such as the young, the less highly educated, and those who have low occupational status may be more likely to adjust their standard downward compared to those in a power advantaged position.[25] However, the above pattern may hold in laboratory studies between strangers but not in non-laboratory studies between intimates. For example, research on marital interaction shows that spouses who have a low status in terms of gender, age, education, and occupation are more likely to express negative behavior in marriage, and it is argued that this action may be an attempt to counteract the view of themselves as unworthy (Stets, 1997; Stets & Burke, 1996). Interaction with an intimate other provides the *opportunity* to challenge unfair treatment. In a laboratory setting, females may be less likely to adjust their standard to the under-rewards if they have the *opportunity* to counteract the implied self-meanings in the situation by interacting with the manager.

In general, the results of this study suggest that the relationship between input and standard meanings in identity theory needs more examination. Emotion may not simply be a function of whether a discrepancy exists, but the size of the discrepancy and how individuals manage the multiple meanings implied by rewards. Further, we need to consider the opportunity to counteract feedback as a factor that may influence how frequent interruptions in the identity process are managed. Research of my own is currently underway to examine these additional features. The goal is to more precisely explain negative and positive emotion for identities that are repeatedly as opposed to seldom disrupted. In general, identity theory is a promising theory to use in studying people's reactions to injustice. It may point to resolving some inconsistencies in how people respond to rewards (goods).

ACKNOWLEDGMENTS: This research was supported by National Foundation Grant SES-9904215. Direct all correspondence to Jan E. Stets, Department of Sociology, University of California, Riverside, CA 92521-0419; email: jan.stets@ucr.edu

REFERENCES

Adams, J. S. (1965). Inequity in social exchange. In L. Berkowitz (Ed.), *Advances in experimental social psychology* (pp. 267–299). New York: Academic Press.

Bartels, D. J. (1997). *An examination of the primary emotions of anger and sadness in marriage within the context of identity theory.* Unpublished MA, Washington State University, Pullman, WA.

Berger, J., Zelditch, M. J., Anderson, B., & Cohen, B. P. (1972). Structural aspects of distributive justice: A status value formulation. In L. Berkowitz, M. J. Zelditch & B. Anderson (Eds.), *Sociological theories in progress* (pp. 119–146). Boston: Houghton-Mifflin.

Blau, P. M. (1964). *Exchange and power in social life.* New York: John Wiley and Sons.

Burke, P. J. (1991). Identity processes and social stress. *American Sociological Review, 56,* 836–849.

Burke, P. J. (1996). Social identities and psychosocial stress. In H. B. Kaplan (Ed.), *Psychosocial stress: Perspectives on structure, theory, life course, and methods* (pp. 141–174). Orlando, FL: Academic Press.

Burke, P. J., & Cast, A. D. (1997). Stability and change in the gender identities of newly married couples. *Social Psychology Quarterly, 60,* 277–290.

Burke, P. J., & Reitzes, D. C. (1981). The link between identity and role performance. *Social Psychology Quarterly, 44,* 83–92.

Burke, P. J., & Reitzes, D. C. (1991). An identity theory approach to commitment. *Social Psychology Quarterly, 54*(3), 239–251.

Burke, P. J., & Stets, J. E. (1999). Trust and commitment through self-verification. *Social Psychology Quarterly, 62,* 347–366.

Cast, A. D., & Burke, P. J. (2002). A theory of self-esteem. *Social Forces, 80,* 1041–1068.

---

[25]See a lengthier discussion on the relationship between status and identity processes by Callero (this volume) and Hunt (this volume).

Cate, R. M., Lloyd, S. A., & Long, E. (1988). The role of rewards and fairness in developing premarital relation-shps. *Journal of Marriage and the Family, 50*, 443–452.

Cooley, C. H. ([1909] 1962). *Social organization.* New York: Scribner.

Fiske, S. T., & Taylor, S. E. (1991). *Social cognition.* New York: McGraw-Hill.

Hegtvedt, K. A. (1990). The effects of relationship structure on emotional responses to inequity. *Social Psychology Quarterly, 53*, 214–228.

Heise, D. R. (1979). *Understanding events: Affect and the construction of social action.* Cambridge: Cambridge University Press.

Homans, G. C. (1961). *Social behavior: Its elementary forms.* New York: Harcourt Brace and World Inc.

Jasso, G. (1980). A new theory of distributive justice. *American Sociological Review, 45*(1), 3–32.

Jasso, G. (1983). Fairness of individual rewards and fairness of the reward distribution: Specifying the inconsis-tency between the micro and macro principles of justice. *Social Psychology Quarterly, 46*(3), 185–199.

Major, B. (1987). Gender, justice, and the psychology of entitlement. In P. Shaver & C. Hendrick (Eds.), *Sex and gender* (pp. 124–148). Newbury Park: Sage.

Markovsky, B. (1985). Toward a multilevel distributive justice theory. *American Sociological Review, 50*, 822–839.

McCall, G. J., & Simmons, J. L. (1978). *Identities and interactions.* New York: Free Press.

Powers, W. T. (1973). *Behavior: The control of perception.* Chicago: Aldine Publishing.

Sedikides, C. (1993). Assessment, enhancement, and verification determinants of the self-evaluation process. *Journal of Personality and Social Psychology, 65*(2), 317–338.

Serpe, R. T., & Stryker, S. (1987). The construction of self and reconstruction of social relationships. In E. Lawler & B. Markovsky (Eds.), *Advances in group processes* (pp. 41–66). Greenwich, CT: JAI Press.

Shott, S. (1979). Emotion and social life: A symbolic interactionist analysis. *American Journal of Sociology, 84(6)*, 1317–1334.

Smith-Lovin, L., & Heise, D. R. (1988). *Analyzing social interaction: Advances in affect control theory.* New York: Gordon and Breach Science Publishers.

Steil, J. M. (1994). Equality and entitlement in marriage: Benefits and barriers. In M. J. Lerner & G. Mikula (Eds.), *Entitlement and the affectional bond* (pp. 229–258). New York: Plenum Press.

Stets, J. E. (1997). Status and identity in marital interaction. *Social Psychology Quarterly, 60*, 185–217.

Stets, J. E., & Burke, P. J. (1996). Gender, control, and interaction. *Social Psychology Quarterly, 59*, 193–220.

Stets, J. E., & Burke, P. J. (2000). Identity theory and social identity theory. *Social Psychology Quarterly, 63*, 224–237.

Stets, J. E., & Tsushima, T. (2001). Negative emotion and coping responses within identity control theory. *Social Psychology Quarterly, 64*, 283–295.

Stryker, S. (1980). *Symbolic interactionism: A social structural version.* Menlo Park: Benjamin Cummings.

Stryker, S. (1987). *The interplay of affect and identity: Exploring the relationships of social structure, social interaction, self, and emotion.* Chicago: American Sociological Association.

Stryker, S., & Burke, P. J. (2000). The past, present, and future of an identity theory. *Social Psychology Quarter-ly, 63*, 284–297.

Stryker, S., & Serpe, R. T. (1982). Commitment, identity salience, and role behavior: A theory and research exam-ple. In W. Ickes & E. S. Knowles (Eds.), *Personality, roles, and social behavior* (pp. 199–218). New York: Springer-Verlag.

Stryker, S., & Serpe, R. T. (1994). Identity salience and psychological centrality: Equivalent, overlapping, or complementary concepts? *Social Psychology Quarterly, 57*(1), 16–35.

Swann, W. B., Jr. (1990). To be adored or to be known?: The interplay of self-enhancement and self-verification. In E. T. Higgins & R. M. Sorrentino (Eds.), *Handbook of motivation and cognition* (pp. 408–450). New York: Guilford.

Swann, W. B., Jr., Griffin, J. J., Predmore, S. C., & Gaines, B. (1987). The cognitive-affective crossfire: When self-consistency confronts self-enhancement. *Journal of Personality and Social Psychology, 52*(5), 881–889.

Swann, W. B., Jr., & Hill, C. A. (1982). When our identities are mistaken: Reaffirming self-conceptions through social interaction. *Journal of Personality and Social Psychology, 43*(1), 59–66.

Thibaut, J. W., & Kelley, H. H. (1959). *The social psychology of groups.* New York: John Wiley and Sons Inc.

Thoits, P. A. (1983). Multiple identities and psychological well-being: A reformulation and test of the social iso-lation hypothesis. *American Sociological Review, 49*, 174–187.

Thoits, P. A. (1991). On merging identity theory and stress research. *Social Psychology Quarterly, 54*, 101–112.

Thoits, P. A. (1995). Identity-relevant events and psychological symptoms: A cautionary tale. *Journal of Health and Social Behavior, 36*(1), 72–82.

Tsushima, T., & Burke, P. J. (1999). Levels, agency, and control in the parent identity. *Social Psychology Quar-terly, 62*, 173–189.

Utne, M. K., Hatfield, E., Traupmann, J., & Greenberger, D. (1984). Equity, marital satisfaction, and stability. *Journal of Social and Personal Relationships, 1*, 323–332.

Walster, E., Walster, G., & Berscheid, E. (1978). *Equity theory and research.* Boston: Allyn and Bacon.

Chapter **8**

Feeling Good, Feeling Well
Identity, Emotion, and Health

LINDA E. FRANCIS

INTRODUCTION

Over the past decade, health psychologists have been finding empirical evidence that negative emotions and unexpressed emotions have negative effects on physiology and health (Kubzansky & Kawachi, 2000; Mayne, 1999; Baum & Posluszny, 1999). Correspondingly, other studies have found that the interpersonal expression of negative emotion about stressful or traumatic events produces health improvements (Pennebaker & Beall, 1986; Smyth et al., 1994). These findings are bolstered by results in the social support literature regarding psychological and emotional distress (Tyler & Hoyt, 2000; Lechner, 1993; Whelan, 1993; Thoits, 1995). However, to date, no explanation has been developed to explain why expressing emotion to others produces such positive health outcomes. Drawing on Identity Theory (Stryker, 1980; Stryker and Statham, 1986), Affect Control Theory (Heise, 1979; 1999), and sociological theories of emotion management (Francis, 1997; Thoits, 1996; Hochschild, 1983), this paper attempts to address this issues. In this chapter, I will develop a theoretical explanation of social interaction to suggest the utility of understanding the role of identity and affect in health.

STRESS, EMOTION, AND HEALTH

Findings over the past two decades on the social status gradient in health has lead to new interest in the social psychological impact of social structure. Research has found that controlling for all known health risks, including physical environment, genetics, health-related behavior (exercise, smoking, drinking, diet, etc.), and culture, and the lower that group's social status on any dimension (race, class, gender, etc.), the worse that group's average morbidity and mortality (Evans, Barer, and Marmor, 1994) . In addition, the lower the social status, the more prolonged and unrelieved are the physical symptoms of stress in reaction to social demands. Studies in biology have related such long-term stress to immune and endocrine anomalies, as well as such concrete outcomes as heart disease. In theory, then, it is this stress that is the connection between the universal health gradient and status. In other words, the negative emotional experiences of those of lower social status contribute substantively to their comparatively early deaths (Evans, Barer, and Marmor, 1994).

Sociologists have covered in detail the effects of social status gradients on emotions. In terms of class differences, Ochs and Schiefflin (1984) have demonstrated that children of different social classes are socialized to recognize and express different emotions. Hochschild (1983) has illustrated the demands of emotional labor among middle class service jobs such as flight attendants and bill collectors. Copp (1998) has further illuminated the impossible emotional labor asked of workers in low skilled social services jobs. Lively (1998) has shown that status differences within an office result in status differentials in the amount of emotion work required and the support given for it. Hochschild has also demonstrated gender differences in the demands placed on women compared to men in our society that have emotional repercussions. Steele (1994) has illustrated the management of identity and emotion that is required of a middle class black man in U.S. culture. Sociology, then, is well-versed in the relationship between social status and emotions.

We have some success as well in our studies relating emotions and social psychology to health (Ensel, 2000; Turner and Avison, 1992; Wickrama et al., 1997). For instance, research on stress and mental health has demonstrated the central importance of coping and social support resources in preventing or ameliorating psychological distress (Aneshensel, 1992; Ensel and Lin, 1991). Other studies have shown the social distribution of stress and health and mental health outcomes (Turner, Wheaton, and Lloyd, 1995; Turner and Lloyd, 1999; Williams, 1990; Ensel, 2000). However, with few exceptions (Peyrot et. al., 1999), results frequently reflect data from self-report measures, which are susceptible to social desirability, stigma, and even mood. Such findings could be strengthened by associations with empirical results from other fields which do collect physiological data, and build bridges that help to illustrate some of the consequences of our social environment.

On the other side of the social psychological divide, the field of health psychology has excelled in empirically demonstrating the connection between negative emotions and physical health. Indeed, one of the more interesting and consistent sets of findings in the field of health psychology has been the confirmation that emotions and emotional expression do indeed have direct impact on human physiology. Gross (1999), for instance, has demonstrated that suppressing negative emotion produces the types of physiological stress that are associated over the long term with heart disease. O'Sullivan (1999) has found that using a repressive coping style characterized by minimizing or denying stressful emotions has negative effects on the sympathetic nervous system. Ernst et al. (1999) have found clinical evidence that alexithymia (a form of dysfunctional expression of emotion) can be expressed as chronic pain.

Even more interesting, a number of health psychologists have found that certain forms of emotional expression can improve health outcomes. For instance, Spiegel et al. (1994) have shown that group therapy among metastatic cancer patients has not only positive psychosocial effects, but actually increases longevity. Frasure-Smith et al. have found that depression, anxiety, anger and emotional social support predict recovery from and relapse of myocardial infarction (1995). Pennebaker and his associates (1999; Spera, Buhrfiend and Pennebaker, 1994; Smyth et al., 1999; Greenberg, Wortman and Stone, 1996) have found that writing about severe negative emotional experiences has dramatic physical health benefits, including significantly fewer physician visits for illness, reductions in symptoms among sufferers of asthma and rheumatoid arthritis, reduced depressive symptoms and faster reemployment, and decreased psychological symptoms among trauma victims.

Over the course of several years, many scholars considering the effects of writing (Pennebaker, Greenberg et al., etc.) have sought to determine the mechanism through which expressing emotion impacts upon health. In other words, what are people doing in their emotional writing that generates such health benefits? What is the difference between those who improve their health and those who do not? Various psychological studies have examined this question, but with only modest success. Greenberg et al. (1996) have tested the hypothesis of catharsis and largely ruled it out. James Pennebaker and Martha Francis have studied word choice and writing structure, and drawn some conclusions that use of more positive emotion words and causation words are associated with increased positive health outcomes (Pennebaker & Francis, 1996). These findings have lead the authors to speculate about the role of creating a structured narrative or story of the event in resolving the associated emotional distress (Pennebaker & Seagal, 1999).

Such a speculation has immediate resonance for a symbolic interactionist. By giving symbolic representation to an event, an emotion, a situation, we have, in a very real sense, created it. And what we have created, we can recreate. Indeed, that is a fundamental tenet of symbolic interactionism and has formed the basis of much of the work done on emotions in sociology. From work first done in the seventies and eighties by Heise (1979, 1987), Hochschild (1978, 1983), Thoits (1985, 1986), Kemper (1978) and Scheff (1977, 1988), to more recent studies by Cahill (1994), Copp (1998), Konradi (1999), Robinson and Smith-Lovin (1999), and Lois (2001), we see the fundamental notion that emotions can be created and recreated in response to social stimuli.

EMOTION AND IDENTITY

It is my argument that from the study of social psychology in sociology, we can draw the tools to answer some of the questions raised by health psychologists on the connection between emotion, behavior, and health. A key feature of the expression of emotion in health psychology studies is that it is consistently emotional communication in question— that is, the research involves the verbal or written discussion of the emotion-causing experiences of the self and others. Thus, in some form, this expression is taking place in interaction between the self and others. Even in the case of writing, one is always writing to some objectified audience, even if only imaginary, or only reflexively to one's self. Given this communicative basis, theories of self and interaction are potential sources of theory for explaining the tie between emotions and health. In particular, I argue for the utility of Identity Theory, Affect Control Theory, and theories of emotion management (Hochschild, 1983; Thoits, 1986, 1996; Francis, 1997) in explaining how health outcomes are influenced by identity and emotion in interaction.

A number of sociologists have argued that emotion management often entails a cognitive or physical change in the situation in which the undesirable emotion has occurred. Hochschild (1983) argues that when a worker's experience of emotion is intractable, he or she will focus on those aspects of the situation which justify the emotion. Thoits (1985) also discusses cues of emotion that can be changed in order to change emotion, included situational cues. She makes the case that self-identity is one cue to an emotional situation that can be changed, potentially resulting in self-labeling. Heise (1979, 1990) has demonstrated that when faced with unexpected events, people are motivated to act in ways to return the situation to expected dimensions or seek new cues to explain the deflection away.

Research has illustrated how this process can occur interpersonally as well. Thoits (1996), for instance, has demonstrated how members of an encounter group manage each others' emotions to fit the norms of the group. In my own work (Francis, 1997), I have argued that support group leaders attempt to help their group members recover through redefining the situation until the members must enact new identities to fit the new definition. Irvine (1999) demonstrates how redefinition and restructuring of situations and emotions occur in a codependency support group.

In this paper, I explore the idea that a similar process is going on in health psychology studies of emotion: subjects are engaging in emotion management that reduces/eliminates the physiological effects caused by unresolved severe, traumatic, or chronic stress.

AFFECT CONTROL THEORY AND EMOTION MANAGEMENT

Symbolic interactionists believe that a situation can be redefined cognitively by focusing on different aspects of that situation. Affect control theory (Heise, 1979,1987; Heise & Weir, 1999; MacKinnon, 1994; Smith-Lovin, 1990; Smith, Matsuno and Ike, 2001) forthcoming) extends Mead's paradigm by demonstrating that the emotional elements of the situational definition can be altered in a similar fashion.

Heise (1979, 1987) has drawn on Osgood, May, and Miron (1975) to argue that people interpret the world in terms of three "EPA" dimensions: evaluation (good-bad, nice-awful), potency (strong-weak, large-small), and activity (lively-calm, fast-slow). People learn to associate certain enduring EPA ratings with certain identities. Thus a mother is rated as quite good, quite powerful, and neither particularly lively nor calm, while a gangster is rated as extremely bad, potent, and lively (Heise 1987). These enduring ratings are called "sentiments." When identities are enacted under various circumstances, events will occur which produce "transient" feelings that either confirm or conflict with the EPA sentiments associated with the identities. For example, a mother saving a baby confirms the sentiments associated with "mother," whereas a gangster saving a baby conflicts with the sentiments surrounding "gangster." The emotion that the agent experiences is due to this confirmation or conflict.

According to ACT, when a conflict or "deflection" occurs, the person is motivated to seek explanation and to find some means of returning the conflict to a confirmation of sentiments. Thus people seek for ways to qualify the situation and remove the deflection. For instance, Heise (1987) points out that people might look more closely to see whether the gangster actually kidnapped the baby rather than saving it. Alternatively, observers might discover that the gangster had children of his own, so the relevant identity is "father" rather than "gangster." A father saving a baby and a gangster kidnapping one confirm the sentiments respectively associated with "father" and "gangster."

In ACT terms, people may use emotion management along the EPA dimensions to resolve emotional deflection. I would argue, for instance, that the subjects in many of these health psychology experiments brought to the situation a ready-made deflection caused by a conflict between a transient feeling and an accustomed EPA sentiment. In many cases, this deflection is self-evident, such as a serious illness that calls into question the person's ability to continue as they have in the past. These subjects have been unable to resolve this deflection, or, alternatively, have resolved the deflection in such a way as to take on a label that harms his or her self-esteem or emotional well-being (Thoits, 1985; Heise and Britt,

1992). In addition, the health psychologists cited above would lead us to suspect such a long-standing deflection would have negative impact upon physical health as well.

In the course of explaining this deflection in support groups, writing, or therapy, people attribute specific identities, actions, and emotions to the actors in the situation. That is, actors reconstruct the situation in detail, possibly for the first time. As Pennebaker and Seagal (1999) have argued, memories are often comprised more of images and sensory impressions than of specific cognitive structures. Therefore creating a narrative is a means of defining the situation.

Once the situation is defined, the actor has the opportunity to explain the actions and feelings of all actors involved. This invites a thorough evaluation of the sentiments and disconfirmations of sentiments that have occurred. The person is asked to make sense of why the actors thought, felt, or behaved the way they did. Under these circumstances, others are requiring that the actor look closely at an uncomfortable disconfirmation of sentiments, which provides a prime opportunity to explain away or resolve that disconfirmation. In writing or talking to a receptive audience of similar others, a person can define (and refine) the elements of the situation so as to reduce the deflection and transform the experience into a confirmation of sentiments.

Most of ACT focuses on the affective changes that take place in every day interaction—usually common place situations with deflections that the person is able to resolve immediately, alone, and largely unaware. However, under some circumstances, deflections are not so easily addressed. Severe negative life events, are, by definition, highly stressful and emotional events that have enduring consequences. Under these conditions, resolving a deflection is likely to be much more difficult.

Heise (1979) has demonstrated that the size of the deflection—that is, the degree of difference between transient emotions and established sentiments—is a fundamental factor in explaining severity of emotion. In addition, as Stryker (1987) and Thoits (1991) argue, an additional crucial predictor of severity is the salience of the identity being affected.

IDENTITY THEORY AND EMOTIONAL INTENSITY

According to Identity Theory (Stryker, 1980, Serpe, 1987, Stryker and Serpe, 1994, Stryker and Burke, 2000), identities are arranged in a salience hierarchy. Salience is influenced primarily by commitment, or the degree to which each identity is enacted in interactions with others. As people will seek opportunities to enact salient identities, commitment to those identities remains high, thereby reinforcing their salience.

Similar to Thoits' (1991) argument about stress, I suggest that if a deflection occurs affecting a salient identity, it will generate a more intense emotion than will a similar deflection in a less salient identity. Heise has, of course, addressed this idea by demonstrating that salient identities are more positively evaluated, and disconfirming negative events create larger deflections (1979). However, in framing the point through Identity Theory, we can construct an argument for the persistence of deflections as well.

A highly salient identity, is one to which a person is highly committed and which they frequently enact with others. If a negative event occurs which compromises the enactment of this identity, it will have wide repercussions for the individual. In a sense, the deflection will be reinforced each time the individual encounters a situation where he or she would normally depend on that identity for interactional purposes. The person is then experiencing a persistent deflection, one that continues unresolved over time.

To cope with this kind of persistent deflection, the person has two choices: to resolve the deflection through redefinition, even if it means altering the identity affected (up to and including self-labeling); or to escape the deflection by avoiding interaction that produces commitment to the affected identity. In this case, salience drops, and the degree of deflection is reduced. Indeed, as I have argued in other research (1997, 1998), in cases of very stressful life events, a person may engage in both strategies.

The latter strategy, that of escaping the deflection, is not always possible, of course. If the life event in question is a serious health problem, for instance, such a strategy would require denial of the problem, an approach which is neither beneficial nor effective in the long term. The first strategy, that of resolution, is therefore the strategy of choice. It is, however, not likely to be an easy endeavor to redefine situations involving a highly salient part of the self.

EMOTION MANAGEMENT AND HEALTH

Given the above argument, a person's attempts at managing emotion resulting from threats to salient identities are likely to involve other techniques of emotion management first. Thoits (1986) and Pollak and Thoits (1989) have identified several possible ways that people try to manage emotion. There are four cues of emotion that people depend upon to identify and change their emotions: physiological cues, expressive gestures, cultural labels, and situational cues. Each of these cues also reflects a domain which can be changed either cognitively or behaviorally in order to manage undesirable emotions. For instance, a person might change their expressive gestures behaviorally by suppressing a smile, or taking a deep breath to keep from crying. In another case, a person could cognitively change their cultural label, saying they are not angry just disappointed. As both Thoits (1989) and Hochschild (1983) note, changing the situation (whether cognitively or behaviorally) is liable to be the most difficult and complex task, because it frequently involves the actions of other people. As a result, that technique is often the last resort.

Modification of cues from the first three domains, physiology, expressions, and labels, does not lead to resolving the deflection that caused the emotion in the first place. That is, those cues are not addressing the source of the emotion directly. These kinds of actions could arguably fall under the category of what health psychologists call the "suppression" of emotion (Martin et. al., 1999; Lehrer, 1998; Petrie et al., 1998). This kind of "suppressive" emotion management, then, can itself have negative health effects, above and beyond the stress of the persistent deflection. In cases of severe life events involving salient identities, using suppressive emotion management techniques over the long term could potentially exacerbate health problems and symptomology.

HEALTH OUTCOMES AND THE
(RE)DEFINITION OF THE SITUATION

Returning to the original argument that unexpressed and suppressed negative emotions have negative physiological consequences, we can now make a direct connection to the health benefits of expressing emotion. We can argue that negative emotions result from negative deflections from accustomed sentiments. Managing the resulting emotions without eliminating the source of the emotion is suppressive, and therefore can produce potential harmful health outcomes. Resolving deflections, on the other hand, would ameliorate negative affect at the source. At minimum, this should have positive health consequences, by eliminating the negative health effects caused by the negative affect and its suppression. Expression allows a return to cognitive, emotional, and physical equilibrium.

Drawing from the preceding arguments, I suggest a key to improving health outcomes through emotional expression is the resolution of persistent deflections affecting salient identities. As stated earlier, resolving such deflections involves fundamental redefining of the situation in which that identity is enacted. This is a difficult task, and one that people may not know how to undertake on their own. This is where the communication of emotion to others is helpful. The process of communication to others requires that the event be structured into a coherent narrative, with explanations or attributions about why circumstances occurred as they did. Such a structured, conscious, deliberate effort at definition requires more concentration and thought than reviewing memories of events internally. Such effort can clarify the respective relations of actors, actions, and motivations of the event producing the deflection, and encourage redefinition of the situation.

The two ways that this kind of emotional communication has been studied, through support groups (Spiegel, 1998) and through writing (Pennebaker, 1993; 1999), are both likely to produce redefinition. In support groups, the experiences of similar others give them insight that helps in the definition process. This may be why social support is most effective from similar others: they are more than merely sympathetic, they understand how the deflections might best be resolved. In this light, social support could be conceptualized as "assisted deflection resolution." Social support, then, is a resource people can use to aid them in the difficult task of resolution rather than suppression.

In writing, the same opportunity for redefinition and resolution exists. While the person does not have the help of supportive others, they have other advantages. Writing, for instance, entails even more structure and coherency than does speaking. It also allows for uninterrupted thought, and anonymity allows some protection from embarrassment or other negative emotions. Regardless of the mechanism, both forms of the communication of emotion provide a venue to undertake the difficult task of resolving persistent deflections involving salient identities. In other words, we would expect that emotional narratives *should* have a positive effect on health.

MODEL

On the basis of this argument, I propose a model of the connection between identity, emotional communication and health. When a negative event occurs affecting a salient identity and producing a deflection from established sentiments, the result is liable to be very negative, stressful emotions. If the actor does not resolve the deflection, that person can manage the negative emotion in one of two ways: (1) by avoiding enactment of the affected identity, which will reduce identity salience, thereby reducing the severity of the deflection and making the emotions easier to suppress; or (2) by engaging directly in suppressive emotion management. Suppressing negative emotions will have a negative influence on health outcomes. Only by redefining the event (e.g., through communication) can it be resolved, resulting in a return to established sentiments and the elimination of negative health effects. This process is illustrated in Figure 1.

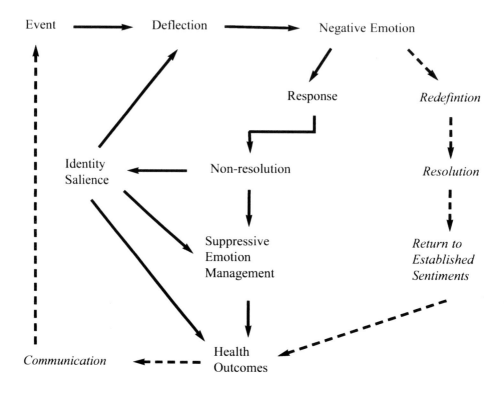

Figure 1. Emotions to Health Process.

DISCUSSION

Some of the interesting implications of this model lie in their congruence with on-going research by Pennebaker and his associates (Pennebaker and Seagel, 1999, Niederhoffer and Pennebaker, 2002). Recent works by Pennebaker and his students have shown that writing emotional essays increases working memory and reduces intrusive thoughts. In addition, these effects are most significant when writing about negative events, and indeed, the greater the negative stress, the greater the effect.

The model proposed here provides potential explanations for all of these findings. First, as Heise (2002) has observed, negative deflections are more likely to produce more stress for more people:

> ... for individuals with positive selves, good events like becoming a parent or getting a promotion can be stressful, but bad events generate more deflection and in general are more stressful than good events. On the other hand, both good and bad events are stressful for individuals with negative selves, and such individuals thereby are susceptible to more stress and more of the consequences of stress than are individuals with positive selves (p. 3).

If negative events are generally more stressful for all people, then leaving the associated emotions unexpressed or suppressed will have a greater physiological impact than the emotions of positive events. Resolving negative events, then, will produce a larger amelioration in returning to equilibrium, and therefore a greater potential health improvement.

Returning to equilibrium by resolving a deflection also offers a potential explanation for why disclosing should reduce intrusive thoughts and increase working memory. A deflection is caused by an emotional variation from accustomed sentiments about a person, action or object. Leaving such a variation unresolved means that a piece of one's picture of the environment in which one lives is not in harmony with the rest. It is askew, and thus potentially a source of psychological discomfort and distraction when present, just as something physiologically askew causes physical discomfort and distraction. Imagine having a bad cavity in one's tooth. While it might not be actively painful all the time, relevant situations (eating, drinking hot or cold beverages, brushing teeth) produces discomfort and a reminder that something is not right. This inspires a tendency to repeated poke at the tooth with the tongue, shy away from certain activities, and generally worry about things that might cause pain. The sense of psychological discomfort due to an unresolved deflection could potentially be akin to this kind of perpetual stress of discomfort and of avoiding situations with the potential to activate the discomfort. Such stress would be distracting and intrusive, especially if the stress involved a salient (and frequently enacted) identity.

Resolving such a deflection would remove the psychological irritant, thereby eliminating the distraction and reducing intrusive thoughts. By allowing the person to revert to accustomed sentiments, resolution would reduce cognitive conflict and allow habitual patterns of thought to reassert themselves. The individual would no longer need to waste energy (and working memory) on avoiding, coping with, or managing emotions regarding the deflection. Thus resolving a substantial negative deflection in a salient identity would logically free a person from intrusive thoughts and increase working memory. The greater the stress from the event, the greater the benefit. Pennebaker's findings, therefore, support the theoretical model of this paper.

CONCLUSION: IDENTITY, EMOTION, AND HEALTH

Thus do I offer a sociological explanation of a heretofore psychological and biological phenomenon. From this stems the subtitle of my chapter: "Identity, Emotion, and Health." Improved health outcomes, in the model proposed here, are a product of the resolution of deflection and the elimination of the negative health consequences of enduring stress and suppressed emotion. Following the argument of the paper, however, the appropriateness of the primary title, "Feeling Good, Feeling Well," becomes less clear. It is indeed the case that one must return to positive sentiments in order to have health benefits from disclosure? Or would it also work to return to accustomed sentiments that are negative? The answer may lie in whether the experiencing person has positive sentiments about the salient identity in question. This, however, must remain unclear until the model is empirically tested.

A final point about this model is its utility in pointing out the relevance of Identity theory to a much wider realm of applications than heretofore studied. For instance, if this model is valid, then identity becomes an important medical as well as social psychological construct. It achieves useful practical as well as theoretical purposes. For Sociology and the social sciences, however, the significance is yet greater. Identity Theory can be seen as a critical lynchpin connecting multiple fields of study. Such an interdisciplinary mosaic opens whole new vistas of study in the area of connections between stress, emotion, and health.

REFERENCES

Aneshensel, C. S. (1992). Social Stress: Theory and Research. *Annual Review of Sociology*, 18: 15–38.

Aneshensel, C. S. and Rutter, C. M. (1991). Social Structure, Stress, and Mental Health: Competing Conceptual and Analytical Models. *American Sociological Review*, 56(2): 166–178.

Baum, A., and Poluszny, D. M. (1999). Health Psychology: Mapping biobehavioral contributions to health and illness. *Annual Review of Psychology*, 50: 137–163.

Cahill, S. E. (1999). Emotional Capital and Professional Socialization: The Case of Mortuary Science Students (and Me). *Social Psychology Quarterly*, 62(2): 101–116.

Christensen, N. J., Jensen, E. W. (1994). Effect of Psychosocial Stress and Age on Plasma Norepinephrine Levels: A review. *Psychosomatic Medicine*, 56(1):77–83.

Copp, M. (1998). When Emotion Work Is Doomed to Fail: Ideological and Structural Constraints on Emotion Management. *Symbolic Interaction*, 21(3): 299–328.

Donnelly, D.A., & Murray, E.J. (1991). "Cognitive and Emotional Changes in Written Essays and Therapy Interviews." *Journal of Social and Clinical Psychology*, 10, 334–350.

Ensel, W.M. (2000). Age, the Stress Process, and Physical Distress: The Role of Distal Stressors. *Journal of Aging and Health*, 12(2): 139–168.

Ensel, W. M. and Lin, N. (1991). The Life Stress Paradigm and Psychological Distress. *Journal of Health and Social Behavior*, 32(4): 321–341.

Ernst, H., Key, J. D., and Koval, M.S. (1999). Alexithymia in an adolescent with agenesis of the corpus callosum and chronic pain. *Journal of the American Academy of Child & Adolescent Psychiatry*, 38(10): 1212–1213.

Evans, R.G., Barer, M. L. and Marmor, T. R. (1994). *Why Are Some People Healthy and Others Not?: The Determinants of Health of Populations*. New York: Aldine de Gruyter.

Francis, L.E. (1997). Ideology and Emotion Management: Redefining Identity in Two Support Groups. *Social Psychology Quarterly*, 60(2): 153–171

Frasure-Smith, N., Lesperance, F., Talajic, M. (1995). The Impact of Negative Emotions on Prognosis Following Myocardial Infarction: Is it more than depression? *Health Psychology*, 14(5): 388–398.

Greenberg, M.A., Wortman, C. B., and Stone, A.A. (1996). Emotional Expression and Physical Health: Revising Traumatic Memories or Fostering Self-Regulation? *Journal of Personality and Social Psychology*, 71(3): 588–602.

Gross, J. (1999). Emotion regulation and health. Keynote address at the *Second International Conference on the (Non)Expression of Emotions in Health and Disease*. Tilburg, The Netherlands.

Heise, D. R. (2002). *Affect Control Theory: Likelihoods*. Retrieved September 19, 2002, from Indiana University Department of Sociology Web Site: www.indiana.edu/ ~socpsych/ACT/acttutorial/likeliho.htm

Heise, D. R. (1999). Controlling Affective Experiences Interpersonally. *Social Psychology Quarterly*, 62(1) March: 4–16.

Heise, D. R. (1979). *Understanding Events*. New York: Cambridge University Press.

Heise, D. R. (1987). Affect Control Theory: Concepts and Model. *Journal of Mathematical Sociology*, 13:1–33.

Heise, D.R., and Weir, B. (1999). A Test of Symbolic Interactionist Predictions about Emotions in Imagined Situations. *Symbolic Interaction*, 22(1): 139–161.

Hochschild, A.R. (1979). Emotion Work, Feeling Rules, and Social Structure. *American Journal of Sociology*, 85:551–75.

Hochschild, A.R. (1983). *The Managed Heart: The Commercialization of Human Feeling*. Berkeley and Los Angeles: University of California Press.

Konradi, A. (1999). I Don't Have to Be Afraid of You: Rape Survivors' Emotion Management in Court. *Symbolic Interaction*, 22(1): 45–77.

Kemper, T. D. (1978). *A Social Interaction Theory of Emotions*. New York: Wiley and Sons.

Kubansky, L. D., and Kawachi, I. (2000). Going to the Heart of the Matter: Do negative emotions cause coronary heart disease? *Journal of Psychosomatic Research*, 48(4–5): 323–337.

Lechner, V. M. (1993). Support Systems and Stress Reduction among Workers Caring for Dependent Parents. *Social Work*, 28(4): 461–469.

Lehrer, P. M. (1998). Emotionally Triggered Asthma: A review of research literature and some hypotheses for self-regulation. *Applied Psychophysiology & Biofeedback*, 23(1): 13–41.

Littrell, J. (1998). Is the Reexperience of Painful Emotion Therapeutic? *Clinical Psychology Review*, 18(1): 71–102.

Lively, K. J. (2001). Emotions in the Workplace: Research, Theory, and Practice. *Work and Occupations*, 28(4)501–504.

Lois, J. (2001). Managing Emotions, Intimacy, and Relationships in a Volunteer Search and Rescue Group. *Journal of Contemporary Ethnography*, 30(2)131–179.

MacKinnon, N. J. (1994). *Symbolic Interaction as Affect Control*. Albany: SUNY Press.

Martin, R., Wan, C. K., David, J. P., Wegner, E. L., Olson, B. D., Watson, D. (1999). Style of Anger Expression: Relation to expressivity, personality and health. *Personality and Social Psychology Bulletin*, 25(10): 1196–1207.

Mayne, T. J. (1999). Negative Affect and Health: The importance of being earnest. *Cognition and Emotion, Special Issue: Functional Accounts of Emotion*, 13(5): 601–635.

Murray, E.J., Lamnin, A.D., and Carver, C.S. (1989). Emotional Expression in Written Essays and Psychotherapy. *Journal of Social & Clinical Psychology*, 8: 414–429.

Niederhoffer, K. G. and Pennebaker, J. W. (2002). Sharing One's Story: On the benefits of writing or talking about emotional experience. Pp. 573–583 in Snyder, C.R. and Lopez, S. J. (Eds.) *Handbook of Positive Psychology*. London: Oxford University Press.

Osgood, C., May, W.H., and Miron, M.S. (1975). *Cross-Cultural Universals of Affective Meaning*. Urbana: University of Illinois Press.

Pennebaker, J. W. (1999). The Health Benefits of Narrative. *Journal of Clinical Psychology*, October, 1999.

Pennebaker, J. W. (1993). Putting Stress into Words: Health, linguistic, and therapeutic implications. *Behavior Research and Therapy*, 31(6): 539–548.

Pennebaker, J.W. and Beall, S.K. (1986). Confronting a Traumatic Event: Toward an Understanding of Inhibition and Disease. *Journal of Abnormal Psychology*, 95: 274–281.

Pennebaker, J. W. and Francis, M. (1996). Cognitive, Emotional, and language Processes in Disclosure. *Cognition and Emotion*, 10: 601–626.

Pennebaker, J. W. and Seagal, J. D. (1999). Forming a Story: The Health Benefits of Narrative. *Journal of Clinical Psychology*, 55(10): 1243–1254.

Petrie, K. J., Booth, R. J., Pennebaker, J.W. (1998). The Immunological Effects of Thought Suppression. *Journal of Personality and Social Psychology*, 75(5): 1264–1272.

Pollak, L. H. and Thoits, P.A. (1989). Processes in Emotional Socialization. *Social Psychology Quarterly*, 52(1): 22–34.

Robinson, D. T. and Smith-Lovin,L. (1999). Emotion Display as a Strategy for Identity Negotiation. *Motivation and Emotion*, 23(2): 73–104.

Scheff, T. J. (1999). *Emotions, the Social Bond, and Human Reality*. Cambridge: Cambridge University Press.

Serpe, R. T. (1987). Stability and Change in Self: A Structural Symbolic Interactionist Explanation. *Social Psychology Quarterly*, 50(1)44–55.

Smith-Lovin, L. (1990). Emotion as the Confirmation and Disconfirmation of Identity: An Affect Control Model. In T. D. Kemper, (Ed.), *Research Agendas in the Sociology of Emotions*, Albany: SUNY Press.

Smyth, J. M., Stone, A. A., Hurewitz, A., and Kaell, A. (1999). Effects of Writing about Stressful Experiences on Symptom Reduction in Patients with Asthma or Rheumatoid Arthritis. *Journal of the American Medical Association*, 281(14): 1304–1309.

Spiegel, D., Bloom, J. R., Kraemer, H. C., and Gottheil, E. (1994). Effect of Psychosocial Treatment on Survival of Patients With Metastatic Breast Cancer. Pp. 468–477 in Steptoe, A. and Wardle, J. (Eds.) *Psychosocial Processes and Health*. Cambridge: Cambridge University Press.

Spera, S. P., Buhrfeind, E. D., and Pennebaker, J. W. (1994). Expressive writing and coping with job loss. *Academy of Management Journal*, 37(3): 722–733.

Staske, S. A. (1998). The Normalization of Problematic Emotion in Conversations between Close Relational Partners: Interpersonal Emotion Work. *Symbolic Interaction*, 21(1): 59–86.

Stryker, S. (1980) *Identity Theory: A Social Structural Version*. Menlo Park: Benjamin/Cummings Co.

Stryker, S. and Burke, P. (2000). The Past, Present, and Future of an Identity Theory. *Social Psychology Quarterly*, 63(4): 284–297.

Stryker, S., and Serpe, R.T. (1994). Identity Salience and Psychological Centrality: Equivalent, Overlapping, or Complementary Concepts? *Social Psychology Quarterly*, 57(1)16–35.

Thoits, Peggy A. 1985. "Self-Labeling Processes in Mental Illness: the Role of Emotional Deviance." *American Journal of Sociology* 91: 221–49.

Thoits, P. A. (1986). Social Support as Coping Assistance. *Journal of Consulting and Clinical Psychology*, 54: 416–23.

Thoits, P. A. (1989). The Sociology of Emotions. *Annual Review of Sociology*, 15: 317–342.

Thoits, P. A. On Merging Identity Theory and Stress Research. *Social Psychology Quarterly*, 54(2): 101–112.

Thoits, P. A. (1996). Managing the Emotions of Others. *Symbolic Interaction*, 19(2): 85–109.

Thoits, P. A. (1995). Stress, Coping, and Social Support Processes: Where Are We? What Next? *Journal of Health and Social Behavior*, extra issue: 53–79.

Turner, J. R., and Lloyd, D. A. (1999). The Stress Process and the Social Distribution of Depression. *Journal of Health and Social Behavior*, 40(4): 374–404.

Turner, J. R., and Avison, W.R. (1992). Innovations in the Measurement of Life Stress: Crisis Theory and the Significance of Event Resolution. *Journal of Health and Social Behavior*, 33(1): 36–50.

Turner, J. R., Wheaton, B., and Lloyd, D. A. (1995). The Epidemiology of Social Stress. *American Sociological Review*, 60(1): 104–125.

Tyler, K. A., and Hoyt, D. R. (2000). The Effects of an Acute Stressor on Depressive Symptoms among Older Adults: The Moderating Effects of Social Support and Age. *Research on Aging*, 22(2): 143–164.

Whelan, C. T. (1993). The Role of Social Support in Mediating the Psychological Consequences of Economic Stress. *Sociology of Health and Illness*, 15(1): 86–101.

Wickrama, K. A. S., Lorenz, F. O., Conger, R. D., Matthews, L., and Elder,G., Jr. (1997). Linking Occupational Conditions to Physical Health through Marital, Social, and Interpersonal Processes. *Journal of Health and Social Behavior*, 38(4): 363–375.

Williams, D. R. (1990). Socioeconomic Differentials in Health: A Review and Redirection. *Social Psychology Quarterly*, 53(2): 81–99.

Chapter **9**

Interaction, Emotion, and Collective Identities

Edward J. Lawler

INTRODUCTION

This chapter poses the question: *How do emotional aspects of social interaction affect the emergence and salience of collective identities?* I assume that social interaction inherently involves an implicit or explicit joint task—namely to accomplish some result that can only be produced with others. The most fundamental "task" of social interaction can be construed as the coordination and alignment of behavior, such that actors successfully conclude the interaction episode. Essential to this task is a working consensus about definitions of self and other in the social situation, i.e., consensual self-other identities. A central component of my argument is that social interaction has emotional effects that vary with the success of actors at accomplishing this fundamental task. This paper theorizes the conditions under which emotional effects of social interaction promote collective identities that bridge or transcend self-other role identities.

A joint task implies at least two actors in interaction who are aware of each other and who orient their behavior to each other. Examples of joint tasks include two friends deciding how to spend an evening together in a mutually-satisfying way; two academic departments developing a cross-disciplinary program for students; or a couple dividing responsibility for child care. A more complicated example is a merger between two large corporations, which actually involves a vast array of more specific joint tasks that need to be accomplished for the merger to "come off." Regardless of the particular task content, social interaction inherently entails one of more *joint* tasks that may or may not be accomplished by the actors. I argue that the *jointness* of the interactional task is the fundamental basis for the emergence or activation of a collective identity. This ostensibly occurs when individual actors interpret their own feelings, emanating from an episode of social interaction, in collective terms (see also Durkheim 1915; Collins 1981, 1989; Lawler and Thye 1999; Lawler 2001).

Emotions are defined as transitory positive or negative evaluative states that have neurological and cognitive features (Kemper 1978; Izard 1991). The focus here are emotions or feeling states that are detected and perceived by the actors. I assume that such emotions both stimulate and respond to cognition and, as a result, they are a component of actors' "definition of the situation." Important to my approach is a distinction, in Weiner's (1986) attribution theory of emotion, between *global* (i.e., "primitive" in Weiner's terms) and *specific* emotions (see also Lawler 2001). Global feelings are initial emotional responses such as pleasure, enthusiasm, displeasure, and sadness. Specific emotions have targets—self and other—and include shame, anger, gratitude, and pride. According to Weiner, global feelings are not under the control of actors; they simply happen to them (Hochschild 1979); whereas, the specific emotions develop from an interpretation (attribution) of the global emotions, thereby making more concrete the meaning of more global feelings. Following a recent "affect theory of social exchange," (Lawler 2001), I adopt this distinction and use it to show how the emotional aspects of social interaction are involved in role and collective identities.

To address the theoretical question above, I integrate ideas from exchange theories of commitment (e.g., Cook and Emerson 1984; Kollock 1995; Lawler and Yoon 1996) with ideas from structural identity theories (Stryker 1980; McCall and Simmons 1978; Burke 1991). The main claim from research on exchange is that repetitive exchange among the same actors enhances their commitment to one another over time (Kollock 1995, Lawler and Yoon 1996). The main claim from identity theory is that interactional or affective commitments determine the salience of different role-based identities (Stryker 1980; Stryker and Serpe 1994). The backdrop for this paper is a deduction from these two claims—namely, that repetitive exchange should affect the salience of actors' identities. Repeated interaction to solve joint tasks generates emotions that objectify and make salient actors' common or collective identities. Broadly, an underlying objective of this paper is to identify, analyze, and build on points of similarity and complementarities between exchange and symbolic interaction perspectives on how micro orders develop (see Lawler 2002).

BACKGROUND

One of the most enduring contributions of symbolic interaction in sociology is an unequivocal and single-minded focus on social interaction as a foundation of social life. No other sociological tradition takes social interaction more seriously or accords it more power or force in the social world. Interaction is highly problematic and thus there is much "cognitive" or "interpretive" work for actors as they enact their action plans and adapt them continuously. This general image of social interaction is consistent with our assumption that interaction is inherently a joint task, however the task of interacting, as conceived by symbolic interaction theory, can be rather daunting. Many symbolic interactionists conceptualize social interaction as so tenuous, fluid, and unpredictable, that it is not clear how people could have the reserves of energy to continually "construct interaction" almost *de novo* (Blumer 1969). Careful attention to *social context*, however, mitigates this "excessive fluidity" problem. The social context provides language, standard meanings, background expectations, rules, and roles, expectations, and so forth; these elements of the context make social interaction possible and the construction of identities easier. *Contextualizing* social interaction has been a pervasive problem for symbolic interactionist theory.

This problem can be traced George Herbert Mead's (1934) classic analysis of the "generalized other." Mead posited that people develop ties or relationships not only with specific others but also with symbolic social units (groups, communities, societies). The concept of generalize other was Mead's way to give social interaction context. In fact, there is an affinity between Mead's notion of specific and generalized others to Parsons' (1951) argument that person-to-person and person-to-group ties are dual sources of social order. Of special relevance to this paper, Mead's analysis suggests the importance of distinguishing self-other ("role") identities, that are primarily person-to-person, and collective identities, that are primarily person-to-group (see Stryker 2000).

In a recent edited volume, linking identity and social movement theories, Stryker (et al 2000) puts forth several definitions that guide this paper. An identity is defined as " . . . an internalized set of meanings attached to a role played in a network of social relationships . . . " (p. 6). Identities are structurally based in positions or roles, and the salience of identities varies (Stryker 1980). "Role identities" capture the generic meaning of identities in structural symbolic interaction (see also McCall and Simmons 1978). Collective identities are "emergent, shared beliefs about membership, boundaries, and activities . . . " of a group (p. 6). They are constructed in social interaction, organized around or directed at shared interests and purposes, and activated by specific issues, experiences, or tasks. Collective identities are tenuous and impermanent but, once formed or activated, they orient and organize social interaction among those who share the given collective identity. In other words, collective identities involve a sense of "we-ness;" they bridge the more enduring structurally-based identities that generate a sense of "me-ness" (Thoits and Virshup 1995; Snow and McAdam 2000).[1]

The work of structurally oriented symbolic interactionists, such as Stryker (1980), Burke 1991, and Heise (1979), carefully nest social interaction in the roles actors occupy. I suggest that such identities are an important backdrop for interactions that generate and sustain overarching collective identities. Role identities are based on structural interdependencies. A parent cannot enact and sustain his or her role identity as a parent without the "help" of offspring, just as the role identity of child cannot be enacted and affirmed without the parent. The parent has to enact the role of parent and the child has to treat the parent like a parent; moreover the parent has to see that the child is treating them as a parent, and the child has to see that the parent is acting like a parent. Role identities, while strongly structural, can only be enacted and affirmed jointly with others and, in this sense, they are joint tasks in themselves (McCall and Simmons 1978).

To summarize and elaborate, there are several differences between role and collective identities, important to my analysis. First of all, role-identities are relatively fixed in the social structure; the roles enacted are in part "made" by the actor's but the force of the larger structure on the behavior of the actor's remains strong (Stryker 1981; Turner 1962, 1978). Collective identities are relatively fluid, evolving features of self-other definitions. They accentuate social characteristics held in common, interpret and affirm shared experiences, and give meaning to group memberships (Melucci 1995; Klandermans and de Weerd 2000). Stryker's (1980, 1981; Stryker and Serpe 1994). Second, role definitions generally contain fundamental cultural expectations for occupants, and these are exogenous. Collective identities and

---

[1] Role and collective identities are distinguished from personal and social identities. A personal identity is a definition of self on personal dimensions or characteristics (e.g., honest, hard-working), whereas a social identity is a definition in terms of meaningful social categories (e.g., gender, race, education). Group identities are treated as social categories in the social identity literature (Tajfel and Turner 1986). Following Stryker 2000) and others (Thoits and Virshup 1995), we treat them as collective identities.

associated expectations are endogenous and develop around common tasks, goals, and interests. They can be construed as "localized" overarching symbols of common activities and experiences based partly on the emotions felt and shared with others (see Collins 1989). Third, collective identities are the basis for "weak ties," that cross or bridge existing structural dimensions or cleavages; whereas role identities imply strong ties forged and maintained in part by social structures. Collective identities can be viewed as an important source of non-institutional connections among roles.

This chapter theoretically links the emotional effects of social interaction to the development of collective identities. Social interaction has emotional consequences for individuals (positive or negative), and to the degree that these emotions are attached to a social unit, membership in that unit becomes a salient collective identity. Collective identities are connected to role identities, in part because enacted role identities can have the same emotional effects as consummated exchange. Reaching a consensual definition of self and other is a joint task, similar in form to negotiating an explicit exchange, and we expect the emotional effects to be similar as well. To theorize the emotion-to-collective identity process, the analysis draws heavily from the social exchange perspective, in particular the theory of relational cohesion (Lawler and Yoon 1993, 1996; Lawler, Thye, and Yoon 2000; Thye, Yoon, and Lawler 2002) and a recently formulated "affect theory of social exchange" (Lawler 2001, 2002). Broad areas of convergence between exchange and symbolic interaction perspectives frame the theoretical analysis, and I now turn to these.

Social Exchange and Symbolic Interaction Approaches

Social exchange and structural symbolic interaction make different fundamental assumptions about people and social interaction. Exchange theorists assume self-interested actors who respond to rewards (payoffs) and costs (punishments). Actors are dependent on one or more others for access to outcomes they value; and structures of interdependence determine who is likely to interact and exchange with whom (Molm and Cook 1995). Social interaction is a process through which actors provide valued benefits to one another. A *successful* interaction, therefore, is one in which actors provide each other more benefits than they can achieve from alternative others.

In contrast, symbolic interactionists assume actors who ascribe meaning to self and other in the context, and act in accord with these meanings. At the outset of an interaction episode, meanings or definitions are provisional. Actors develop initial expectations by applying "names" to self and other (Stryker 1980). These then are further refined in the interaction, as actors define themselves with reference to the particular other and the other with reference to themselves. These self and other definitions are interdependent. A *successful* interaction, therefore, is one in which actors establish and act in terms of consensual definitions of self and other.

In exchange theory, social structures entail exogenous incentives, whereas in structural symbolic interaction, social structures are objectified definitions of self and other with both exogenous and endogenous aspects. From exchange theory, actors pursue rewards and avoid punishments in the context of structural constraints and opportunities. In symbolic interaction, actors pursue meaning and the affirmation of self-other identities in the context of socio-cultural roles (Stryker 1980, 1981). In both theoretical perspectives, underlying interdependencies are the structural foundation for interaction, cognitive processes intervene between structure and behavior, and some form of consensus or concurrence is the relevant outcome.

I focus here on a particular tradition of symbolic interaction: *identity theory*. Turner's (1962) classic work treats the self in terms of roles that entail structural givens but principally are "made" by the actors in interaction with others. McCall and Simmons (1966,1978) develop an explicit "role-identity model" that assumes the self is composed of a set of role-based identities with some being more prominent (central) than others. They argue that identities are imagined, idealized role behaviors or performances, and that these require continual legitimation and affirmation. The focus of McCall and Simmons is the dramaturgical dynamics of the joint activity in which identities are negotiated and renegotiated.

Stryker's (1980) approach strengthens the structural theme in Turner's (1962) work, arguing that identities are based in roles that carry with them "names" and associated cultural expectations. Heise (1979) develops an affect-control theory of the self in which the "naming" of each other is role-, group-, or individual-based. His is a relational approach in which people bring fundamental identities to any situation, and redefine situational identities in this context. Maintaining consistency between fundamental (trans-situational) identities and transient (situational) identities is a core tendency produced by the emotional response to inconsistency. Burke (1991) develops a cybernetic model of identity that emphasizes reflexivity and feedback. His focus is how individuals' process and react to reflected appraisals and how identities therefore evolve and change over time in relationships. The comparison of reflected appraisals with identity standards is central to this argument. With all of the above theoretical approaches to identity, actors integrate fixed, structural features of the situation (roles) with actions and reactions of others (reflexivity) and develop definitions of self and other for that situation.

In this context, my theoretical argument is built on four areas of convergence between exchange theorists (Emerson 1972, 1981) and structurally-oriented symbolic interactionists (Stryker 1980, 1981). First, social interaction is assumed to be problematic. For symbolic interaction, the key "task" facing each actor is defining the situation, especially who they and the others are or will be in the situation. For exchange theory, the main problem is uncertainty about the other's and even one's own intentions, goals, and constraints (Emerson 1981; Cook and Emerson 1984). While these notions are complementary, the symbolic interactionist conception is broader than and can subsume the uncertainty problem of exchange theory. Identities and identity affirmations are key ways to handle the uncertainty problem posed by exchange theory, because having a consensual view of self and other renders the behavior of each predictable.

Second, social interaction occurs in the context of structural constraints and opportunities, involved in interdependent roles (Stryker 1980) or positions (Emerson 1981). For exchange theory, benefits or outcomes are interdependent, while for symbolic interactionists, identities are interdependent. Reward structures are the foundation for interdependencies in the former, and role structures are the foundation for them in the latter. Just as the outcomes of social exchange are joint social products of the interaction, the identities affirmed and shaped in an interaction are joint social products. For both theoretical perspectives, structures are exogenous, but also modified or changed in the course of social interaction.

Third, for each theory, choice is a central activity for individuals (see Emerson 1981; Stryker 1981). From exchange theory, actors choose partners (if alternatives exist) and make choices about what to give and what to expect the other to give. From symbolic interaction theory, actors choose which identities to act in terms of and how exactly to enact them in a concrete social situation, e.g., a parent decides whether to spend the afternoon with his or her children or with friends (Stryker 1980; McCall and Simmons 1978).

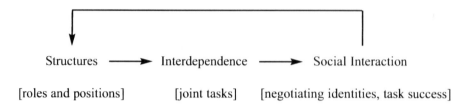

Figure 1. Convergence of Symbolic Interaction and Exchange Theory.

The nature of these choices is different. Choosing a partner in exchange does not necessarily imply a choice of identity because the choice could be among others with the same identity (e.g., a graduate student choosing a faculty advisor); whereas, choosing an identity does not necessarily imply a particular partner with whom to interact.

The diagram in Figure 1 captures the fundamental points of convergence between symbolic interactionist and social exchange approaches, that this paper builds on. From the figure, social structures create interdependencies among actors that lead them to interact with one another. Roles and positions are key elements of the social structure, joint tasks and products are key aspects of interdependence, and social interaction entails a negotiation of both identities and outcomes. The "negotiation" of identities or of exchange terms has a reciprocal effect on social structure (McCall and Simmons 1978; Willer 2000). This reciprocity of interaction and structure reflects the larger dynamic of self and society, assumed by symbolic interactionists (Stryker 1980), and of micro and macro processes, assumed by exchange theorists.

BASIC THEORETICAL ARGUMENT

An Expanded Model

This section builds on the convergent model, portrayed by Figure 1, in two ways. The first is by adding the idea that roles and positions are socially embedded in overarching social units, e.g., small groups, organizations, communities, and societies. The importance of the group context is an obvious point, but it has not been subject to much explicit theorizing in either the social exchange tradition or the structural tradition of symbolic interactionism. Exchange theorists treat *networks* of exchange as the larger context of primary concern with only occasional reference to social units with membership boundaries, shared goals or activities, and sustained interaction among members. For structural symbolic interaction, roles are embedded in the larger society, and initial definitions of self and other are tied to the cultural meanings of the role "names" (e.g., parent, husband, co-worker). Role identities are a juncture at which there is a mutual reciprocity between the larger society and social interaction, but the relevant social units are left in the background.

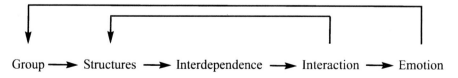

Figure 2. Expanded Model of Convergence.

My theoretical argument is that through an emotional-affective process, social interaction generates stronger or weaker attachments to a given social unit (e.g., relationship, network, organization, community, society) and *indirectly* to the role identities one enacts in that social unit or group (Lawler 1992; Lawler, Thye, and Yoon 2000). Stryker and colleagues (e.g., Stryker and Serpe 1994) theorize and empirically show that interactional and affective commitments to a role enhance the salience of that role for the actor and leads her to enact it more often, when opportunities arise. I propose that if actors are more strongly and affectively attached to a group, they will be even more committed to the roles that they occupy within that group. In this context, the enactment of role identities can generate and affirm collective identities, i.e., enacting "me's" may promote a sense of "we," in the terms of Thoits and Virshup (1995).

The second addition to the model (see Figure 2) indicates that the "me-to-we" process operates through the emotional effects of social interaction, as these emotions have feedback effects on group attachments. Following recent theory and research on relational cohesion in social exchange (e.g., Lawler and Yoon 1996), we hypothesize that social interaction has emotional effects on individual actors tied to the degree that the interaction successfully aligns actors' behavior. The resulting emotions involve global feelings of pleasure/displeasure, elation/enthusiasm, comfort and confidence, sadness or depression, and so forth (see Weiner 1986; Izard 1991; Collins 1981, 1989). If the interaction is "successful," the emotions felt are positive; if the interaction is "unsuccessful," the emotions felt are negative. These global emotions constitute an important mechanism that generates or renders salient a collective identity.

Feedback Loops

As the feedback loops in Figure 2 indicate, a collective identity forms or becomes salient when there is a feedback loop from the emotion experienced in social interaction to the group or larger social unit. If the emotions individuals experience are associated with the group, this should effect how actors feel about their membership in that group—i.e., the feedback loop is present (see also Collins 1981). This association should occur if actors perceive the group as responsible for the interaction that makes them feel good or feel bad (Lawler 1992, 2001). Positive individual feelings from interaction yield stronger group attachments, and negative feelings yield weaker group attachments (see Lawler 1992; Lawler and Yoon 1996; Lawler 2001, 2002), i.e., positive or negative feedback loops. Moreover, groups that are repeatedly a context for positive emotional experiences should take on more intrinsic value, and those that are a context for negative emotional experience should have less value to actors. Thus, the global emotional effects of interaction can enhance or diminish the value of a group membership or affiliation. The argument offered here is complementary to Stryker's—specifically, that identity commitments are stronger when the role identities are embedded in groups to which actors are affectively attached.

Social exchange and symbolic interaction theories offer different perspectives on how and when the feedback loop from emotion-to-group occurs? Based on exchange theory, the feedback loop would be contingent on the reinforcing properties of the emotions produced by social interaction (Lawler 2001). Feeling good is rewarding in itself and feeling bad is punishing in itself, i.e., emotions are internal rewards and punishments (Bandura 1997). Thus, actors should be motivated to reproduce the positive feelings and avoid the negative feelings just as they continue behaviors that are reinforced and eliminate those that are punished (Emerson 1972a).[2]

The tenets of symbolic-interaction indicate that people will interpret these internal stimuli, as they do other stimuli, and respond to their interpretation, rather than to the stimuli, as such (Mead 1934; Blumer 1969). The ambiguous nature of initial global feelings, experienced by the actors, is an important impetus for such interpretive efforts, and because these emotional responses are not under actors' control, they tend to look outside of themselves to interpret them. The range of social stimuli (i.e., self, other, relation, group, or society) to which they might be attributed is vast, and this makes the interpretive processes pivotal to when the feedback loop from emotion to group occurs. In sum, exchange theory suggests a reinforcement basis for the actors motivation to understand the source of their feelings, while symbolic interaction suggests that "vocabularies of motives" involved in definitions of self, other, and society (generalized others) are the prime basis for actors' understanding.

The expanded model, if viewed dynamically, has several noteworthy implications. There are two avenues by which structural role identities are modified or shaped: (1) through the self-other definitions developed in the interaction (i.e., *directly* through the feedback from interaction to structure), or (2) through the emotional/affective consequences of the social interaction (i.e., *indirectly* by promoting or undermining group attachments). The first avenue, by also increasing the level of interdependence, could enhance the strength of the emotions produced by future interaction. There could be a threshold of interdependence beneath which the emotional/affective consequences do not occur; but once the threshold reached, social interaction should generate emotions that increasingly promote group attachments (in the case of positive emotions) or diminish them (in the case of negative emotions).

Overall, we argue that emotions produced by social interaction are rewarding or punishing to actors and thus motivate interpretive processes to understand them. In accord with exchange theory, actors strive to experience good feelings again and avoid the bad feelings; and, in accord with symbolic interaction, actors attribute meaning to the emotions by fitting them into the *social* context, that is, by interpreting them in terms of relevant social objects, i.e., self, other, and the social unit. Symbolic interaction makes it clear why social objects, such as self and other, might be targeted in actors' interpretive processes, but it is not clear about how and when overarching collectivities or groups are targeted (see Stryker, Owens, and White 2000 for recent work on this issue). An "affect theory of social exchange," recently developed (Lawler 2001), can be adapted to deal with the latter issue.

ELABORATION OF THEORETICAL ARGUMENT

The affect theory of social exchange builds on the theory of relational cohesion and related research (e.g., Lawler and Thye 1999; Thye, Yoon, and Lawler 2002). The empirical evidence on relational cohesion consistently supports the theoretical argument as follows. More frequent exchange among the same actors has been shown to generate more positive

---

[2]Traditional Skinnerian notions that Emerson used as a foundation for exchange theory suggest that internal emotional responses would not add anything to the impact of extrinsic reinforcements and punishments, i.e., they are epiphenomenal (Lawler 2001). More recent models of social learning (Bandura 1997) attribute an independent role to internal (self) reinforcements, and emotional responses can be viewed as an instance of self-reinforcement.

feelings about their joint activity (i.e., the negotiation of exchanges). Successfully reaching agreements makes them feel pleasure/satisfaction, and not reaching agreements makes them feel displeasure/dissatisfaction. Positive global feelings, in turn, foster a sense of cohesion in their relationship (Lawler 1993, 1996) or group (Lawler, Thye, and Yoon 2000); and, the result is commitment behavior, such as giving each other gifts, staying in the relationship despite alternatives, and being more inclined to participate in a joint venture involving the risk of malfeasance by the other (Lawler and Yoon 1993, 1996, Lawler, Thye, and Yoon 2000). This emotion-based commitment process is stronger when actors have equal rather than unequal power or dependence and when they are highly interdependent (Lawler and Yoon 1996, 1998). The key moments in the relational cohesion process—*exchange-to-emotion-to-cohesion*—have considerable empirical support.

Lawler and associates (Lawler and Yoon 1993, 1996; Lawler and Thye 1999; Lawler, Thye, and Yoon 2000; Thye, Yoon, and Lawler 2002) infer from the evidence that repeated exchange promotes "incipient group formation" or micro social orders (Lawler 2002) which is tantamount to a sense of "we-ness" in Thoits and Virshup's (1995) terms. There is indirect evidence for this in the patterns of behavioral commitment (i.e., more relationship- or group-oriented behavior) and from questionnaire data (i.e., more value attributed to the social unit, greater perceived group-ness). The logic behind this is that emotions, felt individually, make actors aware of and responsive to relevant group affiliations or memberships, i.e., promote psychological group formation in social identity terms (Tajfel and Turner 1986; Isen 1987). Collins (1981, 1989) develops a similar argument for the emotional effects of social interaction, in general.

An important question is: When do collective or group affiliations and identities become salient? The fundamental answer, offered by the "affect theory of social exchange (Lawler 2001)," is that this should occur when one or more social units are perceived as a primary source, cause, or context for the emotions felt—positive or negative—as a result of an exchange. However, this answer raises another question: What social conditions lead actors to implicate social units in their emotional experiences? It is these conditions that should underlie the emergence or activation of collective identities. Collins (1981) argues that this is an inherent consequence of recurrent joint activities among the same people. Such activities ostensibly create shared emotional experiences that objectify group affiliations or memberships. In identity terms, this also should make collective or group identities more salient. The "affect theory of social exchange" (Lawler 2001), however, implies that the effect of emotions on identity salience is contingent on and varies with the nature of the joint activity.

Joint Activities or Tasks

The "affect theory of social exchange" identifies two properties of joint tasks that are important to the collective objectification and identity process, one structural and one perceptual. The *structural* dimension is the degree that individual contributions to the task cannot be identified and distinguished. This has been termed, "non-separability" by Williamson (1985:245–247) in his analysis of governance structures. Williamson argues that when labor is organized in this manner, the result is a greater sense of common endeavor and fate among employees. I propose a parallel argument for social interaction in general (Lawler 2001).

The *perceptual* dimension of joint tasks is the degree that the task fosters a sense of shared responsibility among the actors. In the theory (Lawler 2001), these perceptions are tied to and caused by objective, structural conditions of "nonseparability." The argument is that perceptions of shared responsibility for the results of recurrent interaction episodes lead actors to view their individual feelings as mutually and interdependently generated. Such jointly produced feelings create a sense of something larger, enduring, and transcendent; this could be a relationship, group affiliation, or a social category with cultural meaning. Under such conditions, common affiliations or memberships and related collective identities should become more salient than otherwise and constitute a plausible interpretation for the jointly generated emotional experiences. The feedback loop from emotion to group attachment (see Figure 2), therefore, is stronger and the collective identity more salient.[3]

Shared responsibility should have even stronger effects to the degree that these perceptions mitigate the well-known tendency of actors to make self-serving attributions for success or failure—namely that people credit self for good results and blame the other for bad results (e.g., Weiner 1986). There are good reasons for predicting countervailing effects for perceptions of shared responsibility. If the contributions of each individual's behavior are difficult to distinguish, it is also more difficult for self-serving attributions of the emotions to dominate. Individual and collective experience is more intertwined when structural conditions entail tasks with the property of nonseparability. In this context, repeated interaction—because of the emotions generated and the desire of actors to experience positive and avoid negative feelings—should activate collective identities.

A larger theoretical rationale for the joint task-to-shared-responsibility effects on collective identity is suggested by the "affect theory of social exchange." Lawler (2001) argues that successfully-completed joint tasks affirm individuals' sense of self-efficacy while also suggesting to actors that their own efficacy is mediated by their involvement in the collective or group activity, i.e., self efficacy is "socially mediated." The more actors perceive a shared responsibility for social-interaction outcomes, the more they perceive their own individual efficacy as being tied to collective efficacy. This leads to a major inference: *If self and collective efficacy are interwoven by social interaction, collective identities become salient and shape role identities, in particular the expectations attached to them.* Perceptions of shared responsibility have collective-identity effects in part because they reflect an interconnection of self and collective efficacy.

The *relative* salience of role and collective identities may stem, in part, from the connections actors' perceive between self and collective efficacy.[4] On the one hand, if these are in tension, it is reasonable to suspect that role identities will be most salient. By definition, role identities foster a sense of "me-ness" (Thoits and Virshup 1995); they can be construed as socially sanctioned and legitimated frameworks of self-interest. In addition, under these conditions, there would be no counterweight against self-serving attributions for success/failure and resulting emotions. On the other hand, if self and collective efficacy are unrelated, both role identities and collective identities can exist side-by-side and be relatively independent. An example is a friendship group consisting of people who work together in the same organization but in which joint activities are solely nonwork-related.

---

[3]To test the effects of a joint activity or task, one could use either objective measures of nonseparability (task interdependence) or perceptual measures of shared responsibility. The latter reflects the social-constructionist feature and is the proximal cause of collective or group identity, but for practical and theoretical reasons, either could serve as a proxy for the nonseparability-to-shared-responsibility process.

[4]Stryker (2000) argues that one of the problems with the uses of identity in the social movement literature is the tendency to either assume only collective identities are operating or to fuse, by theoretical assumption, group, social-category based, and role-based identities. We subscribe to Stryker's (2000) position and argue that the *affect theory of social exchange* helps understand how closely connected or distant are collective and role-based individual identities for actor.

Their work identities may be the original basis for nonwork collective activities, but the latter could conceivably take on a life of their own, especially under conditions (shared responsibility) that generate a collective identity.

Emotions Directed at Self and Other

Role identities are a structural basis for self-serving attributions of emotions. Such attributions affect the specific emotions likely to develop from actors' interpretation of the global feelings (see Weiner 1986; Lawler 2001). The affect theory of social exchange emphasizes four specific emotions: *pride* or *shame* directed at self and *gratitude* or *anger* directed at the other. If only role identities are salient, pride in self for successful interaction may be stronger and gratitude toward the other weaker; similarly, failure would generate greater anger toward the other and less shame in self. With salient role identities, emotional attributions across self and other are essentially zero-sum. However, given a joint task and a sense of shared responsibility for it, a successful interaction fosters *both* pride in self and gratitude toward the other; whereas, unsuccessful interaction produces both shame in self and anger toward the other (see Lawler 2001 for more discussion). Pride in self and gratitude toward the other go together, as do shame and anger, implying a nonzero sum relationship between the emotions directed at self vs. other. Collective identities emerge from and, in turn, promote a nonzero sum relationship between emotions directed at self and other.

The specific emotions, directed at self and other, reflect individual inferences about their own role and their relationship to others with complementary roles. A supervisor and subordinate in an organization, who repeatedly interact and produce positive results, may make attributions to their relationship or group, but also to self and other. The supervisor feels good about herself (pride) but also a sense of gratitude toward the subordinate, and vice versa. Gratitude expressed by one to the other would enhance the pride felt by the other. A pride-gratitude cycle, in which the actors essentially share the credit for their joint activities and the resulting emotional benefits, should enhance further the salience of the particular role identities, but not necessarily at the expense of a collective identity emergent around their joint activities. Pride-gratitude cycles build relationships or groups and, by implication, foster associated collective identities, whereas shame-anger cycles weaken overarching social units and associated collective identities.[5]

Dynamics underlying specific emotions elaborate how role identities can generate overarching collective identities that in turn reciprocally impact role expectations. Assume, as explained earlier, that developing consensual self-other role identities is a fundamental underlying joint task in social interaction. If a working consensus is reached, global pleasant feelings result, and these are ostensibly interpreted with reference to social units in which the roles are enacted, and in part with reference to the expectations of their role. Consensual self-other definitions affirm and make salient one's role identity and generate feelings of pride, but, under the conditions articulated here, they also generate gratitude toward each other. In this sense, perceptions of shared responsibility for joint tasks sets the stage for role-based interactions to generate collective identities and foster the mutual expression of positive feelings (or negative feelings).

---

[5]Negative emotions, jointly felt and shared, can be a source of collective-action frames and group identity if directed at third parties (Gamson 1995). For example, Taylor (2000) studies self-help groups for post-partum depression and shows how individuals in these groups jointly transformed guilt and shame into pride by the fact that they dealt with their ordeal and anger toward gendered concepts of motherhood.

A final point is that a collective identity, when salient, should motivate actors to undertake collectively oriented behaviors, because self-efficacy is socially mediated. However, based on Gecas (1986), self-efficacy is one of only three motivational dimensions of the self, the others being esteem, and authenticity. Gecas states, ". . . by virtue of having a self concept the individual is motivated to maintain and enhance it, to conceive of it as efficacious and consequential, and to experience it as meaningful and real." (1986: 138). Applied to the "affect theory of social exchange," a joint task that affirms the efficacy of the individuals also should enhance self-esteem and "authenticity." Thus, I infer that *collective identities should have the greatest salience when they not only mediate actors' individual sense of self-efficacy but also generate self-esteem and self-affirmation (i.e., authentication).*

THEORETICAL PROPOSITIONS

My theoretical analysis in this paper suggests a number of central claims or propositions, and these are summarized below.

1. Success at social interaction with another produces simple everyday emotions. Because the emotions are rewarding/punishing but also global and ambiguous, actors are motivated to interpret what are their causes, where they come from? This becomes part of the actors "definition of the situation" (Lawler and Thye 1999).

2. If interaction with the same others repeatedly generates such feelings, actors are prone to interpret and attach the emotions to self, other, or the social unit (Lawler and Yoon 1996; Collins 1981). Stable patterns of emotion attributions tend to develop in the context of repeated interaction.

3. Attributions to the social unit are most likely when the task is joint and entails high interdependence. Under these conditions, the relevant social unit (e.g., relation, group, organization) is perceived as a cause of emotions felt by an actor (Lawler, Thye, and Yoon 2000; Lawler 2001) and, as a result, the collective group identity is activated.

4. Attributions to self and other are most likely when actors can easily separate their contributions to or involvement in the interaction. Under these conditions, role identities become salient and interpretive processes lead to more specific emotions: pride or shame in self, gratitude or anger toward the other (Lawler 2001).

5. If specific emotions of pride in self and gratitude toward the other are nonzero sum, these role-based emotions strengthen the salience of the collective identity, whereas if pride and gratitude are negatively related, self-serving attributions weaken collective identities.

6. Role identities are intertwined with collective identities to the degree that actors' sense of self-efficacy is tied to and mediated by their joint activities or tasks. This is more likely when the interaction tasks foster a sense of shared responsibility for the results of the interaction.

7. Role identities strengthen collective identities when role occupants are highly dependent on each other, interact frequently, and engage in joint tasks in which their individual contributions are non-separable; conversely, collective identities strengthen role identities especially when enacting joint tasks enhances individuals' self efficacy, self esteem and self affirmation (authenticity). These reciprocal

effects operate through an emotional/affective process, specified by relational cohesion theory (Lawler and Yoon 1996; Thye, Yoon, and Lawler 2002).

8. The most salient identities are those that actors interpret as the strongest source of positive feelings in social interaction, whereas the least salient identities are those actors interpret as the strongest source of negative feelings in interaction. Thus, the emotional effects of social interaction and actors' interpretation of these affect the salience of multiple identities.

CONCLUSION

This chapter aims to understand how and when social interaction in the context of role identities generates a collective identity. Collective identities are viewed as emergent, shared beliefs about person-to-group memberships or affiliations. They emerge from and within interaction, and they are organized around particular activities or tasks. Durkheim (1925), in his classic study of religion in a preliterate society, suggested that collective activities (ritual) generate feelings of elation or effervescence that affirm actors' membership in a group and are important sources of solidarity. Collins (1975, 1981, 1989) generalizes this idea in his theory of "interaction ritual chains," by arguing that a common focus and common mood in social interaction fosters a sense of something larger, i.e., a common group membership or affiliation. Finally, Lawler and associates (Lawler and Yoon 1996; Lawler and Thye 1999; Lawler, Thye, and Yoon 2000; Lawler 2001, 2002) indicate that such emotional effects explain how and when repetitive exchange among the same actors will generate commitments to a relation or group. Based on this prior work, I argue here that interaction-to-identity processes are mediated by emotions and feelings, and these shape actors identification with and attachment to a social unit.

My argument in brief is that perceptions of mutual, shared responsibility for interaction is an underpinning of collective identities, whereas perceptions of individual responsibility are an underpinning of role identities. The former generates a sense "we," the latter a sense of "me" (Thoits and Virshup 1995). In this context, identities that are perceived by actors as a frequent source of positive emotional experience (and infrequent source of negative feelings) should be valued more than those that generate infrequent positive or frequent negative feelings. This idea is applicable to structurally based identities as well as to emergent collective identities. By implication, the salience of multiple identities, available to actors in a given context, depends on the degree that actors associate their identities with social interactions that, on a global level, make them feel good (or bad), and that on a specific level, make them feel pride or shame in self and gratitude or anger toward the other.

Broadly, the implications of this paper are that social interaction is a source of a collective identity under several conditions: (1) The interaction entails a joint task in which actors have difficulty separating or distinguishing their individual contributions or responsibilities for its success or failure. (2) The social interaction affirms actors' self-efficacy, but because this occurs through collective activities that neither can accomplish alone, self-efficacy is intertwined with collective efficacy. (3) The interaction generates positive or negative global feelings, and actors' interpretation of these feelings generates specific emotions (e.g., pride, gratitude) directed at self and other. Overall, if actors interpret their individual emotions in terms of what they share or have in common, a collective identity becomes more salient.

ACKNOWLEDGMENTS: The author expresses appreciation to Shane Thye and Jeongkoo Yoon for helpful comments. Communications should be sent to the author at School of Industrial and Labor Relations, Cornell University, Ithaca, New York, 14853.

REFERENCES

Bandura, Albert. (1997). *Social Learning Theory.* Englewood Cliffs, NJ: Prentice Hall.
Blumer, Herbert. (1969). *Symbolic Interaction: Perspective and Method.* Englewood Cliffs, NJ: Prentice Hall.
Burke, Peter. (1991). Identity Processes and Social Stress. *American Sociological Review, 56,* 836–849.
Collins, Randall. (1981). On the Microfoundations of Macrosociology. *American Journal of Sociology, 86,* 984–1014.
_____. (1989). Toward a Neo-Median Sociology of Mind. *Symbolic Interaction,. 12,* 1–32.
Cook, Karen S. & Emerson, Richard M. (1984). Exchange Networks and the Analysis of Complex Organizations. In S. B. Bacharach and E. J. Lawler (Eds.) R*esearch on the Sociology of Organizations*, vol. 3, (pp. 1–30). Greenwich, CT: JAI Press.
Durkheim, Emile. (1915). *Elementary Forms of Religious Life.* New York: Free Press.
Emerson, Richard M. (1972a). Exchange Theory Part I: A Psychological Basis for Social Exchange. In J. Berger, M. Zelditch, Jr., and B. Anderson (Eds.), *Sociological Theories in Progress*, vol. 2, (pp. 38–57). Boston, MA: Houghton-Mifflin.
_____. (1981). Social Exchange Theory. In M. Rosenberg and R. H. Turner (Eds.), *Social Psychology: Sociological Perspectives* (pp. 30–65). New York: Basic Books.
Gecas, Victor. (1986). The Motivational Significance of Self Concept for Socialization Theory. In E. J. Lawler (Ed.), *Advances in Group Processes 3* (pp. 131–56). Greenwich, CT.: JAI Press. .
Heise, David R. (1979). *Understanding Events.* New York, Cambridge.
Hochschild, Arlie R. (1979). Emotions Work, Feelings Rule, and Social Structure. *American Journal of Sociology, 85,* 3, 551–75.
Isen, Alice. (1987). Positive Affect, Cognitive Processes, and Social Behavior. In L. Berkowitz (Ed.), *Advances in Experimental Social Psychology* vol. 20, (pp. 203–253). New York: Academic Press.
Izard, Carroll E. (1991). *The Psychology of Emotions.* New York: Plenum Press.
Kemper, Theodore D. (1978). *A Social Interactional Theory of Emotions.* New York: Wiley.
_____. (1987). How many Emotions are There? Wedding the Social and the Autonomic Components. *American Journal of Sociology, 93,* 263–89.
Klandermans, Bert. (1997). *The Social Psychology of Protest.* Cambridge, MA: Blackwell Publishers.
Klandermans, Bert & de Weerd, Marga. (2000). Group Identification and Political Protest. In Sheldon Stryker, Timothy J. Owens, and Robert W. White (Eds.), *Self, Identity, and Social Movements* (pp. 41—67). Minneapolis: University of Minnesota Press.
Kollock, Peter. (1994). The Emergence of Exchange Structures: An Experimental Study of Uncertainty, Commitment, and Trust. *American Journal of Sociology, 100,* 315–45.
Lawler, Edward J. (1992). Choice Processes and Affective Attachments to Nested Groups: A Theoretical Analysis. *American Sociological Review, 57,* 327–39.
Lawler, Edward J. (2001). An Affect Theory of Social Exchange. *American Journal of Sociology, 107,* 321–52.
Lawler, Edward J. (2002). Micro Social Orders. *Social Psychology Quarterly, 65,* 4–17.
Lawler, Edward J. & Yoon, Jeongkoo. (1993). Power and the Emergence of Commitment Behavior in Negotiated Exchange. *American Sociological Review, 58,* 465–81.
_____. (1996). Commitment in Exchange Relations: Test of a Theory of Relations Cohesion. *American Sociological Review, 61,* 89–108.
_____. (1998). Network Structure and Emotion in Exchange Relations. *American Sociological Review, 63,* 871–894.
Lawler, Edward J. & Thye, Shane R. (1999). Bringing Emotions into Social Exchange Theory. *Annual Review of Sociology, 25,* 217–44.
Lawler, Edward J., Thye, Shane R., & Yoon, Jeongkoo. (2000). Emotions and Group Cohesion in Productive Exchange. *American Journal of Sociology,* in press.
McCall, George J. & Simmons, J.L. (1966/1978). *Identities and Interactions: An Examination Of Human Associations in Everyday Life.* New York: Free Press.
Mead, George Herbert. (1934). *Mind, Self, and Society.* Chicago: University of Chicago Press.

Melucci, Alberto. (1995). The Process of Collective Identity. In H. Johnston and B. Klandermans (Eds.), *Social Movements and Culture* (pp.41–63). Minnesota: University of Minnesota Press.

Molm, Linda & Cook, Karen. (1995). Social Exchange and Exchange Networks. In K. S. Cook, G.A. Fine, and J.S. House (Eds.), *Sociological Perspectives on Social Psychology* (pp. 209–235). Boston: Allyn and Bacon.

Parsons, Talcott. (1951). *The Social System.* New York: Free Press.

Snow, David A. & McAdam, Doug. (2000). Identity Work Processes in the Context of Social Movements: Clarifying the Identity/Movement Nexus. In Sheldon Stryker, Timothy Owens, & Robert White (Eds.), *Self, Identity and Social Movements* (pp. 41–67). Minneapolis: University of Minnesota Press.

Stryker, Sheldon. (1980). *Symbolic Interactionism: A Social Structure Version.* Menlo Park, CA: Benjamin/ Cummings Pub. Co. Stryker, Sheldon,. Owens, Timothy J., & White, Robert W. (Eds.). (2000). *Self, Identity and Social Movements.* Minneapolis: University of Minnesota Press.

Stryker, Sheldon & Serpe, Richard T. (1994). Identity Salience and Psychological Centrality: Equivalent, Overlapping, or Complementary Concepts. *Social Psychology Quarterly, 57,* 16–35.

Tajfel, Henri & Turner, John C. (1986). The Social Identity Theory of Intergroup Behavior. In Steven Worchel & William G. Austin (Eds.), *Psychology of Intergroup Relations* (pp. 7–24). Chicago: Nelson-Hall.

Taylor, Verta. (2000). Emotions and Identity in Women's Self-Help Movements. In Sheldon Stryker, Timothy Owens, & Robert White (Eds.), *Self, Identity and Social Movements* (pp. 271–299). Minneapolis: University of Minnesota Press.

Thoits, Peggy A. & Virshup, Lauren K. (1995). Me's and We's: Forms and Functions of Social Identities. In Richard Ashmore & Lee Jussim (Eds.), *Self and Identity: Fundamental Issues* (pp. 106–133). New York: Oxford University Press.

Thye, Shane, Yoon, Jeongkoo & Lawler, Edward J. (2002). The Theory of Relational Cohesion: Review of a Theoretical Research Program. In *Advances in Group Processes: Studies of Cohesion and Solidarity* volume 19, (pp. 139–166). New York: Elsivier Press.

Turner, Ralph. (1962). Role Taking: Process versus Conformity. In A. M. Rose (Ed.), *Human Behavior and Social Processes* (pp. 20–41). Boston: Houghton-Mifflin.

Weiner, Bernard. (1986). *An Attributional Theory of Motivation and Emotion.* New York: Springer-Verlag.

Williamson, Oliver. (1985). *The Economic Institutions of Capitalism.* New York: Free Press.

Chapter 10

Using Identity Discrepancy Theory to Predict Psychological Distress

KRISTEN MARCUSSEN AND MICHAEL D. LARGE

INTRODUCTION

An important goal of stress research is to clarify the processes by which external conditions result in psychological distress (e.g., Burke, 1991b 1996; Holmes and Rahe, 1967; Mirowsky and Ross, 1989; Thoits, 1991). In addition to specifying the relationship between stress and distress, mental health scholars have become increasingly interested in predicting specific forms of distress (Aneshensel, 1992; Mirowsky and Ross, 1989). Sociological social psychologists in general, and identity theorists in particular, have focused on the relationship between self and social structure to explain how external conditions impact emotional states. Although some theorists have linked identities with psychological distress (Burke, 1991b; 1996; Simon, 1992; Thoits, 1986; 1991), the impact of identity meanings on stress processes, as well as the ability to predict specific distress outcomes, deserves further attention.

We offer an identity model of distress that allows for differentiation between distress outcomes. Our model (Large and Marcussen, 2000) represents an extension of Burke's identity control model (1991b, 1996), which incorporates ideas from self-discrepancy theory (Higgins 1987; 1989; 1996) in order to explain the form and degree of distress. We have incorporated ideas from self-discrepancy theory because it specifies the origins of distress and predicts distinct outcomes, that is, depression and anxiety. Depression and anxiety are regarded as the most common and general consequences of stress (Mirowsky and Ross, 1989) and research suggests they differ in both their causes and consequences. Therefore, our initial model is directed at predicting these disorders.

Self-discrepancy theory, while it predicts anxiety and depression, focuses on a global concept of the self. Consequently, it does not explicitly locate the source of stress in a social context. Identity theory, on the other hand, explains how distress arises from different social roles. Focusing on identities promotes emphasis on the meaning a position in the social structure holds for the self-concept. This point is critical to our theory because we explain the form of distress as a function of the meaning that social roles hold for individuals. In merging these theories then, we attempt to explain two major forms of distress (depression and anxiety) in the context of (1) social roles that are embedded in social structure and (2) the meanings of those roles for individuals.

In this chapter, we review the identity control model and self-discrepancy theory, and present an integrated identity discrepancy theory of distress. We also offer some preliminary data which test the basic propositions of the model using three identities: student, child, and friend. We conclude by suggesting directions for future research linking identities and distress.

BACKGROUND

Identity Control Model

The identity control model specifies four components of an identity: the identity standard, self-relevant perceptions, a comparator, and output (Burke, 1991b; 1996). The identity standard is the content or meaning the identity holds for the individual. Self-relevant perceptions are situational elements that inform the individual about the self, and constitute the input into the identity system. Self-relevant perceptions include both an individual's perceptions of the situation as well as the individual's perception of how others view the situation (Riley and Burke, 1995). The comparator is the process by which the congruence between the identity standard and the self-relevant perceptions is assessed (Burke, 1991b; 1996). The output is the consequence of this assessment. It is action toward the social situation that is meaningful in terms of the same dimensions of meaning relevant to the identity standard and self-relevant perceptions.

The identity process involves a continual assessment of the consistency between the identity standard and self-relevant perceptions (Burke, 1991b; 1996). Individuals are motivated to achieve semantic congruence, that is, a match between the standard for an identity and self-relevant perceptions in the situation. When there is incongruence between the standard and self-relevant perceptions, the individual acts on the social situation in order to alter that situation and thereby change the feedback from the social situation to be more consistent with the identity standard. For example, a person with a student identity that means that he should be organized has the criterion "organized" as part of his identity standard for his student identity. Comments from friends, parents, or teachers relevant to his identity-standard meaning (organized) would constitute the self-relevant perceptions in the identity system. For instance, the student's roommate might suggest that he is not organized enough to get his term paper done. The identity-relevant comments from the roommate are compared to the student's identity standard, which specifies that he be organized. The output is the person's response to any discrepancy between the identity standard and the self-relevant perceptions. Perhaps the student will try to explain to the roommate his seemingly messy, but highly sophisticated system of organization. In general, the identity process operates smoothly, making minor adjustments as necessary. When the process is disrupted, however, distress occurs.

Interruption Theory

Interruption theory (Mandler, 1975; 1982) suggests that interruption of an organized action or thought process results in some degree of autonomic activity (such as changes in heart rate or skin temperature). The impact that an interruption has on an individual increases with (1) the degree of organization of the interrupted process (that is, how habitual the process has become), and (2) the severity of the interruption (Mandler, 1982). An interruption is severe if it is persistent, or if the process or activity is highly salient. The individual experiences this autonomic activity as distress. The type of distress experienced is determined by the subjective meaning applied to the interrupting event (Berscheid, 1983).

Identity Interruption Theory

Identity interruption theory (Burke, 1991b; 1996) integrates interruption theory and identity theory, explaining distress as an interruption of the normal operation of an identity process. For example, an identity process may be interrupted because others in the social situation do not respond to the individual's outputs. This may occur when an individual's behavior is misunderstood or ignored, and therefore does not produce the intended effect of bringing the feedback from others back in line with the identity standard. The essential consequence of interruption is that semantic congruence is not achieved.

The amount of distress an individual experiences from identity interruption is a function of (1) the degree of organization of the identity, and (2) the severity of the interruption (Burke 1996). Severity of the interruption is determined by the persistence of the interruption and the salience of the identity. Salience refers to the likelihood of an identity being activated in a given situation or across situations (Stryker, 1980; Stryker and Serpe, 1994), that is, how available an identity is for activation. Interruption of an identity should be more distressing for identities that are highly salient compared to those that are less salient (Burke, 1991b; 1996; Thoits, 1991). Identity interruption theory provides a useful model for explaining distress, but does not provide an adequate means to distinguish the forms of the distress. Self-discrepancy theory (Higgins, 1987; 1989) focuses on such distinctions.

Self-Discrepancy Theory

Self-discrepancy theory (Higgins, 1987; 1989) distinguishes three domains of the self: actual, ideal, and ought. The actual self refers to a representation of the attributes that the individual (or some other) believes he or she possesses. The ideal self refers to a representation of the attributes that the individual (or some other) wishes or hopes for the individual to possess. In essence, the ideal self reflects *aspirations* for the individual. The ought self refers to a representation of the attributes that the individual (or some other) believes the individual should possess. In other words, the ought self reflects our feelings of *obligation*. Higgins also distinguishes between two standpoints on the self: own and other. However, the distinction between standpoints on the self is intended to allow distinction between particular subtypes of agitation-related emotions (e.g., fear, guilt) or dejection-related emotions (e.g., disappointment, shame). Because this distinction does not bear on the current formulation, we will focus only on the three domains of the self. The actual-self in Higgins' theory relates to the self-relevant perceptions in Burke's identity model. The ideal and ought selves are self-guides, that is, self-motivating standards. Self guides relate to identity standards; they are gauges against which self-relevant perceptions are measured.

Higgins (1987; 1989) assumes individuals compare their self-concept to self-guides, and are motivated to achieve a state of congruence between their self-concept and relevant self-guides. This notion, based on consistency theories (Festinger, 1957; Heider, 1946), is analogous to the assumption of Burke's identity theory (1991b; 1996) that people are motivated to achieve "semantic congruence" and Heise's (1977, 1979) argument that people try to minimize "deflections" between fundamental and transient sentiments. Self-discrepancy theory predicts an emotional reaction to a discrepancy between the self-concept and the self-guides, depending on which self-guide is discrepant with the actual self. In general, discrepancies between the actual self and the ideal self produce dejection-related emotions. Alternatively, discrepancies between the actual self and the ought self produce agitation-related emotions. The rationale for this distinction in emotional consequences is that the actual-ideal discrepancy represents the absence of positive outcomes, while the actual-ought discrepancy represents the presence or threat of negative outcomes (Higgins, 1987). These discrepancies indicate interruptions of the identity process in identity theory terms (Burke, 1996). That is, sustained incongruence between social feedback and self guides with respect to a given identity maps onto what Burke calls identity interruption. When congruence is not achieved, self-discrepancy theory predicts specific psychological outcomes (depression or anxiety) depending on which self-guide is inconsistent with the actual self.

Self-discrepancy theory (Higgins, 1987; 1989) predicts the strength of the emotional reaction as a function of the magnitude and accessibility of the discrepancy. The magnitude of a self-discrepancy depends on the degree of divergence between the two incongruent self-representations. Accessibility refers to how readily a self-discrepancy may be activated, or used in information processing. Accessibility corresponds to salience in identity theories (Stryker, 1991; Stryker and Serpe, 1994), though Higgins uses accessibility in reference to discrepancies while identity theorists attend to the salience of identities, not discrepancies. Higgins (1987) hypothesizes that the magnitude and accessibility of a given type of self-discrepancy are positively related to the experience of emotion associated with that type of self-discrepancy. This general hypothesis from self-discrepancy theory has been supported in a number of empirical studies (e.g., Alexander and Higgins, 1993; Higgins et al., 1986; Strauman, 1992).

An Extension of an Identity Theory of Distress

Symbolic interactionists indicate that meanings associated with a role derive from social structure (Stryker, 1980). A person's location in the social structure impacts the interactions through which that person generates and affirms self-meaning. Whereas identity theory has called attention to the importance of meaning to the study of social roles, we add that identity meanings also include a dimension of self-aspirations, and that they too are anchored in social structure. Previous theorists (Burke, 1996; Stryker, 1991) have noted that incorporating ideas from self-discrepancy theory would allow for prediction of the specific forms of distress experienced, an important goal of stress research. For these reasons our extension of Burke's identity theory incorporates (1) types of self-guides, (2) specific emotional responses based on incongruence between the actual self (self-relevant perceptions) and particular self-guides (identity standard), and (3) the relation between discrepancy magnitude and the degree of distress experienced.

We start with a conceptualization of the self as comprising multiple identities, and refine this notion by suggesting that each identity includes identity standards which contain, to some degree, beliefs that reflect both aspirations and obligations. That is, rather than treating the aspiration and obligation domains as separate components of a single, global self, we consider them aspects of each specific identity. For example, a person may have a "friend" identity containing both aspirations (e.g., "I wish to amuse my friends") and obligations (e.g., "I should be supportive of my friends"). Thus, a person can have an identity standard heavily constituted of aspirations and/or obligations. Such a conceptualization of the self will allow an extension of identity theory that specifies more precisely the anticipated composition of distress.

Assumptions and Hypotheses

From identity interruption theory (Burke, 1996) we assume that interruption of a highly organized identity process results in increased distress. We also assume that distress is a function of the persistence of the interruption and the salience of the identity being interrupted.

From self-discrepancy theory we draw the argument that the magnitude of the discrepancy is also important in determining distress. Interruption based on a slight discrepancy should be less distressing than interruption deriving from a large discrepancy. That is, we assume that the magnitude of the discrepancy is positively related to distress. From these assumptions we can predict that interruptions of an identity process will result in some degree of distress. This forms our first hypothesis.

> **Hypothesis 1**: The greater the magnitude of the discrepancy between self-relevant perceptions and the identity standard, the greater the distress experienced by the individual.

Our goal, however, is not only to predict when distress will occur and to what degree, but also to what degree specific forms of distress will occur. To do so we must consider the meaning of the identity. Just as the behavioral response to incongruence between the standard and self-relevant perceptions is significant in terms of the meaning of the identity, the emotional response to an identity interruption also depends on the meaning of the identity. For example, if your "child" identity means you aspire to be respectful of your parents, then discrepancies between that aspiration and feedback from others will motivate you to engage in behavior to alleviate that discrepancy (for example, following household rules). If the discrepancy is not alleviated, then the type of distress experienced is contingent on the type of the meaning (aspiration and/or obligation) that is not being verified. In this example the meaning is an aspiration, so the predicted result is depression. That is, we assume that depression is a function of discrepancy with the aspiration dimension of the identity standard. This leads to our second hypothesis.

> **Hypothesis 2**: The greater the discrepancy with respect to aspirations, the greater the depression.

Further, while we are predicting a general effect of discrepancies on distress, we are also trying to differentiate the forms of distress, depression and anxiety in particular. Consequently, we suggest that aspiration discrepancies should be more closely associated with depression than with anxiety, and offer the following ancillary hypothesis.

> **Hypothesis 2a**: The aspiration discrepancy will have a greater impact on depression than it will on anxiety.

When the meaning of the identity is represented more in terms of obligations, then an interruption in the identity process would entail an actual-ought discrepancy in Higgins' terms. For example, if your friend identity means you ought to be dependable, but you avoid your friends when they are feeling down, the consequence will be an anxiety-related emotion. Thus, we assume that anxiety is a function of discrepancy with the obligation dimension of the identity standard. From this we propose the following hypothesis.

Hypothesis 3: The greater the discrepancy with respect to obligations, the greater the anxiety.

We also assume that obligations are more strongly associated with anxiety than they are with depression. This leads to the following ancillary hypothesis.

Hypothesis 3a: The obligation discrepancy will have a greater impact on anxiety than it will on depression.

These assumptions constitute a modification of Burke's theory providing for prediction of anxiety and/or depression, depending on the meaning of the identity. Given the meaning of the identity and relevant social feedback, we predict a particular distress outcome. This allows prediction of the amount of depression and anxiety that may be associated with each of the person's identities. This formulation implies that the activated identity standard may contain ideals, obligations, or both, and that the individual with a discrepancy may experience depression, anxiety, or both.

DATA AND METHODS

Sample

Data for these analyses come from 308 self-administered questionnaires completed by undergraduate students at a Midwestern university. Although limited in terms of its generalizability, this sample allows us to examine empirically some of the basic theoretical propositions we have advanced (Large and Marcussen, 2000). Due to the nature of our sample, we measured identities that were most likely to be held by a student population: student, child, and friend.

Psychological Distress

We examined different measures of depression and anxiety in this study. The first set of measures taps *global* depression and anxiety. For the global measures we used items from the Center of Epidemiological Studies-Depression (CES-D) scale and the General Social Survey (GSS). Consistent with Strauman and Higgins (1988), we found that only a small number of items from the CES-D and GSS discriminated well between depression and anxiety. Although a substantial correlation between depression and anxiety is common in mental health research, our goal is to predict these disorders differentially. For that reason, we attempted to create scales with the least amount of overlap between constructs. To accomplish this, we selected items from the CES-D and GSS that appeared to reflect our conceptualizations of depression and anxiety and loaded on these components in a factor analysis. This produced four items for each scale.

For each measure of distress, respondents were asked to report how many days in the past week they experienced a number of symptoms. For depression, the items included: (1) I was bothered by things that usually don't bother me, (2) I felt that I could not shake off the blues even with help from my family or friends, (3) I felt depressed, and (4) I felt sad. For anxiety, the items included: (1) I felt so restless that I couldn't sit long in a chair, (2) I felt worried a lot about little things, (3) I felt anxious and tense, and (4) I had trouble keeping my mind on what I was doing. Response categories ranged from zero to seven days (Cronbach's alpha = .92 for depression and .77 for anxiety).

The second set of measures for depression and anxiety consist of role-specific semantic differential scales to assess distress in the student, child, and friend identities. Respondents were asked to think about each identity and describe the extent to which pairs of adjectives describe them using a scale ranging from 0 to 10. For depression, the following pairs were presented to respondents: (1) depressed to cheerful, (2) dejected to joyful, (3) hopeful to hopeless, and (4) happy to sad. Cronbach's reliability ranged from .86 to .92 for the identity-specific depression scales. Using the same rating technique, items used to assess anxiety for each identity were: (1) relaxed to anxious, (2) apprehensive to not apprehensive, (3) agitated to at ease, and (4) calm to tense. Cronbach's reliability for the identity-specific anxiety scales ranged from .73 to .77.

Discrepancy Scores

Respondents were asked to describe themselves with respect to three identities: student, child (son or daughter), and friend. For each identity, respondents were given a list of adjectives and were asked to report the extent to which these adjectives described them in terms of (a) how they thought others view them (self-relevant perceptions), (b) how they aspired to be (aspirations), and (c) how they thought they should be (obligations). For the *student identity*, the adjectives included the following: (1) disorganized, (2) social, (3) irresponsible, (4) studious, and (5) intense. For the *child identity* the adjectives were (1) disobedient, (2) friendly, (3) caring, (4) dependent, and (5) truthful. For the *friend identity* the adjectives were (1) funny, (2) honest, (3) protective, (4) undependable, and (5) communicative. Response categories for each identity ranged from 0 "not at all" to 10 "extremely." The adjectives for each identity were selected based on a pilot test that asked students to identify the characteristics they believed to be relevant to these roles. For each identity two sets of discrepancy scores were calculated by taking the absolute differences between the scores on aspiration items and obligation items from scores on corresponding self-relevant perceptions. Descriptive statistics for discrepancy and distress scales are presented in Table 1.

Table 1. Descriptive Statistics for Model Variables

	Mean	SD	Range	α
Dependent Measures				
Global Depression	8.82	7.04	0–28	.92
Global Anxiety	11.26	6.04	0–28	.77
Role Specific Depression—Student	15.54	6.90	4–36	.89
Role Specific Depression—Child	11.92	6.29	4–36	.86
Role Specific Depression—Friend	11.24	6.50	4–36	.92
Role Specific Anxiety—Student	20.32	6.41	4–36	.77
Role Specific Anxiety—Child	14.56	6.24	4–36	.73
Role Specific Anxiety—Friend	13.30	5.99	4–36	.77
Identity Discrepancies				
Aspiration Discrepancy—Student	10.69	6.59	0–35	—
Aspiration Discrepancy—Child	8.11	6.18	0–47	—
Aspiration Discrepancy—Friend	6.41	4.94	0–36	—
Obligation Discrepancy—Student	12.91	6.72	0–37	—
Obligation Discrepancy—Child	4.76	4.32	0–30	—
Obligation Discrepancy—Friend	5.46	5.46	0–40	—

RESULTS

Zero-order correlations among discrepancy measures and among distress measures were examined in order to assess the relationships among identity standards, as well as to determine how well the measures discriminate the theoretical concepts in the model. The correlations among aspirations and obligations can be found in Table 2a. As might be expected, the correlations between obligation and aspiration discrepancies within identities were rather high, ranging from .73 for the student identity to .82 for the friend identity. Though theoretically distinct, these high correlations reveal a good deal of overlap in our measures of aspirations and obligations. Additionally, the correlations among the distress measures were in some cases quite high, as shown in Table 2b. The global measures of depression and anxiety correlated at .63, and the correlations between role-specific measures of depression and anxiety were higher.

Our hypotheses were assessed with structural equation models (using AMOS) in order to take advantage of multiple indicators of the theoretical constructs and assess the impact of identity discrepancy on depression and anxiety simultaneously. Our basic analytic model is presented in Figure 1. As indicated in the figure, we controlled for gender and allowed error terms for depression and anxiety to be correlated. The exogenous variables were also correlated, allowing us to assess the unique effects of aspirations and obligations. This analysis was adopted despite a limited sample size because the ability to predict depression and anxiety differentially is central to our formulation, and this analytic strategy allows for a stringent assessment of the independent effects of aspirations and obligations on non-shared variation in depression and anxiety. Each identity was modeled separately.

In this initial test of the theory, we examined the impact of discrepancies between individuals' self-relevant perceptions and their aspirations and obligations on psychological distress. We discuss the overall effect of each type of identity discrepancy on distress, as well as findings for the relationship between type of discrepancy (aspirations and obligations) and specific forms of distress (depression and anxiety). Table 3 presents the results of these analyses.

Table 2a. Correlations for Aspiration and Obligation Discrepancies for Student, Child, and Friend Identities

	(1)	(2)	(3)	(4)	(5)	(6)
(1) Student Aspiration Discrepancy	1.00					
(2) Student Obligation Discrepancy	.73	1.00				
(3) Child Aspiration Discrepancy	.47	.42	1.00			
(4) Child Obligation Discrepancy	.41	.41	.80	1.00		
(5) Friend Aspiration Discrepancy	.33	.39	.56	.52	1.00	
(6) Friend Obligation Discrepancy	.25	.39	.46	.49	.82	1.00

Table 2b. Correlations for Global and Role Specific Depression and Anxiety

	(1)	(2)	(3)	(4)	(5)	(6)	(7)	(8)
(1) Global Depression	1.00							
(2) Global Anxiety	.63	1.00						
(3) RS Student Depression	.47	.35	1.00					
(4) RS Student Anxiety	.38	.48	.66	1.00				
(5) RS Child Depression	.38	.23	.44	.25	1.00			
(6) RS Child Anxiety	.25	.21	.28	.29	.68	1.00		
(7) RS Friend Depression	.44	.28	.45	.32	.58	.36	1.00	
(8) RS Friend Anxiety	.37	.27	.39	.35	.50	.45	.86	1.00

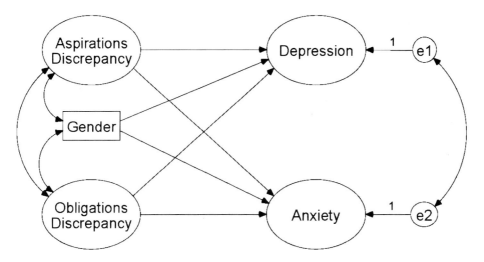

Figure 1. General Analytic Model Used to Test Identity Discrepancy Theory.

Aspiration Discrepancies

Looking first at the overall effects of aspiration discrepancies on anxiety and depression, we found only limited support for Hypothesis 1. Aspiration discrepancies were significantly associated with role-specific depression (β = .36) and role-specific anxiety (β = .30) for the student identity only. Aspiration discrepancies were not significantly associated with role-specific distress for either the child or friend identity. Moreover, there does not appear to be a significant association between aspiration discrepancy and global distress for any of the three identities.

The second hypothesis we investigate in these analyses pertains to the relationship between aspiration discrepancy and depression. As noted above, this relationship is significant with respect to role-specific depression in the student identity only. Finally, we examine the extent to which the relationship between aspiration discrepancies are related to depression *more so* than anxiety (Hypothesis 2a). Focusing only on the one significant effect of aspirations on depression, we find some support for this hypothesis. Specifically, the relationship between aspiration discrepancy and role-specific depression (β = .36) is stronger in magnitude than the relationship between aspiration discrepancy and role-specific anxiety (β = .30) for the student identity.

Obligation Discrepancies

As is the case for aspiration discrepancies, the results for obligation discrepancies and distress indicate only mixed support for Hypothesis 1. Obligation discrepancies are positively associated with global anxiety (β = .19) for the student identity. Discrepancies between obligations and self-relevant perceptions are associated with role-specific depression for the child identity (β = .19) and friend identity (β = .31), as well as with role-specific anxiety (β = .23) for the friend identity.

Hypothesis 3 focuses more specifically on the relationship between obligation discrepancies and anxiety. Here we find only two significant relationships in the student and friend identities. Interestingly, obligation discrepancy is associated with global anxiety for the student identity and with role-specific anxiety for the friend identity.

Table 3. Standardized Coefficients for Aspiration and
Obligation Discrepancies on Depression and Anxiety[a]

	Depression		Anxiety	
	Global	Role-Specific	Global	Role-Specific
Aspiration Discrepancy				
Student	.037	.357**	.063	.299*
Child	.138	.149	.119	.176
Friend	.023	.170	-.011	.161
Obligation Discrepancy				
Student	.157	-.034	.193*	.024
Child	.079	.190*	.139	.110
Friend	.158	.309**	.190	.228*

*** $p < .001$, ** $p < .01$, * $p < .05$
[a] All models control for gender.

Hypothesis 3a states that the obligation discrepancies will result in higher levels of anxiety than depression. Considering the two significant effects of obligations on anxiety, we found that (1) the student obligation discrepancy predicted global anxiety more so than global depression, but (2) contrary to our expectations, the relationship between obligation discrepancy and distress is stronger for role-specific depression than role-specific anxiety for both the friend and child identities.

DISCUSSION

We have described an identity model of distress that gives focus to the relation between role identities and the social environment. We began with Burke's (1996) identity interruption theory and incorporated notions from self-discrepancy theory (Higgins, 1987) to predict that when an identity process is disrupted, the meaning of the identity (aspirations and/or obligations) in relation to the meaning of the self-relevant perceptions determines the type of emotional response (anxiety and/or depression) experienced. Our conception of identity meanings includes aspirations and obligations as aspects of the identity standard used to interpret self-relevant information, and maintains the critical relationship between social structure and self.

In the analyses reported in this chapter, we found only modest support for the theory. Our first hypothesis focused on the general relationship between discrepancies and psychological distress. This hypothesis was supported for both types of identity discrepancies, across all three identities. With respect to aspirations, student identity discrepancies appeared to be more associated with role-specific than global measures of distress. Obligation discrepancies were also primarily related to role-specific distress for the child and friend identity. In addition to the overall impact of identity discrepancies on distress, we examined more specifically the extent to which aspiration and obligation discrepancies were associated with depression and anxiety, respectively. As alluded to above, aspirations significantly predicted depression only with respect to the relationship between student aspiration discrepancy and role-specific depression. Obligation discrepancies were related to global anxiety (for the student identity) and role-specific anxiety (for the friend identity). Finally, we examined whether aspiration discrepancies predict depression *more so* than anxiety, and if obligation discrepancies predict anxiety *more so* than depression. These hypotheses were supported in the case of the student identity. Specifically, aspiration discrepancies were more strongly associated with role-specific depression than role-specific anxiety, and obligation discrepancies in this role were more strongly associated with global anxiety than with global depression.

Although the majority of the associations between discrepancy and distress were not significant in the analyses presented here, it is worth noting that the general pattern of effects was consistent with the predictions of Hypotheses 2a and 3a. That is, with very few exceptions the magnitude of the effects between aspiration discrepancies and distress were stronger for depression than anxiety, and the relationships between obligation discrepancies and distress were more predictive of anxiety than depression. Furthermore, when looking at the significant coefficients only, the strongest support for this set of hypotheses lies with the student identity, where aspiration discrepancies were more strongly associated with depression than anxiety. Moreover, the evidence most inconsistent with Hypotheses 2a and 3a was found in the friend identity, where the association between obligation discrepancy and distress was stronger for depression than anxiety. We think this is especially relevant because where the correlation between aspirations and obligations is weakest (the student identity) we found the greatest support for the theory, and where the overlap was greatest between aspirations and obligations (the friend identity) the effects tended to be counter to our predictions. In other words, the more independent the aspirations and obligations for an identity, the more the findings regarding that identity provided support for the hypotheses.

Reflecting on these findings, the measurement of the key theoretical constructs warrants consideration. While aspiration discrepancies are expected to be related to obligation discrepancies, they are theoretically distinct. However, high correlations (from .73 to .82) between aspiration and obligation discrepancies within role identities (seen in Table 2a) call into question the discriminant validity of the measures. We speculate that this is at least partially a product of how the dimensions were obtained. That is, students identifying the dimensions they think relevant for these roles may well be predisposed to think in terms of social expectations in this context. This would mean that though respondents in this study were answering questions about aspirations, they were doing so on dimensions that tend to be more associated with obligations.

The associations among the role-specific distress measures also reveal a pattern worthy of some attention. Though it is clear from prior research that depression and anxiety covary significantly, the correlations between depression and anxiety *within* identities is particularly high. Table 2b shows correlations between role-specific depression and role-specific anxiety ranging from .66 for the student identity to .86 for the friend identity. Corrected for measurement error, these correlations run from .79 for the student identity to virtually 1.0 for the friend identity. Thus, these measures do not adequately tap independent aspects of role-specific distress.

The correlations between depression and anxiety within a role are higher than correlations within a type of distress across roles. This pattern implies that distress is, in fact, linked to roles, and that role-specific distress may be more telling than global measures of distress in this research. This points to the importance of a clear understanding of how role-specific distress relates to global distress, which further emphasizes the necessity of clean measures of role-specific distress.

FUTURE DIRECTIONS

There are a number directions this research can take that we find compelling. First and foremost, future tests of the model should incorporate components of the theory that were not tested in this chapter, including the impact that the persistence of identity interruption and identity salience have on the magnitude of distress. Our theory predicts that salience will moderate the effect of discrepancies on distress. Because we test only the basic model in this chapter, we did not include moderating variables. Moreover, we believe identifying effects of salience might be especially challenging when individuals are asked to "think about" particular identities in terms of self-relevant perceptions, aspirations, and obligations. This issue should be attended to in future work on identities and distress.

Work on identity discrepancies and distress would also benefit from focused attention on the measurement issues noted above. We have speculated that the high correlations between types of discrepancies may be at least in part a method effect. In this study, the discrepancy measures were obtained using characteristics specified without regard to aspirations or obligations, and therefore might be more related to one than another. We suggest that exploration of how best to tap the aspiration and obligation dimensions would be valuable. For instance, it may be more appropriate to allow the respondent to identify the characteristics relevant to the aspiration and obligation dimensions of the identity standard for a given identity.

In addition to the high correlations between types of discrepancies, strong associations between role-specific depression and anxiety also raise important measurement concerns. Certainly the high correlations between these distress measures suggest that identity interruptions often involve both aspirations and obligations, but to an extent they may also reflect inadequacies in our measurement strategy. It is possible that these correlations are high in part because we used somewhat focused definitions, and consequently measures, of role-specific anxiety and depression. It may be that depression and anxiety are more easily distinguished when symptoms such as somatization are considered, as well as additional dimensions of anxiety such as social anxiety, guilt, and shame. The relative utility of using more inclusive measures of distress should be investigated. A second potential reason why these role-specific measures did not discriminate well between depression and anxiety is that we used the same general items to measure role-specific distress across different identities. Using items that are more explicitly linked to the specific identities may more effectively reveal independent aspects of role-specific depression and anxiety.

Future studies should also consider examining additional identities. Because we used a college student sample in the present analyses, we focused on a limited number of identities. However, investigating a broader array of identities should help clarify the relationship between identities and well-being more generally, and in particular may provide valuable insight into the relationship between aspirations, obligations, and social roles. For instance, some identities may comprise more aspirations and others more obligations. Furthermore, it may be the case that aspirations and obligations are more difficult to disentangle for some identities than for others. Examining these dimensions of the identity standard in a greater number of social roles may shed light on variation in the composition of identities in terms of aspirations and obligations, and how this variation impacts mental health.

Finally, we believe it would be useful to explore the implications of different sources of self-relevant perceptions. This work has attended only to reflected appraisals as a source for self-relevant perceptions. However, we have suggested that system input may derive from other sources (e.g., comparison to reference groups) as well (Large and Marcussen,

2000). These sources may influence the type and magnitude of discrepancies that occur, and subsequently the form of distress experienced.

In this chapter, we presented a theoretical model that predicts distress from discrepancies in the identity process, and provided some empirical evidence in support of this argument. The theory also elaborates the link between the meanings of identities and distress; and thereby allows for prediction of specific distress outcomes. While the findings presented here are somewhat mixed, the patterns in the data are suggestive. We believe these results provide insight into, and pose challenges for, future research on identity processes.

ACKNOWLEDGMENTS: The authors' contributions are equal. We wish to thank Peter J. Burke and Richard T. Serpe for helpful comments and suggestions.

REFERENCES

Alexander, M.J., & Higgins, E.T. (1993). Emotional trade-offs of becoming a parent: How social roles influence self-discrepancy effects. *Journal of Personality and Social Psychology 65,* 1259-1269.

Aneshensel, C.S. (1992). Social stress: Theory and research. *Annual Review of Sociology18,* 15-38.

Berscheid, E. (1983). Emotion. In H.H. Kelley, E. Berscheid, A. Christensen, J.H. Harvey, & T.L. Huston (Eds.), *Close relationships* (pp. 110-68). New York: W.H. Freeman.

Burke, P.J. (1991a). Attitudes, behavior, and the self. In J.Howard & P. Callero (Eds.), *The self-society dynamic: Cognition, emotion, and action* (pp.189-208). New York: Cambridge University Press.

Burke, P.J. (1991b). Identity processes and social stress. *American Sociological Review 56,* 836-49.

Burke, P.J. (1996). Social identities and psychological stress. In H. Kaplan (Ed.), *Psychosocial stress: Perspectives on structure, theory, life course, and methods* (pp. 141-174). Orlando: Academic Press.

Festinger, L. (1957). *A theory of cognitive dissonance.* Stanford: Stanford University Press.

Heider, F. (1946). Attitudes and cognitive organization. *Journal of Psychology 21,*107-12.

Heise, D. (1977). Social action as the control of affect. *Behavioral Science 21,*163-177.

Heise, D. (1979). *Understanding events: Affect and the construction of social action.* NewYork: Cambridge University Press.

Higgins, E.T. (1987). Self-discrepancy: A theory relating self and affect. *Psychological Review 94,*319-40.

Higgins, E.T. (1989). Self-discrepancy theory: What patterns of self-beliefs cause people to suffer. In Berkowitz (Ed.), *Advances in experimental social psychology* (pp. 93-135). San Diego: Academic Press.

Higgins, E.T. (1996). The "self-digest": Self-knowledge serving self-regulatory functions. *Journal of Personality and Social Psychology 71,* 1062-1083.

Higgins, E.T., Bond, R.N., Klein, R., & Strauman, T. (1986). Self-discrepancies and emotional vulnerability: How magnitude, accessibility, and type of discrepancy influence affect. *Journal of Personality and Social Psychology 51,*5-15.

Holmes, T. H. and Rahe, R. H. (1967). The social readjustment rating scale. *Journal of Psychosomatic Research 11,* 213-18.

Large, M.D., & Marcussen, K. (2000). Extending identity theory to predict differential forms and degrees of psychological distress. *Social Psychology Quarterly, 63,* 49-59.

Mandler, G. (1975). *Mind and emotion.* New York: Wiley.

Mandler, G. (1982). Stress and thought processes. In L. Goldberger and S. Breznitz (Eds.), *Handbook of stress: Theoretical and clinical aspects* (pp. 88-104). New York: Free Press.

Mirowsky, J. & Ross, C.E. (1989). *Social causes of psychological distress.* New York: Aldine.

Riley, A. & Burke, P.J. (1995). Identities and self-verification in the small group. *Social Psychology Quarterly 58,* 61-73.

Simon, R.W. (1992). Parental role strains, salience of parental identity, and gender differences in psychological distress. *Journal of Health and Social Behavior 33,* 25-35.

Strauman, T. J. (1992). Self-guides, autobiographical memory, and anxiety and dysphoria: Toward a cognitive model of vulnerability to emotional distress. *Journal of Abnormal Psychology 101,*87-95.

Strauman, T. J. & E. Tory Higgins. (1988). Self-discrepancies as predictors of vulnerability to distinct syndromes of chronic emotional distress. *Journal of Personality, 56,* 685-707.

Stryker, S. (1980). *Symbolic interactionism: A social structural version.* Menlo Park: Benjamin/Cummings.

Stryker, S. (1991). Exploring the relevance of social cognition for the relationship of self and society: Linking the cognitive perspective and identity theory. In J.Howard & P. Callero (Eds.), *The self-society dynamic: Cognition, emotion, and action* (pp.19-41). New York: Cambridge University Press.

Stryker, S. & Serpe, R.T. (1994). Identity salience and psychological centrality: Equivalent, redundant, or complementary concepts? *Social Psychology Quarterly 57*, 16-35.

Thoits, P.A. (1986). Multiple identities: Examining gender and marital status differences and distress. *American Sociological Review 51*, 259-72.

Thoits, P.A. (1991). On merging identity theory and stress research. *Social Psychology Quarterly 54*, 101-12.

Part IV

Multiple Identities

Chapter **11**

Self, Identity, and Interaction in an Ecology of Identities

LYNN SMITH-LOVIN

Arguably, one of the most significant theoretical accomplishments of the 1960's was Sheldon Stryker's (1968, 1980) linking of symbolic interactionist ideas with mainstream sociological concerns about social structure. In a sense, Stryker rescued the study of symbolic interaction from a somewhat counterproductive fascination with idiosyncratic, creative, atypical behavioral productions in ill-defined, unconstraining behavioral settings. He reasserted the ability of the basic symbolic interactionist principle—that society shapes self which then shapes social behavior—to inform a powerful theoretical view of how social structure and the individuals that exist within it effect and constitute one another. Following role theory in concentrating on the stable, reoccurring interactions in our social system, Stryker once again made social psychology relevant to the mainstream concerns of our discipline. By linking the role patterns with the internalized meanings that roles had for individuals, he provided the connection between social structure, meaning and action that drives structural symbolic interaction today.

Particularly important was research conducted by Stryker and Richard Serpe (1982; Serpe, 1987) that developed an explicitly ecological understanding of the multiple-identity self. This work showed how a change in environment (from high school to college) led to two parallel developments. First, identities motivated students to seek out groups in the new environment that would allow the expression of identities that had been salient in their high school lives. Individuals largely recreated themselves in the new environment. Second, the social structure of the new environment had an impact on the selves that could be sustained in that setting. When groups were not available to reaffirm old identities, those identities withered and decreased in salience. This dynamic ecology of individual agency and social structural resources gave us a powerful picture of how selves and social environments sustain and shape one another.

We have not seen substantial development in this very productive line of work in the past couple of decades. In the 1970's, David Heise (1978, 1979) introduced another very powerful idea into structural symbolic interactionist thought—affect control theory. He

167

used William Power's (1973) control model to show how identity meanings acted as a reference signal to control behavior. The emphasis in this new theory was on how stable identity meanings, acquired through past experiences in one's culture and evoked through definitions of social situations, were compared to current impressions that were produced by social interaction. The central premise of the theory was that people acted to maintain the alignment of their identity meanings with the impressions created by the local social interaction, either through actions or through cognitive reinterpretation of events. Peter Burke (1991) later developed his own version of this control model in the context of identity theory.

The focus of work in structural symbolic interaction shifted rather completely from a central concern with the ecology of the self and society to a research program that focused on one identity at a time and how it was maintained in interaction. In a sense, affect control theory had no model of the self. It implicitly accepted Stryker's theoretical view of a multiple-identity, hierarchically organized self that made predictable choices about what identity would be salient within the context of any given situation. The control theories of identity were concerned only with the behaviors, attributions, and emotions that occurred once a situation had been defined (and relevant self-identities within that situation determined) (Smith-Lovin and Heise 1988). In a sense, we had a theory of social situations, not of the relationship between individuals and the social structures in which they were embedded.

The same focus largely absorbed the attention of Burke and his colleagues who pursued the more cognitive identity control theory (c.f., Burke, 1991; Stets, 1995; Stets & Burke, 1996). As Stryker and Burke (2000) note in their recent review of identity theory, the "external" and "internal" threads of structural symbolic interaction have proceeded relatively independent of one another, and more emphasis has been given to the latter in recent years. But, just as many of us turned to the interrelationship of emotion, identity and action in the late 1980's, it seems that it is time to once again link social systems with selves and the emotional experiences that they engender. In their review, Stryker and Burke point to the need to develop the potential of a multiple-identity self within the context of our theories. Furthermore, in our research programs, we find that we cannot interpret individuals' actions in a substantial number of situations without analyzing the multiple identities that they hold and how those identities may operate together to form lines of social action. Several of us, relatively independently, have turned to this theoretical puzzle—Stryker (2000) in his consideration of social movement participation, Stets (1995) in her analysis of simultaneously held role- and personal- identities, Burke (1995; this volume) in his analysis of subjects in network exchange experiments and in small task groups, myself in an analysis of mixed emotions (Smith-Lovin, 2002), and a number of psychological researchers as well. It is time to tackle systematically the question of when and how people occupy multiple identities simultaneously. Doing so will help us re-connect our work to important substantive issues like social movement participation and to the important work that people like Peggy Thoits (1983, 1986, this volume) are doing on the ways in which multiple identities affect mental distress and other important outcomes.

In this chapter, I attempt to break the broad question of how multiple identities operate within situations into a manageable set of more specific issues. This formulation allows us to use some well-formed ideas from other research traditions to link social structure and individuals into an ecology of identities. I can then make some rather straightforward arguments, based on affect control theory, about how multiple identities will produce emotions and actions.

QUESTIONS, DEFINITIONS, AND SCOPE

I focus on three basic questions. First, what conditions determine the structure of available identities within a social system, and therefore the likelihood that social actors have relatively complex (multiple identity) selves? Second, when do people occupy two or more identities within the same social situation? Third, how do those simultaneously held identities produce lines of social action and emotional responses?

Before proceeding, I will clarify a few definitions and scope conditions. I use the term "identity" in a somewhat broader sense than Stryker's (1980) identity theory definition. I will include (1) the role-identities associated with positions in the social structure (Stryker, 1980), (2) the social identities that are associated with membership in groups and organizations (Stryker, 2000), and (3) the category memberships that come from identification with some characteristic, trait or attribute (Turner, 1985). For example, when we asked 38 members of the university community at Arizona about their identities in an experiential sampling study I conducted in 1995, they reported 559 distinct identities. These ranged from positional role-identities with clear role alters (e.g., bartender, landlord, sister), to activity-based identities with ambiguous alters (e.g., artist, camper, music lover), to social identities based on group membership (e.g., church member, Greek), to salient personal characteristics (e.g., African-American, believer, responsible person). I argue that this wide range of social entities should be studied together because they represent the ways that people think about themselves in situations. Since cognitive labeling and affective meaning are inextricably intertwined, and lead inevitably to processes of control and identity maintenance (MacKinnon, 1994), I argue that these self-labels should be treated in a single theoretical statement.

In the theoretical argument here, I hope to talk about identities that operate at the same level of the perceptual control system, rather than those that represent higher or lower levels of reference signal. Both Heise (1979) and Burke (Tsushima & Burke, 1999) have noted that multiple levels of control system exist, with shifts at higher levels effectively re-setting the reference levels that are operative at lower levels. Here, I attempt to analyze the relationships among those identities whose meanings directly determine the generation of lines of action and emotional responses to the actions of others, rather than those at higher levels. A rough operational criterion would be the nouns that people might use spontaneously (or when asked) to name themselves within the context of a situation.

What are the conditions, then, that make it more likely that an actor will occupy simultaneously more than one identity in the context of the same situation? I begin by using base rate logic (Mayhew, 1974). Before we explore more complex social processes, it makes sense to consider what conditions will make it more likely *by chance alone* that a person will occupy more than one identity simultaneously. This baseline logic requires that we step back from the typical concerns of individual-level or even interactional-level analysis, and think of identities as entities in a larger social structure. We are asking, essentially, when people are more likely to have more complex selves. Given a larger number of potential self-identities, it is more likely by chance that an actor will enter a situation where more than one of these identities is relevant and operates as an active identity standard for interaction. Logically, multiple identity occupancy should occur more often when the self is relatively complex (that is, when the individual has a relatively large number of identities in his or her salience hierarchy).

SOCIAL STRUCTURE AND COMPLEX SELVES

So, the question becomes: when do people have more or less complex selves? The tentative answers to such a question come from our theoretical understanding of what identities are: they are, at their core, the internalizations of role-identities, group memberships, and individually differentiating characteristics. All three of these identity sources have networks as their source. In the case of role-identities, it is a network relation with an alter that defines a position within a social structure that has rights, responsibilities, and behavioral expectations vis a vis some other position (Stryker, 1980). In the case of group membership, it is a membership tie to a group of alters who are similar in some defined way (Hogg, 1992; Turner, 1985; Tajfel & Turner, 1979). In the case of personal identities, it is network ties with others that create salient differences (Turner, 1985; Berger, Cohen & Zelditch, 1972).

Notice that homophily—the tendency to associate with similar others—does not create self-identities when it is perfectly strong. Most small, isolated, indigenous societies had a name for themselves that we translate roughly as "the people." Race or ethnicity does not appear as a salient identity until one is embedded in a system with *other* national or ethnic groups. It is the contrast, the interaction with dissimilar others, that makes a personal identity out of some personal characteristic (Berger et al., 1972). When homogeneity on a characteristic is very high, we get a taken-for-granted orientation toward that characteristic rather than an identification with it. Perhaps this is why all societies have age and sex categorization systems, and correspondingly salient self-identities for these characteristics (Sanday, 1976). These are the only two features where interactions among non-similar others are certain to occur within even the smallest, simplest society.

The clear dependence of self-complexity on network relations is very useful, for there is a substantial literature about how features of social systems link to network characteristics. The first principle upon which we can draw is the well-known relationship between size and differentiation. In virtually any domain—from the entire social system to the most ill-defined voluntary group—larger size leads to increased internal differentiation, with a concomitant rise in role differentiation (Mayhew, 1983; Mayhew, James & Childers 1972; Mayhew & Levinger 1976; Mayhew, Levinger, McPherson & James, 1972; Kasarda, 1974). Relations between actors shift from Gemeinschaft to Gesellschaft as systems grow large. In larger systems, we interact with those who are functionally interrelated but different from us; in smaller systems, we interact with those who are similar.

McPherson and Ranger-Moore (1992) have made a closely related argument about the dimensionality of the salient socio-demographic space that they call "Blau space." They note that there are few characteristics that distinguish individuals in small, technologically simple societies (primarily age, sex and physical capabilities). As society grows in size and scope, however, the scale of the system requires other dimensions of social life such as wealth, education, and other characteristics to organize social interaction. Perhaps more importantly, McPherson argues that salient dimensions of social differentiation become less correlated in large, modern systems, leading not just to greater diversity in the system as a whole, but allowing the development of distinctive regions (niches) that may be less connected with the rest of the system.

The second general social law that we can use in our argument here is homophily, the fact that social contact among individuals is a declining function of distance in Blau space (McPherson Smith-Lovin & Cook, 2001). Homophily organizes social networks in all known human groups, but the character of the social structure created by homophily changes as systems grow and social dimensions become less correlated. The decreasing correlation of relevant social dimensions has the effect of creating cross-cutting social circles: homophilous interactions on one dimension become more likely to create contacts with alters who are dissimilar on another (Blau 1977).

Both the size—differentiation principle (which should have its largest effect on role-identities) and the unfolding of Blau space in larger, technologically advanced systems (which should have its largest effect on membership- and category-based identities) lead us to predict that there will be more identities and people will have more complex selves in larger social systems. Of course, the differentiation in larger systems also will create lower density of interactions among actors (and segmentation of that interaction). These processes will work against the relationship between system size and identity structure complexity. But even with considerable homophily of interaction, the greater differentiation of larger systems should produce a less unified, more differentiated self structure.

AN ECOLOGY OF IDENTITIES

We can develop a somewhat more subtle view of the relationship between social systems and self structures by using the ecological framework developed by scholars who study the interplay of population distributions, networks and social groups. McPherson (1983) developed an ecological theory that should apply to any social entity that (1) spreads through homophilous network contacts and (2) involves some level of competition for the time or energy of actors. Entities as wide ranging as group memberships (McPherson, 1983; McPherson, Popielarz & Drobnic, 1992; Popielarz & McPherson, 1995), occupations (Rotolo & McPherson, 2001), musical taste communities (Mark, 1998a), cultural traits (Mark, 1998b) and religions (Chaves & Giesal, 2001) have been successfully analyzed using this framework. Since identities within a self structure should meet these criteria, I argue that an ecology of identity is a useful model for examining the relationship between system-level characteristics and the range, diversity and overlap of identities.

In a recent simulation study, McPherson (1999) analyzes the relationship between the level of homophily in a system and a number of outcomes that are directly related to identity—the number of distinct groups, the heterogeneity within groups, and membership overlap (the extent to which actors in the system are members of multiple groups simultaneously). Remembering that "group" here can represent any social entity that spreads through homophilous networks and competes for time and energy, all of these features should be related to the self complexity of actors within the system. In the simulations, a high level of homophily suppresses the extent of overlap of groups and the diversity of people within the groups. Effects on group size and the number of groups (net of system size) are minimal, primarily because homophily has countervailing direct and indirect forces. The direct effect of homophily is to create more, smaller groups. But homophily also has an effect on tie stability—homophilous ties are more likely to survive for longer periods—and the effect of tie stability is to make groups less numerous and larger. When homophily's direct effects on group size and number, and its indirect effects through tie stability, are taken into account, the net effect is near zero.

Therefore, any impact on the complexity of self structures from homophily should come from the overlap of groups or the diversity of groups, both of which should make for a more complex self. Homophily within a social system is likely to be created when sociodemographic dimensions are more correlated, since homophily on multiple dimensions can be optimized simultaneously in such a system. Under such conditions, groups (and other social entities like communities that hold similar tastes, engage in similar activities, etc.) will tend to be small and less diverse, leading to a simpler self.

SELVES IN NETWORKS

By focusing on the dependence of selves and their multiple identities on network ties, we can make use of the extensive literature on density and diversity of networks in different regions of social space to draw implications about self structure. For example, we know from Peter Blau's (1977) structural analysis that numerically smaller categories of people will have more out-group ties than those in larger categories (e.g., African-Americans have more ties with Anglos than Anglos do with African- Americans). Actors higher in the stratification system are more likely to have diverse networks that range further through the social system than those who are lower in the stratification system (Lin, 2001). Each of these well-established empirical facts has an implication for self complexity. Individuals occupying numerically smaller categories will have more complex selves than individuals from numerically larger categories, because they interact with more people who are different from them. Higher status actors will have more complex selves than lower status actors, because they have networks that extend into more distant reaches of the social system.

Having used properties of social systems to draw implications about when actors will have complex selves, I now turn to the more familiar domain of interaction to suggest how these complex selves will be enacted in actual situations.

COMPLEXITY OF SITUATIONS

A complex self is a necessary condition for multiple identities to be enacted in a given situation. Increasing self complexity may make such multiple identity enactment more likely by chance. But there is also the possibility that interactions are segregated in ways that lead complex selves to be played out in relatively simple single-identity interactions. Indeed, Bernice Pescosolido and Beth Rubin (2000) have pointed out mechanisms that vary with historical time that should operate with a countervailing force. They have suggested that the historical trends that I outlined in the section above have progressed beyond an unfolding of salient dimensions to a post-modern society where individuals mostly bridge structural holes, connecting non-overlapping entities. In such a post-modern world, where most network ties are bridging ties, individuals would have complex selves but would seldom encounter situations in which multiple identities were relevant.

Pescsolido and Rubin (2000) suggest that the primary mechanism driving the post-modern "spoke" network structure, where individual actors act as bridging ties between otherwise unconnected groups, is the stability of ties. If ties are stable, long-term relations, the fact that most group memberships are recruited through network ties should lead one bridging tie to become many. Social groups will become cross-cutting social circles if ties persist long enough for new ties to build on the first connection between the groups. Indeed, McPherson's (1999) simulation studies of system-level parameters and their effects on group structure show a clear, strong positive relationship between tie stability and the membership overlap of groups. These simulations also show that tie stability fosters larger, more diverse groups that survive longer (although in smaller numbers). The simulation results from these system-level relationships lead to our first insights for situation-level predictions. A tie that has persisted for longer periods of time is more likely to evoke multiple, overlapping group memberships and, net of other social forces, to result in the simultaneous operation of multiple identities.

The suggestion that interactions in multiplex relationships are more likely to involve multiple identities may sound definitional, but it is not. Stryker's (1968, 1980) original specification of the basic Meadian principle—society shapes self shapes social behavior—focused on role choice behavior. He argued that commitment to an identity (the extent of one's social network ties that are dependent on that identity) influenced salience of an identity in the self hierarchy, which then influenced which role-identity one *chose* to enacted when a given situation allowed for the enactment of more than one self-identity. The clear implication of this thinking is that when multiple identities are options in a given interaction, a choice will be made to enact *one* of them (the most salient one) in preference to the others. A multiplex relationship to an alter does not require a multiple identity interaction. On the contrary, the research traditions spawned by Stryker, Heise and all of their structural symbolic interactionist colleagues typically assume that one identity will prevail and dominate a well-defined interactional setting. Here, I loosen that (often implicit) assumption. Therefore, the suggestion that multiplex relationships are more likely than interactions with alters with whom one has only a single relation to evoke multiple identity standards for behavior is a base rate prediction from the structure of the relationship.

This structural relationship applies most clearly to identities formed from role relationships and, perhaps, from group membership. But multiple identities can also be evoked in a situation by interactions with diverse others. Here, one can make use of arguments about salience of status characteristics in expectation states theory. When interactants are differentiated by one or more noticeable characteristics, those characteristics are likely to become salient (in the sense of organizing expectations and action)—in other words, they are likely to evoke identities that will operate as reference standards in the context of the interaction.

We know that most interactions occur in the context of larger institutional foci, and that the composition of these settings has powerful effects on the direct connections among actors within those settings. McPherson and I have shown that most of the observed similarity among friendship ties that form in groups, for example, is due to the opportunity structure of the group rather than individual choices that are made within the group (McPherson & Smith-Lovin 1985, 1986). Therefore, we can think of setting-level versions of our earlier social system differentiation arguments to predict when interactions will involve alters who differ in some socially-important characteristic (either roles or category memberships): people who interact in large, diverse groups or institutional settings with low internal correlations among social characteristics will be more likely to be embedded in interactions with diverse others, and to occupy multiple identities within those interactions.

Up to this point I have attempted to answer the first two questions posed at the beginning of this chapter, using information from social ecology and network theory to suggest when multiple indentities will be available in self structures and operative within situations. I now move onto more social psychological processes to discuss how multiple identities will be processed in a situation where they are relevant and psychologically accessed. Here, I will draw more explicitly on the "internal" branch of recent identity theories.

MULTIPLE IDENTITIES AND IDENTITY STANDARDS

As Stryker and Burke (2000) noted in their recent review article, the "internal" branches of structural symbolic interaction—affect control theory and identity control theory—largely assumed the problem of multiple identities away, by assuming that one identity becomes paramount in a given interaction and that actors operate to maintain that identity. As we have encountered the obvious shortcomings of this theoretical position, some intermediate solutions have evolved to deal with multiple identities. Affect control theorists, largely following the work of Chris Averett from the late 1970's, have added qualifiers to role-identities (Averett & Heise 1987; Smith, 1999). For example, socio-demographic characteristics can be combined with identities to create amalgams like "a black doctor" or " a rich CEO." The fundamental meanings of these qualified identities can be predicted very accurately using the same empirical paradigm that affect control theory uses to estimate meanings in general: the meanings of both the identity and the qualifying characteristic are assessed on the three dimensional structure (evaluation, potency and activity) developed by Osgood and his colleagues (Osgood, Suci & Tannenbaum, 1957, Osgood, May & Miron, 1975) to measure affective meaning. The meaning of the composite is assessed using the same scales. Then the meaning of the composite is regressed on the meanings of the identity and qualifier in isolation to develop an empirically derived model of how the two combine to form a new fundamental meaning for the composite identity. Not surprisingly, when the attribute closely matches the identity in meaning, the identity is not changed significantly by the addition of a qualifier (e.g., a rich CEO). In this case, the qualifying characteristic is already included in the prototypical meaning of the identity, and is reflected in its affective meaning within the culture. When the qualifier *is* significantly different in meaning, the resulting amalgam (a weighted average of the two) can be substantially different from either of te original meanings. This, then, is one possibility of handling at least some identity combinations—those that link one central identity with some additional, atypical socio-demographic qualifier.

A simple averaging of meanings is not likely to capture the ways in which people operate with multiple identities in all situations. However, there is good reason why it seems to work fairly well as a provisional first step. In the ecology of identities that I discuss in the earlier sections, it is likely that identities that are commonly linked within social systems (i.e., are held simultaneously by a relatively large number of actors within those social systems) have similar meanings in the three dimensional evaluation-potency-activity space. If this were not true, the co-occurrence would lead to pressure for change in the cultural meanings of these identities over time, as we saw people who occupied those identities behave in ways that maintained a very different set of meanings (the other, co-present identity). Therefore, identities that are simultaneously held are likely to be similar in meaning. This pattern is implied strongly by the control system that is necessary to maintain these identities.

When identities are relatively close in meaning, they can be maintained simultaneously by similar actions, no matter what the alters' responses in the context of the situation. Since it is the meaning in the three-dimensional space that determines the actual processing of the event, two identities that are close in the meaning space are *effectively* the same identity. Therefore, it is reasonable to think that two simultaneously held identities that are close in meaning might easily be combined into a slightly different, composite identity standard that will then be maintained through interaction. This will be the typical situation when multiple identities are evoked.

Consider, however, the relatively unusual case where two identities *are* quite different in meaning, but are simultaneously evoked by the situation. In this case, actions (by self or alter) that maintain one identity will be disruptive to the other. In the conceptual language of affect control theory, deflection will result. Since any (weighted) average of the two identities will create a composite that is quite distant in the three-dimensional meaning space from either of the original identities, such an amalgam is unlikely to occur. If we assume that actors may intermittently attend more or less to various identities that they hold within the course of an interaction, such a composite, being quite distant from either of the original identities in meaning, would lead to considerable deflection when one or the other gained temporary foregrounding in cognitive processing. Indeed, the deflection might *create* the attentional shifts that would shift attention toward the individual identities.

A more realistic view would reject the central processing model that currently dominates our models of human psychology, and replace it with a connectionist model (Humphreys & Kashima, 2002). There are several indications in recent theoretical discussions that a connectionist model might be more consistent with the new challenges introduced by multiple identity standards. The distributed representations that are possible within the connectionist model are well suited to characterizing a multiple-identity self. And the parallel processing offers a potential answer to the problem of how multiple identities operate within a given situation. Multiple aspects of the self—multiple role-identities that are potentially relevant to the situation, or a mix of more general self-conceptions and specific role-identity meanings—can be activated by a situation. Events can be perceived and processed simultaneously from the point of view of multiple identities.

If identities rather disparate in meaning are processed in parallel, maintenance in one will result in deflection for the other. To the extent that deflection is experienced psychologically as a sense that the world is unpredictable, not right, or disturbing, one would expect stress to result. Perhaps there also might be a heightened probability of leaving the interaction. One phenomenon that this parallel multiple-identity processing could explain is the common experience of mixed emotions (Smith-Lovin, 2002). If our control models are correct, emotions are experienced primarily as the result of the confirmation or disconfirmation of role-identities that are activated within a setting. If an actor is occupying more than one identity simultaneously, and experiencing events from those multiple perspectives, it is natural that a mixture of emotions (some of which might be quite different in character) would be felt as a result of events. For example, a directive action that would support the identity of "judge" might produce negative deflection on the evaluation and positive deflection on the potency dimension for "woman." This might produce a mixture of feelings of being tense (the judge) and being bitchy (the woman).[1]

I will note in conclusion that the connectionist representation of identity processing is also quite consistent with affect control theory's view of the relationship between individuals and the culture from which they derive identity meanings. Consider the view that each individual represents a variety of self-conceptions (identities) within a parallel distributed processing system, and that the meanings associated with these self-conceptions are shared with other individuals and represented symbolically by cultural artifacts like books, films and language use. This distributed cognition model captures several features that are central to affect control theory and other sociological theories that grew out of

---

[1] These results are from affect control theory simulations using Program INTERACT, which is available on the web at www.indiana.edu/heise/socpsych.

Meadian symbolic interactionism. First, it accurately represents the relationship between the individual and the collective. Individual meanings are developed out of contact with society (in both its personal and artifactual forms). Furthermore, individuals act as both learners, carriers and (within limits) innovators of cultural meanings. Therefore, the ideas presented in this chapter connect to the social system level in two ways. I use ecological theory to suggest the connections among identities that are created by the complex selves that individuals create under varying social structures. Then, I use a connectionist model of individual processing that more accurately represents how individual actors operate as part of an interconnected cultural system. This connectionist model shows how actors process multiple parts of a social system simultaneously in their own interactions, carrying partial representations of a larger interconnected cultural system in their self structures.

ACKNOWLEDGMENTS: This chapter is based on a paper prepared for the Indiana Conference on Identity Theory, Bloomington, IN, April 27–29, 2001. The work has been supported by National Science Foundation grant SBE-0110599.

REFERENCES

Averett, C.P. & Heise, D.R. (1987). Modified social identities: Amalgamations, attributions, and emotions. *Journal of Mathematical Sociology,* 13, 103–132.

Berger, J, Cohen, B.P.,& Zelditch, M Jr. 1972. Status characteristics and social interaction. *American Sociological Review,* 37, 241–55.

Blau, P.M. 1977. *Inequality and Heterogeneity.* New York: Free Press.

Chaves, M., & Giesel, H. 2001. How should we study religious competition? Paper presented at the meetings of the Society for the Scientific Study of Religion, Columbus, OH.

Burke, P.J. 1991. Identity processes and social stress. *American Sociological Review* ,56, 836–49.

Burke, P.J. & Franzoi, S.L. 1988. Studying situations and identities using experiential sampling methodology. *American Sociological Review,* 53, 559–68.

Childers, G.W., Mayhew, B.H. & Gray, L.N. 1971. System Size and Structural Differentiation in Military Organizations: Testing a Baseline Model of the Division of Labor *American Journal of Sociology,* 76, 813–830.

Heise, D.R. 1979. *Understanding Events: Affect and the Construction of Social Action.* Cambridge, U.K.: Cambridge University Press.

Heise, D.R. 1990. Affect control theory: A technical appendix. Pp. 270–280 in T.D. Kemper (ed.), *Research Agendas in Emotions,* New York: SUNY Press.

Heise D.R. & Britt L. 2000. In *Identity, Self and Social Movements,* edited by S. Stryker, T. Owens and R. White. Minneapolis: University of Minnesota Press.

Kasarda, J.D. 1974. The Structural Implications of Social System Size: A Three-Level Analysis. *American Sociological Review,* 39, 19–28.

MacKinnon, N.J. 1994. *Symbolic Interaction as Affect Control.* Albany: SUNY Press.

Mark, N. 1998a. Birds of a Feather Sing Together. *Social Forces,* 77, 455–85.

Mark, N. 1998b. An ecology of culture. Doctoral dissertation, University of Arizona.

Mayhew, B.H. 1974. Baseline models of system structure. *American Sociological Review,* 39, 137–143.

Mayhew, B.H. 1983. Hierarchical differentiation in imperatively coordinated systems. Pp. 153–229 in *Research in the Sociology of Organizations* edited by S. Bacharach. Greenwich: JAI Press.

Mayhew, B.H., James, T.F.& Childers, G.W. 1972. System size and structural differentiation in military organizations: Testing a harmonic series model of the division of labor. *American Journal of Sociology,* 77, 750–765.

Mayhew, B.H. & Levinger, R.L. 1976. Size and the density of interaction in human aggregates. *American Journal of Sociology,* 82, 86–110.

Mayhew, B.H., Levinger, R.L., McPherson, J.M. & James, T.F.1972 System size and structural differentiation in formal organizations: A baseline generator for two major theoretical propositions. *American Sociological Review,* 37, 629–633.

McPherson, J.M. 1983. An ecology of affiliation. *American Sociological Review,* 48, 519–532.

McPherson, J.M. 1999. Modeling change in fields of organizations: Some simulation results. In Ilgen, D. and Hulin, C. (Eds.) *Computational Modeling of Behavioral Processes in Organizations.* American Psychological Association Press.

McPherson M, Popilearz, P. A. & Drobnic S. 1992. Social networks and organizational dynamics. *American Sociological Review,* 57, 153–70.

McPherson, J.M. & Ranger-Moore, J.R. 1991. Evolution on a dancing landscape: Organizations and networks in dynamic Blau space. *Social Forces,* 70, 19–42.

McPherson, J.M. & Rotolo, T. 1996. Testing a dynamic model of social composition: Diversity and change in voluntary groups. *American Sociological Review,* 61, 179–202.

McPherson, M. & Smith-Lovin, L. 1986. Sex segregation in voluntary associations. *American Sociological Review,* 51, 61–79.

McPherson, M. & Smith-Lovin, L. 1987. Homophily in voluntary organizations: Status distance and the composition of facetoface groups. *American Sociological Review,* 52, 370–79.

McPherson, M & Smith-Lovin L. 2002. "Cohesion and membership duration: Linking groups, relations and individuals in an ecology of affiliation." Pp. xx in S. Thye and E. Lawler, *Advances in Group Processes,* JAI Press.

McPherson, M., Smith-Lovin, L. & Cook, J. 2001. "Birds of a feather: Homophily in social networks. *Annual Review of Sociology,* 27, 415–44.

Mirowsky, J, & Ross, C. 1995. Sex differences in distress: Real or artifact?" *American Sociological Review,* 60, 449–68.

Osgood, C.E., May, W.H., & Miron, M.S. 1975. *Cross-cultural universals of affective meaning.* Urbana: University of Illinois Press.

Osgood, C.E, Suci, G.C., & Tannenbaum, P.H. 1957. *The measurement of meaning.* Urbana: University of Illinois Press.

Popielarz, P. & McPherson, M. 1995. On the edge or in between: Niche position, niche overlap and the duration of voluntary association memberships. *American Journal of Sociology,* 101, 698–720.

Powers, W. T. 1973. *Behavior: The control of perception.* Chicago: Aldine.

Ridgeway, C. 1991. The social construction of status value: Gender and other nominal characteristics. *Social Forces,* 70, 367–86.

Ridgeway, C. & Smith-Lovin, L. 1994. Structure, culture and interaction: A comparison of affect control theory and expectations states theory. *Advances in Group Processes,* Vol. 11, JAI Press.

Robinson, D.T., & Smith-Lovin, L. 1992. Selective interaction as a strategy for identity maintenance: An affect control model. *Social Psychology Quarterly,* 55, 12–28.

Rotolo, T., & McPherson, J.M. 2001. The system of occupations: Modeling occupations in sociodemographic space. *Social Forces,* 79, 1095–1130.

Serpe, R.T. 1987. Stability and change in self: A structural symbolic interactionist explanation. *Social Psychology Quarterly,* 50, 44–55.

Smith-Lovin, L. 2002. Role-identities, action and emotion: parallel processing and the production of mixed emotions. In Kashima, Y., Foddy, M. & Platow, M. (eds.), *Self and Identity: Personal, Social, and Symbolic.* New York: Erlbaum.

Smith-Lovin, L. 2000. "Social psychology." In J. Blau (ed.), *Blackwell companion to sociology* Malden, Mass.: Blackwell.

Smith-Lovin, L. 1990. "Emotion as confirmation and disconfirmation of identity: An affect control model." Pp. 238–270 in T.D. Kemper (ed.), *Research agendas in emotions.* New York: SUNY Press.

Smith-Lovin, L. 1987. Impressions from events. *Journal of Mathematical Sociology,* 13, 35–70.

Smith-Lovin, L. & Heise, D.R. 1988 *Affect Control Theory: Research Advances.* New York: Wiley Interscience

Stets, J.E. 1995. Role identities and person identities: Gender identity, mastery identity and controlling one's partner. *Sociological Perspectives,* 38, 129–50.

Stets, J.E. & Burke, P.J. 1996. Gender, control and interaction. *Social Psychology Quarterly,* 59, 193–220.

Stryker, S. 1968. Identity salience and role performance. *Journal of Marriage and the Family,* 4, 558–64.

Stryker, S. 1980. *Symbolic Interactionism: A Social Structural Version.* Menlo Park, CA: Benjamin Cummings.

Stryker, S. 2000. Identity competition: Key to differential social movement involvement."In *Identity, Self and Social Movements,* edited by S. Stryker, T. Owens and R. White. Minneapolis: University of Minnesota Press.

Stryker, S. & Burke P. J. 2000. The past, present and future of identity theory. *Social Psychology Quarterly,* 63, 284–97.

Stryker, S. & Serpe, R.T. 1982. Commitment, identity salience and role behavior: A theory and research example. Pp. 199–218 in *Personality, Roles and Social Behavior,* edited by W. Ickes and Eric S Knowles. New York: Springer-Verlag.

Stryker, S. & Statham, A. 1985. Symbolic interaction and role theory. Pp. 311–78 in *Handbook of Social Psychology*, edited by G. Lindzey and E. Aronson. New York: Random House.

Tajfel, H. & Turner, J.C. 1979 An integrative theory of intergroup conflict." Pp. 33–47 in W.G. Austin and S. Worchel, (eds.), *The Social Psychology of Intergroup Relations*. Monterey CA: Brooks-Cole.

Tsushima, T. & Burke, P.J. 1999. Levels, agency and control in the parent identity. *Social Psychology Quarterly*, 62,173–89.

Thoits, P.A. 1983. Multiple identities and psychological well-bring. *American Sociological Review*, 49, 174–87.

Thoits, P.A. 1986. Multiple identities: Examining gender and marital status differences in distress. *American Sociological Review*, 51, 259–72.

Turner, J.C. 1985. Social categorization and the self-concept: A social cognitive theory of group behavior." Pp. 77–122 in E.J. Lawler (ed.), *Advances in Group Processes, Vol. 2*. Greenwich, CT: JAI Press

Chapter 12

Personal Agency in the Accumulation of Multiple Role-Identities

PEGGY A. THOITS

INTRODUCTION

Identity theory and its parent theory, symbolic interactionism, are based on the fundamental premise that society and self mutually shape and influence each other. In this chapter, I focus especially on the self-affects-society side of this interdependent relationship, because it has been neglected both theoretically and empirically. My goal is to foster greater appreciation of the degree to which individuals are active agents in their own lives and to spell out some of the implications of this observation for the further expansion of identity theory.

To accomplish these tasks, I take as a case in point the often investigated effects of role-identities on individuals' thoughts, feelings, and behaviors. A brief description of the theoretical underpinnings of these studies is useful.

Symbolic interactionist theory assumes that people acquire self-conceptions through the process of taking the role of the other (Blumer, 1969; Cooley, 1902; Mead, 1934; Stryker, 1980); we know who we are, in a social sense, through seeing ourselves in the eyes of other people. Because others define and behave toward us on the basis of our social positions and roles (among other attributes), we come to define ourselves, at least in part, in these terms as well—we accept our positions and roles as identities (or "role-identities"). This is the "society shapes the self" aspect of symbolic interactionism.

Identities in turn have important behavioral consequences. Because we not only know ourselves through the eyes of others, but evaluate our worth, goodness, and competence through others' eyes as well (Cooley, 1902), we are motivated to gain the rewarding approval of other people by anticipating and meeting their expectations. Typically, this means that we conform to the norms attached to the conventional role-identities that we hold: spouse, parent, employee, student, friend, neighbor, and so forth. When we behave in normative ways, albeit with idiosyncratic variations that make our role-related behaviors uniquely characteristic of us (McCall & Simmons, 1978), we in effect reproduce and sustain the social order. This is the "self shapes society" aspect of symbolic interactionist thought.

Although considerable emphasis has been placed on the behavioral consequences of the role-identities that individuals hold (e.g., Stryker, 1980; Stryker & Serpe, 1982, 1994), identities also have important mental health implications, i.e., implications for how individuals think and feel about themselves. I have argued in earlier work (e.g., Thoits, 1983) that because role-identities define who we are, and why and how we are to behave in normatively specified ways, they provide a sense of purpose and meaning in life and behavioral guidance, thus reducing depression and anxiety and promoting the avoidance of non-normative behaviors, such as excessive alcohol or drug use. Competent role-identity performances also generate positive self-appraisals (Cooley, 1902; Rosenberg & McCullough, 1981) and foster beliefs in self-efficacy, i.e., one's ability to produce desired outcomes and avoid undesired ones (Bandura 2001). In short, role-identities are important sources of key aspects of well-being: few psychological symptoms, high self-esteem, and a sense of control or self-efficacy (Ervin & Stryker, 2001). Generally, the more role-identities individuals hold, the more purpose, meaning, behavioral guidance, and approving social feedback they have available, and thus, the better should be their mental health or general well-being.

These implications of role-identities for well-being contradict the predictions of traditional role theorists. Merton (1957), Goode (1960), and Coser (1974), for example, assumed that occupying multiple statuses and roles puts individuals at increased risk of experiencing role conflict and/or role overload. These role strains in turn make more likely the onset of emotional distress (due to individuals' overtaxed abilities to cope) or ill health (due to physical exhaustion). Contemporary stress theory makes similar predictions, particularly with respect to women who hold multiple roles with incompatible or inordinate demands (e.g., Gove, 1984; Menaghan, 1989). Only in recent years have "revisionist" role theorists challenged these assumptions, arguing that holding multiple roles is more beneficial than harmful to mental and physical health. Revisionists have suggested that role accumulation generates additional energy and commitment (Marks, 1977), provides a global sense that life is meaningful and worthwhile (Burton, 1998), bolsters self-esteem (Sieber, 1974), and sustains a sense of positive identity in the face of failures or setbacks (Sieber, 1974; Thoits, 1983).

Consistent with the revisionists' view, studies have repeatedly shown that holding multiple roles has significant positive rather than negative influences on mental health, even when individuals' prior mental health status is controlled (Adelmann, 1994; Baruch & Barnett, 1986; Burton, 1998; Gore & Mangione, 1983; Hong & Seltzer, 1995; Jackson, 1997; Miller, Moen & Dempster-McClain, 1991; Pietromonaco, Manis, & Frohardt-Lane, 1986; Repetti & Crosby, 1984; Spreitzer, Snyder, & Larson, 1979; Thoits, 1983, 1986; Waldron & Jacobs, 1989). This finding has often been critiqued on the grounds that the quantity of roles is not what truly matters for well-being. Rather, it is the quality of experiences within role domains (Barnett & Baruch, 1987; Baruch & Barnett, 1986; Jackson, 1997) and/or the particular gender- or age-appropriate combination of roles held by individuals (Menaghan, 1989; Thoits, 1992) that accounts for variations in physical or mental health.[1] Although these critiques have theoretical merit and have been empirically supported as well, it is important to note that *all* of these investigators have shown (usually in the

---

[1]Jackson (1997) reports that role accumulation and psychological well-being are positively associated for whites and Mexican-Americans but not for African-Americans or Puerto Ricans. She suggests that specific roles and some role combinations are more stressful and/or less meaningful to African Americans and Puerto Ricans than to the other two groups.

same critical articles) that role accumulation itself has significant positive effects on well-being outcomes. In short, the role quality and role combination arguments have validity, but the quantity effect still remains. The quantity effect, however, is found most consistently when voluntary roles (e.g., churchgoer, club member, friend, neighbor) are considered as a subset, in contrast to obligatory roles such as spouse, parent, and worker (Pavalko & Woodbury 2000; Thoits, 1992). This is probably because voluntary roles make fewer or less intense demands on time, energy, and commitment; they are often deliberately acquired for their anticipated benefits; and they can be exited more easily when their costs exceed the rewards that individuals obtain from them.[2]

NEGLECT OF AGENCY

Interestingly, research on multiple roles has focused on the physical or mental health *consequences* of role accumulation and has not examined its *determinants*. Because theorists suspect that prior physical and/or mental health status may affect role accumulation, investigators who have longitudinal data have routinely controlled for individuals' prior physical and psychological states in order to rule out the possibility of reverse causality, or "selection effects." For sociologists, the desire to demonstrate "social causation" rather than selection is an understandable impulse; the discipline's goal is to establish that social arrangements and social relationships have important consequences for human beings that cannot be ignored. Ironically, however, this desire to focus on social causation processes while controlling for or ruling out selection processes (however understandable) diverts attention from the importance of human agency in social life.

In contrast to mainstream sociological approaches, classical interactionists (e.g., Blumer, 1969 Cooley, 1902; Mead, 1934) and contemporary identity theorists (e.g., Burke, 1991, 1997; McCall & Simmons, 1978, Stryker, 1980) all emphasize the indeterminacy in human thought and behavior, attributing that indeterminacy to individuals' free will, spontaneity, or creativity (Mead's "I"). (Emphasis on free will is found in the Marxist tradition as well.) Free will in more current terms is the exercise of "personal agency." As agents, people act intentionally, make choices or decisions, formulate and follow plans of action, set goals and pursue them, and monitor and correct their own progress toward some future outcome (Bandura 2001).[3] If we accept the theoretical premise that individuals can be activists in their own lives (Thoits, 1994), it becomes important to verify selection effects in the relationship between multiple role occupancy and well-being, rather than ruling those effects out with statistical controls. In other words, it becomes important to show that individuals' pre-existing physical and psychological characteristics do influence their subsequent acquisition of role-identities, which in turn embed them more fully in social life. (Taking a symbolic interactionist stance, I will from this point on refer not to roles but to "role-identities," as I have confirmed in prior research [Thoits, 1992] that people indeed conceive of themselves in terms of the roles that they hold, that is, they do view their social roles as identities.)

---

[2]Reitzes & Mutran (1994) reported no relationship between role accumulation and self-esteem in a middle-aged sample of employed men and women. Seven of the twelve roles that they examined were obligatory in nature, outnumbering the remaining five which were voluntary.

[3]The idea of individuals having choice and control, built into symbolic interactionist thought, may reflect larger historical shifts in Western culture toward valuing individualism and agency (Callero in this volume; Giddens, 1991).

Which physical and psychological characteristics are crucial in this agentic process? In stress theory, confidence, a sense of control or mastery, and self-worth are key aspects of personality upon which people draw when they are dealing with challenges and difficulties in their lives (Pearlin & Schooler, 1978; Thoits, 1995). These personality traits allow individuals not only to solve problems but to initiate and persevere in desired lines of action. Not surprisingly, people who are confident, feel a sense of mastery, and have high self-esteem also have good physical and mental health (Turner & Roszell, 1994). Positive personality traits and good physical and mental health can more generally be viewed as personality and well-being resources, respectively, that facilitate seeking entry to and becoming involved in a variety of conventional role-identity domains.

I suggest that individuals who possess more of such personal and well-being resources are more effective in pursuing their values or goals. Effective action in turn should result in the accumulation of more role-identities, both obligatory (e.g., spouse, parent, worker) and voluntary (e.g., community volunteer, church member, friend). Some studies indicate that people select themselves into marriage and employment partly on the basis of their personality characteristics, interpersonal skills, and physical and mental health (Rodgers & Mann, 1993; Ross & Mirowsky, 1995; Thoits, 1994; Turner & Gartrell, 1978). Because voluntary identities are adopted by choice, personal agency is obviously involved in such role acquisition. People with greater resources that enable the exercise of choice and sustained goal-directed activity should acquire more voluntary role-identities over time than those with fewer resources.

However, it is important to qualify these arguments. Selection processes do not only or always reflect the influence of human agency or *self*-determination (Thoits & Hewitt 2001). Entry into roles is often controlled by gatekeepers, such as employers who are filling work positions, chairs of committees seeking active participants, deacons identifying trustworthy church members to handle congregational tasks, and trainers preparing crisis line personnel for emergency calls. Gatekeepers probably select individuals differentially not only on the basis of their formal credentials or past relevant experience, but on the basis of personality, physical health, and emotional maturity, especially when open positions involve responsibility for the welfare of others or risks to the role incumbent (e.g., McAdam, 1988). Thus, personality and well-being resources may not only facilitate *self*-selection into roles but may be influential in the decision-making of gatekeepers, a *social* selection effect.

It is important, furthermore, not to exaggerate selection processes, whether they be self- or social selection. Stryker and Statham (1985) long ago pointed out that virtually all human choices are socially constrained. People's social statuses—gender, race, ethnicity, education, social class, age, religion, and nationality—influence the opportunities they have for role-identity acquisition and accumulation. Regardless of motivation, skill, or preparation, due to their locations in the social structure, some people may be actively barred from entry into role domains, be kept unaware of possibilities for entry, or be discouraged by others from trying. This is a key tenet of symbolic interactionist thought: Humans are both "shapers" of and shaped by their social worlds.

Despite this balanced theoretical view of human behavior, many if not most symbolic interactionists and identity theorists, like role theorists (although see Callero, 1994, for an exception), have tended to focus their research attention on processes through which individuals are socially shaped by, rather than actively construct, their social worlds. Stryker's identity theory, the leading identity approach in the last two decades (Stryker, 1980, Stryker & Serpe, 1982), itself emphasizes the social shaping of individuals' role-identities and role behaviors and de-emphasizes the effects of individuals' thoughts, feelings, and actions on the organization of their own and others' lives. This is reflected in Stryker's characterization of his approach as *structural* symbolic interactionism (my emphasis, Stryker & Burke 2000: 285). In a well-known piece, Stryker and Serpe (1982) argue and show that the number and emotional importance of ties to specific others in people's social networks (their role-identity commitments) influence the probability that individuals will invoke particular role-identities when situations allow a choice among roles (role-identity salience), and this differential probability of invocation in turn predicts the amount of time people will spend in role-identity behavior (and probably predicts the intensity of their efforts to meet role-identity expectations, as well). Influences thus run from the organization of the person's social network to identity salience to in-role behaviors, not from role performance to identity salience to the formation, maintenance, or alteration of people's networks of ties (although see Cast this volume; Ethier & Deaux, 1994; Serpe & Stryker, 1987, for exceptions).

There are good reasons for Stryker's emphasis on social causation processes rather than selection processes: One of Stryker's overriding goals was and continues to be addressing a major gap in symbolic interactionist thought: a lack of explicit attention to social structure. To fill this gap, Stryker elaborated social structural influences on the organization of identities and on identity enactment (Stryker, 1980; Stryker & Burke 2000; Stryker & Statham, 1985). Not surprisingly, then, the thrust of much of Stryker's work has been to demonstrate the crucial importance of people's positional locations (i.e., their social statuses) and their network structures (the extensiveness and intensity of their social ties) for identity salience and identity performance (e.g., Stryker & Serpe, 1982, 1994).

Nevertheless, this emphasis on social causation processes in identity theory, and in sociological work on multiple roles and mental health more generally, has promoted a unidirectional view of the relationship between role-identities (society) and well-being (the person), however inadvertently. This is also true of my own past research on multiple role-identities. Consequently, I explore here both sides of the self-society relationship to support a more balanced theoretical and empirical view.

To illustrate the influence of personality and well-being resources on identity accumulation, especially the accumulation of voluntary identities, I use panel data on a stratified random sample of married and divorced adults residing in Indianapolis. I will demonstrate both selection and social causation effects. I will leave the task of parsing self-selection from social-selection processes to future research; my primary goal is to establish that selection processes do occur.

STUDY DESCRIPTION

The purpose of the Indianapolis panel study was to assess the stress experiences, identities, and mental health of married and divorced adults over time. The first wave of structured face-to-face interviews occurred in 1988 (N = 700) and the second in 1990 (N = 532). Respondents were selected through random digit dialing techniques, with an additional subset of recently divorced persons selected with systematic sampling from the Indianapolis courthouse records.[4] The sample under-represented poor and working class individuals, and this middle-class bias intensified over time. Although the data cannot be generalized to the population of married and divorced adults in Indianapolis as a whole, the relationships that I describe here should still be informative theoretically.

---

[4]The response rate at Time 1 was 66% (a typical response rate for surveys in urban areas) and 80% at Time 2.

Consistent with identity theory (Stryker, 1980), I defined role-identities as positions in the social structure that individuals viewed as self-descriptive. For each of 17 roles (listed below), I asked respondents whether they thought of themselves as a (*name of role, e.g., mother/father/parent*). Possible answers were "yes," "no," or "does not apply to me." Only roles for which individuals said, "Yes, I think of myself as an X," are treated here as role-identities.

For the purposes of this analysis, I subdivided role-identities into obligatory and voluntary types. Previous work showed that obligatory roles are beneficial for mental health only when chronic strains experienced in these roles are low, while voluntary identities significantly reduce psychological distress individually and as a set (Thoits, 1992). Given these differing relationships with well-being, these types of role-identities should be kept distinct.

I conceive of obligatory role-identities as involving long-term ties to others that are often affectively intense and have relatively demanding mutual rights and responsibilities attached to them, making these identities more difficult to exit, both emotionally and instrumentally. When incumbents fail to meet their role responsibilities or when they contemplate exit, they are highly likely to be sanctioned by role partners. The set of obligatory identities assessed in this study includes parent, spouse, worker, student, son/daughter, (other) relative, son/daughter-in-law, stepparent, and caregiver, so obligatory role-identity accumulation ranges in value from 0 to 9. Note that agency is involved in entering several of these roles; people choose to marry, have children, pursue employment, and so on. I classify them as obligatory because of the relative strength of their normative demands on role incumbents.

I view voluntary role-identities as discretionary—one can more easily choose to enter and abandon these identities. Because voluntary ties tend to be shorter-term (compared to obligatory ties), because their affective intensity is usually lower, and because responsibilities to role partners are less demanding and less likely to be sanctioned when unmet, voluntary identities are easier to exit. In the data, the set of voluntary identities consist of friend, churchgoer, boyfriend/girlfriend, neighbor, group member, athlete, hobbyist, and community volunteer, so voluntary role-identity accumulation can vary from 0 to 8.[5]

Table 1 shows the average number of obligatory and voluntary identities held by respondents at the first interview, by marital status. Not surprisingly, married individuals hold two additional obligatory identities than the divorced, on average (about 5.5 versus 3.5). This difference is a direct function of marital status—the married see themselves as spouses and sons/daughters-in-laws while the divorced, who no longer enact these role-identities, do not. In addition to spouse and in-law, the most common identities held by all respondents include parent, relative, son/daughter, and worker. Table 1 also shows that the married and divorced hold equal numbers of voluntary identities, about four on average. The four most frequent for both groups are friend, neighbor, hobbyist, and religious person.

I use five different indicators of personality and well-being resources, all of which have good reliability. *Self-esteem* is a personality resource, measured with Rosenberg's (1979) well-known global self-esteem scale which has ten items (for example, "I take a positive attitude toward myself," "I feel I have a number of good qualities"). Respondents could indicate their degree of agreement with these statements on four-point scales from "strongly disagree" to "strongly agree." All responses were summed so that higher scores indicate higher self-esteem.

---

[5]The friend identity might be an exception to my characterization of most voluntary roles, because friendship ties can be emotionally close, long-term, and include the exchange of valued goods or assistance. However, friendships are usually easier and less costly to exit than marriages, kin relations, or even jobs.

Table 1. Mean Numbers of Obligatory and Voluntary Role-Identities at Time 1 by Marital Status

	Married	Divorced	p
Number of obligatory identities	5.6 (1.3)*	3.6 (1.1)	.001
Number of voluntary identities	3.7 (1.6)	3.8 (1.7)	ns
N of cases	272	252	

* *Note*: Standard deviations are in parentheses.

A *sense of mastery or control*, another personality characteristic, is assessed with Pearlin's (Pearlin, Lieberman, Menaghan, & Mullan, 1981) seven-item mastery scale (e.g., "I have little control over the things that happen to me," "I can do just about anything I really set my mind to"). Again, respondents could "strongly disagree" to "strongly agree" on four-point scales. Higher summed scores indicate a higher sense of mastery.

Good health, a physical resource, is the sum of three items asking respondents to rate, on four-point scales, their health in general (from poor to excellent), their satisfaction with their health (from very dissatisfied to very satisfied), and how often ill health gets in the way of things they want to do (from never to very often). Higher scores indicate better physical health.

Psychological distress represents the relative lack of a psychological resource, in this case, emotional well-being. It is measured as the average of 23 symptoms from the depression, anxiety, and somatization subscales of the Brief Symptom Inventory developed by Derogatis and Spencer (1982). Respondents indicated how much they were distressed by each symptom over the past month (e.g., nervousness or shakiness inside, feeling blue, trouble falling asleep), with response categories ranging along five points, from "not at all" to "extremely." Each respondents' responses are averaged by the number of symptom items he/she answered in order to reduce the number of missing cases (these items were self-administered and some respondents skipped items). Scores on the distress scale therefore range from low (a score of 1) to high (a score of 5) in value.

Finally, *substance use*, an indicator of possible alcohol or drug abuse, is a four-item subscale from the Profile of Adaptation to Life Scale (Ellsworth, 1979). Respondents were asked how often during the past month they have had a drink or taken mood-altering drugs, gotten high on alcohol or drugs, had problems with their families caused by their use of alcohol/drugs, and had problems in thinking clearly caused by alcohol/drugs. Response categories ranged from "not once" to "almost daily" and were summed so that a high score indicated greater substance use.

IS THERE RECIPROCITY IN THE RELATIONSHIP BETWEEN ROLE-IDENTITY ACCUMULATION AND WELL-BEING RESOURCES?

The reader might have noted that, earlier, I did not claim that the relationships between identity accumulation and well-being resources are reciprocal. Because role-identity acquisition is a social process that occurs over time, it seems unlikely that resources and identities will have immediate effects on each other. People with greater physical and psychological well-being at one point in time, say, the first interview (Time 1) should actively maintain and even gain role-identities (especially voluntary identities) as time passes. If there is a personal agency effect, it should not be evident immediately but at later points in time—in this case, in the number of role-identities held at the second interview, two years later (Time 2). Conversely, the meaning, satisfaction, behavioral guidance, and other benefits that are obtained from daily role-identity enactments may "pay off" in greater personality and well-being resources over the longer run, as net costs and rewards of various role-identities may take time to discern and/or to stabilize. Hence, I do not expect simultaneity between identity accumulation and well-being. I checked this assumption by conducting two-stage least-squares analyses of the reciprocal influences of role-identity accumulation and well-being resources at Time 2.[6] The results of this analysis confirmed that identity accumulation and well-being resources were not reciprocally related at the Time 2 interviews. I therefore proceeded to capitalize on the panel design of the study by examining the influences of *Time 1* measures of personality and well-being resources on *Time 2* obligatory and voluntary identity accumulation, and vice versa. Because simultaneous determination was not an issue, all analyses employed ordinary least squares regression.

SOCIAL CAUSATION: THE EFFECTS OF ROLE-IDENTITY ACCUMULATION ON PERSONALITY AND WELL-BEING RESOURCES

Before examining selection processes, I started by confirming the traditional direction of social causation influences, from the possession of multiple identities to personality and well-being resources. Table 2 summarizes the effects of the number of obligatory and voluntary identities respondents held at the first interview on each of the five measures of personal resources at Time 2.

As previous research has shown (Thoits, 1992), the accumulation of *obligatory* identities was unrelated to well-being, with one exception, substance use: People with more obligatory identities at Time 1 used alcohol and mood-altering drugs significantly less often by Time 2. In contrast, individuals with more *voluntary* identities at Time 1 had significantly higher self-esteem, a stronger sense of mastery, better physical health, and reduced psychological distress at Time 2. (But voluntary identities were unrelated to substance use at Time 2.) These results clearly support the social causation argument. People who are in essence socially well-integrated through multiple voluntary identity involvements garner important personality, physical, and psychological resources from those involvements.

Although it may appear that people do not obtain personal or well-being benefits from obligatory roles such as spouse, parent, and worker, as mentioned earlier, other research shows that this absence of effects is due to the counterbalancing positive and negative influences of those roles (Berbrier & Schulte 2000 Stephens, Franks, & Townsend, 1994; Thoits, 1992, 2001). Most people report ongoing strains in obligatory role domains as well as considerable satisfactions in those domains; the effects of these strains and satisfactions on well-being tend to counteract each other, producing a net "no effect" (see also Gove, Style, & Hughes, 1990; McLanahan & Adams, 1987; Umberson & Gove, 1989).

---

[6]The number of obligatory identities held, the number of voluntary identities held, and each indicator of personality and well-being resources at Time 2 were examined in separate 2SLS equations. The instrument for each endogenous variable at Time 2 was its value at Time 1. Sociodemographic variables also were controlled in each equation: dummy variables indicating married women, divorced women, and divorced men (with married men serving as the omitted comparison group), minority group member (coded 0,1), age, years of education, and family income (measured ordinally in $3,999 increments through $76,000 or more).

Table 2. Effects of Obligatory and Voluntary Identity Accumulation at Time 1 on Personality and Well-Being Resources at Time 2[a]

	Self-esteem	Mastery	Time 2 Good Health	Distress	Alcohol/ Drug use
Time 1					
Obligatory identities	.08	.03	.03	.02	-.10[+]
Voluntary identities	.18[***]	.13[**]	.08[+]	-.10[*]	-.03
N	500	498	502	504	500

[a] Standardized coefficients are presented. Also controlled in each equation but not shown are gender, marital status, age, race/ethnicity, education, and family income.

[+] p = .10, [*] p = .05, [**] p = .01, [***] p = .001

SELECTION PROCESSES: EFFECTS OF PERSONALITY AND WELL-BEING RESOURCES ON IDENTITY ACCUMULATION

Selection influences are examined next. Table 3 summarizes the effects of each of the personality and well-being variables, measured at Time 1, on the number of obligatory identities and the number of voluntary identities respondents held at Time 2.

Unexpectedly, people with more personal and well-being resources at Time 1 did not have more *obligatory* identities by Time 2, with one exception: Those in better physical health held more obligatory identities at Time 2. Perhaps because obligatory identities involve long-term relationships that are relatively stable (e.g., spouse, parent, relative, in-law), acquiring more obligatory identities by Time 2 is unlikely. However, those with high self-esteem, a strong sense of mastery over life, good health, and low psychological distress possessed significantly more *voluntary* role-identities at Time 2, as expected. Only the use of alcohol and drugs was unrelated to voluntary identity accumulation. Thus, generally speaking, personality and well-being resources enabled people to select themselves (or to be selected by other people) into greater numbers of voluntary, easy-to-exit role domains. These results are consistent with a selection argument.[7]

CHANGES IN RESOURCES AND IDENTITIES OVER TIME

Up to this point, I have demonstrated that *voluntary* role-identities produce subsequent personality, physical, and psychological benefits, and conversely, personality and well-being resources generate a larger accumulation of *voluntary* role-identities. I have not examined changes in these variables over time, as my argument thus far has focused on *levels* of resources and identity accretion at each time point. It is straightforward to extend these ideas to changes over time. Gains in the number of identities people hold, especially gains in the number of voluntary identities, should augment personality and well-being resources (a social causation process). Conversely, increases in personality and well-being resources should expand the number of identities that people hold over time, especially voluntary identities, as these are easier to enter as well as to exit (a selection process).

---

[7]It should be noted that all effects are quite modest in size. The five resource variables together explain 1% and 5% of the variance in the number of obligatory and voluntary identities at Time 2, respectively.

Table 3. Effects of Personality and Well-Being Resources at Time 1 on
the Accumulation of Obligatory and Voluntary Identities at Time 2[a]

	Number of *Obligatory* Identities, Time 2				
Time 1					
Self-esteem	.00	—	—	—	—
Mastery	—	.01	—	—	—
Good health	—	—	.06+	—	—
Psychological distress	—	—	—	.03	—
Substance use	—	—	—	—	.01
N	510	509	512	512	508
	Number of *Voluntary* Identities, Time 2				
Time 1					
Self-esteem	.14**	—	—	—	—
Mastery	—	.12**	—	—	—
Good health	—	—	.12**	—	—
Psychological distress	—	—	—	-.08+	—
Substance use	—	—	—	—	.02
N	510	509	512	512	508

+ p = .10, * p = .05, ** p = .01, *** p = .001

[a] Standardized coefficients are presented. Also controlled in each equation but not shown are gender, marital status, age, race/ethnicity, education, and family income.

Table 4 summarizes social causation processes, in this case, changes in each resource variable over time produced by initial levels of and changes in the numbers of obligatory and voluntary identities, respectively. Table 5 reports selection effects. For Table 5, changes in the number of obligatory and voluntary identities are regressed separately on initial levels of and changes in each resource variable over time.

In Table 4, we see that the number of *obligatory* role-identities and changes in the number of those identities over the two year period do not affect changes in personality or well-being resources, with one exception: The more obligatory identities held at Time 1, the more self-esteem increases over time. However, initial levels of and changes in *voluntary* identities are significantly related to changes in several personal resources. Specifically, the more voluntary identities held at Time 1 and the more voluntary identities acquired from Time 1 to Time 2, the more the person's self-esteem and sense of control over life are enhanced. Further, as the person's number of voluntary involvements accrue, his or her psychological distress scores decrease over time. (Changes in physical health and substance use are unrelated to changes in voluntary identities.) In general, these results mirror the those found for levels of obligatory and voluntary identities (in Table 2): changes in obligatory identities are typically unrelated to changes in personality and well-being resources, while adding voluntary identities is associated with improvements in personal well-being.

Turning to selection processes, we see in the top part of Table 5 that changes in well-being resources from Time 1 to Time 2 are unrelated to changes in the number of *obligatory* identities that individuals hold. The bottom part of Table 5 shows, however, that initial levels of and increases in self-esteem and mastery add to the person's number of *voluntary* role-identities over time. Changes in psychological distress are also significantly and inversely related to changes in voluntary identities: lowered distress increases the number of voluntary involvements over time.

Table 4. Social Causation Processes: Changes in Resources over Time as a Function of Changes in Role-Identities[a]

	Self-esteem	Mastery	Time 2 Good Health	Distress	Alcohol/ Drug use
Time 1					
T1 Resource variable	.57***	.52***	.63***	.60***	.63***
T1 Obligatory identities	.08+	.08	-.08	.06	-.03
Change in obligatory ids	.06	.05	-.06	-.00	-.04
T1 Voluntary identities	.11**	.08+	.01	-.02	-.04
Change in voluntary ids	.12**	.08+	.06	-.09*	-.05
N	491	488	494	496	489

+ p = .10, * p = .05, ** p = .01, *** p = .001

[a] Standardized coefficients are reported. Sociodemographic variables are also controlled in each equation but not shown.

Table 5. Selection Processes: Changes in Obligatory and Voluntary Role-Identities Over Time as a Function of Changes in Resources[a]

Number of *Obligatory* Identities, Time 2					
T1 Obligatory identities	.55***	.55***	.54***	.55***	.56***
T1 Self-esteem	.01	—	—	—	—
Change in self-esteem	.05	—	—	—	—
T1 Mastery	—	.01	—	—	—
Change in mastery	—	.05	—	—	—
T1 Good health	—	—	.00	—	—
Change in good health	—	—	-.06	—	—
T1 Psychological distress	—	—	—	-.00	—
Change in distress	—	—	—	-.02	—
T1 Substance use	—	—	—	—	.05
Change in substance use	—	—	—	—	-.02

Number of *Voluntary* Identities, Time 2					
T1 Voluntary identities	.52***	.52***	.52***	.53***	.52***
T1 Self-esteem	.09*	—	—	—	—
Change in self-esteem	.13**	—	—	—	—
T1 Mastery	—	.08+	—	—	—
Change in mastery	—	.09*	—	—	—
T1 Good health	—	—	.07	—	—
Change in good health	—	—	.06	—	—
T1 Psychological distress	—	—	—	-.03	—
Change in distress	—	—	—	-.09*	—
T1 Substance use	—	—	—	—	.01
Change in substance use	—	—	—	—	-.05

+ p = .10, * p = .05, ** p = .01, *** p = .001

[a] Standardized coefficients are reported. Sociodemographic variables are also controlled in these equations.

In general, Tables 4 and 5 show that changes in resources (self-esteem, mastery, and psychological distress) and changes in voluntary involvements are dynamically related to one another over time. It is relevant to note that most theorists connect feelings of self-worth (or self-confidence) and the belief that one has control over one's life to notions of personal agency, or the ability to initiate self-change (e.g., Kiecolt, 1994; Lazarus & Folkman, 1984). Thus, although not all changes in resources are associated with changes in voluntary involvements, those that are conceptually closest to the notion of personal agency certainly are.

DISCUSSION

Personality, physical, and psychological resources allow individuals to accumulate multiple *voluntary* identities over time, and those *voluntary* identities in turn foster higher levels of resources.[8] By definition, voluntary roles are assumed by choice and these choices tend to have positive consequences for the person. These dynamics are especially evident for personality characteristics that are most closely linked to personal agency: self-esteem and a sense of control over one's life. These illustrative findings support what has been called the "role benefits" or "role expansion" argument (Froberg, Gjerdingen, & Preston, 1986). When feasible, individuals seek more role-identities for the various gratifications that they can offer (Marks, 1977; Sieber, 1974). This process deepens individuals' social integration, and social integration, in turn, helps to sustain the social order.

In many ways, the patterns summarized in this chapter are unremarkable (and it should be noted that all effects are modest in size). That people exercise agency in the construction and re-construction of their lives is an accepted and honorable symbolic interactionist point, one that sets the framework off from other sociological theories. Interactionists hold that society shapes the self *and* the self in turn shapes society. Despite this tenet, mental health researchers, stress theorists, and even identity theorists have persistently focused on the social causation side of the framework (society shapes the self) to the relative neglect of its reverse (with some exceptions, e.g., Ethier & Deaux, 1994; Pavalko & Woodbury 2000; Serpe, 1987). Processes that maintain or even change the social order have thereby been less often investigated.[9] This chapter takes a step in that neglected direction, documenting that individuals act to expand their social and community ties. (As yet unaddressed is the degree to which *self*-selection versus *social* selection processes operate in the acquisition of such voluntary involvements.[10])

It should be noted that there are two major ways in which my approach to the self-society dynamic departs from contemporary identity theory. I focus on multiple identities, rather than singular identities, and I focus on generalized consequences, rather than identity-specific consequences, of role-identity performances. These differences are clearest when contrasted with the recent merger of Stryker's and Burke's approaches to identity theory (Stryker & Burke, 2000).

---

[8]The same patterns of findings are obtained when married and divorced respondents are analyzed separately.

[9]Because Stryker and Burke (2000), for example, focus on in-role behaviors as consequences of identity salience or identity-relevant feedback, one could argue that they are in fact assessing how the self maintains the social order through the performance of social roles. However, these authors dwell less on the "self sustains society" than the "society guides the self" implications of their theory and findings. This is in part because their goal, especially Stryker's goal, is to explicate the *structural* aspects of symbolic interactionism.

[10]Conversely, Pavalko and Woodbury (2000) show that individuals select themselves out of highly demanding or stressful roles (e.g., caregiving) when circumstances allow.

As described earlier in this chapter, Stryker explains the frequency of in-role behavior as an outcome of identity salience, which in turn depends on the properties of individuals' social networks (i.e., their density and affective intensity). Burke picks up at the point of role-identity enactment, arguing that in-role behaviors are goal-directed or motivated efforts. Individuals behave in ways that they believe will match their identity standards, which are learned from the culture and reinforced in social interaction. When feedback from the social environment reveals a discrepancy between how the self ought to act (the identity standard) and how the self actually behaves in the situation, the person will alter the current situation, or seek and create a new situation, to bring self-relevant meanings back in line with identity standards (Burke, 1997; Stryker & Burke 2000: 288). In short, individuals deliberately alter their situations, their role behaviors, or even their role incumbencies because they perceive that they are not meeting internalized, culturally shaped identity standards. Note that for both Stryker and Burke, these processes apply to in-role behaviors that actualize *specific* identities.

Rather than considering processes that apply to role-identities taken one at a time, I examine the determinants and consequences of identity aggregation. (Note that Burke's and Smith-Lovin's creative chapters on "multiple identities" in this volume refer to situations in which two or more identities are *simultaneously activated*, not to identity accumulation.) One might plausibly argue that I investigate aggregations of identities that vary in the degree of commitment that they require. My sets of "obligatory identities" are quite similar to Stryker's concept of "high commitment identities": They involve relatively long-term relationships in higher density networks; these ties are often affectively intense; responsibilities or demands are relatively high (Berbrier & Schulte 2000); and, I would add, these ties are often instrumentally valuable because identity partners typically exchange material goods or practical services with the individual. In contrast, "voluntary" or "low commitment identities" are shorter-term relationships, less often emotionally intense, include relatively fewer responsibilities or demands, and may or may not include an exchange of valuable goods or services. So in Stryker's terms, I might be described as studying the consequences of holding sets of identities that are high or low in commitment. But also unlike Stryker and Burke, I do not focus on specific in-role behaviors but the *generalized byproducts of various identity performances*. (It is relevant to note that Ervin & Styrker [2001] have recently elaborated the theoretical implications of *particular* identity performances for global self-esteem, self-competence, and psychological well-being.)

A number of generalized consequences can flow from multiple identity enactments. These include global self-esteem, drawn from positive feedback from various role partners (Cooley, 1902); a sense of mastery or control over life, derived from successful problem-solving in many role domains (Gecas & Burke, 1995; Thoits, 1994); good health, sustained by physically demanding tasks performed in several domains; low symptoms of distress, due to identity-affirming interactions with role partners and a sense of purpose in life derived from "mattering" to them (Burke, 1991; Burton, 1998; McCall & Simmons, 1978; Rosenberg & McCullough, 1981; Thoits, 1983); and abstinence from excessive alcohol or drug use, due to the behavioral expectations of, and the social controls exerted by, various role partners (Burke, 1991; Thoits, 1983). These are by no means the only possible consequences of role performances, but all are at least consistent with symbolic interactionist thought or are derivable from it. In short, my focus is on more general personality, physical, and psychological consequences of a variety of in-role behaviors which can be carried into a wide array of situations, rather than, for example, an examination of tension states that prompt efforts to better meet identity standards in a single role such as marriage (Burke, 1991; Burke & Stets, 1999).

Certainly these general resources can also enhance people's performances in specific role-identity domains. But because they are broader personal characteristics, not tied to particular role domains, they allow individuals to initiate self-change—for example, by altering identity standards, adopting new identities, or dropping old ones. And herein lies a final subtle difference in emphasis between Stryker and Burke on the one hand and myself on the other.

In current statements of identity theory, people's reasons for performing in-role identity behaviors *and* their reasons for changing identities are inherently social. People are embedded in social networks that exert behavioral demands, and people want to meet the expectations of both their specific role partners and the generalized other (i.e., their identity standards) in order to obtain approval or other social rewards (e.g., prestige, respect, status, power). If individuals' performances are poor, or if they fail to meet internalized standards, they will change the situation or even change identities in order to regain social approval or other social rewards. I agree that such rewards are powerful motivators. However, by this argument, personal agency becomes invested primarily in the process of attempting to meet others' expectations or to accrue markers of their approval. Personal agency ceases to be creative, innovative, playful, and/or motivated by factors other than social ones, such as the intrinsic gratifications obtained from performing a role or learning a new one. I am suggesting instead, more in keeping with the idiosyncratic and renegotiable nature of the self suggested by McCall and Simmons (1978), that people acquire, relinquish, and change role-identities not only because they seek social rewards (or are painfully failing to meet internalized standards), but because they want to try something new, they want different challenges, they find new interests, they want to grow as persons, or, in relinquishing roles, they just need some free time for themselves. Role-identity performances generate personality and well-being resources that can be used and elaborated across a *variety* of activity domains and that can facilitate deliberate changes made for reasons *other* than social approval or prestige, and even *despite* social disapproval and sanctions. In short, generalized resources that are derivable from multiple social involvements can, paradoxically, also set people free.

ACKNOWLEDGMENTS: I appreciate the comments of Larry Griffin on this chapter.

REFERENCES

Adelmann, P. K. (1994). Multiple roles and psychological well-being in a national sample of older adults. *Journal of Gerontology: Social Sciences, 29,* S227–S285.

Bandura, A. (2001). Social cognitive theory: An agentic perspective. *Annual Review of Psychology, 52,* 1–26.

Barnett, R. C., & Baruch, G. K. (1987). Social roles, gender, and psychological distress. In R. C. Barnett, L. Biener, & G. K. Baruch (Eds.), *Gender and stress* (pp. 122–143). New York: Free Press.

Baruch, G. K., & Barnett, R. (1986). Role quality, multiple role involvement, and psychological well-being in midlife women. *Journal of Personality and Social Psychology, 51,* 578–585.

Berbrier, M., & Schulte, A. (2000). Binding and nonbinding integration: The relational costs and rewards of social ties on mental health. *Research in Community and Mental Health, 11,* 3–27.

Blumer, H. (1969). *Symbolic interactionism: Perspective and method.* Englewood Cliffs: Prentice-Hall.

Burke, P. J. (1991). Identity processes and social stress. *American Sociological Review, 56,* 836–849.

Burke, P. J. (1997). An identity model for network exchange. *American Sociological Review, 62,* 134–50.

Burke, P. J., & Stets, J. E. (1999). Trust and commitment through self-verification. *Social Psychology Quarterly, 62,* 347–66.

Burton, R. P. D. (1998). Global integrative meaning as a mediating factor in the relationship between social roles and psychological distress. *Journal of Health and Social Behavior, 39,* 201–215.

Callero, P. 1994. From role-playing to role-using: Understanding role as resource. *Social Psychology Quarterly, 57*, 228–243.

Cooley, C. H. (1902). *Human nature and social order.* New York: Scribner's.

Coser, L. (with R. L. Coser). (1974). *Greedy institutions.* New York: Free Press.

Derogatis, L. R., & Spencer, P. M. (1982). *The Brief Symptom Inventory (BSI): Administration, scoring and procedures manual-1.* Baltimore: Clinical Psychometric Research, Johns Hopkins University School of Medicine.

Ellsworth, R. B. (1979). *Holistic profile of adaptation to life.* Institute for Program Evaluation, Box 4654, Roanoke, VA 24015.

Ervin, L., & Stryker, S. (2001). Theorizing the relationship between self-esteem and identity. In T. J. Owens, S. Stryker, & N. Goodman (Eds.), *Extending self-esteem theory and research: Sociological and psychological currents* (pp. 29–55). Cambridge: Cambridge University Press.

Ethier, K. A., & Deaux, K. (1994). Negotiating social identity when contexts change: Maintaining identification and responding to threat. *Journal of Personality and Social Psychology, 67*, 243–251.

Froberg, D., Gjerdingen, D., & Preston, M. (1986). Multiple roles and women's mental and physical health: What have we learned? *Women and Health, 11*, 79–96.

Gecas, V., & Burke, P. J. (1995). Self and identity. In K. S. Cook, G. A. Fine, & J. S. House (Eds.), *Sociological perspectives on social psychology* (pp. 41–67). Boston: Allyn & Bacon.

Giddens, A. (1991). *Modernity and self-identity: Self and society in the late modern age.* Stanford: Stanford University Press.

Goode, W. J. (1960). A theory of role strain. *American Sociological Review, 25*, 483–496.

Gore, S., & Mangione, T. (1983). Social roles, sex roles and psychological distress: Additive and interactive models of sex differences. *Journal of Health and Social Behavior, 24*, 300–312.

Gove, W. R. (1984). Gender differences in mental and physical illness: The effects of fixed roles and nurturant roles. *Social Science and Medicine, 19*, 77–91.

Gove, W. R., Style, C. B., & Hughes, M. (1990). The effect of marriage on the well-being of adults. *Journal of Family Issues, 11*, 4–35.

Hong, J., & Seltzer, M. M. (1995). The psychological consequences of multiple roles: The nonnormative case. *Journal of Health and Social Behavior, 36*, 386–398.

Jackson, P. B. (1997). Role occupancy and minority mental health. *Journal of Health and Social Behavior, 38*, 237–255.

Kiecolt, K. J. (1994). Stress and the decision to change oneself: A theoretical model. *Social Psychology Quarterly, 57*, 49–63.

Lazarus, R. S., & Folkman, S. (1984). *Stress, appraisal, and coping.* New York: Springer.

Marks, S. (1977). Multiple roles and role strain: Some notes on human energy, time, and commitment. *American Sociological Review, 42*, 921–936.

McAdam, D. (1988). *Freedom summer.* New York: Oxford University Press.

McCall, G. J., & Simmons, J. L. (1978). *Identities and interactions.* New York: Free Press.

McLanahan, S., & Adams, J. (1987). Parenthood and psychological well-being. *Annual Review of Sociology, 13*, 237–257.

Mead, G. H. (1934). *Mind, self, and society.* Chicago: University of Chicago Press.

Menaghan, E. G. (1989). Role changes and psychological well-being: Variations in effects by gender and role repertoire. *Social Forces, 67*, 693–714.

Merton, R. K. (1957). The role set: Problems in sociological theory. *British Journal of Sociology, 8*, 106–120.

Miller, M. L., Moen, P., & Dempster-McClain, D. (1991). Motherhood, multiple roles, and maternal well-being: Women of the 1950's. *Gender and Society, 5*, 565–582.

Pavalko, E. K., & Woodbury, S. (2000). Social roles as process: Caregiving careers and women's health. *Journal of Health and Social Behavior, 41*, 91–105.

Pearlin, L. I., Lieberman, M. A., Menaghan, E. G., & Mullan, J. T. (1981). The stress process. *Journal of Health and Social Behavior, 22*, 337–356.

Pearlin, L. I. & Schooler, C. (1978). The structure of coping. *Journal of Health and Social Behavior, 19*, 2–21.

Pietromonaco, P. R., Manis, J., & Frohardt-Lane, K. (1986). Psychological consequences of multiple social roles. *Psychology of Women Quarterly, 10*, 373–381.

Reitzes, D. C., & Mutran, E. J. (1994). Multiple roles and identities: Factors influencing self-esteem among middle-aged working men and women. *Social Psychology Quarterly, 57*, 313–325.

Repetti, R. L., & Crosby, F. (1984). Gender and depression: Exploring the adult-role explanation. *Journal of Social and Clinical Psychology, 2*, 57–70.

Rodgers, B., & Mann, S. L. (1993). Re-thinking the analysis of intergenerational social mobility: A comment on John W. Fox's "Social class, mental illness, and social mobility." *Journal of Health and Social Behavior, 34,* 165–172.

Rosenberg, M. (1979). *Conceiving the self.* New York: Basic Books.

Rosenberg, M., & McCullough, B. S. (1981). Mattering: Inferred significance and mental health among adolescents. *Research in Community and Mental Health, 2,* 163–182.

Ross, C. E., & Mirowsky, J. (1995). Does employment affect health? *Journal of Health and Social Behavior, 36,* 230–243.

Serpe, R. T. (1987). Stability and change in self: A structural symbolic interactionist explanation. *Social Psychology Quarterly, 50,* 44–55.

Serpe, R. T., & Stryker, S. (1987). The construction of self and reconstruction of social relationships. In E. Lawler & B. Markovsky (Eds.), *Advances in group processes* (pp. 41–66). Greenwich: JAI Press.

Sieber, S. (1974). Toward a theory of role strain. *American Sociological Review, 39,* 567–78.

Spreitzer, E., Snyder, E. E., & Larson, D. L. (1979). Multiple roles and psychological well-being. *Sociological Focus, 12,* 141–148.

Stephens, M. A. P., Franks, M. M., & Townsend, A. L. (1994). Stress and rewards in women's multiple roles: The case of women in the middle. *Psychology and Aging, 9,* 45–52.

Stryker, S. (1980). *Symbolic interactionism: A social structural version.* Menlo Park: Benjamin/Cummings Publishing.

Stryker, S., & Serpe, R. T. (1982). Commitment, identity salience, and role behavior: Theory and research example. In W. Ickes & E. Knowles (Eds.), *Personality, roles, and social behavior* (pp. 199–218). New York: Springer-Verlag.

Stryker, S., & Serpe, R. T. (1994). Identity salience and psychological centrality: Equivalent, overlapping, or complementary concepts. *Social Psychology Quarterly, 57,* 16–35.

Stryker, S., & Burke, P. J. (2000). The past, present, and future of an identity theory. *Social Psychology Quarterly, 63,* 284–297.

Stryker, S., & Statham, A. (1985). Symbolic interaction and role theory. In G. Lindzey & E. Aronson (Eds.), *Handbook of social psychology* (3rd edition, pp. 311–378). New York: Random House.

Thoits, P. A. (1983). Multiple identities and psychological well-being: A reformulation and test of the social isolation hypothesis. *American Sociological Review, 48,* 174–187.

Thoits, P. A. (1986). Multiple identities: Examining gender and marital status differences in distress. *American Sociological Review, 51,* 259–272.

Thoits, P. A. (1992). Identity structures and psychological well-being: Gender and marital status comparisons. *Social Psychology Quarterly, 55,* 236–256.

Thoits, P. A. (1994). Stressors and problem-solving: The individual as psychological activist. *Journal of Health and Social Behavior, 35,* 143–159.

Thoits, P. A. (1995). Stress, coping and social support processes: Where are we? What next? *Journal of Health and Social Behavior, Extra Issue,* 53–79.

Thoits, P. A. (2001). *Identity changes in response to stress.* Unpublished manuscript, Department of Sociology, Vanderbilt University.

Thoits, P. A., & Hewitt, L. N. (2001). Volunteer work and well-being. *Journal of Health and Social Behavior, 42,* 115–131.

Turner, R. J., & Gartrell, J. W. (1978). Social factors in psychiatric outcomes: Toward the resolution of interpretive controversies. *American Sociological Review, 43,* 368–382.

Turner, R. J., & Roszell, P. (1994). Psychosocial resources and the stress process. In W. R. Avison & I. H. Gotlib (Eds.), *Stress and mental health: Contemporary issues and prospects for the future* (pp. 179–210). New York: Plenum.

Umberson, D., & Gove, W. R. (1989). Parenthood and psychological well-being: Theory, measurement, and stage in family life course. *Journal of Family Issues, 10,* 440–462.

Waldron, I., & Jacobs, J. A. (1989). Effects of multiple roles on women's health: Evidence from a national longitudinal study. *Women and Health, 15,* 3–19.

Chapter **13**

Relationships among Multiple Identities

PETER J. BURKE

It is almost a truism to say that people have multiple identities. Certainly, it is this idea to which William James (1890) was referring when he said that each person has as many selves as others with whom they interact. Having noted that, however, very little has been theorized or investigated about the way in which these multiple identities relate to each other, or activated, or jointly operated to influence behavior. Most identity research focuses on one or another identity that people have without asking questions about how those identities relate to each other or what the implications are for understanding behavior that such behavior may function to verify (or not) more than one identity. I begin with a brief review of work that has begun to address these issues more directly, as well as work that, while not addressing such issues directly, nevertheless makes an indirect contribution to our understanding.

In doing this, I distinguish between two different issues in the relationship between and among multiple identities. These two issues have to do with what might be termed the internal and external foci that have developed within identity theory (Stryker & Burke, 2000). The external focus addresses how the multiple identities that an individual has are tied into the complexities of the social structure(s) in which the individual is embedded.[1] It is also concerned with the impact of social structure on the salience and activation[2] as well commitment[3] to the multiple identities. From this perspective, the relationship between multiple identities is an issue of the link between social structure and the individual. The

---

[1] This is the approach taken by Smith-Lovin (Chapter 11).

[2] The salience of an identity is its probability of being activated in a situation (Stryker, 1980). Activation refers to the condition in which an identity is actively engaged in the self-verification process as opposed to being latent and inactive.

[3] Commitment is the strength of the tie that an individual has to an identity. There are really two sources to commitment, as Stryker has made clear (Stryker & Serpe, 1982). The first is the number of persons to which one is tied by holding a given identity (extensive commitment) and the other is the emotional attachment to the others to which one is tied. The overall commitment is a combination (perhaps product) of these two forms, and represents the strength of the forces that influence people to maintain congruence between the meanings in their identity standards and self-relevant meanings in the situation (Burke & Reitzes, 1991).

internal focus attends to issues of how the multiple identities that an individual has function together within the self, or within the overall self-verification process, and the implications of the self-verification process for the multiple identities held. From this second perspective, the relationship between multiple identities is an issue of the mechanisms by which all identities function within the self and the entire perceptual control system of an individual. Also at issue is the internal organization of the identities in terms of their relative salience.

Identities are the meanings that individuals hold for themselves—what it means to be who they are. These identities have bases in being members of groups (social identities), having certain roles (role identities), or being the unique biological entities that they are (personal identities). I am a member of the university faculty (social identity), a professor (role identity), and a person with high standards (personal identity). What it means to me to be a faculty member, a professor, and a person with high standards are the contents of these three identities that I have. In most of what follows I will not be dealing with the third basis of identity, that is, the person, but will focus on those identities that are tied more directly to elements of the social structure: groups and roles. I begin the discussion with the internal focus, that is, on the internal mechanisms that are involved when considering multiple identities within the perceptual control system because what happens at that level influences the way in which the multiple identities manifest themselves within the larger social structure.

ISSUES OF MULTIPLE IDENTITIES WITHIN THE PERCEPTUAL CONTROL SYSTEM

When considering the relationship between identities within the hierarchical perceptual control system in which all identities are thought to reside, at issue are questions of how multiple identities relate to each other, how they are switched on or off, and, when they are on, how the person manages to maintain congruence between perceptions and standards for each identity. Included in this last part is the question of what happens when behavior cannot maintain perceptions congruent with their standards.

Beginning with the idea of how identities relate to each other, most prior work on the relationship between multiple identities has focused on the way in which identities do or do not share meanings. For example, Linville's (1985; 1987) self-complexity theory dealt with the idea that individuals with more complex selves were better buffered from situational stresses. The complexity of the self was defined as the number of "distinct self-aspects" that one has. Distinct self-aspects are roles, relationships, traits, or activities that do not share attributes or meanings. In this way, problems that develop with respect to the attributes or meanings that relate to one "identity" do not spill over to others.

Related to this is the idea that multiple identities may have beneficial effects in their multiplicity rather than how they do or do not relate to each other (Thoits, 1983; 1986). While this hypothesis has received mixed support, especially relative to an alternative suggestion that it is particular combinations of identities that are more influential in terms of increasing or decreasing stress or well being (Reitzes & Mutran, 1995), when applied to *voluntary* as opposed to *obligatory* role identities support is much stronger (Thoits, this volume).

Stets (1995) looked at the relationship between gender role identity and mastery, a personal identity, and suggested that the two are related through common dimension of meaning concerning the degree to which the person controls aspects of their environment. This idea of relating identities by the degree to which they share meanings was also put forward by Hoelter (1985) in his proposed methodology for conceptually linking identities in semantic space as defined by the "universal" dimensions of evaluation, potency, and activity (Osgood, Suci, & Tannenbaum, 1957). This idea is also at the heart of affect control theory (Heise, 1979; Smith-Lovin & Heise, 1988) in which identities not only act to change meanings in the situation, but are also activated, and sometimes chosen to fit the meanings of the situations. Deaux (1992; 1993) also proposed this idea of common characteristics among social and personal identities. She used the concept of common "traits," though one could substitute the idea of common meanings with the same effect.

Shared among all of these researchers is the idea that identities that have common meanings are likely to be activated together whenever those meanings are present in the situation, and that multiple identities might work together in the self-verification process to control those meanings in the situation. Additionally, Deaux suggests that identities that share many meanings are located near the top of a prominence hierarchy and may work together to control the meanings of identities lower in the hierarchy.

I develop this idea of the hierarchy of control of meanings from the point of view of identity control theory. For this, we need to understand the hierarchical nature of the overall perceptual control system in which identities are located. The overall perceptual control system is composed of an interlocking set of individual control systems at multiple levels (Tsushima & Burke, 1999).[4] At the "lowest" level, outputs of the individual control systems (identities) are behaviors in the situation. These are illustrated in Figure 1 with control systems two and three. The figure illustrates these outputs as being merged since there is a single individual engaged in behavior, although the behavior is guided by multiple individual control systems. This implies that the behavior of an individual must "satisfy" several individual control systems simultaneously by altering the situation in ways that change the self-relevant meanings perceived by all of the different individual control systems.

What is the relationship between these control systems and identities? The answer to this is partly conceptual. If we think of an identity as the set of all meanings and expectations held for oneself in terms of, for example, a particular role, then an identity standard might be thought of as that set or vector of meanings, each of which acts as a goal for perceptions. Strictly, each meaning is part of a separate control system, but conceptually it is easier to think of the set or vector of meanings of an identity as part of a single control system. In this more aggregated view, each control system in Figure 1 represents a single identity. The lower control systems (two and three) can be thought of as two identities that influence behavior (more) directly. The two lower-level identities might represent multiple identities that have been activated in a situation, each of which is acting to control relevant perceptions by altering behavior in the situation.

At levels other than the "lowest," outputs of each individual control system are standards for identities that are at lower levels in the control system. This is illustrated in Figure 1 by control system one. The higher control system (one) represents a (more abstract) identity (Tsushima & Burke, 1999). For these control systems that are not at the lowest level, control of their perceptions is maintained by altering one or more[5] standards at lower levels, each of which in turn alter standards at lower levels until, ultimately, at the lowest level behavior alters the situation and thus perceptions of that. It is through the operation

---

[4]This hierarchical organization of identities in the overall perceptual control system should not be confused with the salience hierarchy of identities (Stryker, 1968). The latter refers to the relative likelihood that identities will be activated.

[5]Although the figure shows the output of the higher identity acting as a standard for a single lower identity, the output of the higher-level identity may be the standard for several lower-level identities, each controlling different perceptions.

of the control systems at higher levels that the control systems of particular identities have their standards (self-meanings) changed.

Thus, the hierarchical perceptual control system in identity theory acts to maintain self-relevant perceptions close to their identity standards at all levels simultaneously. For a single identity, this means that the set of all self-meanings for an identity is conceptualized as a standard for the identity, and that the perception of the set of self-relevant meanings in the situation is maintained as close as possible to its standard through meaningful social behavior. The comparators shown in Figure 1 act to measure closeness. The outputs of these comparators (each a function of the difference between perceptions and standards) change behaviors in the situation, or, for higher levels, change the standards at lower levels. This is the self-verification process, which is a dynamic, ongoing, continuous process of counteracting disturbances that occur in the situation. Such disturbances may be the result of others' behaviors in the situation, one's own behavior in the situation, or ongoing physical processes in the situation.

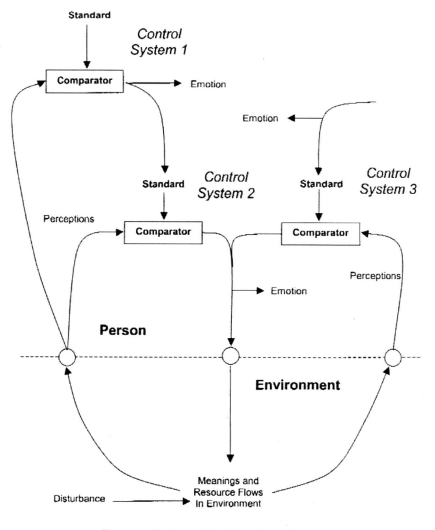

Figure 1.   Identity Model of Three Control Systems.

Through the self-verification process, actions (output behaviors acting on the meanings and resources flows in the environment) are taken to alter the situation and hence the self-relevant meanings in that situation to bring them into congruence with the standards held in the identity. To the extent that process succeeds or fails, and perceived self-relevant meanings are or are not brought into congruence with their standards, two concurrent outcomes result. First, emotional reactions that are positive when the discrepancy is decreasing or non-existent and negative when the discrepancy exists or increases. At the same time of this ongoing emotional response, there occur changes in behavior as well as in higher-order control systems. Behavior changes the situation and moves one's perception toward the standard, while identity changes (changing meanings held in the identity standards) move the standard toward the perception (though at a much slower rate). In the longer run, the identity system moves toward congruence between perceptions and the identity standards through the operation of both mechanisms.[6]

This process occurs for all activated identities in a situation, so that perceptions of all of the self-relevant meanings of all of the activated identities are simultaneously controlled. For this to happen, all of the meanings must be either orthogonal or aligned. They cannot remain in opposition. Were, for example, two self-relevant meanings perceived in the situation to be in opposition with each other, as one was brought into alignment, the other would be moved out of alignment. One cannot both be good and bad, for example, or both strong and weak. When different identity standards require oppositional meanings, the system is put into an impossible situation in which one or both identity standards cannot be verified. To the extent this happens, the standards themselves shift as outlined above. People re-identify themselves, changing their self-meanings as held in their identity standards.

When identity meanings are orthogonal or unrelated to each other, an action that changes one will leave the other unaffected. It is, of course, possible that while the meanings are cognitively unrelated they are situationally related. For example, the meanings involved in task leadership may be unrelated to the meanings involved in social emotional (SE) leadership. Yet, in an empirical instance one may use a limited period of time to engage in behavior that has strong task leadership implications and consequently not use that time to engage in behavior that has SE leadership implications, thus forcing a link between the two in that instance (Stryker, 2000).[7] Additionally, it is possible that while the self sees Task and SE meanings as independent, others may perceive a particular behavior as having positive SE leadership meanings but negative task leadership meanings. For example, acting in a friendly manner may situationally be seen as lacking the directiveness and strength needed for task leadership yet at the same time it may be seen as fulfilling aspects of the social-emotional leadership role.[8] Because the self exists in a situation in which others also perceive and act on meanings, for coordinated behavior to occur, the meanings must become shared over time (Riley & Burke, 1995).

According to the theory, having two oppositional identities activated at the same time should result in much distress because the verification of one necessarily increases the discrepancy for the other. However, it also should result in change. First, one or both standards may slowly shift as the meanings in the identity standards change as suggested

---

[6]It is, of course, possible that an identity will be dropped and the individual will no longer consider himself or herself to have that identity. For example, Cast and Burke (2002) show that spouses who have trouble verifying their spousal identity are more likely to become divorced.

[7]Over time, to maintain their independence, the choices toward task or SE leadership ought to be random.

[8]It is also possible that the reverse of this is true in some instances; others perceive identities that share meanings for an individual as independent and responded to accordingly.

above. Second, one or the other identity may become less important, or salient, or the commitment to the identity may become lower as the person withdraws from relationships involved with the identity. Finally, one may avoid situations in which both identities are likely to be simultaneously activated. In all likelihood, all of these processes would occur to varying extents. Over time, however, I would expect that such incongruities would be worn away, so to speak, and that most of a person's identities would become at least independent of each other, and the relationships among the various meanings of the different identities would become shared with others in the situations in which we act.

When two identities share common meanings the situation is much simpler. Control of the situation to change self-relevant perceptions on the shared dimension of meaning helps both identities. Verifying one of the identities will help verify the other. For example, consider a married person with children. If the spousal identity includes standards for providing material support for one's spouse, and if the parent identity includes standards for providing material support for one's children, then getting a well-paying job will help verify both identities.

Finally, it should be noted that having multiple identities also creates a nexus of those identities that are affected by the fact that a single individual holds them. Events and conditions that affect the individual have the capacity to affect all the identities held by that individual. For example, the individual may become overwhelmed by events with respect to one identity and suffer performance degradations with respect to other otherwise unrelated identities, as when work suffers while an individual is going through a divorce, or an individual who is sick may have trouble verifying many of their identities.

ISSUES OF HOLDING MULTIPLE IDENTITIES WITHIN THE SOCIAL STRUCTURE

As Stryker and Burke (2000) note, sociology has long conceptualized persons as occupying multiple positions or roles within the organized matrix of social relations we call the social structure (Linton, 1936; Merton, 1957; Parsons, 1949; Turner, 1978). That these multiple positions may come into conflict with each other within the individual was a logical next step that has been explored in a number of ways using the ideas of role conflict (Gross, Mason Ward, & McEachern, 1958), role strain (Secord & Backman, 1974), and status inconsistency (E. Jackson, 1962; E. F. Jackson & Burke, 1965; Lenski, 1954).[9]

While this work was conceptualized in terms of the multiple positions that people hold and the multiple sets of expectations held for them rather than the multiple identities of those individuals, a translation to the latter perspective is fairly straightforward. Indeed many of the effects of role conflict or status inconsistency (for example, to create distress of one sort or another) only make sense when the individual cares about the conflicting expectations, having internalized them as standards for themselves—an idea that is very close to our current understanding of the concept of identity (cf, Burke, 1980).

The viewpoint that identities are tied to social structural positions (i.e., that individuals' memberships and roles in the groups, organizations, and networks to which they belong form the basis of many of their identities) grows out of the ideas of structural symbolic interaction theory (Stryker, 1980). This perspective suggests a number of ways in

---

[9]Stryker and Statham (Stryker & Macke, 1978; Stryker & Statham, 1985) have nicely summarized of much of this work.

which the identities may relate to each other in terms of the way in which the positions are connected within the social structure. For this I note three different conditions (1) persons may have multiple role identities within a single group (2) persons may have the same role identities but in different groups (3) persons may have different role identities within intersecting groups.

In all of these situations or conditions, we are talking about multiple identities that are simultaneously activated. If an identity is not activated, I suggest it has no effect, since no self-verification is taking place, and no behavior is being used to control perceptions relevant to that identity. For this reason, the abstract concept of multiple identities makes sense only in that there may be multiple identities for people to call up (activate) on different occasions. The overall number of identities held by a person may influence the likelihood that activated identities may conflict with each other. It is likely that, aside from sleep or otherwise being inattentive, one or more identities is always activated, providing guidance for our perceptions and behaviors. The question then is what are the conditions for multiple identity activation?

Multiple identities within a single group. There are two forms of this condition. One may have several roles within a group (e.g., husband, father, son, and brother within an extended family group, or task leader and social emotional leader in the same group). In this case, these different identities will often be concurrently activated. The concurrent activation will have both internal and external consequences. Internally, I hypothesize that being activated concurrently will, over time, lead to these identities having similar levels of salience and commitment for the individual, as well as shared meanings. Similar levels of salience will develop because the identities are often activated together, while similar levels of commitment will develop because they are activated in the presence of common others. Externally, with the identities being concurrently activated, others in the group are likely to develop expectations about the way one engages in behavior relevant to each of the identities such that the identities will be consistent and mutually reinforcing. In this way each of the identities becomes tied to the overall structure of the group in ways that make the self-verification processes for all of the identities much more coordinated.

The second form of multiple identities within a single group exists when a person has an activated identity in one group and something in the situation activates an identity that the person has in another group. This is the perspective that Stryker (2000) seems to suggest in his analysis of competing identities within the context of social movements. With both identities activated, the person engages in behavior that attempts to verify both identities with the result that each is influenced by the requirements of the other.[10] For example, I am at a faculty meeting and my faculty identity is activated. At that meeting someone mentions that they had seen and enjoyed a movie playing in town. This information is relevant to my spousal identity, as my wife and I had been contemplating seeing the movie. As a result, my spousal identity becomes activated and I store away the information about the movie to convey to my spouse at a later time. However, while the spousal identity is activated, I am engaging in self-verification processes with respect to that identity as well as the faculty member identity, with the result that I may attempt to speed up the faculty meeting in an attempt to accompany my wife to the movie that evening. In this way, each of the activated identities may influence the salience and commitment of the other, with the likelihood that the more salient identity will influence the less salient identity to a greater extent.

---

[10]Levels of commitment to each identity, as well as situational demands, would influence which identity is dominant in the situation even though both are activated.

Identities based on a common role within multiple groups. In this case the multiple identities are multiple in a sequential sense, and not necessarily activated at the same time. For example, a person may have the identity "friend" in separate non-overlapping groups, or "treasurer" in several non-overlapping voluntary association. Because each of these role identities resides in the same individual, and because many of the meanings of these identities are already shared having arisen in a common culture (what it means to be a friend to A is similar to what it means to be a friend to B), I would expect that any differences in the friend identities for any one person would diminish over time. Parsimony would argue that where the friend identities did not have to be different, they would become alike reducing the information load for carrying around different expectations and meanings. Additionally, I would expect that such identities would become highly salient because of the extended network of connections to others though the identities (commitment).

Multiple identities in intersecting groups. In this case, the different identities that a person has in different groups become simultaneously activated if and when the different groups come into contact or overlap in some way. For example, a person may have the identity "friend" to a peer and "daughter" to her parents. The two groups may intersect when the peer visits in the person's home while her parents are present. Within this situationally aggregated set of persons, both identities will be activated and sets of meanings and expectations from both identities will be relevant. This is often the situation when role conflict is present. The meanings and expectations for each identity come into conflict when both identities are activated. Under such conditions, I would expect the identity standards involved to shift meanings with the more salient or more committed identity shifting the least. On the other hand, to the extent that the identities share meanings, the commonality of the meanings and expectations should reinforce each other. The increased ties in the larger network of others (parents and peer) should increase the level of commitment to the shard meanings and hence the identities that share those meanings.

There is a second form of this condition that results because people are the carriers of identities. Identities meet and interact when people meet and interact. One can meet others because of a shared group membership (for example, belonging to the same union) or role relations (for example, doctors meet patients, nurses, drug salesmen, etc.). Because individuals hold many identities, when one individual with a certain identity meets another because of the context of that identity, the identities of the two persons other than the ones that brought them together may become relevant and activated in unexpected ways.[11] Consider, for example, the father of my daughter's kindergarten friend. We may meet picking up our daughters at school and initially know each other as the father of my daughter's friend. Over time, however, other of our identities may become activated and known to each other. He may know though his work identity of a job opportunity that I with my work identity could fulfill. Through this mechanism, there is a random element to the way in which identities are interconnected both within and between people that results from both the structural arrangements of society, the connection of individuals to those structures, and the multiple identities that are housed within any given individual. Highly salient identities become activated and known to others who may then find additional ways to relate to the person through activating other identities of their own. Thus the network of relations expands as identities find new ways of verifying themselves by activating relevant identities in other individuals. Lovers may meet at church, skiers at work, friends in voluntary association meetings, and co-workers at fraternal gatherings.

---

[11]Additionally, identities that one does not want known may also become known.

The Issues

Bringing together the above discussions on the variety of ways in which multiple identities of individuals may be linked, activated and connected (both within and between individuals), and the way in which the perceptual control system operates to verify all active identities, there are a number of general principles that can be listed and offered as hypotheses to guide future research.

1. Situations are sought out to verify activated identities.
2. Situations will contain meanings that activate (other) relevant identities.
3. Identities with common meanings will tend to be activated together.
4. Identities often activated together will develop similar levels of salience and commitment.
5. Identities will adjust to the pressures of the situations, the other identities concurrently activated, and the meanings and expectations of others in the situation.
6. Multiple identities held by persons in different positions in the social structure will have different demands, expectations, and meanings placed on them with the result that the multiple identities of a person in one position will relate to each other differently than the multiple identities of a person in another position.
7. Identities higher in the salience hierarchy will take preference in the verification process over identities lower in the salience hierarchy.
8. Identities with higher levels of commitment will take preference in the verification process over identities with lower levels of commitment.

In the present paper, I begin this program of research by testing the sixth of these general principles through an examination of the task and social emotional (SE) leadership identities and roles within task-oriented groups. I look at these identities for persons who hold the position of coordinator compared to those who do not hold that position.

The Discussion Groups

In these task-oriented discussion groups, each individual holds two separate identities: task leadership and social emotional leadership. While these may in some sense be thought of as two sets of meaning "packets" for a single leadership identity, their apparent independence or at times oppositional character (Bales & Slater, 1955; Burke, 1972) suggests they are separate roles with separate identities.

I examine how these two identities play themselves out for persons who are in two structurally different locations in the groups and therefore subjected to different meanings and expectations. Each group has a designated person who is the coordinator of the discussion. The persons who occupy this structural position will be contrasted with the persons who do not occupy this position. The theory of task and social emotional role differentiation notes that expectations for task activity from persons who are in the legitimated coordinator role are different from the expectations for task activity held for persons who are not in the legitimated coordinator position (Burke, 1972).

Specifically, task leadership activity from official coordinators is much more accepted and viewed as legitimate, while task leadership activity from others is less accepted and tends to violate expectations. The theory of task and social-emotional leadership role differentiation suggests that it is the negative reactions to non-legitimate task leadership performance that, in turn, prevents those non-legitimate task leaders from engaging in social emotional activity. The consequence of this is to allow or encourage someone else to engage in more of the social emotional activity, creating a likelihood that this other person would be the social emotional leader. The result of this step is the emergence of task and social emotional leadership role differentiation. The focus in the present context is to examine the way in which these role performances are influenced by the identities behind them and the context in which they occur.

PROCEDURES

Sample

Forty-eight four-person laboratory groups, each composed of two males and two females, were formed from a random sample of undergraduate students at a large Midwestern university. The students were invited to participate in a study of communication in small groups. They arrived at a general meeting (of 50–60 students at a time) at which the study was explained in general terms as a study of communication in groups and the factors that influence communication. The students were told that they would be paid $10.00 for filling out a background questionnaire at the general meeting and participating in a discussion group at some point in the next two weeks.

After this, they filled out a schedule of times they would be available, and then filled out the background questionnaire that took about 20 minutes to complete. During this time, the investigator constructed groups randomly from the persons who were available at the specific times, with the added constraint that there be two males and two females in each group. After the questionnaire was completed, group assignment times were given to each person along with a reminder slip. All subjects were called the day prior to their scheduled meeting to remind them of that meeting.

The group discussion sessions were held over the next two weeks following the general meeting. Each group of two males and two females participated in four different discussions using group polarization or choice dilemma protocols (two that usually showed a shift to risk and two that usually showed a shift to conservatism). The choice dilemma problems were used to provide the groups with a task in which they had to reach a consensus.

The four discussions were contained in the one session that the group met. Each session lasted about an hour and a half, with each discussion lasting from ten to twenty minutes. Each of the discussions followed the same format. Prior to the discussion, the individual members read the choice dilemma and wrote down their personal recommendation. Following this, the members were instructed to discuss the problem and come to a group consensus for making a group recommendation. After each discussion was completed, subjects filled out a questionnaire evaluating the discussion and rating each other on a series of items measuring the degree to which they performed various activities during the discussion.

In half of the groups, chosen randomly, one person was designated as the coordinator. This person was told to moderate the discussion and was given a sheet on which to record the group's consensual answer. In the other half of the groups, no one was designated the coordinator and the sheet on which to record the group's answer was simply placed on the table in front of all participants with an indication that the group's final answer was to be recorded there. In this way, one person in half the groups was given legitimacy to act in a leadership manner, while no one had this legitimacy in the other groups.

Measures

From the background questionnaires, measures of task leadership identity and social emotional leadership identity were taken (see Table 1). The measure of task leadership identity consists of five items that tap self-meanings of task leadership in groups. An example item is "when I work on committees, I like to take charge of things." These items form a single factor with an omega reliability of .74. Seven items that tap self-meanings of social leadership in groups measure the social emotional leadership identity. These include items such as "most people would think of me as outgoing and sociable," and "I try to have close personal relations with people." These items form a single factor with an omega reliability of .83.

Table 1. Item Analysis of Task and Social Leadership Identity and Performance Measures

Task Leadership Identity	Item Total Correlations
I try to maintain my own opinions even though many other people may have a different point of view	.54
When I work on committees I like to take charge of things	.70
I try to influence strongly other people's actions	.64
When I work with a group of people, I like to have things done my way	.70
I try to be the dominant person when I am with people	.71

Omega reliability of scale: **.74**

Social Emotional Leadership Identity	
My personal relations with people are cool and distant (R)	.64
It is hard for me to start a conversation when I am with strangers (R)	.70
Most people would think of me as outgoing and sociable	.77
I feel nervous in situations where I have to meet a lot of people (R)	.60
I try to have close personal relations with people	.52
I have fewer friends than most people my age (R)	.65
I am an enthusiastic person	.64

Omega reliability of scale: **.83**

Task Leadership Performance	
Providing fuel for the discussion by introducing ideas and opinions for the rest of the group to discuss	.91
Guiding the discussion and keeping it moving effectively	.86
Attempting to influence the group's opinion	.87
Standing out as the leader of the discussion	.94

Omega reliability of scale: **.94**

Social Emotional Leadership Performance	
Acting to keep relationship between members cordial and friendly	.82
Attempting to harmonize differences of opinion	.80
Intervening to smooth over disagreements	.84
Making tactful comments to heal any hurt feelings that may have arisen during the discussion	.63

Omega reliability of scale: **.80**

Table 2. Means, Standard Deviations, and Correlations[1] of the Variables

Variables	Coordinator Mean	Std. Dev.	Non-coordinator Mean	Std. Dev.	(1)	(2)	(3)	(4)	(5)	(6)	(7)	(8)	(9)	(10)
(1) Task Leadership Identity	.00	.52	.00	.70	1.00	-.18	.29	.11	.18	.07	.28	-.01	.16	.01
(2) SE Leadership Identity	.07	.08	-.09	1.05	.13	1.00	.02	.15	.11	.16	.06	.24	-.06	.18
(3) Task Performance 1	.50*	1.05	-.17*	1.02	.38	.13	1.00	.41	.52	.19	.47	.17	.47	.17
(4) SE Performance 1	.40*	.97	-.21*	1.05	.01	.15	.24	1.00	.26	.53	.24	.41	.21	.44
(5) Task Performance 2	.44*	.83	-.15*	.98	.24	.10	.57	.18	1.00	.28	.54	.28	.48	.11
(6) SE Performance 2	.42*	.96	-.06*	1.05	-.08	.00	.26	.58	.31	1.00	.29	.56	.25	.42
(7) Task Performance 3	.26*	.93	-.09*	.98	.28	-.02	.46	-.04	.50	.00	1.00	.32	.53	.18
(8) SE Performance 3	.01	.84	-.07	.97	-.08	-.03	-.06	.38	.26	.36	.30	1.00	.20	.38
(9) Task Performance 4	.14	.98	-.05	.99	.27	.20	.53	.03	.41	-.04	.47	.13	1.00	.23
(10) SE Performance 4	.29*	.91	-.03*	.95	-.06	.19	.13	.44	.12	.31	-.03	.48	.48	1.00

* Differences between coordinators and non-coordinators: $p \leq .05$

[1] For the correlations, coordinators are below the diagonal, non-coordinators are above the diagonal.

The post discussion questionnaires included ratings of each member by all the members (including self-ratings) on eight items designed to measure task and social emotional leadership performance. The task leadership performance items are also given in Table 1, and include, for example, "guiding the discussion and keeping it moving effectively," and "providing fuel for the discussion by introducing ideas and opinions for the rest of the group to discuss." The four items form a single factor with an omega reliability of .94.

Finally, the social emotional leadership performance items, also given in Table 1, include, for example, "acting to keep relationships between members cordial and friendly," and "intervening to smooth over disagreements." The four items form a single factor with an omega reliability of .80. Table 2 contains the means, standard deviations, and correlations for the scales on which the analysis is based.

The Model

Figure 2 shows the model that was used in the present research. Each leadership identity influences the corresponding set of leadership behaviors, which behaviors are also influenced by other things in the discussion, including the behaviors of other persons in the discussion. Structural equation modeling was used to estimate the effects for the model.

RESULTS

I begin with the hypothesis that role identity meanings create role performances with corresponding meanings. While this is not new, having been documented many times, it provides a starting point. We see from the results in Table 3 that for task and social emotional leadership identities, the greater the leadership identity the greater is the corresponding role performance (paths tt and ss). There are differences in the degree to which each of the identities influences the behaviors, but this may be a question of the quality of the measurement of each as well. There are no differences in this effect between those in and not in the coordinator position.

The second hypothesis is that when role performances are disturbed so that their meanings do not fully correspond to the meanings implied in the identity, people will act to counteract the disturbances. Persons who, as a result of disturbances, perform more of the behavior than indicated by the meanings in their identity will act to reduce their level of performance. In a similar fashion, should disturbances lead to a performance less than expected given their identity meanings, people will act to increase their performance level. This is the agentic part of an identity in which people attempt to resist outside pressures in order to maintain consistency between their identity standards and self-relevant perceptions of self-relevant meanings in the situation.

This can be shown in two ways. The more traditional way allows sequential errors on the performance measures to correlate. A negative correlation would indicate that a large positive performance residual (performing more than expected) at one time is associated with a smaller residual at the next time. Similarly, a larger negative residual (performing less than expected) should be associated with a smaller residual at the next time. When this analysis is done in the present research, the expected negative correlations among adjacent error terms are observed for both task and social emotional performances, and for both coordinators and non-coordinators, thus indicating the sequential adjustment of leadership performances to reduce discrepancies.

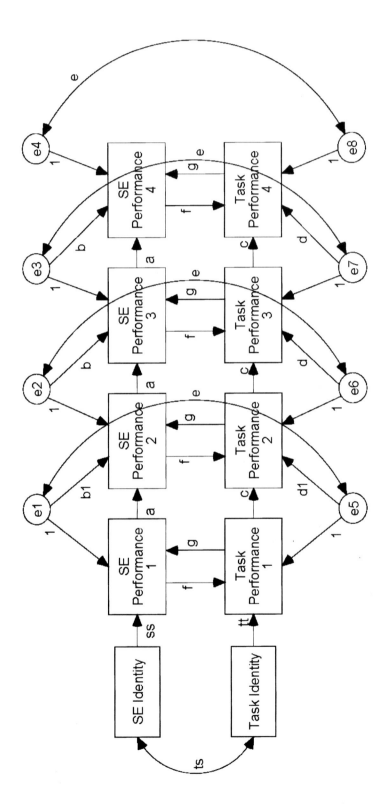

Figure 2. Model of the Relationship between Task and Social Emotional Leadership.

Table 3. Unstandardized Path Coefficients and Covariances for
Coordinators and Non-Coordinators under the Model of Figure 1[a]

Path[b]			Coordinators	Non-coordinators	Path label
seid	→	se1	.17[*]	.17[*]	ss
tskid	→	tsk1	.38[*]	.38[*]	tt
e1	→	se2	-.38[*]	-.38[*]	b1[‡]
e2	→	se3	-.58[*]	-.58[*]	b
e3	→	se4	-.58[*]	-.58[*]	b
e5	→	tsk2	-.59[*]	-.59[*]	d
e6	→	tsk3	-.59[*]	-.59[*]	d
e7	→	tsk4	-.59[*]	-.59[*]	d
se1	→	se2	.86[*]	.86[*]	a
se2	→	se3	.86[*]	.86[*]	a
se3	→	se4	.86[*]	.86[*]	a
tsk1	→	tsk2	.96[*]	.96[*]	c
tsk2	→	tsk3	.96[*]	.96[*]	c
tsk3	→	tsk4	.96[*]	.96[*]	c
tsk1	→	se1	-.03	.03	g
tsk2	→	se2	-.03	.03	g
tsk3	→	se3	-.03	.03	g
tsk4	→	se4	-.03	.03	g
se1	→	tsk1	-.07	.06	f
se2	→	tsk2	-.07	.06	f
se3	→	tsk3	-.07	.06	f
se4	→	tsk4	-.07	.06	f

Covariances

seid	↔	tskid	-.04	-.04	ts
e1	↔	e5	.34[*†]	.10[*†]	e
e3	↔	e7	.34[*†]	.10[*†]	e
e2	↔	e6	.34[*†]	.10[*†]	e
e4	↔	e8	.34[*†]	.10[*†]	e

[a] Chi-Square for Model of Figure 2: 87.2, df = 77, p = .2.

[b] The variables seid = SE leadership identity, tskid = Task leadership identity, se1–se4 = social emotional leadership performance, tsk1–tsk4 = task leadership performance, e1–e3 = SE leadership performance discrepancy, e5–e7 = task leadership discrepancy.

[*] p ≤ .05

[†] diff. between Coordinators and Non-coordinators: p ≤ .05

[‡] diff. between paths b1 and b: p ≤ .05

However, a more direct and theoretically driven way of showing the response to discrepancy between actual performance levels and levels set by one's identity places a path from the error term (residual) at one time to the performance level at the next time. This is the model shown in Figure 2. In this way the magnitude and direction of the discrepancy (as reflected in the error term) are allowed to directly influence subsequent leadership performance.[12] This model also fits the data very well and shows a strong negative direct effect of residual on later performance. This is true for both the task leadership (path d of Figure 2 and Table 3) and the social emotional leadership (paths b1 and b of Figure 2 and Table 3). Again, a positive residual (performing more than expected), reduces the level of performance next time; conversely a negative residual increases performance at the next time point. Thus, we see the strong counteraction that occurs when performances are pushed out of line with the identity standards.

Thus far, I have shown that identities do influence performance, and that when there are disturbances to that identity-performance relation, individuals change their performance levels to bring them into accord with the levels that would be expected given their identity meanings. The next question concerns the relationship between these two identities. What the present data show is that there is very little relationship between the levels of task leadership identity and the levels of social emotional leadership identity held by the individuals. The correlation of -.10 (covariance of -.04 shown in the bottom of Table 3) is not significant nor is it different between coordinators and non-coordinators.[13] The degree to which people see themselves as task leaders in independent of the degree to which they see themselves a social leaders. Yet, given the above, it is clear that people act to portray themselves consistently with the meanings in both of their identities and attempt to counteract disturbances to both of these self-perceptions.

We also see that while the task and social emotional identities are independent of each other, there is also no direct connection between task leadership performance and social emotional leadership performance (paths f and g in Figure 2 and Table 3). The degree to which one performs task leadership activity had no influence on the degree to which one performs social emotional activity, and vice-versa. This is true for both coordinators and non-coordinators in these groups.

However, that does not mean the task and social emotional leadership activities are independent of each other. As the error correlations between these two activities shows (path e in Figure 2 and Table 3), there is a strong positive residual correlation between the activities for the coordinators. For the non-coordinators there is only a small positive residual correlation between these two leadership activities. Here is where we see the primary difference ($\chi^2 = 9.69$, df = 1, p $\leq$ .05) between coordinators and non-coordinators.

This means that although the meanings contained in the task and social emotional leadership identities are unrelated, and although the task and social emotional leadership role performances do not influence each other directly, there are, nevertheless other external forces in the group that are causing the two performances to become coordinated such

---

[12]The difference between this and the more traditional model is that by correlating adjacent error terms as in the traditional way of modeling, an indirect path is set up between non-adjacent error terms. Thus, with correlated error terms a correlation between e_1 and e_2 and a correlation between e_2 and e_3 allows an implicit correlation between e_1 and e_3. In the model with direct paths from the error at time i to performance at time i+1, no such indirect correlation is assumed. Each of these two models fits the data approximately equally well, and, because they are not hierarchical one to another, there is no way to test whether one is better than the other. The model in Figure 2 is preferred because it represents the theory more closely.

[13]Of course, the coordinators were selected randomly, so there should be no systematic correlation.

that high (low) levels of task leadership accompany high (low) levels of social emotional leadership. There are two important implications of this: one for the theory of leadership role differentiation, the other for the identities in question.

Recall the theory of role differentiation says that non-legitimate task leaders generate hostile, negative reactions in other members that make their social emotional performance suffer. From this we would expect the task performance of non-coordinators to negatively influence their social emotional performance. We do not see this in the data. The two performances are independent of each other, as are the meanings in their two leadership identities. An individual with high levels of task performance is hardly more likely to be a high performer on social emotional leadership activities than a person with low levels of task leadership performance. It does not appear that non-legitimated task leaders are prevented from performing social emotional leadership activity.

Instead, we see that coordinators who are performing higher levels of task leadership activity are also performing higher levels of social emotional leadership activity (and vice-versa), and this is being done not because of any shared meanings between the two activities or because of some causal link between the two activities, but apparently because of the activities and expectation of others in the group (things not included in the model). Thus, it is *not* the presence of some pressure on non-coordinators to prevent them from engaging in both activities (leading to role differentiation), but rather the presence of a pressure on the coordinators *to* engage in both activities (leading to a lack of differentiation). Overall, role differentiation among the non-coordinators appears to result from the relative independence of the roles and meanings.[14] The reduced level of role differentiation among the coordinators appears to result from the behaviors and expectations of others in the group and not the propensity of coordinators to engage in leadership behaviors with common meanings.

There are consequences of this pattern of outcomes for the identities of the participants. Principle two above suggests that people who cannot change their performances to correspond with the meanings implied in their identities will find over time that the meanings implied in their identities shift to correspond to the meanings of their perceptions/performances (Burke & Cast, 1997; Swann, 1997). I expect, therefore, that under this pressure on coordinators to engage in similar levels of task and social emotional leadership, these two sets of meanings will lose their independence and come to share some common core of meaning within the coordinators' identities. This expectation would not hold for non-coordinators inasmuch as they are not subject to the same behaviors and expectations by others in the group. The correlation between their task and SE leadership performances is minimal and there are thus only minimal pressures to bring the meanings together.

DISCUSSION

Identities are control systems in which outputs in the form of behaviors change the situation to bring perceived self-relevant meanings in the situation into alignment with the self-meanings contained in the identity standard; this is the self-verification process. It is understood that this self-verification process, however, operates only for identities that are

---

[14]The focus here is on all non-coordinators, not just those who are performing high levels of task leadership activity. Among these latter persons, there is a tendency for lower than expected levels of SE activity as found in earlier research (Burke, 1972).

activated. Indeed, we may understand that activation can be defined as setting in motion the self-verification process for a particular identity. The fact that the multiple identities of a person operate within the overall perceptual control system and often share meanings imposes constraints on the possible relationships that might exist among them. Because of the systemic aspects of the perceptual control system for all activated identities it would be difficult if not impossible to maintain identities that have contrastive meanings. Such contrastive meanings between activated identities would cause a reorganization and shift in identity meanings to keep them at least orthogonal, so that verifying one would not result in the other becoming more discrepant with self-relevant meanings in the situation. Of course, if the person could act in a way to keep such contrastive identities from being activated at the same time, the problem would not ensue.

Because identities are always activated within the context of the overall social structure in which they exist, they both influence and are influenced by this structure and their position therein. Such positioning helps determine not only levels of commitment and salience for the identities, but also the variations in the meanings contained in the identities. Additionally, the sharing of meanings across identities brings about commonalities in the levels of commitment and salience of the identities that do share meanings, thus feeding back to changing the social structure. Additionally, inasmuch as identities seek out opportunities for their verification, they come to influence the connectedness of persons with others to accomplish that verification which also shapes the social structure.

In the present paper I showed that the way that individuals are tied into the social structure influences the way in which behaviors from two identities are related. While each person independent of position engaged in task and SE behaviors to verify their task and SE leadership identities, and while each person independent of position sought to counteract disturbances to the verification process, those persons in the coordinator position were subjected to different expectations and meanings than those not in that position, with the consequence that their task and SE performances differed. Coordinators came to have more highly correlated levels of performance of task and SE behaviors than non-coordinators even though the two identities were relatively independent. Over time, we would expect this effect of the position of coordinator would lead to adjustments not only in performance (as we have seen) but also in the meanings of the task and SE leadership identities (increasing the amount of shared meaning). Such changes would take time, and unfortunately in the present study these measurements were not taken. Change in identities as the result of situational influences, however, has been documented (Burke & Cast, 1997; Cast, Stets, & Burke, 1999). It remains for future research to show how the multiple identities one holds may come to share meanings in response to the situational and structural conditions in which the identities are played out.

ACKNOWLEDGMENTS: This research was partially supported by a grant from the Division of Social Sciences, National Science Foundation (NSF BNS 76-08381). I would like to thank Jan E. Stets for her helpful comments on an earlier draft of the paper.

REFERENCES

Bales, R. F., & Slater, P. E. (1955). Role differentiation in small decision-making groups. In T. Parsons & R. F. Bales (Eds.), *Family, socialization and interaction process* (pp. 259–306). Glencoe: the Free Press.
Burke, P. J. (1972). Leadership role differentiation. In C. McClintock (Ed.), *Experimental social psychology* (pp. 514–548). New York: Holt Rinehart and Winston.

Burke, P. J. (1980). The self: Measurement implications from a symbolic interactionist perspective. *Social Psychology Quarterly, 43*, 18–29.

Burke, P. J., & Cast, A. D. (1997). Stability and change in the gender identities of newly married couples. *Social Psychology Quarterly, 60*, 277–290.

Burke, P. J., & Reitzes, D. C. (1991). An identity theory approach to commitment. *Social Psychology Quarterly, 54*(3), 239–251.

Cast, A. D., & Burke, P. J. (2002). A theory of self esteem. *Social Forces, 80*, 1041–1068.

Cast, A. D., Stets, J. E., & Burke, P. J. (1999). Does the self conform to the views of others? *Social Psychology Quarterly, 62*, 68–82.

Deaux, K. (1992). Personalizing identity and socializing self. In G. M. Blackwell (Ed.), *Social psychology of identity and the self-concept* (pp. 9–33). London: Surry University Press.

Deaux, K. (1993). Reconstructing social identity. *Personality and Social Psychology Bulletin, 19*(1), 4–12.

Gross, N., Mason Ward, S., & McEachern, A. W. (1958). *Explorations in role analysis.* New York: John Wiley and Sons Inc.

Heise, D. R. (1979). *Understanding events: Affect and the construction of social action.* Cambridge: Cambridge University Press.

Hoelter, J. W. (1985). The structure of self-conception: Conceptualization and measurement. *Journal of Personality and Social Psychology, 49*, 1392–1407.

Jackson, E. (1962). Status consistency and symptoms of stress. *American Sociological Review, 27*, 469–480.

Jackson, E. F., & Burke, P. J. (1965). Status and symptoms of stress: Additive and interaction effects. *American Sociological Review, 30*, 556–564.

James, W. (1890). *Principles of psychology.* New York: Holt Rinehart and Winston.

Lenski, G. E. (1954). Status crystallization: A non-vertical dimension of social status. *American Sociological Review, 19*, 405–413.

Linton, R. (1936). *The study of man.* New York: Appleton-Century-Crofts.

Linville, P. (1985). Self-complexity and affective extremity: Don't put all of your eggs in one cognitive basket. *Social Cognition, 3*, 94–120.

Linville, P. (1987). Self-complexity as a cognitive buffer against stress-related illness and depression. *Journal of Personality and Social Psychology, 52*, 663–676.

Merton, R. K. (1957). *Social theory and social structure* (Revised and Enlarged ed.). Glencoe, IL: The Free Press.

Osgood, C. E., Suci, G. J., & Tannenbaum, P. H. (1957). *The measurement of meaning.* Urbana, IL: University of Illinois Press.

Parsons, T. (1949). *The structure of social action.* Glencoe, IL: the Free Press.

Reitzes, D. C., & Mutran, E. J. (1995). Multiple roles and identities: Factors influencing self-esteem among middle-aged working men and women. *Social Psychology Quarterly, 57*, 313–325.

Riley, A., & Burke, P. J. (1995). Identities and self-verification in the small group. *Social Psychology Quarterly, 58*(2), 61–73.

Secord, P. F., & Backman, C. W. (1974). *Social psychology.* New York: McGraw-Hill.

Smith-Lovin, L., & Heise, D. R. (Eds.). (1988). *Analyzing social interaction: Advances in affect control theory.* New York: Gordon and Breach Science Publishers.

Stets, J. E. (1995). Modelling control in relationships. *Journal of Marriage and the Family, 57*(2), 489–501.

Stryker, S. (1968). Identity salience and role performance. *Journal of Marriage and the Family, 4*, 558–564.

Stryker, S. (1980). *Symbolic interactionism: A social structural version.* Menlo Park: Benjamin Cummings.

Stryker, S. (2000). Identity competition: Key to differential social movement involvement. In R. White (Ed.), *Identity, self, and social movements* (pp. 21–40). Minneapolis: University of Minnesota Press.

Stryker, S., & Burke, P. J. (2000). The past, present, and future of an identity theory. *Social Psychology Quarterly, 63*, 284–297.

Stryker, S., & Macke, A. (1978). Status inconsistency and role conflict. *Annual Review of Sociology, 4*, 57–90.

Stryker, S., & Serpe, R. T. (1982). Commitment, identity salience, and role behavior: A theory and research example. In W. Ickes & E. S. Knowles (Eds.), *Personality, roles, and social behavior* (pp. 199–218). New York: Springer-Verlag.

Stryker, S., & Statham, A. (1985). Symbolic interaction and role theory. In G. Lindzey & E. Aronson (Eds.), *Handbook of social psychology* (pp. 311–378). New York: Random House.

Swann, W. B., Jr. (1997). The trouble with change: Self-verification and allegiance to the self. *Psychological Science, 8*(3), 177–180.

Thoits, P. A. (1983). Multiple identities and psychological well-being: A reformulation and test of the social isolation hypothesis. *American Sociological Review, 49*, 174–187.

Thoits, P. A. (1986). Multiple identities: Examining gender and marital status differences in distress. *American Sociological Review, 51*, 259–272.

Thoits, P. A. (2001). *Personal agency in the accumulation of role-identities*. Chapter 11.

Tsushima, T., & Burke, P. J. (1999). Levels, agency, and control in the parent identity. *Social Psychology Quarterly, 62*, 173–189.

Turner, R. H. (1978). The role and the person. *American Journal of Sociology, 84(1)*, 1–23.

Afterword

A Peek Back—and Then Ahead

SHELDON STRYKER

Anticipating my formal retirement, Tim Owens—earlier a Postdoctoral Fellow in a program I directed and later a collaborator in preparing works on self and identity issues—asked whether I would approve an effort to mount a conference and subsequently a volume in my honor. I was careful to emphasize that I would not be pleased by a conference that was intended as a celebration of my work or of me. Appreciating the sentiment inherent in his offer, I suggested that if what he wanted to do was to organize a conference around the concept of identity—subsequent publication of course depending on the quality of the work presented—I would approve of that. I was careful to emphasize that it was not a conference on Identity Theory, meaning by that term the focus of my own work in social psychology over roughly the past forty years, nor even on the concept of identity as I conceptualize or define it, that would please me. Nor, I added, would I be pleased if positive appreciation of my work were used as a criterion when inviting participants in the conference. Rather, what would truly honor me was bringing together a set of persons who have worked or are working the terrain of identity, asking them in the papers they prepared for the conference to deal with the question of where they would have work on identity go, however they have defined, theorized and conceptualized that terrain. Finally, I said, I did not wish to be involved at all in the process of developing a list of possible participants because I did not wish to influence that process in any way.

I do not know whether Tim, before discussing the matter with me, had consulted two of my former colleagues—Peter Burke and Peggy Thoits—and my former student and longtime research collaborator—Richard Serpe—or had enlisted them in the enterprise after talking with me. Whatever may be the case, all four of the editors of this volume have themselves been major contributors to the theoretical and research literature on identity; and all four are my very good friends each of whom has taught me a great deal about self and identity through the years. There is no way I can adequately express my appreciation for their efforts in organizing a highly successful conference and in producing the present volume.

I cannot say that the sets of persons who participated in the conference and who produced the papers making up this volume includes any who might be expected, a priori, to disagree with me in a fundamental way. After all, I have either taught or have been taught by, have collaborated with, or have been a professional colleague of most of the participants. In point of fact, all (with some individual variation, of course!) utilize the structural symbolic interactionist frame from which my own theoretical and research work develops. Too, all seem to accept a conception of self as, in part, comprised of multiple identities, although not all find it necessary to invoke that conception in their proposals for further work on identity.

And almost all specify the content of identities as the meanings entailed in the expectations for behavior derived from others as well as from self, and ultimately from the larger social structure and culture within which others and self are located. I can say, however, that the contributors have produced a set of papers that collectively incorporate a broad and intriguing vision of identity-related matters, and collectively lay out an ambitious research agenda for future work around yet to be answered questions invoking the concept of identity. Part of that vision extends my own in ways that deepens considerably the relevance of the concept of identity for the broader social psychological and sociological enterprise.

In some cases, that extension and deepening applies the ideas of identity theory to "older" problems. Other cases apply these ideas to problems stemming from research traditions and programs that develop from frames other than symbolic interactionism. And still others apply ideas from theory and research outside of identity-related work to problems of identity theory. In all of these cases, the application leads to new and interesting research possibilities, thus each contributes to meeting my hopes with respect to the objective of the volume and the conference that preceded it.

While the authors of the chapters in the volume appear to find my multiple identity conception useful, some raise questions that assert or imply a need to reframe how we think about and use that concept. These questions concern the conceptualization of identity, as well as ways in which human agency enters identty processes. In so doing, they suggest shortcomings in extant work on identity as well as an under-developed potential for contributing to our understanding of social psychological and sociological matters of the formulations they provide. In so doing, they also meet my hopes with respect to the objective of conference and volume. The following discussion distinguishes subsets of chapters that fall into the two classes noted. It begins with chapters that extend, deepen and apply identity theory.

Peter Burke's chapter deals with an "old" problem of identity theory. Burke has long been concerned with the part of identity theory focusing on perceptual control processes internal to self that seek to match behavior to identity standards in the interests of self-verification. Noting that identity work in general holds a multiple identity conception of self, he also notes the paucity of research that incorporates multiple identities as concurrently operative, and he charts a research program based on his earlier work intended to remedy that state of affairs. Burke's past success in developing methods and measures adequate to his research program holds the promise of new methods and measures that are exportable to other research involving multiple identities and of opening a flood of new, theoretically meaningful research.

Alicia Cast also deals with an "old" problem, the reciprocity of identity and behavior, by focusing on changes in the meanings of identities produced through behaviors of newly married persons on entry into a new role relationship. She thus reinforces the strategy of selecting for research on identity processes more generally situations in which either established relationships break down or new relationships build, or both. Explicit consideration of that strategy as researchers think about optimal settings and ways to conduct the research that they wish to undertake should continue to have considerable payoff. Any form of social or geographical mobility and any change in life status is likely to involve changes in persons' social networks, with correlative changes in self and identity. Mobility and change in life status are also likely as well to provide opportunities to construct new networks offering support for older identities as well as new networks offering support for the development of novel identities. Thus the research strategy Cast adopts in her work on new marriages is useful in the study of a wide range of identity questions.

The chapters by Jill Kieckolt and Anna LoMascolo, Edward Lawler, Jan Stets, and Mathew Hunt all open up new arenas of research by applying identity theoretic ideas to issues into which such ideas have at best infrequently entered. At the same time, each does not hesitate to make use of ideas from "outside" identity work when considering how identity theory and concepts may apply in the arenas considered.

Kieckolt and LoMascolo draw on my version of identity theory, George McCall's role-identity frame, and social identity theory to explore a variety of issues connected with family resemblances. When and how do perceived family resemblances or the lack thereof matter, positively or negatively, for the identities of children raised by biological parents, and for the identities of adoptees when their adoptive parents are of the same or different ethnicity? These and other questions raised in the paper suggest intriguing opportunities covering a wide range of identity as well as social relationship issues, some involving identification with family members and others involving dis-identification (to anticipate the contribution of another author, George McCall, discussed below).

Capitalizing on the complementarities of symbolic interactionist theorizing about identities and exchange theorizing about commitment processes, Lawler develops a model of the convergence of the two. That model is used to analyze how collective identities become salient and fused to individual role-identities through a process in which positive emotions emerge and are attached to a collective identity when persons successfully deal with their interdependencies in arriving at solutions to a joint task. Implied in the model are a number of linkages between joint activity and emotion, between emotion and the identification with a collectivity and the emergence of a collective identity, between collective identity and individual identity. These hypothesized linkages are all open to empirical test; to the degree they are evidenced in research, the exchange and the identity theoretic perspectives are both enriched. Further, Lawler's work strongly suggests something that has not been invariably true in the past, namely, that sociologists working from different theoretical frames now understand the potential benefits of making use of one another's efforts.

Jan Stets undertakes a similar journey in her chapter, applying to distributive justice processes a logic that sees persons' behavior as mediated by the emotion generated by confirmation (or disconfirmation) of their identity standards. Distributive injustice, the failures of persons to reap the rewards they believe they deserve, she argues, constitute disconfirmations of identity (whether persons are over-rewarded or under-rewarded relative to their expectations), so should generate negative affect. Distributive justice, receiving rewards consistent with expectations, should generate positive affect. Further, frequently repeated instances of rewards seen as unjust or as just should produce more extreme affective responses. Her findings in an experimental study are clearly more complex than the hypotheses she derives from the current theorizing about affective responses to differences between actual and expected rewards can accommodate, thus offering a variety of new questions for future research.

Using a review of the research literature relating self and identity concepts to stratification issues as a point of departure, Mathew Hunt observes that this research typically employs a relatively unsophisticated conceptualization of self and, in particular, identity. He suggests research using a more sophisticated conception that adopts identity theory's multiple self perspective and (from Peggy Thoits' work) a concept of identity structure as identity salience, identity claims and identity combinations. Doing so, he further suggests, is likely to produce improved knowledge of self as the product of social arrangements and as a force shaping consciousness of and attitudes about social inequalities. The detailed specification of research questions, the methods that could answer these questions and the utility from a variety of points of view of obtaining those answers give credibility to Hunt's suggestions. I would add only that it might be particularly interesting to use the design Hunt develops in examining the effects on behavioral choices of combinations of identities that involve conflicting vs. mutually reinforcing meanings, doing so in the context of differences and similarities in identity salience.

Seeking to explain the persistent finding of health research that expressing emotions to others produces positive health outcomes, Linda Francis assembles ideas of identity theory, affect control theory, and theories of emotional management to produce an account she believes achieves that explanation. Her account argues that unresolved negative emotions has perverse effects on health and that such emotions arise when highly salient identities of persons are contradicted by events they experience. She argues, further, that a key available way of achieving resolution is through persons' redefinitions of themselves, others, or the situations that produce the contradictions, and that persons typically are incapable of resolving such contradictions without outside help. Finally, she sees the key to improving health outcomes is through expressing the negative emotions to others because doing so requires constructing a coherent narrative involving elements that encourage useful redefinitions. Clearly implicated in the process Francis lays out are research hypotheses whose testing can illuminate sociological and social psychological complements to the psychological and biological sources of health and illness.

The chapters by Lynn Smith-Lovin, by Timothy Owens and Richard Serpe, and by Kristen Marcussen and Michael Large expand current work on identity by bringing to bear ideas that have developed from theory and research outside of identity-related work to problems of identity theory.

In an essay of truly extraordinary scope that bridges from societal structure through persons' identities to emotional responses, Smith-Lovin responds to Peter Burke's and my call for work developing identity theory's multiple identity concept of self and by specifying linkages among commitments to networks of relationships, identity salience and identity standards. Her response theorizes the relation of self, identity and interaction as these occur in larger ecologies of identities. Smith-Lovin begins her argument by asking under what societal structural conditions persons are likely to have a complex self incorporating multiple identities and that make it likely the multiple identities will be operative in given situations. She then applies her answers to the further question of when single identity standards will develop from operative multiple identities and when complex, multiple identity standards will be the result. She ends by drawing implications of these prior analyses for emotional experience. Clearly, many research careers could be based on pursuing the implications of the models presented in this essay.

The literatures of self-esteem theory and research and identity theory and research have developed largely independently of one another. Nevertheless, over the years, a number of social psychologists focusing on self have contended that self-esteem ought relate in determinate ways to such identity theoretic variables as commitment and identity salience. It is an understatement to note that demonstrating empirically such a relationship has proved elusive. Owens and Serpe undertake a new examination of the issue in the research reported in their chapter, using data generated in a survey sample comprised of blacks, whites, and Latinos. The results once again show mixed patterns, especially so with respect to commonalities and differences across the three racial/ethnic subsamples. In seeking to understand these patterns, however, the authors propose a set of accounts amenable to test in new research, evidencing the old saw that good research will often open more questions than it solves.

The concept of self tends to have quite different meanings and usages when it appears in the work of psychologists and in the work of sociologists, yet the potential benefits of bringing these usages and meanings together is considerable. Marcussen and Large illustrate these benefits when they seek to extend theorizing about the link of identity processes to stress. What they wish to develop is an identity theory that can predict not only the occurrence of stress but also its magnitude and the affective forms through which it is expressed behaviorally. Their means for building such a theory is to wed Burke's self-verification theory to Tory Higgins' self-discrepancy theory. The former sees failures in verification as the source of stress; the latter sees major affective forms as consequences of the meaning of particular kinds of discrepancies among self domains, with actual-ideal self discrepancies producing dejection-type affective responses (depression), actual-ought discrepancies producing agitation-type responses (anxiety). The empirical results reported by Marcussen and Large, while mixed, justify pursuing the theory and its empirical test over the next years.

Thus far, I have discussed, however briefly, the cases in which authors are not as inclined to critically appraise current work on identity as to extend it in various ways. In other cases, however, the vision offered also constitutes a critical appraisal of much contemporary work, my own as well as that of others, making use of the concept(s) of identity.

So, for example, George McCall's argument that identity theorists and researchers need to pay attention to the "not-me" points to issues that surely have not been adequately addressed by current formulations of the concept of identity. He reminds us that what we seek to distance ourselves from may be as or more salient, may be as or more dependent on our commitments to social networks, and may have as great or greater impact on our interactions and behavior more generally, than what we identify with. Inherent in these reminders is a research agenda that can serve to challenge identity researchers over the next decades. Among the most intriguing of these questions is the relative power of positive and negative identifications to control various kinds of social behaviors.

Peggy Thoits correctly asserts that, while recognizing human agency as a possibility in the person-society relationship, contemporary theorizing about and research on identity overwhelmingly has been concerned with the impact of society on identity rather than the reciprocal impact of identity on society. She also asserts that the sheer accumulation of multiple identities means the existence of multiple resources to meet life's contingencies, that success in meeting contingencies breeds further success and provides persons with generalized personality resources to shape their own identities. In so doing, Thoits reminds identity researchers that their tendency to treat identities in terms of discrete role related meanings carries costs in the form of inadequate understandings of the relation of identity to generalized physical and emotional well-being. She also reminds us, as did Smith-Lovin and others, that role identities do not exhaust the meaning of self. Once more, a significant research agenda—in this case already well embarked upon—is laid out.

Finally, Peter Callero's essay on the political self forcefully criticizes a symbolic interactionism that does not recognize the centrality of power, therefore the political, in modern society and through that failure contributes to legitimating extant institutionalized systems of dominance. Calling for a reconceptualization of self that, in keeping with the "self reflects society" presumption of the interactionist framework, understands the political as constitutive of self, he sees this step as fundamental to a theoretical and research program that is explicitly normative, that addresses the social and political conditions facilitating positive self-development, and that examines the identity resources necessary to an emancipatory, radical participatory democracy. Whether or not one finds Callero's proposal attractive or feasible, his is a serious challenge to more conventional rationales for and ways of "doing" self and identity theory and research. It deserves thoughtful consideration, and it deserves the attention of at least some identity theorists and researchers.

As I finished reading the chapters on which I have just commented, I wondered what I might have added had I been charged with the task presented to their authors. Given the breadth of the vision entailed in the set of chapters, the answer has to be not very much! I have thought a bit, however, about what matters I would be drawn to were I entering the arena of identity theory and research at its current stage of development and as a reasonably young person, and I want to suggest just a few of these. I will do so only briefly and baldly, without justifying elaboration, in part because some were presented not too long ago in a paper by Burke and myself in which we specified a series of important next topics in the future of Identity Theory research.

An early item on my agenda would be to seek non-intrusive behavioral measures of identity salience to augment, perhaps to replace, the paper-and-pencil measures now used. If, as I have argued, identities are cognitive schema sharing the properties of such schema, they ought to be amenable to methods used to measure characteristics of schema more generally. A number of years ago, Russell Fazio and I embarked on research, never really implemented for reasons irrelevant to this discussion, that sought to use response-time measures to stimuli representing features of identities as putative measures of salience. We intended to compare results with measures of identity salience that have been used— whether these measures related to one another, whether they were equivalently reliable and equivalently valid or not, etc. A behavioral measure of salience would not exhaust the theoretical import of the concept of salience; however, it would help allay concerns about problematic aspects of less "objective" measures.

A second priority item would be the development of models that adequately represented the simultaneous operation of more than two or three identities of varying salience and/or of varying meanings, and, correspondingly, with methods of analysis appropriate to data reflecting such multiple identity models. Ideally, these methods would involve more than simulations, although simulations are useful in the absence of empirical alternatives. The starting point in such work could be the "combination" rules developed by Heise in implementing affect control theory models, or those developed by Berger and associates with respect to expectations states theory. Incidentally, I do not pretend to have the training or abilities that would allow more than token representation in research reflecting this priority; had I been smart enough when I was younger I would have sought the training necessary to something more than token representation.

A third priority item, largely implied in the foregoing, would be dealing in a more integrated manner with the meaning and the structure of identities. My sense has always been that to research the structure of identities effectively, researchers had to locate the identities studied in the context of systems of cultural and personal meaning whose content was reasonably well known. For example, effectively researching the idea that identity competition is key to understanding the issue of differences in levels and modes of members' participation in social movement activities requires the simultaneous consideration of the salience of members' multiple identities and the "fit" or lack thereof of the meanings of those multiple identities.

A last, much less abstract, suggestion for future research begins with recalling that the identity theory I presented was deliberately a minimal theory: I sought a testable explanation of role choice behavior using as few concepts as possible. I understood that the three concepts of the theory—commitment, identity salience, and role behavior—would have to be augmented as tests of the theory demonstrated a need for augmentation and as greater explanatory power was sought. A number of the authors of chapters in this volume argue the need to add social and personal identities to the role-identities on which I focused, some suggest the need to add personality variables, and so on. Many years ago a Israeli social psychologist, Gabriel Horencyk, with whom I have lost contact, visited my training program at Indiana. During his visit he presented some preliminary work on an appealing idea of a different order that had to do with circumstances under which behavioral demands of less than highly salient identities could be attended to. His idea was that each person had an identity bank account into which behaviors relevant to identities were deposited. Building a sufficient balance or surplus with respect to highly salient identities allowed persons to be responsive to identities of lower salience. I would love to be able to follow up on that research suggestion; it would be fun!

To return to and to summarize what I have said about the varied chapters in this volume: Each, individually, makes an independent contribution to thinking about the specific issues confronted in them. Collectively, they serve to advance identity theory and research and to suggest an impressive, wide-ranging, and well-grounded agenda that can, and, I hope, will occupy social psychologists interested in pursuing issues of identity from the perspective of sociology well into the new millenium. Nothing could please me more.

Index

226   Index